The Scots Law of Succession

THE SCOTS LAW OF SUCCESSION

Third Edition

Euan Campbell

Bloomsbury Professional

EDINBURGH • LONDON • DUBLIN • NEW YORK • NEW DELHI • SYDNEY

BLOOMSBURY PROFESSIONAL

Bloomsbury Publishing Plc
50 Bedford Square, London, WC1B 3DP, UK
1385 Broadway, New York, 10018, USA

Bloomsbury Publishing Ireland Ltd
29 Earlsfort Terrace, Dublin 2, D02 AY28, Ireland

First published in Great Britain 2026

1

British Library Cataloguing-in-Publication Data

A catalogue record for this book is available from the British Library.

ISBN:	PB:	978-1-52653-566-5
	Epdf:	978-1-52653-568-9
	Epub:	978-1-52653-567-2

Typeset by Evolution Design and Digital Ltd (Kent)
Printed and bound by TJ Books, Padstow

FSC www.fsc.org MIX Paper | Supporting responsible forestry FSC® C013056

For product safety related questions contact productsafety@bloomsbury.com

Foreword

It is an immense privilege to update the *Scots Law of Succession* to its third edition and to follow in Dr Hiram's footsteps. I am grateful to all of those at Bloomsbury for their time and patience in my updates to a crucial book for research, teaching and consultation. I am also most grateful to the property law undergraduate students at the University of Glasgow and the University of Stirling who flagged issues of understanding in the previous edition of this text. This was very helpful in order to understand sections which students struggle to understand. Parts of succession law can be hard, but I hope it is a subject that students enjoy learning, given its importance to every person in Scotland.

The only apt expression to describe the current law of succession in Scotland is to be found in French: *Plus ça change, plus c'est la même chose*. Bar minor statutory amendments, the long-awaited reform of intestate succession has failed to materialise in the Scottish Parliament. Whether this will yet occur remains to be seen, though the view taken is that this should not inhibit the publication of up-to-date materials in the meantime.

It should be noted that in order to 'future proof' this text, it has been assumed throughout this edition that the Trusts and Succession (Scotland) Act 2024 as at Royal Assent (30 January 2024) is fully in force.

Whilst great care has been taken in reviewing and updating all aspects of this text, all errors in updates remain my own.

EC Campbell
Stair Building
University of Glasgow

Contents

Part 2: Intestate Succession

Table of Cases

A

B

C

D

E

F

L

M

R

Table of Statutes

Table of Statutory Instruments

Introduction

All of us will die, and we will all encounter the death of strangers, celebrities, and loved ones. Death is a permanent feature of human life, and all property must pass to someone else on death: our own property to other people on our death; and other people's property to us on theirs. The transfer of property and rights at death is a subject that permeates throughout all of private law and our own personal lives. It is the law of succession that provides the rules for how the deceased's property is to be distributed and who may inherit it. This includes providing default rules for distribution where the deceased has failed to make any formal directions for the distribution of their property, alongside rules respecting any directions that the deceased had made. This book explores these rules as they apply in Scots law.

On one view, the law of succession seems a thoroughly depressing topic. The work of private client[1] solicitors seems to be a never-ending series of deaths, funerals, and executry accounts. Yet in death the transfer of wealth or property can provide the start of new lives. For those that inherit, there are new opportunities. Inheritance can provide the money for a purchase of a home. It helps people to pay off their debts. It allows people to go abroad and explore the world, with its myriad of cultures. It can pay for private medical care or specialist support to change someone's life for the better. It allows for children to go to fee-paying schools or obtain private tutoring. Succession law is typically viewed at the end of life but, in most cases, it provides the start of a new life for those that inherit. It is really a subject concerned with new beginnings.

Succession law as a branch of private law is currently an issue of intense focus. The western world is currently undergoing the 'Great Wealth Transfer',[2] one of the largest intergenerational transfers of wealth

1 'Private client' is the term often used for the department of a law firm in Scotland handling private wealth management, taxation, and estate planning. This is to distinguish it from family law departments, which typically focus on handling divorce, child custody disputes, and other matters arising from relationships.

2 A Brummer, 'The great £5 trillion wealth transfer; A gargantuan inheritance left by Baby Boomers over the next 30 years is set to reshape Britain' *Scottish Mail on Sunday*, 27 July 2025; and R Colvile, 'The Great Wealth Transfer: what will happen when boomers pass on assets' *The Times*, 16 February 2025.

in human history. One financial institution estimates that £5 trillion will pass from the wealthiest older generations to the younger generations in the United Kingdom.[3] This is the 'new age of inheritance' that affects us all and will shape our society for decades to come.[4] It will shape who can easily afford home ownership, who can retire early, and who can afford the luxuries that others cannot. Accordingly, how succession law regulates the distribution of wealth in our society is of central importance.

WHERE DOES SUCCESSION LAW BELONG IN PRIVATE LAW?

At the outset, it falls to be considered how succession law should be classified within the scheme of Scots private law. Succession law might be said to straddle the boundaries of all other branches as it affects each area in some way. However, given it concerns the distribution of property, one might think it solely to be part of property law. This is true, and indeed in many Scottish universities it is taught alongside general property law, but it may also be thought of as part of family law, as the law of succession somewhat functions as a form of family provision.

Until reforms in 1964, family provision on death and on divorce or nullity was based on the same doctrinal principles and, arguably at least, aimed originally at concentrating and preserving resources within families. Whatever the broader social or political motives may have been, succession was also concerned with the fulfilment of familial obligations. For these reasons, Stair terms it as the 'most important title in law'[5] and Bell described that:[6]

> 'No department of municipal law is more intimately connected with the state of society than that which relates to the rights of heirs and the rules of descent.'

3 J Noble, 'Family rifts and double tax: The reality of the Great Wealth Transfer', *The Times*, 9 March 2025.

4 D Goss and B Glover, *A new age of inheritance: What does it mean for the UK?* (2023), Demos research paper.

5 Stair *Inst* III.4.2.

6 Bell, *Prin*, § 1637.

To a large extent the overlap between property law and family law remains the case today, and succession law might be said to sit in the borderland between property law and family law by providing the rules and mechanisms by which property is transferred to the persons whom we consider to be our family, whether we do this expressly through a will, or whether the law decides who is our family and facilitates distribution to them instead. It is the familial aspect of succession law that has made it subject to successive attempts at reform in recent years to, as Bell noted, reflect the state of modern society. The Scottish Law Commission and the Scottish Government have, for several years, attempted to reform the law of intestate succession to reflect changes in society and societal attitudes towards inheritance and families, with some minor successes, but it is an aspiration that largely remains unimplemented.[7]

THE SOURCES OF SUCCESSION LAW

One finds the sources of modern succession law in Scotland in statute, the common law, and the institutional writers. Much of succession law has developed due to a complex history, which will be explored in this text. In some areas the law is archaic and unclear; in other areas the law is tricky and complex. However, the development of succession law in Scotland has largely been a distinctly domestic affair. Aspects of Roman law, Canon law, English law and independent local customs have shaped Scots succession law into the modern system that we have today, but it remains a uniquely Scottish system, and recourse to other jurisdictions, such as those within the other parts of the United Kingdom, to explain Scots succession law is a largely futile endeavour. This point should be borne in mind when embarking on any independent research or using the internet unwittingly.

7 See below at paras **5.4** and **6.6**.

THE STRUCTURE OF SUCCESSION LAW: INTESTATE SUCCESSION, TESTATE SUCCESSION AND LEGAL RIGHTS

What should be understood above all else is that there is no single or unified law of succession in Scotland. The law of succession can be compared to a jigsaw puzzle. As a whole, it forms a distinct and relatively complete area of law; when taken apart, the significance of its individual aspects and their possible connection to each other can disappear.

Like many countries, there are two forms of succession: intestate and testate succession. These phrases will be used throughout this text, so it is important to define them here. Intestate succession is where there is no will or testamentary document regulating the entire distribution of the estate. This can arise in whole, there simply being no will altogether, or it may arise in part where a will or other testamentary device does not distribute the entirety of an estate. In intestacy the law's default rules are imposed in the distributing the deceased's estate. Intestate succession is regulated largely by statute, principally the Succession (Scotland) Act 1964, but supplemented by a set of older common law rules. Intestate succession is the most common form of succession in Scotland, as many people fail to make a will before they die.[8]

Testate succession is where the deceased has died with a will or testamentary document setting out the distribution of their estate. The law of testate succession is based mainly on common law principles and authority, subject to a few statutory modifications such as the Succession (Scotland) Act 2016. In some cases, the will may not provide a complete distribution of the entire estate, leaving a residue. In such cases this residue is known as a partial intestacy and will be distributed by the rules of intestate succession instead. Similarly, if a will is set aside by a court, then distribution of the deceased's estate by intestate succession may arise.

The existence of the twin regimes of testate and intestate succession may reflect the relative wealth of a deceased person – those who have a lot to leave will generally prepare carefully for how it is to pass, when it is to pass and to whom, while those with little are more likely to leave it to go where it will, generally to romantic partners and children. But

8 See the statistical analysis in K Reid, 'Intestate succession in Scotland', in K Reid et al (eds), *Comparative Succession Law, Volume II: Intestate Succession* (2015), 388.

it may also reflect the fact that, regardless of their relative wealth, some people prefer not to think about it at all, while others plan the succession to their property on death down to the last detail and sometimes change their minds many times in the process. For those who do plan it, the law of testate succession provides the framework for making and imposing those choices that exist in a person's approach to the inevitable. For those who do not, the state makes assumptions as to who should benefit and to what extent by, on behalf of the deceased, weighing his or her relationships with partners and children against each other. It imputes to him or her desires, obligations and intentions for its distribution that he or she may or may not have had but which, it is assumed, he or she ought to have had. It is the combination of its emotional, financial and social significance, both to those who are disposing of their property on death and those who live to receive it from them, that gives the rules, presumptions, principles and policies that make up the law of succession its special significance.

What is one unifying feature that spans across both testate and intestate succession? It is one of the oldest features of Scots succession law, a doctrine known as 'legal rights'. This sounds an odd term, for surely all of private law concerns rights and obligations, but the term 'legal rights' in the context of succession law describes the automatic entitlements available to spouses, civil partners, and descendants to be paid from the moveable estate of the deceased. Therefore, in either testate or intestate succession, it is not possible to totally disinherit a spouse, civil partner or descendants in Scotland due to the operation of legal rights.

THE STRUCTURE OF THIS BOOK

Noting how succession law in Scotland is structured, this book is consequently divided into four parts. Part 1 deals with general issues arising at death, the administration of estates, and the operation of legal rights, which all apply regardless of testate and intestate succession. Part 2 then considers the law of intestate succession. Part 3 sets out the law relating to testamentary documents and their execution, and challenges thereof, and describes other types of legal testamentary devices that may dispose of property on death. Part 4 deals with the substantive rules of testate succession and the construction of testamentary deeds, including the thorny issue of the law of vesting. This book is not concerned with the taxation of estates at death,[9] nor the scheme of international private law which determines the applicable law of succession for a deceased person's estate.[10] Whilst vital topics, a treatment of these subjects cannot be offered here.

9 See A Nathan and M Lemos, *McCutcheon on Inheritance Tax*, 8th edn (2025).

10 See E Crawford and J Carruthers, *International Private Law: A Scots Perspective*, 4th edn (2015) Ch 18; and P Beaumont and P McEleavy (eds), *Anton's Private International Law*, 3rd edn (2011) Ch 24.

Part 1:

General issues in succession

Chapter 1

Death, survivorship, and funerary law

INTRODUCTION

1.1 This chapter explores some of the preliminary issues in succession law, including how the law treats someone as dead and the consequences of that determination. These issues apply regardless of whether the deceased died testate or intestate as part of the general principles of the law of succession. The law of succession is concerned with the transmission of rights in property from a person who has died to another living person. Two rules follow from that statement: (1) The person from whom the succession opens must be dead; and (2) the person who will succeed to the estate must be alive or, as it is termed, the person must survive the deceased.[1] These two basic tests must be satisfied before any of the particular rules of succession, whether testate or intestate, may be considered. As Lord McLaren stated:[2]

> 'To the acquisition of a vested interest in succession of any description it is essential that the heir shall have survived the person whose succession is claimed … The survivance of the persons claiming the character of heirs is always a point of the first importance in questions of succession.'

In the vast majority of cases, establishing whether someone has died and whether the person or persons entitled to succeed to his or her estate are still alive will be perfectly straightforward. However, sometimes either death, survivorship, or both, may be difficult to establish. This includes where a person suffers a serious injury and puts them into a comatose or vegetative state. Additionally, missing persons can create a situation

1 A beneficiary need not be alive at the time a right in succession is payable by the executor, but he or she must have been alive at the time the succession right vested in them. In this case, the legacy or other right will be payable to his or her estate: see para **1.13** below.

2 J McLaren, *The Law of Wills and Succession as Administered in Scotland*, 3rd edn (1894), paras 108–110.

whereby their estates cannot be wound up and distributed to others unless or until death is either known or presumed. Further, where two or more people who may be entitled to succeed to the other appear to have died at more or less the same time, it may be impossible to be certain who has survived the other. In all such cases it is impossible to establish death or survivorship on the facts alone, and legal rules and presumptions may have to be applied. This chapter explores such difficult situations. Once death and survivorship has been established, issues arise over who has rights or responsibilities over a person's body and its means of disposal. This chapter will provide a brief introduction to funerary law as the area of law regulating the burial, cremation and handling of bodily remains.

DEATH

(1) Definition of death

1.2 There is no clear accepted definition of death in Scots law.[3] One might say it is the point in which the law considers their legal personality as terminated.[4] However, there remains a question of when exactly this occurs.[5] Leaving aside questions of jurisprudence, when someone is dead as a matter of fact is usually quite easy to determine. In most cases, a corpse is found and that corpse is formally identified as the person in question. One might term that situation as an ascertainable death. Yet, as will be explained below, in some cases death can unascertainable.

3 Though there is a definition in medical practice in the United Kingdom, see the Academy of Medical Royal Colleges, *2008 Code of Practice for the diagnosis and confirmation of death,* (2025 update) available at https://www.aomrc.org.uk/wp-content/uploads/2025/01/Code_of_Practice_Diagnosis_of_Death_010125.pd. The 2008 Code of Practice is often the definition litigated before, or used by, the courts, eg: *St George's University Hospitals NHS Foundation Trust* v *Casey* [2023] EWHC 2244 (Fam); and *Re M (Declaration of Death of Child)* [2020] EWCA Civ 164.

4 'General Legal Concepts (Reissue)' in *The Laws of Scotland: Stair Memorial Encyclopaedia*, para 39.

5 See R Paisley, 'Property Deprivation of an Absentee in Emulation of the Laws of Succession: The Laws of Scotland and South Africa Compared' in E Reid and D Visser (eds), *Private Law and Human Rights: Bringing Rights home in Scotland and South Africa* (2013) 106; and G Gretton, '*Quaedam meditations Caledoniae*: The Property/Succession Borderland' (2014) 3(2) *EPLJ* 109, 115–116.

(2) Proof of death

1.3 The Registration of Births, Deaths and Marriages (Scotland) Act 1965 provides the system for public registration of deaths in Scotland. There is a Register of Deaths in which all deaths in Scotland are to be recorded.[6] This system is overseen by the Registrar-General, *ex officio* the Chief Executive of the National Records of Scotland.[7] District registrars employed by local authorities undertake the routine registration process on behalf of the Registrar-General.[8]

Before a death can be registered, a physician must issue a certificate of cause of death explaining the reason why the person has died.[9] The death must then be recorded in the Register of Deaths at a district-registrar's office. The death is to be registered by any person having a duty to register the death within eight days of death or within eight days of discovering the body.[10] What typically happens is that a family member of the deceased makes an appointment at a local council office with a district registrar. The family member brings the certificate of cause of death and other documentation relating to the deceased. The registrar checks these over and enters the details into the Register of Deaths. The registrar must then issue an extract from the Register of Deaths.[11] This extract is commonly called a 'death certificate', albeit it is really just an extract (copy) of the details entered onto the register.

A death certificate is sufficient but not conclusive proof of death.[12] Where it appears that there may have been a mistaken identity, and a corpse is misattributed to a person who is in fact alive, the onus of proof is on the person seeking to show that the person in question is not dead.

6 1965 Act, Part III. See further 'Registration of Births, Deaths and Marriages (2nd Reissue)' in *The Laws of Scotland: Stair Memorial Encyclopaedia.*

7 The Chief Executive of the NRS is also *ex officio* the Keeper of the Records of Scotland, a role which should not be mistaken with the Keeper of the Registers of Scotland.

8 1965 Act, s 5.

9 1965 Act, s 24. Further legislation deals with the certification process and scrutiny thereof, see the Certification of Death (Scotland) Act 2011.

10 These are a relative, a person present at the death, an executor or the occupier of premises where the death occurred, such as a care home manager, 1965 Act, s 23.

11 1965 Act, s 27.

12 1965 Act, s 41A.

(3) Investigation of deaths

1.4 In cases where the circumstances of death are unusual or unexplained, a physician may be unable to produce a certificate stating the cause of death. In such cases, the local procurator-fiscal will be informed. One of the roles of the procurators-fiscal is to investigate any sudden, suspicious, accidental and unexplained deaths in their jurisdiction. This is a marked difference from the rest of the United Kingdom, and other common law jurisdictions, which have a system of coroners and coroner courts to investigate and determine such deaths.[13]

If it is found that the death is unusual or suspicious, the procurator-fiscal may order a post-mortem and other investigations to be carried out by the police service and other investigatory bodies. The procurator-fiscal may also arrange a Fatal Accident Inquiry before a sheriff for a judicial hearing on the matter.[14] Some types of death, such as deaths at a workplace or deaths in custody, will always have a mandatory Fatal Accident Inquiry.[15]

(4) Unascertainable deaths

1.5 Whilst most deaths are able to be ascertained and resolved by way of the above system of public registration, sometimes death can be unascertainable in the sense that it is unclear whether someone is indeed

13 There have been campaigns for Scots law to adopt such a system, see D Cowan, 'Balcony fall family call for Scots coroner', *BBC News*, 29 April 2021 available at https://www.bbc.co.uk/news/uk-scotland-56929802.

14 Inquiries into Fatal Accidents and Sudden Deaths etc (Scotland) Act 2016. See G Mawdsley, *Sudden Deaths and Fatal Accident Inquiries in Scotland: Law, Policy and Practice* (2023) and A Cubie (ed), *MacPhail's Sheriff Court Practice,* 4th edn (2022) Ch 28. The current system is not without its critics in Scotland, particularly from the families of those who have died whilst in police or prison custody. The Crown Office and Procurator Fiscal Service has come under scrutiny of its handling of FAIs. See the Abercrombie Report, *Deaths in Custody – Independent Review of Fatal Accident Inquiries Report* (2025) available at https://www.gov.scot/publications/report-2025-independent-review-fatal-accident-inquiries-relating-deaths-custody-scotland/documents/ and Scottish Human Rights Commission, *A 'brutal' system: Families' experiences following a death in custody in Scotland* report (2025) available at https://www.scottishhumanrights.com/media/3196/designedpdf-mainreport-policy-fatalaccidentinquiriesfamilylisteningday-2025.pdf.

15 2016 Act, s 2.

dead – whether factually or legally speaking. In those cases, it is also unclear whether the law of succession can operate to distribute the person's property. These difficult situations are outlined below.

(a) Living death

1.6 It is helpful to begin this section with an example. Brian works as a scaffolder. One day at work, he falls at height from a building and lies motionless on the ground. The first aider assesses him and realises that he is not breathing, nor can she feel a pulse. She immediately performs CPR and administers a defibrator to no avail. Paramedics arrive and continue compressions and defibrillation in the back of the ambulance all the way to the hospital. At the Accident & Emergency department, doctors are able to restart Brian's heart and, thereafter, put him on a ventilator to keep his lungs moving and blood circulating around his body. Scans reveal a serious bleed on the brain. Brian's wife and children arrive at the hospital and are told the tragic news that Brian is unlikely to ever wake up, nor would he be able to breathe unaided without medical apparatus. The doctors advise that the best outcome would be to withdraw the ventilator to let his heart naturally stop.

Rather remotely, a lawyer's initial analysis of this situation would include the following questions:

- At what point is, or was, Brian dead? Was it when he fell from height and his heart stopped from the trauma? Was he dead whilst the first aider, paramedics and doctors kept performing compressions and moving blood around his body? Is he dead whilst the life support machine in the hospital keeps his lungs moving, his heart beating, and blood moving around his body?
- If he is still alive during those situations, would he then only be dead when his wife agrees with the doctors to turn off the life support machine?
- Would it be a crime by the doctors or family to willingly turn off the life support machine?[16]

16 That question cannot be answered in this text but see *Law Hospital NHS Trust* v *Lord Advocate* 1996 SC 301 and the discussion in S McLean, 'Giving Up or Letting Go: *Law Hospital NHS Trust v Lord Advocate*' in J Grant and E Sutherland (eds), *Scots Law Tales* (2010). See also A Farrell and E Dove, *Mason and McCall Smith's Law and Medical Ethics*, 12th edn (2023) Ch 17.

- What if Brian's wife refuses to consent to turn off the machine, in the shock and (understandable) vain hope that he might wake up again one day? Would the law consider Brian alive or dead in the months and years that follow, where he lies in a hospital ward or hospice on a ventilation machine?
- What becomes of Brian's property and debts in all of this? When can his wife and children claim his property under the law of succession?

These are some of the difficult legal questions in a tragically all too common situation faced by many families. As Lord Hope observed:[17]

> 'Medical science has now advanced to such a degree that many techniques are now possible which only a generation ago would have been unthinkable. The ability to prolong life by artificial means has reached such a stage that it is possible to nourish the body and preserve it from disease so that life, in the clinical sense, may be continued indefinitely.'

Since it is technically possible to keep a person breathing with the aid of a ventilator and to nourish and hydrate that person for several years while he or she remains unconscious, does this mean that the person is alive?

Even if the ethical questions involved in this type of case are left aside, it is clear that death can be difficult to define. From a medical perspective, death is not a single event but may be described more accurately as a process – in the sense that cellular activity stops and the body begins to decompose.[18] The accepted position in the medical profession is that clinical death arises where there is:[19]

> 'The permanent cessation of brainstem function, whether as a consequence of cardiorespiratory arrest or devastating brain injury, will produce the permanent loss of the capacities for consciousness and for breathing, and thus, the clinical state of death. Therefore, a diagnosis of permanent cessation of brainstem function means the person has died and allows a competent individual to confirm the person's death.'

Unlike heartbeat, respiration is a function of the brain stem. When the brain is deprived of oxygen – for example, when the heart has stopped

17 *Law*, at 307.
18 *2008 Code of Practice* (2025 update), para 2.1.
19 *2008 Code of Practice* (2025 update), para 2.3.

during a cardiac arrest – but the person is revived, the brain may be damaged irreversibly. If the person is unconscious and cannot breathe unaided without artificial respiration, the brain stem is dead. Thus, for the medical profession, brain-stem death means that the person is clinically dead. However, where a person is being kept 'alive' by artificial means, he or she is clinically dead but, in law, the person is still treated as alive.[20] *Law Hospital NHS Trust v Lord Advocate* somewhat recognises that a person in a long-term comatose state continues to be alive for the purposes of the law, despite being in a state of 'living death'.[21]

For the purposes of succession, where it must be determined whether an estate can be distributed, or if a beneficiary of a person's estate has actually survived the deceased, this can raise ethical and practical problems where brain-stem death is involved. If, for example, a husband and wife have been critically injured in an accident and both are now artificially ventilated, how is the order of their deaths to be determined? If death were deemed to be when the machines are turned off, the order of death would be purely arbitrary.[22] On the other hand, if the ventilators of both husband and wife were switched off simultaneously but both were already clinically dead, then death would have occurred before ventilation ceased. It would seem that the moment of death in succession law cannot, therefore, be determined according to the time when machines are switched off and a heart ceases to beat. No clear answer emerges to this conundrum.

(b) Missing persons

1.7 Another difficulty emerges where a person is missing. At which point is it decided that the person has died and their estate is open to distribution under the law of succession? The presumption at common law was that if someone disappeared and was never heard of again, his or her life would continue until the limits of human age. In consequence, it was presumed that the missing person must remain the owner of all of his or her property until such time as natural causes must have brought about his

20 *Finlayson v HMA* 1979 JC 33.

21 S McLean, 'Giving Up or Letting Go: *Law Hospital NHS Trust v Lord Advocate*' in E Sutherland and J Grant (eds), *Scots Law Tales* (2010) 138.

22 It is not unimaginable that the family might potentially choose whose life support machine should be turned off first in order to control how succession rights vest.

or her death. In Stair's opinion the limit of human age was 80 years old; in Bankton's view it was 100.[23] Declarator of death could be granted, but for limited purposes only.[24] Rebuttal of the common law presumption of life depended on the particular circumstances of the case, and the standard of proof was thought to be the criminal standard of beyond reasonable doubt.[25] In effect, declarator could not be granted unless the missing person had been missing for so long that death from natural causes must have occurred. Although the age of the missing person and the health and circumstances of the individual at the time of his or her disappearance were relevant considerations, declarator would be refused where there was insufficient evidence to rebut the presumption of life.

For example, in *Secretary of State for Scotland v Sutherland*,[26] there were no special factors to take into account, and the court held that the applicant's missing husband might merely have been hiding very successfully for 42 years. By contrast, in *Greig v Trustees of the Edinburgh Merchant Company's Widows' Fund*,[27] special factors were taken into account, and declarator of death was granted six years after the missing person was last seen (when he would have been aged 53), on the basis that he had been an alcoholic with a life expectancy of only six to ten years at the time he disappeared. Where the missing person had been engaged in a dangerous or life-threatening activity, the onus of proof was also lighter and declarator more likely to be granted.[28]

Reform was introduced by the Presumption of Life Limitation (Scotland) Act 1881, which gave the right to raise an action of declarator of death to a person entitled to succeed to a missing person's estate, provided that the missing person appeared to be absent from Scotland and had not been heard of for seven years or more. However, the legislation was limited in its scope. No one other than a person entitled to succeed to the missing person's estate could apply to the court; the missing person had to have

23 Stair *Inst* IV.45.17; Bankton *Inst*, IV.34.1; *Secretary of State for Scotland v Sutherland* 1944 SC 79; and *Bruce v Smith* (1871) 10 M 130.

24 See the discussion in Consultative Memorandum on *Presumptions of Death and Survivorship* (SLC CM No 11, 1969), paras 3–7.

25 *McGeachy v Standard Life Assurance Co* 1972 SC 145.

26 *Secretary of State for Scotland v Sutherland* 1944 SC 79.

27 *Greig v Trs of the Edinburgh Merchant Company's Widows' Fund* 1921 SC 76.

28 *Fairholme v Fairholme's Trs* (1858) 20 D 813; *Garland v Stewart* (1841) 4 D 1; *Sands v Her Tenants* (1678) Mor 12645; and *French v Earl of Wemyss* (1677) Mor 12644.

an estate to be disposed of; and that estate must have been situated in Scotland. Different orders might have to be applied for successively for different purposes, and the decree was not good against the world, as it bound only those parties called as defenders to the action.[29]

(c) Current law: The Presumption of Death (Scotland) Act 1977

1.8 As a result of a Scottish Law Commission project on the area, further reforms were introduced by the Presumption of Death (Scotland) Act 1977.[30] The 1977 Act is a useful and effective piece of legislation, replacing both the common law and the Presumption of Life (Limitation) (Scotland) Act 1881.[31] The main provision of the 1977 Act is set out in s 1(1):

> 'Where a person who is missing is thought to have died or has not been known to be alive for a period of at least seven years, any person having an interest may raise an action of declarator of death of that person … in the Court of Session or the sheriff court in accordance with the provisions of this section.'

Section 1(1) makes clear that there are two situations where an action of declarator may be raised:

(1) The first is where a person is thought to have died.[32] In this case, it is not necessary that the person has been missing for seven years. Declarator can be sought and granted immediately if there is sufficient evidence to satisfy the court that on the balance of probabilities, the missing person has died; for example, where no corpse is recovered or a positive identification of the corpse is impossible, perhaps because of the severity of the injuries sustained.

29 See Consultative Memorandum on *Presumptions of Death and Survivorship* (SLC CM No 11, 1969).

30 See Report on *Presumption of Death* (SLC Report No 74, 1974).

31 For further details on how the legislation operates, and the procedures involved, see A Cubie (ed), *MacPhail's Sheriff Court Practice,* 4th edn (2022), paras 20.06 to 20.17; and *Parliament House* (looseleaf, Release 185, October 2025), Vol 8, Div C, Ch 50.

32 As a recent example, see *LM v AM* 2025 SLT (Sh Ct) 84.

(2) The second situation is where there is neither circumstantial nor forensic evidence sufficient to satisfy the court that the missing person has died but neither is there any positive knowledge of his or her being alive. In this case, after seven years, it is not proof of death that is required for decree to be granted but the fact that there is no proof of survivance.

Anyone who has information about the death or survival of the missing person and who is aware that an action of declarator has been raised or an application for a variation order made (if declarator has already been granted) has a duty to disclose that information to the court dealing with the action.[33] There is no duty, however, if the person would be entitled to refuse to give evidence as a witness or would be entitled to refuse on the basis of the law relating to the withholding of information on the grounds of public interest.[34]

Section 2(1) of the 1977 Act provides that the standard of proof required is the ordinary civil standard of the balance of probabilities. Under s 2(1)(a), the court will declare a date and time of death. Where it is uncertain when, within any period of time, a missing person died, it shall be at the end of the period of time within which he or she could have died. Where the person has not been known to be alive for a period of at least seven years, s 2(1)(b) provides that the court will find that the missing person died at the end of the day, occurring seven years after the date on which the person was last known to be alive.

Whilst typically it will be the family of the deceased, such as a spouse or blood relation, raising 1977 Act proceedings, the Act allows any person with an interest to raise proceedings, including the Lord Advocate for the public interest.[35] The missing person themselves should ordinarily be called as the defender, and imitation of the action should be given to the missing person, such as by way of advertisement in local newspapers.[36]

33 1977 Act, s 9.

34 1977 Act, s 9(2).

35 1977 Act, s 17.

36 *Horak v Lord Advocate* 1984 SLT 201. Specific rules are found for the Sheriff Courts in the Ordinary Cause Rules, Ch 37. For the Court of Session, the Rules of the Court of Session, Ch 50.

(c)(i) Jurisdiction

1.9 The Court of Session and the sheriff court both have jurisdiction to entertain an action of declarator of death. Under s 1(3), the Court of Session has jurisdiction:

(a) if the missing person was domiciled in Scotland on the date when he or she was last known to be alive, or had been habitually resident in Scotland throughout the period of one year ending with the date when they were last known to be alive;[37] or

(b) the pursuer in the action is the spouse or civil partner of the missing person and is domiciled in Scotland, or was habitually resident in Scotland throughout the period of one year ending with the date when the missing person was last known to be alive;[38] or

(c) if the pursuer is: (i) the civil partner of the missing person, (ii) the two people concerned registered as civil partners of each other in Scotland, and (iii) it appears to the court to be in the interests of justice to assume jurisdiction in the case.[39]

Under s 1(4), the sheriff court has jurisdiction:

(a) if the provisions of s 1(3)(a), the provisions relating to the missing person's domicile or habitual residence above, are satisfied and the missing person's last known place of residence was in the sheriffdom;[40] or

(b) if the provisions of s 1(3)(b), the provisions relating to the missing person's spouse or civil partner raising the action, are satisfied and the pursuer was resident in the sheriffdom for a period of not less than 40 days ending with the date of raising the action.[41]

A further provision for the sheriff court to found jurisdiction was enacted with the introduction of same-sex marriages into Scots law.[42] Under

37 1977 Act, s 1(3)(a).
38 1977 Act, s 1(3)(b).
39 1977 Act, s 1(3)(c) [as introduced by the Civil Partnership Act 2004, Sch 28, para 45].
40 1977 Act, s 1(4)(a).
41 1977 Act, s 1(4)(b).
42 Marriage and Civil Partnership (Scotland) Act 2014, Sch 1, para 2.

s 1(4A) of the 1977 Act, Edinburgh Sheriff Court is a jurisdiction of 'last resort' where the pursuer is a spouse in a same-sex marriage, and they married in Scotland. If Edinburgh Sheriff Court considers it in the interests of justice for it to assume jurisdiction, then jurisdiction can be so assumed.[43]

(c)(ii) Powers of court

1.10 Section 2 of the 1977 Act lists the powers of the court in any action of declarator. It may:

(a) determine the domicile of the missing person at the date of his or her death;[44]

(b) determine any question relating to any interest in property which arises as a consequence of the death of the missing person;[45]

(c) appoint a judicial factor on the estate of the missing person, notwithstanding what the value of the estate may be;[46] and

(d) determine any incidental questions.[47]

Under s 1(5), a person having an interest in the action who is not the pursuer in the action may lodge a minute seeking a determination or appointment under s 2 of the 1977 Act which is not sought by the pursuer.

Where an action is raised in the sheriff court, a party to the action or the sheriff himself may, at any stage in the proceedings, apply to the Court of Session under s 1(6) of the 1977 Act to have the action remitted to it.

43 The reason for this provision relates to international private law. If the same-sex couple are married in Scotland but later reside in a country which does not recognise same-sex marriage, then it may not be open for a spouse to raise missing person proceedings under the couples' domiciled legal system. Section 1(4A) allows them a remedy in Scotland to raise such proceedings. Similar amendments to protect same-sex couples married in Scotland were made to a range of family law court actions by Sch 1 of the 2014 Act.

44 1977 Act, s 2(2)(a).

45 1977 Act, s 2(2)(b).

46 1977 Act, s 2(2)(c). On judicial factors, see the Judicial Factors (Scotland) Act 2025 which is anticipated to be in force in short course.

47 1977 Act, s 2(3).

The action will be remitted if the Court of Session considers it desirable because of the importance or complexity of the matters at issue.

(c)(iii) Effect of decree

1.11 If decree is granted, it is conclusive in relation to all matters contained in the decree and is effective against any person and for all purposes, including the dissolution of a marriage or civil partnership to which the missing person was a party and the acquisition of rights to or in property belonging to any person.[48] This means that succession to the estate of the missing person, now the deceased, opens and distribution can competently begin following decree.

A dissolution of marriage or civil partnership is not invalidated if the missing person turns out to be alive[49] and, even if declarator of death is neither sought nor granted, it is a defence to a charge of bigamy that at no time during the period of seven years immediately preceding the marriage or civil partnership did the person who has re-married have any reason to believe that his or her spouse or civil partner was alive.[50]

A decree does not provide amnesty for crimes or offences if the missing person turns out to be alive and the criminal responsibility of neither the missing person nor any other person is removed if the missing person was in fact alive at the date specified in decree.[51]

(c)(iv) Recall or variation of decree

1.12 If declarator of death is granted and the missing person later turns out to be alive; decree is not set aside but may be recalled or varied under s 4 of the 1977 Act. Any person having an interest, including the person presumed to have died, may apply to the court for variation or recall of the decree.[52] The court can make orders of the same types specified in s 2

48 1977 Act, s 3(1).
49 1977 Act, s 3(3).
50 1977 Act, s 13.
51 1977 Act, s 3(4). For an illustration of the potential risk for not having such a rule, readers might enjoy the American film, *Double Jeopardy* (1999).
52 1977 Act, s 4(1).

for granting of the declarator of death.[53] As with the original decree, a person who is not the pursuer in the action has the right to lodge a minute in relation to any determination or appointment.[54]

Section 4(5) provides that no variation or recall can be sought in relation to the dissolution of marriage to which the missing person was a party, and the marriage will not be revived.[55] In relation to the missing person's property, however, if decree has been granted and succession to that person's estate has already opened, the estate may have been distributed by the time any application for variation or recall is made. Underscoring the effect of decree set out in s 3(1), s 5(1) provides the general rule that a variation order shall have no effect on rights to or in property acquired as a result of the decree.

Section 5(2) provides an exception: if decree is recalled or varied within five years of its being granted, the court can make an order in relation to property rights as it considers fair and reasonable in all the circumstances.[56] The orders that can be made are limited by the further provisions of Section 5:

(1) First, s 5(2) provides that no order will have an effect on any income accruing between the date of decree and the date of the variation order. This means that even if variation or recall is sought within the five-year period, any right to income is forfeited.

(2) Second, s 5(3) makes certain limitations in relation to property administered under a trust, or for any sums paid out by insurers.

(3) Third, s 5(5) provides that where any person acquires rights to or in property as a result of decree under s 2, or any person derives rights from him or her, and he or she enters into a transaction with another person acting in good faith and for value, that third

53 1977 Act, s 4(2).

54 1977 Act, s 4(3).

55 There is no equivalent statutory provision in relation to civil partners. However, the civil partnership would be dissolved (as with marriage) under s 3(1) by the decree. The absence of equivalent statutory provision appears to be an omission by the parliamentary drafters, and it is unlikely that the law would be such that a civil partnership would be revived by recall of the decree.

56 1977 Act, s 5(4).

party's title shall not be challengeable on the ground that an order for variation or recall under s 5(2) was made.

To mitigate against the risk that the missing person turns out to be alive and seeks recall of the decree once his or her property has been distributed, s 6 of the 1977 Act requires a trustee (or executor or judicial factor) to effect a policy of insurance against any claim which may arise as a result of an order made under s 5(2).

In addition, s 6(3) provides that where a person receives a capital sum representing the proceeds of insurance on the missing person's life, the insurer may require that person to effect an insurance policy in his or her own name against any claim being made if decree is varied or recalled.

In short, the court may, but need not unless it considers it fair and reasonable, make an order recalling or varying the decree within five years of it being granted, but such an order will relate to capital only. A missing person who turns up more than five years after decree is granted has no right to recover any of his or her property. If he or she seeks an order for variation or recall within the five-year period, any right to income that has accrued during the period when he or she was missing is forfeited.

SURVIVORSHIP

1.13 The *sine qua non* of the law of succession is that one person may succeed to the estate of another only if the former is alive and the latter has died. Establishing who survives will determine not only whether a succession opens at all, but who may succeed to the deceased's estate.

As a basic rule, the dead cannot inherit. A successor or beneficiary must survive the deceased in order to inherit. As an example, Lucy left her entire estate to Mary in her will. Lucy dies on 5 January after catching a serious flu. Mary had the same flu and died three days earlier on 2 January. Mary, and her successors, cannot inherit Lucy's estate. The reason for this rule relates to the law of vesting.[57] When Lucy died, succession rights vested in her successors' patrimonies.[58] On the face of it, a succession right could not vest in Mary's patrimony because she is dead. Consequently, the

57 See **Ch 13**.

58 Before the deceased dies, a successor only has a *spes* (a hope) of succession rather than a right (*jus*) of succession. See para **13.2**.

succession right to Lucy's estate is not part of Mary's patrimony or estate. Thus, Mary's own successors cannot claim Lucy's estate.

If a survivor does subsequently die after succession rights have vested in their own patrimony, that does not necessarily mean that the succession rights they hold will lapse. As the succession right was in the (subsequently deceased) survivor's patrimony, the survivor's successors may be able to claim the entitlement. To take another example: Billy dies of a heart attack on 4 February. In his will, Billy had left all his estate to his brother Archie. Archie is ill with bowel cancer and dies on 15 March. Archie's successors can claim Billy's estate. This is because succession rights vested in Archie and his patrimony at the point of Billy's death. The right to Billy's estate is now a patrimonial asset within Archie's own estate. The estate can be claimed from Billy's executor by Archie's executor.

Even if no right ever vested in a predeceasing successor, it may still be possible for their issue (descendants) to claim under limited circumstances. Where this happens, the (deceased) successor may have no vested succession right in their patrimony, but the law allows the successor's descendants to 'step into their shoes' and claim the succession right in their place. This is considered later in this text.[59]

Another exception to the basic rule is that vesting of succession rights may be delayed or postponed to a later date, or the occurrence of a certain event. Where this happens, the survivor may well be alive at the point the deceased died, but no succession rights vested in their patrimony because they had not met specified conditions. This is common in the case of testate succession, where the testator imposes conditions for the vesting of a succession right under a legacy. One common example is for a legacy to require that a successor must be 25 years old at the time of the testator's death for the right to vest. If the successor is not yet 25 years old when the deceased died, then it is arguable that no succession right has vested in their patrimony. Should the survivor then die before they reach the age of 25, then the legacy will lapse and cannot be claimed by the survivor's own successors. These complicated rules are, again, considered later on in this text.[60]

59 See paras **5.7–5.9** on representation in legitim; paras **6.35–6.36** on representation in the intestate estate; and para **11.22** for implied destinations-over under s 6 of the Succession (Scotland) Act 2016.

60 See paras **13.9–13.12**.

Whilst there are exceptions, as a basic rule, no one may succeed at all unless it is first established that: (i) the person from whom a succession opens is dead, and (ii) the successors entitled to succeed to his or her estate were alive at the moment of death of the person whose estate is being distributed. Where the facts of death and survivance cannot be known, legal rules and presumptions are applied. This typically arises in the case of common calamities.

(1) Common calamities

1.14 A long-married husband and wife have wills in favour of each other. One day they go for a drive. On the motorway, a lorry crashes into them and their car flips over and catches fire. Both are pronounced dead when emergency services arrive at the scene. Did the husband succeed to the wife's estate? Or did the wife succeed to the husband's estate? Did neither succeed to the other's estate?

That example is the classic situation of a common calamity. A common calamity refers to where two or more people are killed together in a single event and one victim was entitled to succeed to the other or each victim was entitled to succeed to the other.[61] Since survivorship is a prerequisite of establishing whether one person may succeed to the estate of another, the question to be determined in cases of common calamity is the order of death as between the persons killed. Only then can it be ascertained how each person's estates fall to be distributed.

It is generally impossible to know the exact moment at which any death occurs unless under close medical supervision. Death may not take place at a single point in time but may be a process that takes some time to complete; this is likely even where there appears to be instantaneous and simultaneous destruction of two people. As Lord Porter observed in *Hickman v Peacey*:[62]

61 For a comparative overview of this subject, see R Zimmermann and R Gleim, 'Presumptions of Survivorship or Simultaneous Death in Cases of 'Common Calamity: Scots law Against the Background of European Legal Developments' in A Steven et al (eds), *Nothing so Practical as a Good Theory: Festschrift for George L Gretton* (2017).

62 *Hickman v Peacey* [1945] AC 304, at 337.

> 'I am not sure that the occurrence of two deaths at exactly the same point in time is possible, and still less am I inclined to accept the allegation that it can ever be proved.'

A fraction of a second may be enough to constitute the survivorship of one person over another, but while the fact of survival may in some cases be perfectly clear, it may be entirely incapable of proof in others.[63] To return to the car crash example above, there may be little evidence from the couple's burnt corpses to indicate who died first. It is in these cases that the law must provide a default rule to allow estates to be distributed without undue complexity.

(a) Common Law and the Succession (Scotland) Act 1964

1.15 As with the case of missing persons, it could not be presumed at common law that one person had outlived another as a result of age, sex or state of health, and several cases illustrate the situations that arose and the difficulties that this could cause. In *Drummond's Judicial Factor v Lord Advocate*[64] a husband and wife and their two children were killed by a bomb falling onto their house during the Clydebank Blitz. Both the husband (Mr Drummond) and wife (Mrs Drummond) died intestate, and the question arose as to whether Mr Drummond's siblings or the Crown were entitled to succeed to Mrs Drummond's estate. Although there was no legal presumptions of survivorship in Scots law, the pursuers argued that the court ought to apply presumptions such as existed in other systems of law. They argued that the presumptions of Roman law should be followed, whereby males were preferred to females (so that Mr Drummond would be held to have survived his wife) and a father was presumed to have survived sons under the age of puberty (so that Mr Drummond would be held to have survived his children). Alternatively, there were presumptions in the Napoleonic Code and the English Law of Property Act 1925[65] that could be applied. The Crown argued that Scots law required proof

63 See 'Common calamities and the presumption of death' 1963 *SLT (News)* 101.

64 *Drummond's JF v Lord Advocate* 1944 SC 298.

65 Section 184 of the 1925 Act provides that where two or more persons died in circumstances which rendered it uncertain which had survived the other or others, it should be presumed that the younger had survived the elder.

of survivance and it was now too late to incorporate the Roman law in the law of Scotland; accordingly, Mrs Drummond's property was *bona vacantia* and fell to the Crown as *ultimus haeres*.

The Lord Justice-Clerk (Cooper) held that the rules of other systems cited were 'essentially arbitrary and artificial rules of expediency, and had no fundamental basis in principle or equity'.[66] To adopt them would be an act of judicial legislation which, apart from the issue of its legitimacy, was in any case unnecessary, since Scots law already provided a solution:[67]

> 'Survivance is in every case a matter of proof, and ... when a claimant whose claim depends upon proof of survivorship is unable to establish the fact of survivance, his claim necessarily fails.'

Lord Mackay commented that 'it seems to be taken for granted (but why?) that the children cannot be held or presumed to have survived either parent' and went on to say that while he would like to see easily ascertainable and easily applicable rules of survivorship being recognised, it was not the task of the court to adopt these on a case-by-case basis.[68] The court held that since it was impossible to prove the order of death and no presumptions of survivorship could be applied, the whole family was to be presumed to have died simultaneously, with the consequence that Mrs Drummond's estate fell to the Crown as *ultimus haeres* and not to her husband's heirs.

In *Mitchell's Executrix v Gordon*[69] a husband and wife and one of their three daughters were killed together in a plane crash, survived by the other two daughters and the son of the deceased daughter. Mr Mitchell had died intestate. Mrs Mitchell had made a will in which she directed trustees to hold the residue of her estate for her children equally among them, with vesting in each child postponed until she reached the age of majority. The daughter who had died had reached majority already, and the legacy would vest in her on her mother's death, provided that she survived her. On the basis that survivorship was wholly a matter of proof as established by the evidence and there was no evidence as to survivorship in the instant case, the three deceased were presumed to have died simultaneously. The

66 1944 SC 298, at 301.
67 1944 SC 298, at 302.
68 1944 SC 298, at 302.
69 1953 SC 176.

daughter could not succeed to her parents' estate because she could not be presumed to have survived them; neither could she be presumed to have predeceased them. The consequence of this was that her son could not succeed to either of his grandparents' estates or in his mother's place.[70]

Ross's Judicial Factor v Martin[71] illustrates the situation where the parties have executed mutual wills. Two sisters had each named the other as sole beneficiary to her estate, subject to a destination-over to a named charity in the event of the other's predeceasing. The effect was that when one sister died, the other would succeed to her estate but, if that sister died first, the legacy would be payable to the charity. In the event, both sisters died together as the result of a gas leak. The only conclusion that the court could reach was that each had predeceased the other. Both estates fell into intestacy, and the charity had no entitlement to either of them.

In order to address the difficulties that could arise at common law, Section 31 of the Succession (Scotland) Act 1964 introduced statutory presumptions to be applied in cases of common calamity. To be charitable, these provisions were complex and will not be explored here in any further detail.[72] The complexity did not escape the attention of the Scottish Law Commission who examined potential reform of the common calamity provisions of the 1964 Act.[73]

(b) Current Law: Succession (Scotland) Act 2016

1.16 The Commission's recommended reforms are now contained in ss 9–10 of the Succession (Scotland) Act 2016. The standard of proof under these provisions remains the same as the common law, in that

70 If his mother had been presumed to have survived her parents, her son could have succeeded to his grandfather's intestate estate by way of representation under the Intestate Moveable (Succession) (Scotland) Act 1855 (see para **6.35** on the equivalent provision under the Succession (Scotland) Act 1964, s 5) and to his grandmother's testate estate under the old *conditio si institutus sine liberis decesserit* (see para **11.22**). He could, alternatively, have claimed legal rights by way of representation in both of his grandparents' moveable estates (see para **5.7**).

71 1955 SC (HL) 56.

72 See the second edition of this text at paras 1.17–1.20.

73 Report on *Succession* (SLC Report No 124, 1990), Part V; and Report *on Succession* (SLC Report No 215, 2009), paras 6.54 to 6.60.

when assessing a common calamity, it is dealt with on the balance of probabilities.[74] If it cannot be shown, on the balance of probabilities, that one person survived the other (however short a period that may have been), then ss 9–10 will apply. In a contentious dispute in this area, forensic investigators and pathologists could examine the corpses to offer expert evidence in order to disapply the default provisions in the statute.

Section 9(1) of the 2016 Act provides that where two persons are involved in a common calamity, and it is uncertain as to who predeceased first, each deceased person is treated as failing to survive the other. Thus, to return to the example at the beginning of this section, if a husband and wife die together in a car crash, and it cannot be shown who died first, then the result would be that neither would inherit anything from the other's estate. Each is treated as predeceasing the other, and consequently, no succession rights vested in their patrimony on the other's death.

Whilst the section describes *two* persons, it is really to be treated as a question of two people against one another. If four people died in a common calamity, and it is unclear about who died first, then section 9 would still apply. To take an example, if Cameron, Alliah, Ken and Oliver are killed in an explosion and it is unclear about who died first, then in a question of Cameron's estate, Alliah is treated as predeceasing Cameron. Ken is treated as predeceasing Cameron, and Oliver is treated as predeceasing Cameron. The wording of section 9 is dealing with a matter of perspective for one person's estate against one successor to it.

Section 9(2) provides a rule for common calamities in the case of testate succession. It has complex wording, but it concerns how a destination-over operates in a common calamity.[75] If the husband and wife in the car crash example had a legacy in each of their wills which said 'I leave my entire estate to my spouse, whom failing my son' then s 9(2) deems the spouse to have predeceased – so that the son may inherit the estate. It is a technical extension of the rule contained in s 9(1).

A separate rule is found in section 10. This is rather more fiendish to explain. Its basic idea is to provide equal distribution of certain property at death where two or more persons[76] had the potential to receive that

74 *Lamb v Lord Advocate* (1964) SC 110.

75 For destinations-over, see para **11.17**.

76 This is referred to as a 'group of persons', which is two persons or more than two persons, 2016 Act, s 10(3).

property dependent on who in the group died first. If the group die in a common calamity, then it is unclear as to whose estate should receive that property. The 2016 Act provides for equal distribution of the property amongst the estates of the group in such cases. This is a high-level explanation because the provision is complex. To explain how it operates completely, it is necessary to outline its legislative history.

The Commission's proposals

1.17 The original idea of Section 10 is to be found in the Commission's consultation work on succession law in 1986.[77] The Commission initially had proposed a rule whereby:[78]

> 'Where property is to be transferred to one of two or more persons, depending on the order of their deaths, and does not form part of the estate of either or any of those persons before his death then if those persons have died simultaneously or in such other circumstances that it cannot be established which of them survived the other or others the property or its value should, unless the obligation to transfer contains any provision to the contrary, be divided equally between or among the estates of those persons.'

The Commission proposed that this would apply 'in the situation in which two or more people are entitled to [property] from a third person'.[79] Where the testator themselves was involved in the common calamity then what is now s 9 of the 2016 Act would apply instead.

The examples given by the Commission included where a life insurance company may insure an entire family, with a capital sum payable to the estate of the family member who died first. Should the family all die in a common calamity then it would be unclear as to whose estate should the insurance payout be made over to (if at all).[80] The Commission proposed

77 Consultative Memorandum on *Some Miscellaneous Topics in the Law of Succession* (SLC CM No 71, 1986), para 3.7.

78 Report on *Succession* (SLC Report No 124, 1990), para 5.6.

79 *Written Evidence from the Scottish Law Commission to the Delegated Powers and Law Reform Committee on the Succession (Scotland) Bill* (5 August 2015), para 36.

80 Report on *Succession* (SLC Report No 124, 1990), para 5.6.

solution was that any such property should be divided equally.[81] Thus in the example of the life insurance policy, the monies from the insurer should be paid out equally to the estates of each family member.

Reception in the Scottish Parliament

1.18 This proposal was then taken to the Scottish Parliament, and 'a number of issues arose' in respect of what now forms sections 9 and 10 of the 2016 Act.[82] The Scottish Government sought to make amendments to clarify the exact application of section 10. The result is that the provision is rather cumbersome, though it still intends to provide for:[83]

> 'A narrow and particular set of circumstances... Those circumstances cover where property is to pass to one member of a group of people depending on the order of death and members of the group are involved in a common calamity. All members of the group are potential beneficiaries and have equal status... In those circumstances the new rule provides that the property will be divided equally among their estates.'

The 2016 Act

1.19 Section 10 will operate where there is some form of obligation (be it under a will, trust, insurance policy or other)[84] that means that property was to be transferred to:[85]

(i) the estate of a person who dies first amongst a group of persons;

(ii) the survivor of a group of persons; or

(iii) members of a group equally, or to the surviving member(s) of that group.

81 A proposal carried forward into the Report on *Succession*, (SLC Report No 215, 2009), para 6.60.

82 Delegated Powers and Law Reform Committee, *Stage 1 Report on the Succession (Scotland) Bill* (SP Report 821, 2 November 2015), para 97.

83 Official Report, *Delegated Powers and Law Reform Committee: Succession (Scotland) Bill, Stage 2 Proceedings* (Tuesday 8 December 2015), col 18.

84 Report on *Succession* (SLC Report No 124, 1990), para 5.6.

85 2016 Act, s 10(1)(a).

If two or more of that group die in a common calamity, and the order of death is uncertain, then the property will be distributed equally amongst the estates of the deceased group members.[86] This is a default position which applies in the absence of any specific instructions in the document in question.[87] It is important to note that this only deals with transfers from a third party. If the property is to pass under a will, and the testator has died in the common calamity alongside the group, then section 10 will not operate (and section 9 will operate instead).[88]

Examples

A few examples are offered on section 10's potential application in the absence of any reported judicial treatment:

1. Katie and Phoebe are married. A number of years ago, they purchased a joint-life insurance policy from Glasgow Life Insurance. The policy provides that £100,000 is to be paid out to the survivor of them. Katie and Phoebe are killed in a plane crash in the North Sea. Glasgow Life Insurance would be required to pay £50,000 to Katie's executor and £50,000 to Phoebe's executor.

2. Sandy created a trust for her three sons, Alex, Leo, and Nicholas. This provides for payment of £200,000 to the estate of whichever son died first in order to care for their next of kin. The brothers are keen sailors and go sailing in the Irish Sea. A storm sinks their yacht, and their corpses are recovered by the coastguard a week later. It is impossible to tell who died first. The trustee would be required, under section 10, to pay £66,666.67 to Alex's estate, £66,666.67 to Leo's estate and £66,666.67 to Nicholas's estate.

3. Tasnim, Gordon and Nika are three siblings. Tasnim has a will which leaves her estate to her two siblings equally, and to the survivor of them. One day, whilst skiing, the three are killed by an avalanche. Their bodies are not recovered until the spring thaw a few weeks later. It is impossible to ascertain who died first.

86 2016 Act, s 10(2).
87 2016 Act, s 10(1)(d).
88 2016 Act, s 10(4).

> Section 10 would not apply here because Tasnim, the testator, died alongside the group of potential beneficiaries.[89] Instead, section 9 applies and treats each of the group as predeceasing the other. Neither the estate of Gordon, nor the estate of Nika, could inherit Tasnim's estate as they are treated as failing to survive her.

In 1986, the Commission commented on their proposals that 'such gifts though not common are not unknown'.[90] This tends to suggest this statutory provision may not be one often considered by a court, which is unfortunate given its complexity.

(2) Legacy conditions for survivorship: ambiguity as to survivorship

1.20 It was noted at the introduction to the discussion of survivorship that a testator may insert conditions into legacies to delay the vesting of a right under a legacy. One such common condition is an express survivance requirement, where the testator sets a specific period of survivance as a condition for a legacy to vest.[91] A common example for wills of married couples is that a legatee, the surviving spouse, must survive the deceased for a period of one month in order for the legacy to vest in them.[92]

The reason for this additional qualification is to ensure that property does not pass to a legatee who then dies too soon after the testator. In such situations, without a condition, the legacy would be unlikely to provide any personal benefit to the legatee if they died within a short period after the testator. An unqualified vesting of a legacy could provide a windfall to the legatee's own estate, which may be viewed unfavourably depending on the legatee's own successors. A condition of survivance for a specified period can ensure that the legacy will only be payable if the legatee survives the testator for a certain period, and thus they can enjoy 'the benefit' of the legacy personally.

89 2016 Act, s 10(4).

90 Consultative Memorandum on *Some Miscellaneous Topics in the Law of Succession* (SLC CM No 71, 1986), para 3.7.

91 A Barr et al, *Drafting Wills in Scotland*, 2nd edn (2009), para 5.15.

92 See Scottish Law Commission, Report on *Succession*, (SLC Report No 215, 2009), paras 6.58–6.59.

A final rule of survivance is to be found in section 11 of the 2016 Act dealing with a situation where it is unclear if the legatee survived the deceased for the stipulated period of time. This might occur if, for example, a legatee dies at home alone and no one discovers their corpse for many weeks – such that it is difficult to determine when exactly they died, and whether they did indeed survive for the stipulated period under the legacy.

In such situations, s 11 provides that where it cannot be proven, on the balance of probabilities, whether the legatee survived the testator for the specified period, then the legatee is simply treated as predeceasing the testator so that the legacy cannot be said to have vested in them.

THE CORPSE

(1) Ownership of corpses

1.21 Once someone has died, does anyone hold the right of ownership in the corpse or its constituent parts? Could a family member acquire the right of ownership in a corpse? If someone steals a corpse, does a family member have a vindicatory or possessory remedy in property law to have the corpse returned to them? If a doctor harvests a corpse's liver for transplantation or experimentation without the family's consent, are they committing theft? These are some of the potential questions in this area for which Scots law struggles to answer.

At one stage, it was easy to conclude that no one holds the right of ownership of a corpse or its constituent parts. In recent years, a clear conclusion on the law has become harder to reach.[93] A growing consensus seems to be emerging that body parts detached from a *living* person are capable of being things (*res*) and thus capable of being subject to a right of ownership.[94] However, for the moment, there still seems to be a

93 Much debate can be found in this area but for useful overviews see N Whitty, 'Rights of personality, property rights and the human body in Scots law' (2005) 9(2) *Edin LR* 194; K Reid, 'Body Parts and Property' in D Bain et al, *Northern Lights: Essays in Private Law in Memory of Professor David Carey Miller* (2018); and J Brown, ''Still a part of me': 'functional unity' and the human body in Scots law' (2022) *Jur Rev* 80.

94 K Reid, *The Law of Property in Scotland*, 2nd edn (2026), para 46; Whitty, 'Rights of personality, property rights and the human body in Scots law' (2005) 9(2) *Edin LR* 194, 228–234.

widespread rejection that a corpse, and its constituent parts, could be a *rem* and thus subject to ownership.[95]

The traditional approach of Scots law in rejecting ownership of a corpse is shown by *Robson v Robson*.[96] A widow had given birth to her husband's posthumous child, which then died. Her husband was buried in a lair owned by his father, and she petitioned the court to disinter her dead husband's body in order to move it to a lair which she had bought in the same cemetery as the child's. The court considered the general questions involved:[97]

> 'It appears to be settled in the law of Scotland, as in that of England, that there is no right of property in a dead body.'

This view was more recently endorsed by Lord Brodie in *C v Advocate General*.[98] Developments in Scots criminal law seem less clear. It is a distinct offence, known as violation of sepulchres, to remove a corpse from a grave or final resting place.[99] However, it seems there is authority under *Dewar v HMA* that prior to internment, it is possible that a corpse can be capable of being subject to theft.[100] What follows from that is, from a criminal law perspective, that a corpse is a thing (*rem*) which can be stolen. The implications of this are as Gordon, Chalmers and Leverick explain:[101]

> 'The approach of the court in *Dewar*, therefore, confirms the view that a human body, at least prior to burial, can be owned, and so can be stolen. If that is so, it is possible to hold that it is theft to steal a body which instead of being buried has been gifted to a laboratory, or placed in a museum, or even embalmed and kept in a glass case in the widow's livingroom. Indeed,

95 See the discussion in J Brown, *Corpus Vile or CorpusPersonae? The Status of the Human Body, its Parts and its Derivatives in Scots law,* PhD thesis, University of Strathclyde (2020), Ch 2. Whilst ownership may be rejected, it is possible that a family may have suffered an actionable wrong in delict for interference with a corpse, see *Stevens v Yorkhill NHS Trust* [2006] CSOH 143.

96 *Robson v Robson* (1897) 5 SLT (Sh Ct) 351.

97 ibid 353.

98 *C v Advocate General for Scotland* [2011] CSOH 124, para 63.

99 See *HMA v Coutts* (1899) 3 Adam 50 and J Chalmers and F Leverick (eds), *Gordon's Criminal Law of Scotland*, Vol II, 4th edn (2017), Ch 51.

100 *Dewar v HMA* 1945 JC 5.

101 Chalmers and Leverick (eds), *Gordon's Criminal Law of Scotland*, Vol II, para 21.26.

> the need to protect specimens in laboratories and exhibits in museums is itself a strong argument for treating a body as capable of being owned. It seems unreasonable to suggest that a museum has no property in its mummies, or that an anatomical laboratory has no property in parts of a body it has dissected, and which it has preserved for exhibition.'

Whilst ownership of a corpse remains unclear, statute has better regulated the management and handling of corpses such that this important point may now hopefully be little more than an intellectual curiosity in most cases.

(2) Organ and cadaver donation

1.22 It is now fairly common for people to carry organ donor cards; slightly more unusual are bequests of one's body to medical institutions for the purposes of teaching and research. The question is: Who has the ultimate authority to consent to the donation of organs from, and research on, a deceased person's body?

It is worth noting a scandal which has influenced the law in this area. In the early part of the noughties, it came to light that medical professionals within the United Kingdom had been retaining organs and other bodily tissue after deaths and post-mortems without family members' full knowledge.[102] This was often for research purposes, rather than out of any malicious or grotesque intent. The North Glasgow University Hospitals Trust came under particular scrutiny; it being found to have accrued around 4,500 organs.[103] What was rather sickening was that deceased children's organs had also been retained without parental consent.[104] The Scottish Executive appointed Professor Sheila Maclean of the University of Glasgow to convene a review of the practice and the law in Scotland, whose findings in turn led to reform under the Human Tissue (Scotland) Act 2006.[105]

102 See M Brazier, 'Retained organs: ethics and humanity' (2002) 22(4) *Legal Studies* 550.

103 J Allardyce, 'Hospital staff took cash for organs', *The Times* 29 August 2004.

104 K Scott, 'Inquiry call over babies' organs', *The Guardian* 26 August 2000.

105 Independent Review Group, *Final Report on the Retention of Organs at Post-Mortem* (2001).

The 2006 Act provides that organ or tissue removal from a corpse must be authorised for transplantation, research, education, training, or audit and quality assurance, provided that removal is carried out according to the requirements set out in the Act for each of those purposes.[106] Recent amendments have been made by the Human Tissue (Authorisation) (Scotland) Act 2019 to facilitate the new system of 'opt-out' organ donation, whereby it is presumed that all eligible persons have authorised the use of certain tissue for transplantation.

A full treatment of the 2006 Act cannot be offered here, but, broadly, an adult with capacity may give authorisation of the removal of tissue at their death.[107] Under the opt-out transplantation system, an adult with capacity who is ordinarily resident in Scotland is deemed to have already authorised the removal of certain tissue for the purpose of transplantation.[108] However, it is possible to provide an opt-out declaration to disapply this presumption.[109] Additionally, some tissue is always excepted from transplantation under the opt-out system,[110] though the 'nearest relative' of the deceased can later give consent for its use provided the deceased has not made an opt-out declaration.[111] If the adult is incapacitated, then authorisation can be given by the 'nearest relative' of the adult instead.[112]

Otherwise, an adult is still free to give express oral or written authorisation for transplantation.[113] For all other removals, such as the removal of tissue for research, express authorisation must be given in writing.[114] This can be from the adult themselves prior to death, or by their nearest relative (either orally or in writing) after death.[115]

Children over the age of 12 years old are also entitled to authorise the removal of tissue.[116] A parent may also consent to the removal of tissue for

106 2006 Act, s 3.
107 2006 Act, s 6.
108 2006 Act, s 6D.
109 2006 Act, s 6B.
110 2006 Act, s 6D(2)(c); and The Human Tissue (Excepted Body Parts) (Scotland) Regulations 2020 SSI 2020/388, reg 2.
111 2006 Act, s 6G; and s 50.
112 2006 Act, s 6F; and s 50.
113 2006 Act, s 6(1A)(a).
114 2006 Act, s 6(1A)(b).
115 2006 Act, s 6H.
116 2006 Act, s 8.

these children too after their death, provided this is not inconsistent with the child's known views.[117] For children under the age of 12, a parent may similarly authorise the removal of tissue.[118]

Otherwise, an adult may request their entire body be donated for anatomical examination under the Anatomy Act 1984.[119] This is commonly the source of cadavers used within universities teaching and training medical professionals. Such a request has to be in writing and signed by the donator in the presence of a witness.[120] If the donator is blind or unable to physically sign documents, then execution can be made by another person on their behalf, subject to additional safeguards.[121] A child over the age of 12 can also request in writing that their body be donated too, with additional safeguards that two witnesses attest to the request.[122] Each witness must also certify that the child understood the request and was not acting under undue influence.[123]

(3) Disposal of a corpse

1.23 The law relating to funerals and the disposal of corpses has undergone significant change since the last edition of this text. In 2007, the Burial and Cremation Review Group issued a report advising on updates to funerary law in Scotland. These recommendations have gone on to form the Burial and Cremation (Scotland) Act 2016, though some areas of the statute are still in the process of being brought into force.

Under the 2016 Act, there are three main ways that a corpse may be disposed of in Scotland: (i) burial; (ii) cremation; and (iii) hydrolysis (often termed as water cremation).[124] The 2016 Act makes detailed provision for

117 2006 Act, s 8D.

118 2006 Act, s 10. Other relatives may also be able to consent in the absence or incapacity of parents, s 10A. Special provisions apply under s 10B where the local authority is exercising parental rights and responsibilities.

119 1984 Act, s 4.

120 1984 Act, s 4(1A)(a).

121 1984 Act, ss 4(1A)(b); 4(1B); and s 4(1D).

122 1984 Act, s 4(1C).

123 1984 Act, s 4(1C)(ii).

124 Hydrolysis has been introduced by the Hydrolysis (Scotland) (No. 1) Regulations 2026 SSI 2026/50 and The Hydrolysis (Scotland) (No. 2) Regulations 2026 SSI 2026/51.

all three methods, and a modern treatment has been offered elsewhere.[125] It is also possible to be buried at sea, though the authorisation process is restrictive, complex and cumbersome.[126] In 2023, cremations accounted for 73.07% of disposals in Scotland indicating burials, historically the standard method of disposal in Scotland, continue to diminish in popularity.[127]

(a) The deceased's own wishes

1.24 It is common for a person to contemplate and discuss with those close to them about what they would like their funeral ceremony and final resting place to be. In practice, a person may have subscribed to a paid funeral plan with an undertaker specifying such arrangements, and contributed to the costs during their lifetime. It is also common that a person may have expressed a preference in a will or letter of wishes provided to their executor.[128] Yet the accepted view in Scotland is that the deceased has no absolute right to decide how their corpse is to be disposed of.

However, in *Robson* the court also considered the question of permissible ways of disposal and held that someone may leave instructions as to how they wish their body to be disposed of:[129]

> 'It seems also to be settled that the deceased may leave instructions as to the disposal of his remains, as by burial or cremation, and as regards the place of sepulture, which must be given effect to so far as he has left means for the accomplishment of his wishes, and these wishes are according to public decency and order.'

On a first analysis, one might think that the deceased's wishes must be adhered to strictly. However, Sheriff Vary Campbell's comment seems to

125 See M Boni (ed), 'Burial and Cremation (Reissue)' in *The Laws of Scotland: Stair Memorial Encyclopaedia.*

126 ibid, paras 31–32.

127 The Cremation Society publishes annual statistics based on reporting to the National Records of Scotland, available https://www.cremation.org.uk/progress-of-cremation-united-kingdom.

128 Barr, *Drafting Wills in Scotland* 2nd edn (2009), paras 3.49–3.50.

129 1897) 5 SLT (Sh Ct) 351, 352.

be in respect of a pecuniary legacy, dedicating the 'means' or money for a specific funeral, burial or memorial. Such pecuniary legacies are capable of being honoured, as Lord President Clyde later stated in *Mackintosh's Judicial Factor* v *Lord Advocate*:[130]

> 'I do not think that, in the law of Scotland, there is any doubt that a testamentary provision for the erection of a memorial or monument to the deceased testator is a perfectly valid direction.'

In *Lindsay's Executor* v *Forsyth*, where the deceased left a substantial sum of money for flowers to be placed on graves, Lord Aitchison noted:[131]

> 'If the testatrix had directed that a small sum be set aside to put flowers on her own grave and her mother's for a short period, the Court would have given effect to it, or, if she had directed that a small sum be expended each year for the purpose of keeping the family burial ground in order, I think that also would have been a good bequest. The law has always made a concession to the natural and human sentiments of ordinary people who desire that there should be some memorial of themselves, or who desire that some act of piety which they have performed during their lives should be continued after their death. That is a concession or indulgence shown by the law, but it is conditioned by the consideration that the bequest should not be extravagant to the point of caprice.'

Lord Aitchison had drawn from the opinion of Lord Sands in *Aitken's Trustee* v *Aitken* (which concerned the construction of a large monument in tribute to the deceased and his family):[132]

> 'I adject this further possible qualification, that it may be of public benefit that the reasonable, honourable, or pious wishes of a testator should not be disregarded, even though it may be impossible to qualify any other interest in the carrying out of his wishes. This, perhaps, satisfactorily covers the case of a direction for reasonable sepulchral memorials either to the testator himself or to his predecessors. To discourage regard to such pious sentiments towards the dead may perhaps be considered as detrimental to the moral interests of the living.'

It would seem that a legacy allocating money for a specific funeral, disposal, or memorial could be valid and enforceable provided this does

130 1935 SC 406, 409.
131 *Lindsay's Executor v Forsyth* 1940 SC 568, 571.
132 1927 SC 374, 381.

not offend the Scottish courts' approach to strike down extravagancies.[133] Yet, otherwise, the accepted position seems to be that an expression of wishes *alone* in a will, with no specific allocation of property for those wishes, is *not* binding and need not be followed.[134] Barr seems to be of the view that this is because no person would have an interest in enforcing such a breach of direction by the deceased.[135] With that said, a new requirement has been introduced on the person entitled to make arrangements for disposing of the corpse.

(b) Who may arrange disposal

1.25 An adult may make what is known as an Arrangements on Death Declaration (ADD), nominating a person to arrange disposal of their body after death.[136] An ADD may be made orally or in writing.[137] Having an express nomination in such a manner is intended to deal with a common problem where different family members have different views on how a corpse should be disposed of,[138] which in some cases can lead to court action.[139]

Should the deceased have failed to make an ADD, or should an ADD have been made but it cannot be given effect to, then the 2016 Act provides that the 'nearest relative' of the deceased is empowered to make disposal arrangements instead.[140] The Act provides a ranking list to determine the nearest relative, with the spouse, civil partner, and cohabitant, coming first in the allocation for adults.[141] In the case of a child, the parents of the child (whom failing, the wider family) are empowered to make arrangements

133 See para **12.3**.

134 Barr, *Drafting Wills in Scotland*, 2nd edn (2009), paras 3.49–3.50.

135 ibid, para 3.50.

136 2016 Act, s 65(8).

137 Burial and Cremation (Scotland) Act 2016, Explanatory Notes, para 165.

138 See the examples of disputes in the Inspectors of Burial, Cremation and Funeral Directors, *Annual Report: 2024-25* (2025), para 25.

139 As an example, see the dispute in *C v M* 2014 SLT (Sh Ct) 109 and its accompanying case *C v Advocate General for Scotland* [2011] CSOH 124. Lord Brodie's opinion in the Outer House decision provides a worthwhile exploration of the problems at common law before the introduction of s 65 of the 2016 Act.

140 2016 Act, s 65(2).

141 2016 Act, s 65(3); and s 65(5).

as the nearest relative of the child.[142] The appointed person must have regard to the deceased adult's or child's wishes, however expressed, and any religion or beliefs that the deceased had.[143] The use of 'regard' seems somewhat deliberate here given the discussion above about whether a deceased's wishes must be strictly followed.[144]

In the event of a dispute as to who is entitled to arrange disposal, for example, due to conflicting ADDs issued by the deceased, an interested person can apply to the sheriff court for an order determining the issue.[145] A power is to be found in s 68(2) which enables the sheriff to issue any provisions as part of the order as considered necessary and expedient. In a recent Sheriff Court case, *DP v BR*,[146] this ancillary power was considered not to be such that a court can specify the means of disposal. As Sheriff Matheson observed:[147]

> 'I do not consider that the statute requires the court to have regard to any funeral arrangements specified by the deceased. What I consider the statute to require is for the nearest relative (as determined by the court) to have regard to any wishes expressed by the deceased. There is nowhere imported into the Act a hint that the court should, for example, consider the question of who would be more likely to have regard to the deceased's wishes in determining who the nearest relative is; or any suggestion that the court can or should make an order detailing what it considers the deceased's wishes as regards funeral arrangements to have been.'

If no person, whether chosen by the deceased or as their nearest relative, is able to arrange a funeral and disposal, then a local authority must attend to disposal.[148] This is often termed a 'public health funeral' or, in rather cruel language, a 'pauper's funeral'. Though commonplace, a public health funeral is not an accurate term for a local-authority disposal. Properly speaking, a public health funeral is one carried out under the Public Health (Scotland) Act 2008 where a corpse presents a risk to public health –

142 2016 Act, s 66.

143 2016 Act, s 67(3).

144 'Burial and Cremation (Scotland) Act 2016' (2017) (61) *Scottish Private Client Law Review* 3, 5.

145 2016 Act, s 68.

146 2026 SLT (Sh Ct) 91.

147 2026 SLT (Sh Ct) 91, at para 32.

148 2016 Act, s 87.

such as it being diseased or irradiated.[149] Finally, it should be noted that detailed provision has been put in place for varying arrangements for the disposal of a foetus birthed on or before 24 weeks old,[150] or after 24 weeks old.[151] This was introduced under the 2016 Act in response to the 'Baby Ashes' scandal in Scotland, where the practices of certain crematoria had distressing treatment of miscarried foetuses, still-born babies, and deceased neonatal babies, often without the parent's knowledge.[152]

(4) Funeral directors and undertakers

1.26 The person responsible for disposal of a body will typically instruct a funeral director to arrange funerals, memorial events, and ultimate disposal. Funeral directors and undertakers enjoy a rich heritage in Scotland. Yet, in recent years, there has been greater scrutiny of the industry's trade practices.[153] A new system of public registration and licensing is currently underway in Scotland.

Under the 2016 Act, funeral directors in Scotland must comply with the Funeral Directors' Code of Practice, which details basic standards for the handling of corpses and the arrangement of funerals, memorial events, and disposals.[154] An Inspector of Funeral Directors is tasked with examining the industry and breaches of the Code.[155] New regulations have been passed setting out the inspection process.[156] In the event that the Inspector considers the funeral director to have breached the Code, then an enforcement notice can be served.[157] Failure to comply with the notice can lead to the Scottish Ministers commencing court proceedings for enforcement.[158]

149 2008 Act, s 92.
150 2016 Act, ss 77–84.
151 2016 Act, ss 69–76.
152 See Lord Bonomy's *Report of the Infant Cremation Commission* (2014); and Dame Angiolini's *Report of the National Cremation Investigation* (2016).
153 See Competition & Markets Authority, *Funerals Market Study: Final Report And Decision On A Market Investigation Reference* (2019).
154 2016 Act, s 97.
155 2016 Act, s 89(1)(c).
156 The Burial and Cremation (Inspection) (Scotland) Regulations 2025/26.
157 2025 Regulations, reg 7.
158 2025 Regulations, reg 12.

A new licensing scheme for funeral directors is provided for under the 2016 Act that will complement the Code, though not yet in force.[159] Failure to obtain a licence or operating without a licence will be a criminal offence.[160] A public Funeral Services Register including the details of all funeral directors in Scotland is currently open for registrations whilst the intricate details of the licensing scheme continue to be determined by the Scottish Ministers.

159 2016 Act, Part 5.
160 2016 Act, s 96 [not in force as at the date of publication].

Chapter 2

Families and unlawful killers

INTRODUCTION

2.1 This chapter sets out the legal rules, doctrines and presumptions which must be considered in relation to persons in their capacity as successors, beneficiaries, or potential beneficiaries of a deceased person's estate. As the family of the deceased are typically the successors to an estate, consideration is given to some common issues deriving from family law which influence how succession law operates, particularly the position of romantic partners and children. Additionally, one aspect of the criminal law, that of homicide, falls to be considered here too in respect of the effect of homicide and a killer's entitlement to succeed to an estate of a person whom they have killed.

FAMILIAL SUCCESSORS: GENERALLY

2.2 The entitlement of children, spouses or partners, and cohabitants to succeed at common law has been reformed radically by legislation. It is in this area that the overlap between family law and succession law is most apparent. Much of the reform in succession law in recent years derives from wider reforms to family law. This includes the rights afforded to children of the deceased, and those afforded to their romantic partner.

In respect of children, the status of all children has been equalised incrementally over the years in Scotland, as will be seen in subsequent sections. However, older rules remain relevant in relation to testate succession for deaths that took place, or testamentary documents that were executed, prior to the reforming legislation. Given the timing of this edition of this text, only passing reference is made to these older rules, and readers are directed to previous editions of this text for further analysis.

In respect of adults in romantic relationships, legislation has reformed the status of adults in same-sex and unmarried relationships, often being more generous to them than was the case under the harsh common law.

The Civil Partnership Act 2004 introduced the status of civil partner and assimilated the position of civil partners with that of spouses. Designed initially to allow same-sex couples to enter into a formal relationship, civil partnerships are now available for heterosexual couples to enter into too. Further, marriages are also no longer limited to heterosexual relationships under the Marriage and Civil Partnership (Scotland) Act 2014. For unmarried couples, the Family Law (Scotland) Act 2006, allows surviving cohabitants in either same-sex or heterosexual relationships to claim provision in the intestate succession of their deceased co-cohabitant depending on the claimant satisfying various qualifying conditions.[1] These various forms of relationships will be considered in subsequent sections.

CHILDREN

2.3 This text is not solely concerned with family law, and readers are directed to other texts dealing with the establishment of parentage of a child.[2] However, it is of relevance here to stress that whilst the Children (Scotland) Act 1995 provides a system of determining persons with parental rights and responsibilities as the 'legal parent'[3] of a child, succession law tends to focus on biological parentage, so that the child ordinarily has to be the biological descendant of the deceased in order to inherit from them.[4]

Whilst biological parentage, or a genetic link, was the focus of the common law, and continues to have relevance today in many estates, in modern times non-biological children have been treated more tenderly in succession law by way of reforms made by legislation. The position of adopted children has, largely, been assimilated with that of non-adopted children in relation to adoptive parents – though some anachronisms still remain.

1 See paras **6.26–6.33**.

2 See K MacFarlane, *Thomson's Family Law*, 9th edn (2026), Ch 9.

3 To adopt the terminology used in MacFarlane, *Thomson's Family Law in Scotland*, Ch 9.

4 For wider debates in this field, see K McNorrie (ed), *Law Relating to Parent & Child in Scotland,* 3rd edn (2013), Ch 4; and MacFarlane, *Thomson's Family Law in Scotland*, Ch 9.

Additionally, great emphasis had been placed at common law on whether the child was the product of a marriage between his or her mother and father. Whilst the law no longer discriminates against children because of the marital status of their parents, this anachronism remains important in the construction of older wills and testamentary documents.[5] Consequently, it is necessary to set out the historic position of children born outwith marriage.

Whilst statutory reform has progressed succession law in some ways, it remains the case that step-children, 'accepted children', or those raised in kinship care, such as a child raised by a family friend, step-parent, or by a member of the wider family, may be unable to inherit from whom they consider to be their parent under the default rules of the law. As will be later seen, some rather arcane rules also remain in relation to half-siblings and their succession to another sibling within intestate succession.[6] All of these limitations are why it is constantly advised by practitioners that clients should make a will to reflect who they consider to be their family, and who they would like to inherit.

(1) Posthumous children and the *nasciturus* principle

2.4 A child born after the death of its parent is a posthumous child. In almost all ordinary cases, it will be the father of the child who has predeceased after the conception of a child before his death. It is not impossible, however, that the predeceasing parent may also be a mother. She could die a mere few seconds or minutes before the child is born; or it may be that the mother is brain-stem dead and her life is being sustained in order for the foetus to survive.

Through modern medicine, it is now also possible for a child to be born as a result of posthumous *conception*, where a male's preserved sperm has been utilised or an embryo using his sperm has been implanted after he has died.[7] Otherwise, a female may have had her eggs preserved, with a later

5 See paras **11.7–11.11.**

6 See para **6.40.**

7 For some interesting paternal examples, see *R v Human Fertilisation and Embryology Authority, ex parte Blood* [1997] 2 All ER 687, *L v Human Fertilisation and Embryology Authority* [2008] EWHC 2149 (Fam); and *Warren v Care Fertility (Northampton) Limited* [2014] EWHC 602 (Fam); and *B v University of Aberdeen* [2020] CSIH 62.

fertilisation and implantation carried out within another person's uterus after her own death.[8] The attribution of parentage in such circumstances, and succession thereof, are regulated by the Human Fertilisation and Embryology Acts 1990 and 2008, and is discussed below.

Whether it is the mother or the father who has died before the birth of their child, the general rule of succession that a beneficiary must be alive in order to acquire rights in the estate of a deceased person is, at least nominally, overturned in the case of posthumous children.[9] As a general principle, children *in utero* are to be regarded as being already born for the purposes of rights in succession:[10]

> 'A child in the mother's womb is esteemed as already born, in all things that concern its own interest; *qui in utero est, pro jam nato habetur.*'

This is known as the *nasciturus* principle[11] and Craig states its purpose to be that there is 'no reason in the case of a posthumous child to aggravate the calamity it suffers by the premature death of its father, nor to make that event a ground for diminishing its rights'.[12]

Thus, a legacy to 'all my children alive at the time of my death' will include posthumous children unless expressly excluded by the terms of the will.[13] Where a posthumous child has simply been omitted from a will executed by his or her parent prior to the child's birth, the child may raise the presumption of implied revocation under the *conditio si testator sine liberis decesserit*[14] where it is in his or her interests to do so.

Clearly, a foetus cannot be a carrier of any legal rights or entitlements and must survive to birth in order to acquire them. The *nasciturus* principle

8 For some interesting maternal examples, see *M v Human Fertilisation and Embryology Authority* [2016] EWCA Civ 611; *EF v Human Fertilisation and Embryology Authority* [2024] EWHC 3004 (Fam); and *Jennings v Human Fertilisation and Embryology Authority* [2022] EWHC 1619 (Fam).

9 See para **1.13.**

10 Bankton, *Inst* I.2.7. See also J, *Digest* I.5.7; Erskine *Inst* III.8.76; and Bell, *Prin*, § 1642.

11 For a comprehensive analysis, see R Paisley, 'The succession rights of the unborn child' (2006) 10(1) *Edin LR* 28.

12 Craig, *Ius Feudale* II.13.15, [Lord Clyde's translation, (1934), 643].

13 *Cox's Trustees v Cox* 1950 SC 117.

14 The doctrine applied originally only to posthumous children but has since been extended: see para **7.16.**

is therefore qualified by two requirements. First, the child must be born alive. This rule has been upheld in a variety of circumstances, including where a posthumous child was entitled to legitim from her father's estate[15] and where a posthumous child was entitled to a share in a class gift to 'the children of my sister' found in a will.[16] Second, the child must gain a direct benefit, and the rule cannot be invoked in the interests of a third party. Lord McLaren stated:[17]

> 'The fiction of law, which treats the unborn child as actually born, applies only for the purpose of enabling the child to take a benefit to which, if born, it would be entitled; and, therefore, where the right of a stranger is conditioned to take effect on the birth of a child within a certain time, the right will not accrue unless the child be actually born within the time limited.'

In *Elliot v Joicey*,[18] a reference to 'survivors' within a bequest was in the circumstances construed as not including a posthumous child where only the child's father's estate would have benefited and not the child himself. The court held that while the accrual of the benefit to the father's estate may indirectly benefit the child, in that the father's intestate estate to which he would succeed would be enhanced, this was an insufficient ground on which to apply the fiction.

(2) Adopted children

2.5 Prior to the Succession (Scotland) Act 1964, adopted children could succeed only to the estates of their birth parents and had no right to succeed to the estates of either of their adoptive parents. Introducing reforms which would enable adopted persons to succeed to their adoptive parents had been discussed for some time before the passing of the 1964

15 *Jervey v Watt* (1762) Mor 8170.

16 *Grant v Fyffe* 22 May 1810 FC. See also *Spalding's Trs v Spalding's Trs* (1874) 2 R 237; *Johnstone's Trs v Johnstone* 1936 SC 766; *Allan's Trs v Allan* 1949 SLT (Notes) 3; and *Cox's Trs v Cox* 1950 SC 117.

17 J McLaren, *The Law of Wills and Succession as Administered in Scotland*, 3rd edn (1894), para 1259.

18 1935 SC (HL) 57. See M Meston 'Succession rights of posthumous children' (1970) 15 *JLSS* 33.

Act, but it had been felt that, until the whole law of succession was overhauled, reform was neither worthwhile nor practicable.

The Adoption of Children Act 1949, which had given rights to adopted children in their adoptive parents' estates in England and Wales, had not been applied to Scotland because of the anomalies it would have introduced into the law of succession, but it was the position of adopted children in Scots law which became the catalyst for the appointment of the Mackintosh Committee in 1961. The Committee was charged with reviewing the law of succession and recommending the terms of its reform, and its recommendations led to the passing of the 1964 Act[19] and recognition of adopted children for the purposes of succession to their adoptive parents' estates.

Section 23(1) of the 1964 Act provides a general rule that:

> 'For all purposes relating to—
>
> (a) the succession to a deceased person (whether testate or intestate), and
>
> (b) the disposal of property by virtue of any *inter vivos* deed,
>
> an adopted person shall be treated as the child of the adopter and not as the child of any other person.'

This has two main consequences, subject to certain qualifications set out below. First, adopted persons will have no rights in succession to their birth parents following adoption.[20] Second, they may also have rights in succession to, or in competition with, any adoptive siblings and their descendants. Reference to succession to a deceased person is to be construed as including a reference to the distribution of any property in consequence of the death of the deceased person and any claim to legal rights or the prior rights of a surviving spouse. The rules apply, therefore, to all types of succession, whether testate or intestate.

19 *Law of Succession in Scotland: Report of the Committee of Inquiry* (Cmnd 8144, 1951), 22–23.

20 See *Cameron's Executrix v Gibson* 2006 SC 283 for an interesting case where an adoption order was successfully reduced in order to affect succession rights. In that case, an adoptive child sought reduction of the order in order to be able to inherit from his biological brother's estate.

Subsequent legislation in respect of adoption is to be found in the Adoption (Scotland) Act 1978[21] and the Adoption and Children (Scotland) Act 2007.[22] However, these statutes do not concern succession law, and the provisions of the 1964 Act continue in force for the purposes of succession of an adopted child.[23] The Scottish Law Commission has recommended decanting the provisions of the 1964 Act into the Adoptions Acts in the interests of coherence.[24]

(a) Exceptions for adopted children

2.6 The Succession (Scotland) Act 1964 does not extend to questions of succession of any title, heraldry, honour or dignity transmissible on the death of the last holder.[25] The common law, with its emphasis on blood relationships and the principle of primogeniture, still applies in these areas.[26] This affects the position of any adopted child in a succession to these species of property or status. Section 23(3) provides that where a deed provides that any property or interest in property is to devolve along with a title, honour or dignity, no statutory provision relating to adoption will prevent that property or interest from so devolving. Clearly, however, this will depend on the wording of the deed, and, in any case, the testator may make separate testamentary provision for an adopted child. It may be possible for an adopted child to receive arms relating to their adoptive parent from the Lord Lyon, though with features differentiating them from the adopted parent's own coat of arms.[27]

Adopted children may also be excluded in other situations, though diminishing, where the old law continues to apply. This can arise because,

21 Adoption (Scotland) Act 1978, s 39.

22 Adoption and Children (Scotland) Act 2007, 40.

23 1978 Act, s 44; and 2007 Act, s 44.

24 Report *on Succession* (SLC Report No 215, 2009), para 7.29ff.

25 1964 Act, s 37(1)(a).

26 For criticism, see C Agnew and G Black, 'The significance of status and genetics in succession to titles, honours, dignities and coats of arms: making the case for reform' (2018) 77(2) *Cambridge LJ* 321.

27 *Stewart, Ptr*, 1951 SLT (Lyon Ct) 3 and G Black, 'The Evolution of Scottish Heraldry: From Elitist to Egalitarian', in M Godfrey (ed), *Miscellany Nine* (Stair Society Vol 70, 2024), 341.

under s 23(4), the provisions of s 23(1) do not apply to any deeds executed prior to the commencement of the 1964 Act on 10 September 1964 nor to the devolution of any property consequent on the death of any person who died before that date. In such situations, an adopted person will be excluded from succeeding to the estate of his or her adoptive parents. Such a result is now likely to be few and far between given the passage of time since the commencement of the 1964 Act.[28]

In the event that the adoptive parent died before the coming into force of the 1964 Act on 10 September 1964, then the adoptive child might have been left with no claim in either the estate of the adoptive parent or their biological parent. A remedy for this situation is given under the Law Reform (Miscellaneous Provisions) (Scotland) Act 1966, which provides that if: (i) the adoptive parent died before the commencement of the 1964 Act; but (ii) the biological parent died after the commencement of the 1966 Act (on or after 3 August 1966), then the adoptive child can be treated as a child of their biological parent for the purposes of succession to the biological parent's estate.[29]

Example

June was born in 1950. Her mother, Serena, was only 16 years old when June was born, and was encouraged by authorities to give her up for adoption. June was adopted by Martha in 1952. Martha sadly died in 1963, and June was thereafter raised by Martha's family.

Serena dies in 2026 at the age of 92. June, now 76, is entitled to claim legitim from Serena's estate under s 5 of the 1966 Act.

With the passage of time, this rule will fall into complete disuse. However, the example above shows that it may still be the case that an adoptive parent died before the commencement of the 1964 Act and their biological parent subsequently died after the commencement of the 1966 Act. In

28 Human rights may be at play in respect of s 23(4) and the construction of pre-commencement deeds and potential discrimination in respect of adopted children, see *Pla v Andorra* (2006) 42 EHRR 25, and the discussion of the cases in English law dealing with this issue in A Learmonth et al (eds), *Theobald on Wills,* 20th edn (2026), Ch 26(2). Of particular note for adoption is *In Re Erskine 1948 Trust* [2012] EWHC 732 (Ch) and *In Re Hand* [2017] EWHC 553 (Ch).

29 1966 Act, s 5.

such situations, the adopted child may still yet have a claim against their biological parent's estate. The Scottish Law Commission gives an example where an adoptive parent dies pre-commencement of the 1964 Act, but a biological parent, dying after the 1966 Act came into force, had left a *mortis causa* trust for their 'children'.[30] In such situations, the adopted child may well yet still have a claim for payment under that trust due to the provisions of the 1966 Act.

Where the succession to an adoptive parent arises under a deed (as opposed to claims in intestate succession or a claim to legal rights),[31] the Succession (Scotland) Act 1964, s 23(2) provides that an adopted person is to count as a child of the adopter only if he or she was adopted before the date of execution of the deed in question. Rather confusingly, the date of execution in a *mortis causa* deed is not, in this context, the date of subscription, as 'execution' is commonly understood in Scots legal parlance. Rather, it is deemed to be the date of death of the deceased person since this is when the deed comes into effect.[32] This provision is favourable to the position of adopted persons since, if an adoption order was made after the deed was formally subscribed but before the testator's death, the adopted person will be deemed to have been included in any provisions to, for example, 'my children'.

An adopted person is not, therefore, excluded if he or she was adopted at any time prior to the testator's death, provided there is no express provision to the contrary.

Example

Katie executes a will in 2000. She had two children at that time and bequeaths the residue of her estate 'to my children'. Katie adopts Connor in 2005. Katie later dies in 2020. Connor is entitled to a third of the share of the residue because he was adopted by Katie before the provisions of her will came into effect in 2020 for the purposes of s 23(2).

30 Report *on Succession* (SLC Report No 215, 2009), para 7.31.

31 All children have equal rights in intestate succession and in claims for legitim since these are regulated by statute rather than by private deed.

32 For the purposes of the s 23(2) of the 1964 Act, a deed containing a provision taking effect on the death of any person shall be deemed to have been executed on the date of death of that person.

(b) Construction of deeds with adopted children

2.7 The Succession (Scotland) Act 1964, s 23(2)(a)–(c) sets out in detail the rules of construction to be applied to deeds coming into effect after the making of an adoption order.[33] Essentially, an adopted person is to be treated as the child of the adopter and not as the child of any other person unless the contrary intention appears.[34] A reference to 'issue' in a deed does not display a contrary intention in that it is not to be construed as referring only to blood descendants.[35]

Section 23(2)(a) of the 1964 Act provides that any reference to the child or children of the adopter is to be construed as including a reference to the adopted person. Section 23(2)(b) of the 1964 Act provides that any reference to the child or children of the adopted person's biological parents is to be construed as not including the adopted person.[36] Section 23(2)(c) of the 1964 Act provides that a reference to a person related to the adopted person in any particular degree is to be construed as a reference to

33 Adoption order is one defined by s 38 of the Adoption (Scotland) Act 1978, or s 28 of the Adoption and Children (Scotland) Act 2007 as the case may be. Under these statutes, these can include adoptions made outwith Scotland provided they satisfy the statutory definitions therein.

34 It had been argued that s 23(2) contradicts s 23(1), since s 23(1) contains no qualifications as to the date of a deed. For example, under s 23(2) a bequest to 'the children of A' will include any children adopted by A at the date of the testator's death but none adopted after. However, under s 23(1) a child adopted after the testator's death will be included within the class if he or she was actually born before the testator's death, see A McDonald 'Adopted Persons' (1965) 10 *JLSS* 95. Whether or not s 23 contains such a contradiction, the right of the adopted person to benefit from a legacy to the class will depend on when the legacy vests and whether it vests subject to partial defeasance if additional members of the class emerge after the date of vesting: see para **13.27**. In general terms, s 23(1) has been held to contain the general rule to which all the other provisions in the section are to be seen as ancillary or subordinate: *Salvesen's Trustees, Petrs* 1993 SC 14, 21.

35 *Spencer's Trs v Ruggles* 1981 SC 289. Some debate has been had on this point, but the matter now seems settled that 'issue' should not be taken to indicate a contrary intention to exclude adopted children. On the use of the term 'descendants' in a deed, and whether this includes adopted persons, see the discussion in J Kessler and W Grant, *Drafting Trusts and Will Trusts in Scotland*, 2nd edn (2018), para 4.16. On an expansive view, any use of 'children', 'issue' and 'descendants' should be taken to include adopted persons falling within that category unless expressly excluded.

36 Though see s 5 of the 1966 Act in the limited circumstances in which it applies.

the person who would be related to him in that degree if he were the child of the adopter and not the child of any other person.[37]

If a person is adopted more than once, the previous adoption or adoptions are disregarded in relation to succession to any person dying after the date of the subsequent adoption order and in relation to any deed executed after the date on which a succession arises.[38] It should be noted that the Scottish Law Commission has proposed that the rules of s 23(2) be removed entirely and the general rule in s 23(1) applies instead in questions of construction.[39]

(c) Relationship between adoptee and their siblings

2.8 For the purposes of the law regulating the succession to any property and for the purposes of the construction of any deed under which property devolves, s 24 of the 1964 Act provides rules for determining the relationship between the adopted person and any other natural or adopted child or children of the deceased.

Generally, the relationship between an adopted person and any other children of the adoptive parent(s) will depend on whether the child was adopted by: (i) two spouses, or (ii) all other cases. Where the adopted person (A) was adopted by spouses jointly and the sibling (B) is the biological or adopted child of both spouses, A will be considered a brother or sister of the whole blood to B.

In every other case outwith adoption by two spouses, such as where the adopted child was adopted by one person only (and presumably in the case of adoption by civil partners and cohabitants jointly), the relationship of the adopted child to any other child of the adopter(s) will be as brother or sister of the half blood. This rule has not kept up with reforms to the general law of adoption and there is some imbalance between the Adoption Acts and the 1964 Act.

37 *Salvesen's Trustees, Petrs*. The Scottish Law Commission initially proposed that for the avoidance of doubt, the word 'issue' should be inserted after the word 'children' in s 23(2)(a) and (b) of the 1964 Act and the word 'or way' after the word 'degree' in s 23(2)(c) of the 1964 Act: Report *on Succession* (SLC Report No 124,1990), recommendation 52.

38 1964 Act, s 24(3).

39 Report *on Succession* (SLC Report No 215, 2009), para 7.33.

Under the Adoption (Scotland) Act 1978, a child may have been adopted only by: (i) a married couple, (ii) one person who was unmarried, or (iii) one person who was married but their spouse is missing, estranged, or suffering from ill-health and consequently cannot consent to the application for an order.[40] However, the Adoption and Children (Scotland) Act 2007 liberalises adoptions by allowing not only sole persons and spouses to adopt but also 'certain couples' to adopt a child, with 'certain couples' including spouses, civil partners and persons living together as if husband and wife or civil partners in an enduring family relationship.[41]

Section 24(1) of the 1964 Act makes provision for determining the relationship between an adopted person and other children based on whether the adoption was carried out by: (i) spouses jointly, or (ii) in all other adoptive cases. In the case where civil partners or a cohabiting couple adopted the child, it would seem absurd that another rule applies given the equivalence of marriage with cohabitation and civil partnerships elsewhere by the 2007 Act. However, this provision has not yet been amended. Similar criticism can be made of the 1964 Act where a single person adopts a child, why should the adoptee be treated any differently in respect of their new siblings in succession based on how many adoptive parents they have under the adoption order? It is one part of the 1964 Act, among others, which requires reform.

Accordingly, an adopted person can only be related as a brother or sister of the full-blood if he or she has been adopted by spouses jointly and the brother or sister is also the child or jointly adopted child of both spouses. In all other cases, if a child has been adopted into a family, and the adopter(s) have other children, the adopted child will be deemed to be a half-blood to those other children. This distinction between relationships of the full and half-blood has particular significance where claims are made by siblings for a share in a deceased sibling's intestate estate.[42]

A further complex rule by s 24(1A) is provided if, under any deed or by operation of law, any members of a class on whom a right is conferred, or an obligation is imposed, are adopted and their relative seniority has to be determined. This can be the case where a deed sets out, for example, that a legacy is to be left to 'my oldest child' or to 'the youngest of Mary's

40 Adoption (Scotland) Act 1978, ss 14–15.

41 Adoption and Children (Scotland) Act 2007, s 29(3).

42 See para **6.40.**

children'. In cases involving adopted children, subsection (1A) provides that an adopted person's age shall be determined as if he or she had been born on the day of their adoption. If more than one child has been adopted on the same date, seniority as between them is determined in accordance with their respective times of birth. It will be apparent to any reader that this rule is a total nonsense. The Scottish Law Commission recommended that this section be repealed in order to avoid the absurdity that where an adopted child who is older than another child of the deceased (whether adopted or not) is adopted at a later date than the adoption or birth of the other child, the other child is deemed to be older.[43] In the words of the Commission it is hard to escape the conclusion that 'the age of an adopted person should always be taken to be their actual age'.[44]

(3) Children born outwith marriage

2.9 At common law, the terms 'bastard' or 'illegitimate child', and variants thereof, are often to be found in describing children born out of marriage or wedlock alongside harsh rules dealing with the treatment of such persons in family and succession law. It was only with the coming into force of the Family Law (Scotland) Act 2006, s 21 that the status of 'illegitimacy' was finally abolished in Scots law. The real significance of s 21 was not in reforming substantively the legal effects of a person's parents not being married – this was already achieved by the Law Reform (Parent and Child) (Scotland) Act 1986 – but, more fundamentally, in consigning the very concept of 'illegitimacy' to history.[45] Section 21 did not introduce new substantive rules but amended significantly the terms of the 1986 Act, which remains, as amended, the basis of the law relating to the status of children of unmarried parents. Because these Acts are not retroactive,[46] three key periods of time emerge:

43 Report on *Succession* (Scot Law Com No 124,1990), recommendation 53(b).

44 Report on *Succession* (SLC Report No 215, 2009), para 7.34.

45 Titles, honours, dignities and coats of arms are still regulated by the older rules of legitimacy under s 9(1)(c) of the 1986 Act. For criticism, see Sir Crispin Agnew and G Black, 'The significance of status and genetics in succession to titles, honours, dignities and coats of arms: making the case for reform' (2018) 77(2) *Cambridge LJ* 321, 333ff.

46 1986 Act, s 1(4)(b).

(i) The estates of persons dying, or deeds executed, before 8 December 1986 must be interpreted with the common law and the earlier legislation.[47]

(ii) The estates of persons dying, or deeds executed, from 8 December 1986 to 4 May 2006 must be interpreted in line with unamended 1986 Act.

(iii) The estates of persons dying, or deeds executed, after 4 May 2006 must be interpreted in line with the 1986 Act, as amended by the 2006 Act.

The rights of children of unmarried parents therefore fall, in particular, under wills or testamentary documents,[48] to be determined according to the rules in force at the relevant time, and there will still be cases where the succession rights of children of unmarried parents will be excluded or restricted unless expressly included within the terms of an older testamentary document.[49] Children who have been 'legitimated', either at common law or under the Legitimation (Scotland) Act 1968, are still entitled to succeed on intestacy or as members of a class of 'children' where the 1986 Act (as enacted, or as amended by the 2006 Act) does not apply.

(a) Common law

2.10 At common law, in keeping with Scotland's religious influences, children born outwith marriage, or conceived outwith marriage, were treated harshly.[50] In succession law, a child of unmarried parents was a *filius nullius* (child of no one). As such, they could not inherit from either

47 See the Scottish Law Commission's consideration of the possibility of assimilating the rules for existing deeds with the proposed reforms for new deeds in Report on *Legitimacy* (SLC Report No 82, 1984), para 9.8.

48 See paras **11.7–11.11.**

49 Again, there may be questions of human rights compliance in interpreting such deeds in this manner today. See A Learmonth et al (eds), *Theobald on Wills*, 20th edn (2026), Ch 26(2).

50 For a historical overview, see P Cowan (ed), *Fraser's Treatise on the Law of Scotland Relative to Parent and Child*, 2nd edn (1866), Ch V.

their mother or father.[51] Erskine stated the reason for this rule was that they were 'procreated of an unlawful conjunction'[52] and in *Clarke v Carfin Coal Co*, Lord Watson noted that 'the mother is as much as the father an utter stranger in blood to her child'.[53]

Children of unmarried parents were considered, therefore, to be unrelated to their parents or to any siblings born of the same parents, and in construing any reference to 'children' or 'issue' in a testamentary deed, any such children were excluded unless the terms of the deed or the surrounding circumstances indicated the contrary.[54] It was never the case, however, that gifts to children of unmarried parents were actually prohibited. Where a testator gave a legacy to a named child whose parents were unmarried, or to children of unmarried parents as a class, such a bequest would be valid since the testator intended clearly that they be beneficiaries. In the absence of express intention, however, the rule was that a reference to 'children' could be construed to mean only such children as were protected by the law of marriage. Thus, a reference to 'issue', 'children' or 'descendants' without further description would be taken to include only *lawful* or legitimate children.[55] A child could be 'legitimated' *per subsequens matrimonium* if the parents married after the birth of the child, but only if they were free to marry at the time when the child was conceived, thus excluding the children of adulterous or incestuous relationships.[56]

(b) Earlier legislation and reform

2.11 Reform has taken place in incremental and piecemeal fashion, the 2006 Act representing the endpoint of a process reflecting changing

51 Until the passage of the Bastards (Scotland) Act 1836, where it was considered 'just, humane, and expedient' to enact reform, an illegitimate child could not even make a will of their own estate.

52 Erskine, *Inst*, III.10.8. Following Roman law, Stair, *Inst,* IV.7.1), and Bankton, *Inst,* I.11.4, thought there may be succession to the mother's moveable estate but this appears to have been overridden by Erskine's formulation. See also M Meston 'Bastards in the law of succession' 1966 *SLT (News)* 197.

53 *Clarke v Carfin Coal Co* (1891) 18 R 63 at 70.

54 *Allan v Adamson* (1902) 9 SLT 404; and *Purdie's Trs v Doolan* 1929 SLT 273.

55 J McLaren *The Law of Wills and Succession*, 3rd edn (1894) paras 1256–58.

56 Erskine, *Inst*, I.4.52; Bankton, *Inst,* V.57.8.

social attitudes and political will. Earlier reforms included the Legitimacy Act 1926 which enabled a mother and her child to succeed to each other, although the father was still presumed to have predeceased the child.

The Succession (Scotland) Act 1964, as enacted, provided under s 4 that a child of unmarried parents had a right to succeed to his or her mother's free estate on intestacy but only providing that she had no lawful issue. In this case the right was payable but, if she were married, only after deduction of claims on her estate by her husband.[57]

The Legitimation (Scotland) Act 1968 superseded the common law rules of legitimation *per subsequens matrimonium* except in the case of hereditary titles. Under ss 1 and 4 of the 1968 Act 'legitimation' took place at the date of the marriage of the parents, whether or not they were free to marry at the time of the child's conception. If the child died before the parents married, the rights and obligations of persons alive at the date of the marriage fell to be determined as if the child had been 'legitmated'.[58] Where, however, any rights vested in another person at the date of the child's 'legitimation', the change of status of the 'legitimated' person did not prejudice these rights.[59] The 1968 Act applied to marriages which took place prior to the date of its coming into force on 8 June 1968 but did not apply to prior deeds.[60]

The Law Reform (Miscellaneous Provisions) (Scotland) Act 1968 introduced further reforms in relation to deaths occurring after 25 November 1968.[61] It amended s 4 and added a new s 10A to the 1964 Act. Under the amended s 4 of the 1964 Act, children of unmarried parents became entitled to succeed to the father's as well as the mother's estate on the same basis as any children of any marriage they may have made; similarly, both parents became entitled to succeed to the free estate of the child should the latter predecease. Section 10A of the 1964 Act gave a right to legitim from the estates of both parents but the child still could

57 If the husband was also father of the child, the child would have been 'legitimated' *per subsequens matrimonium* and his or her claim would not then be postponed: see para **2.10**.

58 ss 3 and 8(1).

59 *Dunbar of Kilconzie v Lord Advocate* 1986 SC (HL) 1.

60 *Wright's Trs v Callender* 1993 SLT 556.

61 Implementing the recommendations of the Report of the *Committee on the Law of Succession in Relation to Illegitimate Persons* (Cmnd 3051, 1966).

not succeed to grandparents or to collaterals. If he or she died intestate, their siblings (whether of the half or the full blood) remained barred from succession to the estate.

(c) The 1986 Act (as enacted)

2.12 The Law Reform (Parent and Child) (Scotland) Act 1986 was a product of the work of the Scottish Law Commission's major project on family law reform.[62] Section 1(1) of the 1986 Act provided that:

> 'The fact that a person's parents are not or have not been married to one another shall be left out of account in establishing the legal relationship between the person and any other person; and accordingly any such relationship shall have effect as if the parents were or had been married to one another.'

Sections 4 and 10A of the Succession (Scotland) Act 1964 were repealed, along with all other references to 'illegitimacy', with the consequence that children of unmarried parents acquired rights in succession identical to those of children born within marriage.

References in a deed executed after its commencement to 'children' or 'issue' were to be construed as inclusive of all children and remoter descendants unless the contrary appeared from the wording of the deed. For example, in *Russell v Wood's Trustees*[63] the testator had bequeathed his estate in liferent to his wife and to 'any children born or to be born of our marriage'. On the wife's remarriage or predecease, trustees were directed to hold the estate 'for behoof of my children' and to apply income and capital for the maintenance of 'my said children'. His wife predeceased him, and the testator then had a child outwith marriage. The trust disposition and settlement had been executed after the coming into force of the Legitimation (Scotland) Act 1964 and Lord Cullen held that:[64]

> 'The natural meaning of the expression 'my children' is any children of the deceased whether by the marriage referred to in the trust deed or any subsequent marriage or illegitimate children whensoever born.'

62 Report on *Legitimacy* (SLC Report No 82, 1984).
63 1987 SLT 503.
64 1987 SLT 503 at 505.

(d) The 2006 Act

2.13 Section 21 of the 2006 Act amended s 1 of the Law Reform (Parent and Child) (Scotland) Act 1986 and, in so doing, changed legal language and legal thinking in a fundamental way. Section 1 of the 1986 Act now states:

> 'No person whose status is governed by Scots law shall be illegitimate; and accordingly the fact that a person's parents are not or have not been married to each other shall be left out of account in-
>
> (a) determining the person's legal status; or
>
> (b) establishing the legal relationship between the person and any other person.'

There are three very significant consequences of this amendment. First, the repeal of the Legitimation (Scotland) Act 1968 underscores the fact that 'legitimation' is now a redundant process. Second, all children cannot be excluded from a legacy in any subsequent deed by construing 'children' as 'lawful' children alone, since this classification of person is now meaningless.[65]

Third, outwith a matter relating to titles, coats of arms, honour or dignity, it is now incompetent to bring an action of declarator of legitimacy, legitimation or illegitimacy. Succession to any title, coat of arms, honour or dignity remains, however, untouched by the legislation[66] and the Law Reform (Parent and Child) (Scotland) Act 1986 (both as enacted and as amended) is not retrospective.[67]

In the case of a deed executed before 4 May 2006, any reference to 'lawful' children will still be taken to refer only to children born to parents

65 Though a conscious choice to expressly exclude children born outside of marriage may still be able to be made, see the suggested drafting in J Kessler and W Grant, *Drafting Trusts and Will Trusts in Scotland*, 2nd edn (2018), paras 4.18ff.

66 Law Reform (Parent and Child) (Scotland) Act 1986, s 9(1)(c). The Scottish Law Commission recommended that s 9(1)(c) be repealed, see Report on *Family Law* (SLC Report No 135, 1992), para 17.11.

67 Law Reform (Parent and Child) (Scotland) Act 1986, s 1(4). The Act does not apply to deeds executed or deaths that occurred before 8 December 1986 but it applies to any power of appointment granted prior to that date. Thus, a power of appointment granted before but exercised at any time after 8 December 1986 may not exclude the provisions of the 1986 Act: see s 4.

married to each other, and a reference to children in such terms remains effective in excluding children of unmarried parents.[68] The justification for this exclusion under the Act, as passed in 1986, was the principle of testamentary freedom, a testator being free to exclude from the succession any person he or she chooses. In the case of deeds executed after 4 May 2006, the issue no longer arises since any distinction between 'lawful' and 'unlawful' children has been abolished.

Because rights to legitim (both directly and by way of representation) and to the intestate estate are regulated by statute under the Succession (Scotland) Act 1964, rather than by private deed, all children are entitled equally where the death from which the succession arises occurred after 8 December 1986.

(4) Stepchildren, accepted children, and kinship care children

2.14 It can be the case that the deceased may have had in their immediate family a non-biological child. However, it is not always the case that this child was formally adopted by the deceased under the Adoption Acts. For example, the deceased may have raised a stepchild deriving from their spouse, cohabitant, or partner. Otherwise, a child belonging to someone in their wider family has been raised by the deceased in 'kinship' care.

Without a formal adoption, these children have no direct succession rights to their accepted parent or step-parent by default of the law. Such children are not entitled to legitim from their step-parent or accepted parent's moveable estate or to a share in their intestate estate under the Succession (Scotland) Act 1964.[69]

In testamentary documents, such children are not to be included within the construction of 'children', 'descendants' or 'issue' in the deceased's will, even where he or she had accepted the child as a 'child of the family'

68 See paras **11.7–11.11.**

69 It is not possible to have an adult-adoption for a person over the age of 18 under the Adoption Acts [though there is a limited exception where the procedure has commenced before the child was 18, 2007 Act, s 28(2)]. Permitting adult adoptions in Scots law has been the subject of a political campaign, see BBC News, 'MSPs hear evidence on adult adoption campaign', 27 September 2018, available at https://www.bbc.co.uk/news/uk-scotland-45652209.

within the meaning of the Family Law (Scotland) Act 1985.[70] With this said, it may be possible that in a case of ambiguity such a term could be constructed in favour of a step-child or accepted child.[71]

Otherwise, the deceased would have to ensure that they have made express provision for that child in their will instead and avoid placing them into a general class, such as 'to my children'. This point is often not considered by the deceased in their lifetime, which can lead to perceived injustices after death where the accepted child or stepchild receives nothing from the deceased's estate.

The Scottish Law Commission has previously considered whether step-children or accepted children should be afforded succession rights in intestacy.[72] It commissioned research which asked the public whether and to what extent step-children ought to be entitled to a share in a stepparent's estate.[73] 75% of the respondents thought stepchildren should receive something from a stepparent's intestate estate, and 68% agreed that they should be treated equally with the stepparent's own children. 65% agreed that young stepchildren ought to be protected from disinheritance in like manner to the stepparent's own children. However, the Commission ultimately concluded that 'disadvantages of a change in the law outweighed the advantages' and recommended that no change in the law be made in respect of stepchildren or accepted children in intestate succession.[74]

The current legal position for stepchildren or accepted children has been the subject of continuing commentary elsewhere.[75] On the one hand,

70 1985 Act, s 27(1), definition of 'child'. By contrast, in English law a person who was treated by the deceased as a child of their family (and in turn, the deceased was treated as their parent) has the right to apply under the court's equitable jurisdiction for modification of the will or the rules of intestacy for reasonable financial provision from the deceased's estate: Inheritance (Provision for Family and Dependants) Act 1975, s 1(1)(d).

71 As a comparative example of such a result, see *Reading v Reading* [2015] WTLR 1245.

72 Report *on Succession* (SLC Report No 215, 2009), paras 2.31–2.34.

73 *Attitudes Towards Succession Law: Finding of a Scottish Omnibus Survey* (SERC, 2005), paras 2.11–2.13, and 2.24.

74 Report *on Succession* (2009), para 2.33.

75 K Norrie 'Reforming succession law: intestate succession' (2008) 12(1) *Edin LR* 77; D Reid, 'From the cradle to the grave: politics, families and inheritance law' (2008) 12(3) *Edin LR* 391, 413ff; D Reid and N Sweeney, 'Land reform, inheritance rights and unintended consequences' (2015) 27(4) *Child and Family Law Quarterly* 403. For further empirical analysis, see N Sweeney, *Public Attitudes to Inheritance in Scotland,* thesis, University of Glasgow (2018), Chs 5–7.

reforming the law to allow stepchildren or accepted children to inherit under a class of 'children' in a legacy, or by claiming legitim or as a distinct right in intestate succession, may well be a fairer outcome. However, the complexity that follows, and the likely litigious atmosphere that it would create, for example in determining who was indeed 'accepted' by the deceased as a child, may mean that it would complicate an estate from being distributed timeously and without acrimony. No clear conclusion or solution emerges from this difficult issue.[76]

(5) Children born from assisted reproduction

2.15 The Human Fertilisation and Embryology Act 1990 regulates the relationship of the deceased to any child born by way of artificial conception or assisted reproduction between 1 August 1991 and 5 April 2009. The Human Fertilisation and Embryology Act 2008 regulates relationships to a child conceived by such means after 6 April 2009.[77] The Acts are broadly similar and can impact a determination of which children can succeed to an estate, outwith succession to titles, coats of arms or dignities,[78] as they provide rules to determine the mother and father of the child. Assisted reproduction can include surrogacy, but this arrangement is given a treatment of its own below.

(a) Relationship to men

(i) 1990 Act

2.16 Generally, providing sperm for artificial conception does not automatically mean that the donating male is to be treated as the father of

76 The Scottish Government consulted on the SLC's conclusions on this aspect several times. On the issue of stepchildren and accepted children in 'blended families', see Scottish Government, *Law Of Succession: Consultation* (2019), paras 2.15 to 2.22. Consultation responses continue to indicate no clear consensus on reform, Scottish Government, *Law Of Succession: Consultation Response* (2020).

77 2008 Act, s 57(1); and Human Fertilisation and Embryology Act 2008 (Commencement No.1 and Transitional Provisions) Order 2009 SI 2009/479, reg 6.

78 1990 Act, s 29(5); and 2008 Act, s 48(8).

the subsequent child.[79] This includes situations where the sperm was used after the man's death.[80] To be considered as the father under the 1990 Act, there are two possible situations:

(1) A husband was married to a woman at the time of an insemination, using the sperm of another man, and the husband consented to the insemination.[81] In such situations, the husband is deemed to be the father.

(2) If treatment was performed in a licensed clinic for a couple, married or not, and the sperm was not his own, then the man in that relationship is to be treated as the father.[82]

If fatherhood is determined in either such manner, then the child will be entitled to succeed to the man on his death irrespective of the child's biological parentage.[83] The 1990 Act has a limited retroactive effect in this regard.[84] If a deed or document refers to a legacy such as 'to my children', irrespective of the date that the document was executed, then a child conceived by artificial conception on or after 1 August 1991 is entitled to inherit under such legacies or other provisions.

Further rules to determine fatherhood were introduced for posthumous conceptions under the 1990 Act by the Human Fertilisation and Embryology (Deceased Fathers) Act 2003. This legislation arose in part due to the interesting *Ex P Blood* litigation,[85] where a woman sought to use her husband's sperm for posthumous conception after his death. The provisions of the 2003 Act are complex,[86] but largely symbolic in that it only facilitates recognition of posthumous fatherhood in the Register of Births.[87] Recognition of posthumous fatherhood in this manner does not give rise to succession rights to his estate.[88]

79 1990 Act, s 28(6).
80 1990 Act, s 28(6)(b).
81 1990 Act, s 28(2).
82 1990 Act, s 28(3).
83 1990 Act, s 29(1).
84 1990 Act, s 29(3).
85 [1999] Fam 151.
86 1990 Act, ss 28(5A)–(5D).
87 1990 Act, s 28(5I).
88 1990 Act, s 29(3A)–(3C).

(ii) 2008 Act

2.17 The 2008 Act is broadly similar to the 1990 Act in its approach in determining fatherhood, and succession rights to a deceased man, though it has been updated to reflect changes in society. Once again, providing sperm for artificial conception does not automatically mean that the donor is to be treated as the father of that child.[89] Instead, there are set conditions that must be satisfied for the law to consider the man as the father in artificial conception cases:[90]

(1) If a female is in a marriage of civil partnership with a man, and receives a fertilised embryo or sperm from another man who was not her husband or civil partner, then provided the spouse or civil partner consents to such treatment, the spouse or civil partner is deemed as the father of the subsequent child.[91]

(2) In other cases, such as unmarried couples or cohabitants, a man can be deemed a father if the 'agreed fatherhood conditions' of the 2008 Act are met and the treatment is performed in a licensed clinic.[92]

Where either route establishes fatherhood, the child is treated in succession law as the man's own child.[93] Being determined as the father under the 2008 Act will therefore impact on questions of succession to him. This has retroactive effect in respect of any deeds or documents already executed by the man.[94]

In the case of posthumous conception using the deceased male's sperm, special provision is again made for his symbolic recognition as the father on the Register of Births.[95] Such registrations do not have any constitutive effect for succession rights.[96] A similar symbolic rule is provided for the

89 2008 Act, s 41.
90 2008 Act, ss 35–38.
91 2008 Act, s 35(1).
92 2008 Act, s 37.
93 2008 Act, s 48(1).
94 2008 Act, s 48(5).
95 2008 Act, s 39.
96 2008 Act, s 41(2); and s 48(3).

male spouse, civil partner or intended parent, though not providing sperm for the conception, who predeceases the birth of the intended child.[97]

(b) Relationship to women

2.18 It may be thought easier to determine who is the mother in an artificial conception, but difficulties can arise if the gametes or eggs come from a woman who is not the carrier of the foetus. The donor of an egg would have a genetic link to the eventual child born, and a question could arise as to whether that child should have succession rights to their biological mother.

(i) 1990 Act

2.19 Under the 1990 Act it is the woman who carries the foetus following insemination or fertilisation that is deemed to be the mother.[98] This applies irrespective of the donor of an egg or gamete. The carrier of the child is deemed as the mother and therefore the child acquires succession rights to her.[99] Once again, this is retroactive, so it may affect any prior deeds or documents executed, regardless of their date.[100]

(ii) 2008 Act

2.20 The 2008 Act is similar to the 1990 Act by recognising the carrier of the embryo as the mother of the child and the consequent impact that this has on succession rights.[101] However, the 2008 Act recognises that the second parent may also be a woman. This could arise in a lesbian relationship, where the intended second parent is also a woman. In cases where another woman is the intended second parent, then the Act facilitates her being deemed as the child's second mother or, more neutrally, as the

97 2008 Act, s 40(4).
98 1990 Act, s 27(1).
99 1990 Act, s 29(1).
100 1990 Act, s 29(3).
101 2008 Act, s 33 and s 48(1).

'second parent'.[102] This would include creating succession rights to her.[103] This can apply where:

(1) The woman is in a marriage or civil partnership with the woman receiving the embryo or artificial insemination.[104] Provided the non-inseminated woman consents to the treatment of her partner, then she can be deemed as the second mother.

(2) Otherwise, if the couple are being treated together in a licensed clinic and provided the 2008 Act's 'agreed female parenthood conditions'[105] are met, then the non-inseminated woman can be deemed as the second mother.

It can be the case that the second mother was also the donator of the egg. However, despite the genetic link, the woman cannot be treated as the mother of the child unless the above routes are satisfied, or the woman adopts the child.[106] If a second mother predeceases the birth of a child, then it is possible for her to be symbolically named as the second mother in the Register of Births provided the conditions in Section 46 of the 2008 Act are satisfied.[107] Once again, this does not establish succession rights, as the Act merely seeks to give a symbolic note of the second mother in the Register of Births.[108]

(6) Children born from surrogacy

2.21 Surrogacy has existed for some time, but the law has not kept up with changes in society.[109] To utilise the language of the Law Commissions,[110] surrogacy can either be 'traditional' in that a woman provides an egg for the intended parent(s), which is inseminated through sexual intercourse

102 2008 Act, ss 42–45.
103 2008 Act, s 41(1).
104 2008 Act, s 42(1).
105 2008 Act, s 44.
106 2008 Act, s 47.
107 2008 Act, s 46(4).
108 2008 Act, s 48(4).
109 See the work of the Scottish Law Commission and Law Commission of England & Wales in this area in Joint Report on *Surrogacy* (SLC Report No 262, 2023).
110 Joint Report on *Surrogacy* (SLC Report No 262, 2023), Vol 1, para 1.8.

or artificial insemination. Otherwise, there is 'gestational surrogacy' where a woman merely carries a foetus for the intended parent(s) without providing her own egg.

Gestational surrogacy can cause problems with succession and the attribution of parenthood. Surrogacy is partly regulated by the 1990 and 2008 Acts as a form of assisted reproduction. Regardless of who is intended to be the parent(s) of the child, the rules noted above under the 1990 and 2008 Acts will apply to determine legal parenthood. Thus, if a surrogate and her spouse agree that she will carry a child for two other people, the 2008 Act or (in older cases) the 1990 Act will determine that the surrogate and any spouse are the mother and father of the child – not the intended parents. There is no mechanism to alter such an outcome as it applies from the moment of birth under the current law. Surrogacy agreements, where the parties contract to an agreement for the carriage, birth, and upbringing of an intended child, are currently unenforceable in Scots law.[111]

Instead, the intended parent(s) must obtain, or have obtained, a parental order under the Acts to become the legal parent of the child.[112] The Law Commissions note that such orders are low in Scotland,[113] which tends to suggest that many parents availing themselves of surrogacy are not appropriately reconciling the factual outcome of a surrogacy, where the intended parents are acting as parent, with whom the law considers to be the legal parent of the child. The consequence of this is seen with its impact on succession law, alongside many other areas.

Without a parental order, the law may not consider the child related to the intended parent(s). Therefore, no succession rights can arise in intestacy or by legitim for that child. Similarly, a legacy to a class, such as 'children', 'issue' or 'descendants', cannot be properly said to include the child who was the product of a surrogacy. Conversely, the child would have succession rights to the surrogate and any person deemed the father or second parent under the Embryology Acts. The problems are as summarised by the Commissions:[114]

111 Surrogacy Arrangements Act 1985, s 1A.
112 1990 Act, s 30; and 2008 Act, ss 54–55.
113 Joint Report on *Surrogacy* (SLC Report No 262, 2023), Vol 1: Summary, 4.
114 Joint Report on *Surrogacy* (SLC Report No 262, 2023), Vol 2, para 15.133.

'Succession law in Scotland is therefore problematic in the context of current surrogacy agreements. If the surrogate dies before the intended parents have obtained a parental order, then the surrogate-born child has an indefeasible claim on her estate by way of legal rights and possibly free estate, or (in preference to legal rights) a share in a legacy. This can then diminish the amount that her other surviving children and family members receive from her estate, even though the surrogate will typically intend that the surrogate-born child should be treated as the child of the intended parents. Conversely if an intended parent dies before the order the child will not inherit from their estate at all unless the intended parent dies testate with a legacy to the child.'

The Commissions, amongst many other recommendations in respect of surrogacy, have recommended that the child can be treated as a child of the intended parent(s) from the point of birth where a sanctioned surrogacy agreement is in place.[115] In addition, what may be seen as an extension of the *nasciturus* principle will allow an *in utero* surrogated child to be treated as a child of the intended parent(s) in the event that one of them predeceases birth. Whether these reforms will be carried forward in the UK Parliament remains to be seen.

ADULT PARTNERS

(1) Spouses

2.22 Marriage continues to fall in popularity in formally recognising one's relationship with their chosen romantic partner.[116] Despite this trend, marriage has an important role in providing succession rights in Scots law under the rules of intestate succession alongside legal rights in both testate and intestate succession.[117]

Formerly, changes in marital status – from unmarried to married or from married to divorced – had no effect on the terms of wills made either prior to or during the marriage. This remains partly true today. If, for example, a single woman makes a will in favour of her nieces and

115 ibid, para 15.144.

116 For wider policy discussions, see E Sutherland, *Child and Family Law, Vol 2: Intimate Adult Relationships,* 3rd edn (2022), Ch 1.

117 See **Ch 5** and **Ch 6.**

nephews, then subsequently marries but makes no testamentary provision for her husband thereafter, he does not have a right to challenge the will *in toto* simply because he has been excluded. However, if a surviving spouse is not provided for in a will (whether it was executed before the marriage or not), he or she retains entitlement to claim legal rights as a partial relief from disinheritance.[118]

The Scottish Law Commission recommended in 1990 that while marriage should not revoke a will, divorce or annulment should revoke provisions by one spouse in favour of the other, whether made by will, or under a nomination or special destination[119] unless the contrary is indicated.[120] This has been achieved by way of s 1 of the Succession (Scotland) Act 2016.[121] Under s 1, a termination of marriage by divorce or annulment has the effect of meaning that the spouse is treated as predeceasing the spouse in any provision in a will.[122] An exception is provided under this provision where the testator has made clear that the spouse should still inherit or should act as trustee or executor of the estate (or have power of appointment of the same).

Section 2 of the 2016 Act makes a similar provision in respect of the effect of the termination of marriage on a special destination.[123] Some doubt had been expressed on how this provision operated.[124] The Trusts and Succession (Scotland) Act 2024 has intended to resolve such doubts by amending the relevant wording of the 2016 Act.[125]

118 See **Ch 5**.

119 On special destinations, see paras **7.12.1ff.**

120 Report *on Succession* (Scot Law Com No 124, 1990), recommendation 17. Under English law, marriage revokes a will unless the will was made in contemplation of the marriage: Wills Act 1837, s 18. This provision has been the subject of scrutiny and recommendation for reform, see Law Commission of England & Wales, Report on *Modernising Wills Law* (LC Report No 419, 2025). On divorce, any provisions in favour of the spouse are revoked, with the surviving spouse being deemed to have predeceased the testator: Wills Act 1837, s 18A.

121 An earlier provision was introduced under s 19 of the Family Law (Scotland) Act 2006 in respect of the effect of divorce or annulment on a special destination.

122 2016 Act, s 1(2).

123 On special destinations, see **7.19–7.25.**

124 J Robbie, 'Death, divorce and defective drafting' (2018) 22(2) *Edin LR* 307; and S Wortley, 'The Meaning of Succession (Scotland) Act 2016, section 2: statutory interpretation and survivorship destinations' 2022 *Jur Rev* 179.

125 Trusts and Succession (Scotland) Act 2024, s 76.

It is important to stress that these provisions of the 2016 Act will only operate with divorce or annulment. Without such a court order, the surviving spouse is entitled to legal rights, and in intestate succession, prior rights and rights to the intestate free estate of the deceased spouse.[126] This point can often come as a shock in situations where the deceased is estranged from their spouse but the pair failed to attend to divorce before one of the party's death.[127]

(a) Irregular marriage

2.23 Until the passing of the Family Law (Scotland) Act 2006, a person who had not undergone a marriage ceremony with the deceased but had lived with him or her and held him or herself out as the deceased's husband or wife could seek a declarator of marriage by habit and repute.[128] If granted, this would entitle the survivor to claim the automatic entitlements available only to spouses, including prior rights out of the deceased's intestate estate, legal rights whether the deceased died intestate or not, and certain benefits such as pension rights.

The abolition of this last surviving form of irregular marriage by s 3 of the Family Law (Scotland) Act 2006 ended the possibility (though some relationships may still subsist on this basis as the 2006 Act could not terminate existing irregular marriages altogether).[129] Despite its repeal, it is still common today to hear the general public speaking of 'common law marriage' in the belief that not being married can be treated the same as being married.[130] The only way now open to individuals to obtain provision as a surviving unmarried or non-civil partnered partner is to

126 See **Ch 6.**

127 For discussion, see J Kerrigan, 'Separated spouses and the retention of rights of intestate succession' 2019 *SLT (News)* 93.

128 See further Sutherland, *Child and Family Law, Vol 2: Intimate Adult Relationships*, 3rd edn (2022), paras 2-187 to 2-201; and for a historical exposition, see W Sellar, 'Marriage by Cohabitation with Habit and Repute: Review and Requiem?' in H Macqueen (ed), *Continuity, Influences and Integration in Scottish Legal History: Select Essays of David Sellar* (2021).

129 2006 Act, s 3(2).

130 Report *on Cohabitation* (SLC Report No 261, 2022), paras 1.6–1.7.

make a claim under s 29 of the 2006 Act as a cohabitant of the deceased, but that remedy is only available if the deceased died intestate.[131]

(2) Civil partners

2.24 The Civil Partnership Act 2004 introduced the status of civil partner, initially enabling two people of the same sex who are unmarried to register their relationship. Following a decision of the Supreme Court,[132] it is now possible for heterosexual couples to enter into a civil partnership too.[133] There have been calls to allow non-romantic relationships, such as siblings, to be formally recognised in such a manner too.[134]

The main effect of civil partnership in succession law is to confer on civil partners the same rights that apply to spouses. The 2004 Act contains two main provisions achieving this aim. First, s 131 confers the right to a share of the deceased moveable estate in like manner as a surviving spouse's right to *ius relicti* or *ius relictae* on civil partners. Since legal rights arise at common law and the common law does not recognise civil partnership, the inclusion of the provisions in s 131 of the Act is a necessary statutory addition.

Section 131(5) of the 2004 Act amends s 36(1) of the Succession (Scotland) Act 1964 so that legal rights are defined as *jus relicti*, *jus relictae*, legitim, and rights under s 131 of the Civil Partnership Act 2004. Second, Schedule 28, Part 1 amended those sections of the Succession (Scotland) Act 1964 that refer to spouses to include references to civil partners. Thus, civil partners are entitled to prior rights in intestate succession and to the intestate estate where there are no prior relatives, both on a par with spouses.[135] Schedule 28, Part 2, amends *inter alia* ss 24–25 of the Family Law (Scotland) Act 1985 to include civil partners, which is also important for the purposes of succession law. Similar protections as spouses enjoy also apply in respect of treating a former civil partner as predeceasing the

131 See paras **6.9ff.**

132 *R (on the application of Steinfeld and Keidan) (Appellants) v Secretary of State for International Development* [2018] UKSC 32.

133 The Civil Partnership (Opposite-sex Couples) Regulations 2019, SI 2019/1458.

134 *Civil Partnership Act 2004 (Amendment) (Sibling Couples) Bill* [House of Lords Bill 25, Session 2017–19].

135 See **Ch 6.**

deceased following formal termination of the partnership in respect of a will or special destination under the Succession (Scotland) Act 2016.[136]

(3) Cohabitants

2.25 With more people now choosing not to marry, or enter into a civil partnership, the position of cohabitants in succession law is somewhat unsatisfactory. A limited remedy exists under Section 29 of the Family Law (Scotland) Act 2006, which can be far less generous than the outcomes where a couple marries or enters into a civil partnership.[137] Despite this pessimism, it is worthwhile to begin by recognising s 29's merits.

Prior to the coming into force of the Family Law (Scotland) Act 2006, cohabiting partners had no rights arising by operation of law to succeed to any part of their deceased partner's estate unless they could prove marriage by habit and repute. The 2006 Act introduced the presumption that cohabitants own household goods in equal shares[138] and confers on them the right to apply to the court for provision on intestacy.[139]

Unlike a surviving spouse or civil partner, a cohabiting partner has no right to fixed shares of the intestate estate, or to any share of a testate estate under legal rights. It is here that the criticism can be raised, as it places cohabitants in a less favourable position than those who choose to marry or enter into a civil partnership.[140] Further, any award made to a cohabitant out of the deceased's intestate estate depends on certain qualifying criteria being satisfied, and the value of the award will be determined at the discretion of the court as guided by certain specified factors.[141]

In order for a cohabitant to make a claim for a share in the deceased cohabitant's intestate estate, he or she must first establish that he or she is

136 Succession (Scotland) Act 2016, ss 1–2.

137 For discussion, see G Christandl, 'Succession rights for cohabitants' (2020) 24(1) *Edin LR* 138; and Sutherland, *Child and Family Law, Vol 2: Intimate Adult Relationships*, 3rd edn (2022), paras 7–118ff.

138 See para **4.10.**

139 See paras **6.26–6.33**.

140 Clearly, however, the deceased partner may have made provision for the survivor in a testamentary disposition or the partner may be entitled to acquire property belonging to the deceased under a will substitute; see **Ch 7.**

141 See further para **6.30.**

a 'cohabitant' within the terms of the Act. Section 25(1), as amended by s 4(4) of the Marriage and Civil Partnership (Scotland) Act 2014, defines a 'cohabitant' as a heterosexual or same-sex relationship where the couple are living together as if married. Section 25(2) goes on to set out how the status, if such it can be called, of a cohabitant is to be determined in any particular case. The court is to have regard to:

(a) the length of the period during which the couple have been living together (or lived together);

(b) the nature of their relationship during that period; and

(c) the nature and extent of any financial arrangements subsisting, or which subsisted, during that period.

It should be noted that the Scottish Law Commission has proposed amending the definition of cohabitation in respect of s 28 claims for financial provision following *inter vivos* terminations of cohabitation.[142] However, the recommendations do not currently extend to amending the definition for s 29 claims in light of continuing debate on wider reform of intestate succession.[143]

UNLAWFUL KILLERS

2.26 The preceding sections have considered the entitlement of persons to succeed based on their familial status to the deceased. The final class of person to be considered, the unlawful killer, has a kind of *quasi*-status in the law of succession. If it be the case that a person has unlawfully killed someone from whom they were due to inherit, then any rights of succession held by the killer to that estate are forfeit. As will be seen, 'forfeit' is perhaps not the most accurate term, as succession rights are not forfeited to the state or the Crown as the term might immediately suggest. However, the 'forfeiture rule' is the term of choice used to describe this rule of law.

Whilst forfeiture of an unlawful killer's succession to an estate is a longstanding rule, the law in this area has been criticised, and the Law

142 Report *on Cohabitation* (SLC Report No 261, 2022).
143 See para **6.3.**

Commissions of both Scotland and England and Wales have each considered how the cases of unlawful killers ought to be dealt with.[144] Reform has followed in Scotland by way of the Succession (Scotland) Act 2016, and in England and Wales under the Estates of Deceased Persons (Forfeiture Rule and Law of Succession) Act 2011.

The forfeiture rule itself is one found in the common law and has been developed from the common law of England and Wales.[145] Statutory reforms in Scotland merely clarify its application and effect. Formerly, Scots law had a piece of legislation, the Parricide Act 1594, which provided that anyone convicted of killing his father, mother, grandfather or grandmother shall be disinherited along with all his or her descendants.[146] The effect of the 1594 Act was limited in several ways: the killer must have been convicted of the crime; it appeared to disqualify the killer from succeeding to heritable property only; and the only class of victim specified was ascendants. Despite these limitations, it has come to be accepted that this statute affected the development of an independent rule at common law regarding the unworthiness of a killer to inherit.[147] As a result, the Scottish courts, principally in *Smith, Ptr*,[148] looked to English law and adopted the development of 'forfeiture' in respect of unlawful killers in England into the Scots common law.

The source of the doctrine of forfeiture is medieval in origin, deriving from the doctrines of escheat and attainder in English law,[149] and within English law it has been adapted into the general principle that no person is entitled to benefit from his or her own wrong, as a matter of public

144 For the Scottish Law Commission recommendations, see Report on *Succession* (SLC No 124, 1990), paras 7.2ff; and Report on *Succession* (SLC No 215, 2009), paras 7.1ff. For the very similar recommendations of the Law Commission of England and Wales, see Report on *the Forfeiture Rule and the Law of Succession* (2005 Law Com No 295).

145 See the historical account in J MacLeod and R Zimmermann 'Unworthiness to inherit, public policy and forfeiture: The Scottish story' (2013) 87(4) *Tulane Law Review* 741.

146 This has been repealed by s 17 of the Succession (Scotland) Act 2016.

147 MacLeod and Zimmermann 'Unworthiness to inherit, public policy and forfeiture: The Scottish story', 764.

148 1979 SLT (Sh Ct) 35.

149 On the history of the rule in England, see A Reppy, 'The slayer's bounty – history of problem in Anglo-American law' 1942 *NYULQ Rev* 229–69.

policy, equity and morality.[150] In *Re Crippen*,[151] Crippen had murdered his wife and under the English law of intestate succession her estate fell to be distributed to her husband. Prior to his execution for her murder, Crippen executed a will in which he appointed his mistress as his executor and the sole beneficiary of his estate. His wife's family challenged Crippen's right to his wife's estate, which would have enlarged his own estate. The court upheld the relatives' claim, holding that:[152]

> 'No person can obtain, or enforce, any rights resulting to him from his own crime; neither can his representative, claiming under him, obtain or enforce any such rights. The human mind revolts at the very idea that any other doctrine could be possible in our system of jurisprudence.'

The forfeiture rule was subsequently defined in statute by the Forfeiture Act 1982 as 'the rule of public policy which in certain circumstances precludes a person who has unlawfully killed another from acquiring a benefit in consequence of the killing'.[153] This Act also applies in Scotland, as will also be further explored below.

The scope of the forfeiture rule has been widened to include culpable homicide and manslaughter, as well as murder.[154] In *Re Hall*, Hamilton LJ stated that to distinguish between murder and manslaughter in applying the forfeiture rule would be to encourage 'a sentimental speculation as to the motives and degree of moral guilt of a person who has been justly convicted and sent to prison'.[155] In *Smith, Ptr*[156] Sheriff MacVicar noted that 'the rule is absolute in cases where there has been a conviction for murder, manslaughter, or culpable homicide'.[157]

The two homicide offences are now not the only basis for engaging such a rule, it has been seen to apply in death by dangerous driving offences.[158] In a recent case, it was determined that aiding and assisting

150 *Smith, Ptr* 1979 SLT (Sh Ct) 35, at 36; and *Hunter's Exrs, Petrs* 1992 SC 474, per Lord Ross at 478.
151 [1911] P 108.
152 *Re Crippen* [1911] P 108, at 112.
153 1982 Act, s 1(1).
154 *Burns v Secretary of State for Social Services* 1985 SC 143.
155 *Re Hall* [1914] P1.
156 1979 SLT (Sh Ct) 35.
157 1979 SLT (Sh Ct) 35, at 36.
158 *Re Amos* [2020] EWHC 1063 (Ch).

the killer in hiding the weapon used to kill the deceased was insufficient to engage forfeiture.[159] It is entirely possible that the rule can be applied in cases where no criminal conviction has even been obtained, provided that an unlawful killing can be established on the facts in a civil court.[160] At one time, it was thought possible that the rule may not apply in 'lesser' offences where the moral turpitude of the killer was not great. Thus, in *Burns*, Lord President Emslie noted that:[161]

> 'It is a recognised principle of the jurisprudence both of England and Scotland that a person may not benefit from his own crime. This is the general rule but it is not an absolute one. Not every crime will require the general rule to be applied to deny a claim for benefit.'

In English law, that approach has now since been abandoned, and the courts now engage in an assessment of turpitude when examining whether to *modify or waive* the rule under the 1982 Act – rather than evaluating turpitude as part of assessing the application of the forfeiture rule entirely.[162] It would be suggested that Scots law may be required to follow this development and to return to Sheriff MacVicar's observation that 'the rule is absolute' and the degree of moral culpability of the killer is, in general, irrelevant in relation to whether the forfeiture rule ought to be engaged.

(1) Exceptions to the forfeiture rule

2.27 There are two main exceptions to the application of the rule. These exceptions excuse the rule from applying, rather than a court later determining to waive or modify any forfeiture (which process is carried out under the 1982 Act).

The first is where the requisite guilty mind is absent so that the killer was not acting unlawfully. This would be apparent in a case where the

159 *Tannock v Tannock* 2013 SLT (Sh Ct) 57.

160 On this see the discussion in A Learmonth et al, *Williams, Mortimer & Sunnucks on Executors, Administrators and Probate,* 22nd edn (2023), paras 64-02 and 64-06.

161 1985 SC 143, 148.

162 See the discussions in A Learmonth et al (eds), *Williams, Mortimer & Sunnucks on Executors, Administrators and Probate,* 22nd edn (2023), para 64-04; and J Glister and J Lee, *Hanbury and Martin on Modern Equity*, 23rd edn (2024), para 12-023.

accused is found not guilty of a crime or has no case to answer on the basis of a necessity of the killing, such as self-defence. The same may be said if the death is truly an accident to which no unlawfulness could be ascribed. Alternatively, the accused may have been suffering from such severe mental impairment that it could not be said their act was unlawful as they had a total lack of capacity. In such cases, the forfeiture rule, as a consequence of an unlawful killing, would not apply.

The second exception to the application of the forfeiture rule is in the case of homicide involving motor vehicles, such as reckless driving. Even when these actions cause the death of a third party, that does not bar the killer from relying on the indemnity provided by a motor insurance policy[163] unless the killing was deliberate.[164]

(2) Legal effect of forfeiture

2.28 Formerly, the precise legal method by which the right of a killer to succeed to his or her victim is forfeit was somewhat obscure. In earlier forfeiture cases such as *Re Crippen*,[165] the courts took the approach of deeming the killer to have predeceased. The legal consequence of a beneficiary predeceasing is that while the person cannot, quite clearly, benefit personally, other relatives may be entitled to claim the entitlement instead.[166] The outcome in *Re Crippen* was that the killer's being deemed predeceased resulted in the deceased wife's relatives being entitled to her intestate estate instead.

However, the approach of treating the killer as predeceasing the deceased was then disapproved of in both the Scottish and the English courts. In *Hunter's Executors, Ptrs*[167] a husband had murdered his wife. They had no children, but the husband had a son from his previous marriage. The wife had made a will bequeathing her whole estate to her husband if he

163 *Tinline* [1921] 3 KB 327; *James v British General Insurance Co Ltd* [1927] 2 KB 311; and *Marles v Philip Trant & Sons Ltd* [1954] 1 QB 29.

164 *Hardy v Motor Insurers' Bureau* [1964] 2 QB 745.

165 [1911] P 108.

166 Whether under a destination-over (see paras **11.12** and **11.22**) or by way of representation in legitim (see para **5.7**) or intestate succession (see **Ch 6**, in particular paras **6.34–6.42**, and **6.45**).

167 *Hunter's Executors, Prs* 1992 SLT 1141.

survived her, and to her sister and her stepson equally if he did not. There was no question that the husband's rights under the will should not be forfeit, but the court was asked to consider whether the estate should be distributed as if the husband had predeceased the wife (in which case the alternative provisions of the will came into effect) or whether the estate had fallen into intestacy.

The court held that public policy required the forfeiture rule to be applied only as far as necessary to achieve the objective sought. For the destination over to the sister and stepson to come into effect, the husband must have predeceased the testator. Relying on the English case of *Re Callaway*[168] the court held that there had been no such predecease and public policy did not require the use of the fiction that there had been. The killer was disqualified simply as a result of the unlawful killing. As a consequence, the legacy lapsed and the estate fell into intestacy:[169]

> 'The general rule of public policy on this branch of the law is the same in England as in Scotland, and should be applied in the same way in each jurisdiction … in England, the general rule of public policy prevents any vesting taking place in the killer, but there is no reason to deem that the killer has predeceased his victim; the rule of public policy should be carried no further than is necessary to achieve that object. The will should be construed literally.'

Hunter's Executors was cited with approval by the English court in *Jones v Midland Bank Trust Co*[170] which also rejected the fiction of predecease. Here, a destination to nephews in the event of the predecease of a son who had been found guilty of the manslaughter of his mother was ineffective; the son had not actually predeceased his mother, and to deem that he had would be to effectively re-write the deceased's will. Again, in *Re DWS Deceased*,[171] the court rejected the fiction, albeit on the basis of statutory interpretation rather than principle,[172] so that the son of a man who had murdered his parents was held not to be entitled

168 [1956] 2 All ER 451.
169 *Hunter's Exrs*, per Lord Justice-Clerk Ross at 1143.
170 *Jones v Midland Bank Trust Co* [1998] 1 FLR 246.
171 [2001] Ch 568.
172 The court relied on a literal interpretation of s 47(1) of the Administration of Estates Act 1925.

to his grandparents' intestate estates since his father had not actually predeceased them.

In light of these cases, the Scottish Law Commission recommended that a person who is responsible for killing the deceased should automatically forfeit his or her rights of succession to the deceased's estate and rights to property held in trust devolving on the deceased's death by being treated as predeceased – thus attempting to return to the earlier caselaw.[173] This has now been given statutory effect by the Succession (Scotland) Act 2016.[174] A killer is now to be treated as predeceasing the deceased in questions of succession rights to an estate, or as a right as a beneficiary under a trust made by the deceased, or under the operation of a special destination.[175] By treating the killer as predeceasing, it may mean that the killer's issue can represent the killer and claim instead.[176] This is under the principle that 'the killer's issue should not be tainted by their ancestor's forfeiture'.[177]

As the killer is treated as predeceasing, this is why 'forfeiture' is not the most appropriate term to describe the operation of this rule. The succession rights are not forfeited or involuntarily transferred away from the killer to the Crown or to another person; instead, the killer is simply treated as failing to survive the deceased, and therefore the general rules of survivance take effect to determine how the property is to be distributed. Subject to the operation of the doctrine of representation, no rights of succession will vest in the killer as they are artificially treated as not surviving the deceased.

In the event that the property has already been distributed to the killer, say before the killer's culpability in the death became known, then it would seem the remedy would be, subject to negative prescription, a claim made under unjustified enrichment by the executor to have the property returned to them – as akin to an *ultra vires* payment to a mistaken

173 Report on *Succession* (SLC No 124, 1990), paras 7.15ff; and Report on *Succession* (SLC No 215, 2009), para 7.3.

174 Succession (Scotland) Act 2016, s 12.

175 2016 Act, s 12(3).

176 Under an implied destination-over under s 6 of the 2016 Act (see para **11.22**) or by way of representation in legitim (para **5.7**) or intestate succession (para **6.35**).

177 Report on *Succession* (SLC No 124, 1990), para 7.17.

beneficiary.[178] The Explanatory Notes of the 2016 Act speak of a 'duty to return the property to the estate' in such situations.[179] However, there is a protection for third-party purchasers in good faith who purchased any inherited property from the killer whilst unaware of the killer's title being invalidated by forfeiture.[180] In the event the killer refuses to sign any documents, then a power is given to the sheriff clerk to execute deeds on behalf of the killer.[181]

(3) Burden of proof

2.29 As noted above, the killer need not have been convicted of a crime in order for the forfeiture rule to apply[182] but, where he or she has been convicted, the conviction carries a presumption that the killer is guilty.[183] Conversely, an acquittal does not carry a presumption of innocence. In *Gray v Barr*[184] the applicant had been acquitted at his criminal trial but the civil court found that he had indeed carried out a manslaughter. Lord Denning held that:[185]

> 'There is no doubt, to my mind, that Mr Barr was guilty of manslaughter. I know that at the criminal trial he was acquitted altogether. But that was a merciful verdict, and in this civil action we must, when called upon, give the true decision according to law.'

Where civil proceedings are brought, the fact of the killing must be proved to the civil standard of proof of the balance of probabilities, rather than the criminal standard of beyond reasonable doubt.[186]

178 Report on *Succession* (SLC No 124, 1990), para 7.19. *See Armour v Glasgow Royal Infirmary* 1909 SC 916. In respect of the executor's own liability in such situations, see s 33 of the Trusts and Succession (Scotland) Act 2024.
179 2016 Act, Explanatory Notes, para 47.
180 2016 Act, s 13.
181 2016 Act, s 14.
182 This may be because the killer has committed suicide before a conviction has been obtained: see, eg, *Re Sigsworth* [1935] Ch 89; *Re Pollock* [1941] Ch 219; and *Dunbar v Plant* [1999] Ch 412.
183 Law Reform (Miscellaneous Provisions) (Scotland) Act 1968, s 10.
184 *Gray v Barr* [1971] 2 QB 554.
185 *Gray v Barr* [1971] 2 QB 554 at 568.
186 *Re Dellow's Will Trusts* [1974] 1 All ER 771.

(4) Waiver or modification of the forfeiture tule

2.30 Not every unlawful killing should require the result that the killer is treated as predeceasing the deceased. In some cases, this may be harsh and create injustice. A classic example may be a wife who has suffered severe domestic abuse from her husband to such extent that one day she, in an act of defence, fights back and kills her husband. A conviction of culpable homicide might mean that the wife is then to be treated as predeceasing her spouse and denied succession to his estate under the forfeiture rule. That outcome may leave the spouse homeless or destitute depending on the financial situation and relationship of the spouse and deceased. In such circumstances, is it entirely fair that she is deprived of any inheritance from the husband's estate?[187]

The Forfeiture Act 1982 gives the court discretion to modify the effects of the rule in the interests of justice so that in some cases the application of the forfeiture rule may be excluded, either wholly or partially. Forfeiture is thus a two-stage process. First, it must be determined whether the forfeiture rule be applied in a given case. As noted above, it may be said there is an absolutist approach in which this question can be determined without questions of moral turpitude. The proving, on the balance of probabilities, of the killing will engage the forfeiture rule.

If the rule is engaged, the second stage is that the killer may then, in certain circumstances, raise proceedings to determine whether its effects ought to be modified under the provisions of the 1982 Act. It is at this second stage that the question of the petitioner's moral culpability, rather than his or her criminal responsibility for the killing, is relevant. Section 2 of the 1982 Act empowers the court to make an order modifying the rule. This can include exclusion of the forfeiture rule altogether. Under s 2(2) of the 1982 Act, the court shall not make an order unless it is satisfied that, having regard to the conduct of the offender and of the deceased and to such other circumstances as appear to the court to be material, the justice of the case requires the effect of the rule to be so modified.

187 In *Burns v Secretary of State for Social Services* 1985 SLT 351, it was noted that the judge at the appellant's criminal trial had stated that the accused seemed to be 'more sinned against than sinning'. See also *Challen v Challen* [2020] EWHC 1330 (Ch).

The court has no discretion to modify the rule where the killer has been convicted of murder; here, total forfeiture always applies.[188] Where modification is possible, s 2(3) of the 1982 Act provides that where a person stands convicted of an offence of which unlawful killing is an element, proceedings for modification must be brought within six months of the appeal window closing for the conviction or, indeed, the conclusion of any appeal against conviction.[189] Compassion for the killer is not a relevant factor,[190] rather:[191]

> 'The court is entitled to take into account a whole range of circumstances relevant to the discretion, quite apart from the conduct of the offender and the deceased: the relationship between them; the degree of moral culpability for what has happened; the nature and gravity of the offence; the intentions of the deceased; the size of the estate and the value of the property in dispute; the financial position of the offender; and the moral claims and wishes of those who would be entitled to take the property on the application of the forfeiture rule.'

(5) Scope of modification

2.31 The interests in property referred to in the Forfeiture Act 1982, s 2(1) are defined in s 2(4)(a) to include any right towards property which the offender would, apart from the forfeiture rule, have acquired either under a testamentary disposition, the law of intestate succession, a nomination or special destination, *mortis causa* donation, a trust or by way of legal rights. Section 2(5) of the 1982 Act allows the forfeiture rule to be modified in either or both of two ways in relation to such interests.

Section 2(5)(a) of the 1982 Act provides that where the applicant would acquire more than one interest in property in consequence of the death, the rule may be excluded in respect of any, but not all, of those interests. For example, the killer may be entitled to a legacy under the deceased's will, have been nominated as the person entitled to receive the proceeds of an insurance policy on the deceased's life[192] and be entitled to the deceased's

188 1982 Act, s 5.
189 1982 Act, ss 2(3)–(3A).
190 *Dalton v Latham* [2003] EWHC 796 (Ch) at para 45.
191 *Dunbar v Plant* [1999] Ch 412, at 427.
192 See para **7.26**.

share of ownership in heritable property under a special destination.[193] He or she has, therefore, three potential interests arising from the death of the deceased but may, at the discretion of the court, be precluded under s 2(5)(a) from taking all of them. The Act does not provide any formula or set of criteria to determine how any particular right, where there is more than one, is to be excluded from modification and remain forfeit. Section 2(5)(b) provides that in respect of any such interest in property, the court may exclude the application of the rule in respect of part or all of the property.

It is within the discretion of the court to determine the extent to which the forfeiture rule ought to be modified in respect of any interest. If, for example, the killer would be entitled to the whole of the deceased's intestate estate but for the forfeiture rule, the court may exclude any proportion of the total value it deems appropriate.

(6) Assisting suicide

2.32 The Forfeiture Act 1982, s 1(2), provides that a reference within the 1982 Act to a person who has unlawfully killed another includes a reference to a person who has unlawfully aided, abetted, counselled or procured the death of that other person. In *Dunbar v Plant*[194] the applicant and her fiancé had made a suicide pact as a result of which the fiancé died. Phillips LJ held that the words of s 2(1) of the 1982 Act could only have been intended to apply to the Suicide Act 1961, s 2(1), which makes it a criminal offence for a person to aid, abet, counsel or procure the suicide of another.[195] Although there had been no violence or threats of violence on the part of the applicant, these were not necessary for the forfeiture rule to be applied; it was sufficient that a serious crime had been committed deliberately and intentionally and the particular means used were not a necessary ingredient of the rule.[196]

The Forfeiture Act 1982 applies in both Scotland and England, but the Suicide Act 1961 applies only to England. This raises the point that

193 See paras **7.19–7.25**.

194 *Dunbar v Plant* [1998] Ch 412.

195 [1998] Ch 412 at 437.

196 [1998] Ch 412 at 425, approving *Whitelaw v Wilson* [1934] OR 415 where the rule was applied to the survivor of a suicide pact in which both the husband and wife had drunk poison.

although aiding, abetting, counselling or procuring the suicide of another is not a specific crime in Scots law, it is an unlawful killing in terms of the 1982 Act. The 1982 Act does not refer specifically to suicide but provides that unlawful killing includes aiding, abetting, counselling or procuring the death of another.

If Phillips LJ is correct that the provision of the 1982 Act can refer only to the provisions of the Suicide Act 1961, this would mean that s 1(2) of the 1982 Act does not apply in Scotland. This would seem a rather unlikely reading of the statute. The better position in Scotland would appear, therefore, to be that while s 1(2) applies in Scotland, the interpretation in *Dunbar v Plant* that it is synonymous with the 1961 Act does not. How then is this subsection to be reconciled with Scots law? Given that assisted suicide can lead to a prosecution of murder,[197] or culpable homicide,[198] it would seem that such assistance could *prima facie* satisfy the engagement of the forfeiture rule if a successor attempts to assist the deceased in terminating their own life.

In recent years, the courts in England seem more willing to afford relief under the Forfeiture Act 1982 in the case of assisted suicide. It has been common for some time that many ill people wish to end their own life with the assistance of another. In most cases, this involves assistance from a family member to allow them the dignity of a peaceful death. If a family member helps the deceased travel to Switzerland or another jurisdiction which permits assisted dying, should it be the case that they are treated as an unlawful killer under the forfeiture rule and deprived of their inheritance? The courts in England appear to suggest relief is appropriate for assisted suicide where there is little moral reprehensibility.[199] Each case will turn on its own facts and the turpitude of the 'killer', but it is likely a similar approach to relief could be reached by the courts in Scotland.

197 *Gordon v HM Advocate* 2018 SCCR 79.

198 See the discussion in J Chalmers, 'Clarifying the law on assisted suicide? *Ross v Lord Advocate*' (2017) 21(1) *Edin LR* 93.

199 *Macmillan Cancer Support v Hayes and Long* [2017] EWHC 3110 (Ch); *Ninian v Findlay* [2019] EWHC 297 (Ch); *Withers Trust Corp Ltd v Goodman's Estate* [2023] EWHC 2780 (Ch); and *Morris v Morris* [2024] EWHC 2554 (Ch).

Chapter 3

Executors and executry law

INTRODUCTION

3.1 From a property law perspective, the law of succession is concerned with distributing and exhausting the deceased's patrimony. The patrimony of the deceased is known as 'the estate'. The estate comprises the deceased's property and their debts, and detailed consideration of the contents of an estate is given in **Chapter 4**. However, this chapter considers the mechanics of distributing the property within an estate and the mechanisms for creditors to satisfy their debts.

It is important to understand that, as a generality, there is no instantaneous transfer of ownership of the deceased's property to successors in Scots law. Scots law generally has an indirect system of transfer, in which a person (the executor or the executrix, depending on their sex) must transfer the deceased's estate to successors.[1] Additionally, there is no automatic transfer of ownership to the executor at the moment of death. Approval from the local sheriff court is required in order for the executor to obtain ownership and distribute the deceased's estate. The effect of that requirement is that as soon as someone dies their estate becomes a *haereditas jacens*[2] (a dormant estate) and the

1 Exceptions exist to this general rule, such as where the deceased has used a testamentary device or *quasi*-will (see paras **7.18–7.29**), a transfer of a residential tenancy (see paras **4.21–4.22**) or the ability of executors or legatees under a will to complete title to heritable property using a will alone, see G Gretton and K Reid, *Conveyancing*, 5th edn (2018), para 26-04.

2 As to the status of ownership of property during the *haereditas jacens*, see G Gretton, '*Quaedam meditations Caledoniae*: The property/succession borderland' (2014) 3(2) *EPLJ* 109, 115, and K Reid, 'Administration of Estates in Scotland' in K Reid and R Zimmermann (eds), *Comparative Succession Law: Volume 4: Administration of Estates* (2025), 444. For a comparative overview of the *haereditas jacens*, see the German language article by J Schmidt, 'Von Monstern, Nebelgestalten und Seelenwanderungen' in N Jansen and S Meier (eds), *Iurium itinera: Historische Rechtsvergleichung und vergleichende Rechtsgeschichte – Historical Comparative Law and Comparative Legal History. Reinhard Zimmermann zum 70 Geburtstag am 10 Oktober 2022* (2022).

ownership of the deceased's property is believed to be temporarily 'vested in no one'.[3]

This chapter explores some of the aspects of executry law, being the name for the law relating to executors, and the procedural aspects which an executor must comply with in order to validly distribute the estate. Executry law is a subject in its own right but the fundamental principles are explored here to provide context for the remaining parts of this book.[4] It should be noted that this discussion proceeds on the basis that the Trusts and Succession (Scotland) Act 2024 is fully in force. The chapter begins by exploring some of the fundamental distinctions in property and succession law. Aspects of the history of succession law are considered here too, the purpose of which is not to digress into areas of mere academic curiosity, but the history is a necessary prerequisite to cover in order to fully understand the current system for the distribution of estates in Scotland today.[5]

HERITABLE PROPERTY AND MOVEABLE PROPERTY

3.2 Before considering succession law, matters of general property law require to be considered.[6] In Scots law, property or a thing (a *rem*) can be classified as either being heritable property or moveable property. Heritable property comprises land, real rights in land, and other

3 D Walker, *Principles of Scottish Private Law*, Vol 1, 4th edn (1988), Book III, 207.

4 The leading text in this area is E Scobbie, *Currie on Confirmation on Executors*, 9th edn (2011). The latest edition is slightly outdated but remains a worthwhile resource.

5 For a fuller history and interesting expositions, see W Sellar, 'Succession Law in Scotland: A Historical Perspective' in K Reid et al (eds), *Exploring the Law of Succession: Studies National Historical and Comparative* (2007); I Kotlyar, 'The Evolution of the Scots Law and Practice of Succession' in M Gigliola di Renzo Villata (ed), *Succession Law, Practice and Society in Europe across the Centuries* (2018); and K Reid, 'Administration of Estates in Scotland' in K Reid et al (eds), *Comparative Succession Law: Volume 4: Administration of Estates* (2025).

6 Naturally a book on succession law cannot consider general property law in significant detail but see G Gretton and A Steven, *Property, Trusts and Succession*, 5th edn (2024), paras 1.15 to 1.26. For an advanced understanding, see K Reid, *The Law of Property in Scotland*, 2nd edn (2026), Ch 2.

miscellaneous rights.[7] Moveable property are things which can be moved 'without injury or change of nature in itself, or the subject with which it is connected'.[8]

Straddling this distinction is a further categorisation: corporeal and incorporeal property. Corporeal property are physical things, thus land is corporeal, as is a car, a bike, a laptop, a bar of chocolate, or a necklace. Incorporeal property are things with no physical presence and essentially are rights that a person holds within their patrimony. Thus, a tenant's right of lease is incorporeal, and so is a right under a contract, or a right to the copyright of a book.

Taking these two distinctions, heritable and moveable, and corporeal and incorporeal, together, four categories, or species, of property emerge:

1. Corporeal heritable property.
2. Incorporeal heritable property.
3. Corporeal moveable property.
4. Incorporeal moveable property.

Difficulties in classifying property into these distinctions are noted further below in **Chapter 4**.[9] However, the distinction between heritable property or moveable property (whether either also corporeal or incorporeal) is of utmost importance in modern succession law. Historically, until the passage of the Succession (Scotland) Act 1964, Scots law effectively operated two separate succession regimes depending on the species of the deceased's property and whether it was heritable property or moveable property. In having this distinction, different rules applied in intestate succession where the deceased died with no will, with the result that property may have passed to very different persons at death. This old

7 It has debated for some time on whether to abandon the term 'heritable' for immoveable property or land in Scots law. Many jurisdictions simply refer to land as 'immoveables' However, the term 'heritable' and 'heritage' is still in use within the current generations of the legal profession and will likely be for some time yet. It should be noted that heritable property is, in its strict sense, wider than just land and real rights in land, see K Reid, *The Law of Property in Scotland,* 2nd edn (2026), para 42.

8 Bell, *Prin,* § 1472.

9 See paras **4.28–4.32.**

distinction has, to some extent, constructed the system of succession law as we understand it today.

THE OLD DIVISION OF HERITABLE AND MOVEABLE SUCCESSION LAW

(1) Heritable succession and the heir

3.3 The basis for the distinction between heritable and moveable property is rooted in the (now abolished) feudal system of land tenure. It is here that the term 'heritable' derives. Heritable property was property that could not be bequeathed by will, instead it had to be inherited under the rules of intestate succession. This affected land because it was not possible to bequeath land in a will until 1868.[10] Separate rules also existed for the distribution of land acquired during the deceased's lifetime, such land known as 'conquest', until the distinction between heritable land and conquest land was abolished in 1874.[11]

A feudal holding would be distributed by the rules of intestate succession and would pass to the 'heir-at-law' at death. Who was to be determined as the heir was based on primogeniture, in which the eldest first-born son would typically inherit the entire heritable estate. Stair justified primogeniture on the ground that:[12]

> 'The expediency of primogeniture is partly public, and partly private: the public expediency is, that the estates of great families, remaining entire and undivided, they with their vassals and followers, may be able to defend their country, especially against sudden invasions … The private expediency is, for the memory and dignity of families, which, by frequent division of the inheritance, would become despicable or forgotten.'

This discriminatory system was abolished by the Succession (Scotland) Act 1964 but the rules of heritable succession emerged in a period when by far the most important source of personal wealth was land[13] and by defining it to include its fruits (such as rent), the continuing wealth of the

10 Titles to Land (Consolidation) (Scotland) Act 1868, s 20.
11 Conveyancing (Scotland) Act 1874, s 37.
12 Stair *Inst*, III.4.22.
13 See T C Smout *A History of the Scottish People 1560–1830* (1972), Ch 6.

bloodline of a family would be ensured. Whether incorporeal property was heritable or moveable, and therefore a right transmissible directly to the heir, came to hinge on the question of whether the subject of the right could be seen as comparable to a feudal estate in land. Tests of the status of a thing were developed, concerned mainly with incorporeal rights relating to land which existed over a tract of future time (such as feudal superiorities, rents, leases and securities). By extension, heritable rights came to include the interest on capital on the basis that the interest could be regarded similarly to the fruits[14] and principles were adopted into the law in order to determine how and when a thing could alter its nature to become heritage.[15] Certain things, including household goods or tools that related to the house or farm to which the heir would succeed, were classified as 'heirship moveables' and passed along with the heritable property to the heir.[16]

For the heir to obtain a succession right to the heritable estate, they would have to formally enter as heir.[17] This could be done by way of the feudal superior accepting the heir and granting a writ (and later deed) of *clare constat* which the heir could use to attend to the necessary conveyancing to complete title to land. Otherwise, and every case where the feudal superior was the Crown, the heir had to utilise a judicial process known as 'service of heir' for a formal hearing to declare them as the person entitled to the heritable estate before they could attend to the necessary conveyancing with their feudal superior. Until such time as either mechanism was used, the entitled person was, until 1874, considered an 'apparent heir' and had a limited range of rights and remedies in respect of the deceased's heritable estate.[18] The mechanism for service of heir was removed by the Succession (Scotland) Act 1964. However, the 1964 Act is not retrospective, and it may be the case that land is discovered in the property registers that is still recorded in the name of a person who died before the commencement of the Succession (Scotland) Act 1964 on 10 September 1964. In such cases, the current heir must obtain a declarator of succession to the land from the

14 Erskine *Inst*, I.2.4–I.2.13.

15 See K Reid, *The Law of Property in Scotland*, 2nd edn (2026), paras 40–43.

16 This may be the origin of things considered as heirlooms; see para **6.19.**

17 See H Monteath, 'Heritable rights – from early times to the twentieth century' in *Introduction to Scottish Legal History* (Stair Society vol 20, 1958), 169ff.

18 Apparent heirs were abolished by s 9 of the Conveyancing (Scotland) Act 1874.

little-known and often-forgotten Sheriff of Chancery at Edinburgh sheriff court under the Titles to Land Consolidation (Scotland) Act 1868.[19]

(2) Moveable succession, next of kin, and the executor

3.4 In contrast to the heavily feudalised system of heritable succession that revolved around land and power, succession to moveable property was a matter of family law, and like other aspects of familial relations and personal status was historically considered to be spiritual affair and the domain of the Catholic Church.[20]

Moveable property would be inherited in intestate succession by the deceased's 'next-of-kin'.[21] In practice the heir and the next-of-kin might have been the same person, such as a sole surviving child of the deceased, but not always, and there could be markedly different distributions depending on who was deemed the heir, and who was deemed the next of kin. Unlike land, it was possible for the deceased to leave moveable property under a will. Intestate succession was 'deplored by religious thought',[22] and one of the most important things for a person to do, to avoid punishment by the Church, was to make a will appointing an executor to distribute the moveable property at death by way of testate succession.[23]

If no executor was appointed or nominated by the deceased, then the Church would appoint an executor instead. The executor would then need to be 'confirmed' by the local Church clergy and its officials in order to distribute the estate. The executor would have to prepare an inventory of the deceased's estate in order for the Church to calculate the correct

19 1868 Act, s 26A. There are some conceptual difficulties as to who is to be considered as the heir and the role of the Succession (Scotland) Act 1964 in determining who may be the current heir today, see G Gretton 'Trust and executry conveyancing' (1986) 31 *JLSS* 111, 114–15; and D Allan, 'Completion of title' (1978) 23 *JLSS* 438.

20 See T Green, 'The Sources of Early Scots Consistorial Law' in M Godfrey (ed), *Law and Authority in British Legal History, 1200–1900* (2016); and J Fergusson, *Treatise on the Present State of the Consistorial Law in Scotland* (1829).

21 As to who qualified as the next-of-kin, see J Irvine-Smith, 'Succession' in *Introduction to Scottish Legal History* (Stair Society vol 20, 1958), 210ff.

22 J Irvine-Smith, 'Succession' in *Introduction to Scottish Legal History* (Stair Society vol 20, 1958), 211.

23 See A Anton, 'Medieval Scottish executors and the courts spiritual' (1955) 67 *Jur Rev* 129.

payment of 'the quot', which essentially was a form of tax payable to the Church. The quot was a significant motive for the Church requiring confirmation, as it provided a revenue stream to it.

With the coming of the Reformation, the Church, its officials and ecclesiastical courts, lost their role in regulating executors. Queen Mary established a commissary court at Edinburgh with commissaries to manage executors and oversee the process of confirmation of executors among other areas of law.[24] Edinburgh was the paramount commissary court, and inferior commissary courts were later established throughout Scotland. Each inferior commissary court had a territorial jurisdiction (a commissariot) within which it had the power to oversee the confirmation of executors for people dying within their jurisdiction. In 1609, the Court of Session acquired appellate jurisdiction over the commissary courts.[25]

Despite the removal of the bishops from confirming executors and overseeing the administration of estates directly, the commissary courts were not entirely secular. The bishops and archbishops continued to have powers of appointment of commissaries. They also continued to receive the quot, and procurators-fiscal of the commissary courts would review deaths in their commissariot and charge the deceased's family to confirm an estate in order to exact payment. If the family failed to do so, the procurators-fiscal would seek confirmation instead. Such charges were later prohibited by statute in 1690.[26] After several suspensions and reinstatements, the bishops finally lost the right to receive the quot in 1700 as part of the separation of the commissary courts from religious control over the course of the end of the seventeenth century.[27] However, the secularised commissary courts continued to exact another form of duty, known as composition dues, instead.

In the nineteenth century, the commissary courts were slowly divested of their jurisdiction until all that remained of their function was the appointment and confirmation of executors. In 1876, the commissary courts were totally abolished and sheriffs assumed their role.[28] In modern

24 On this history of the commissary courts, see *Third Report of the Commissioners of Inquiry of the Courts in Scotland* (11 February 1818).

25 Commissariats Act 1609 (RPS 1609/4/20).

26 Confirmation Act 1690. This Act remains in force.

27 Discharging the Quots of Testaments Act 1700 (RPS 1700/10/243).

28 Sheriff Courts (Scotland) Act 1876, ss 35–40.

times, each sheriff court has a commissary department, and the sheriffs sit *qua* commissary in respect of the appointment and confirmation of executors.

(3) The death of heirs and the rise of the executor

3.5 Whilst the oversight of executors came to be centralised with the abolition of the commissary courts, the separate succession regimes for heritable and moveable property remained until the Succession (Scotland) Act 1964. As part of the package of reform introduced by the 1964 Act, heirs-at-law were abolished for all deaths after 10 September 1964, and the distribution of an estate (both heritable and moveable property) is now carried out entirely by an executor.[29] The 1964 Act also provided new assimilated rules for intestate succession for both heritable and moveable property and is discussed below in **Chapter 6**.

MODERN EXECUTORS

3.6 In present times, the executor is the person responsible for distributing the majority of the deceased's estate beyond any direct transfers of property by way of testamentary devices.[30] It is common to hear of executorship spoken of as if it is a formal office.[31] This is true, and there are duties incumbent on an executor, but in practice an executor is often a family member, friend, or the deceased's solicitor, rather than some form of independent third-party or state official. Formerly, the executor carried with it a form of benefit, in that there was an ability to retain the residue of the estate for themselves, but this entitlement has been removed by successive statutes, and the office of executor is a fiduciary role.[32]

29 1964 Act, ss 14–15.

30 See para **7.18**.

31 Erskine, *Inst*, III.9.41.

32 Estates of Minors Deceased Act 1526 (RPS ref: 1526/6/40); Intestate Succession Act 1540 (RPS ref: 1540/12/95); Executors Act 1617 (RPS ref: 1617/5/28); Intestate Moveable Succession (Scotland) Act 1855, s 8; and *Smart v Smart* 1926 SC 392, per Lord Smart at 402.

As such, an executor is now regarded as a form of trustee. In Scots law, there are two main types of executor. There are executors-nominate and executors-dative. These are considered below.

(1) Executors-nominate

3.7 An executor-nominate is one appointed by the deceased in their will. Formerly, the appointment of an executor-nominate was one of the main aims of a will, rather than the detailed list of legacies or bequests that set out the intended distribution of the estate as is now found in modern wills today.[33] Appointment as executor-dative may be express, implied, or constructive.[34] In the ordinary case, the deceased will have a simple clause at the beginning of their will expressing, for example:[35]

> I appoint Thomas Jones, residing at 22 University Gardens, Glasgow G12 8QQ to be my executor.

In practice the deceased may appoint anyone they wish to act as executor, whether a juristic person, or an adult[36] with capacity. Law firms typically have a separate company constituted in order for that company to act as executor or trustee, rather than any employed solicitor personally.[37]

The testator, the person making the will, may wish to give the executor an honorarium of a small legacy as a token of thanks for acting as executor of the estate. Similarly, a solicitor acting as an executor may wish to be renumerated for this service. Such express legacies are permissible, but generally as a form of trustee, the executor cannot take any personal benefit in the administration of the estate, for example, selling or gifting the deceased's property to themselves, to avoid a breach of their fiduciary

33 A Anton, 'Medieval Scottish executors and the courts spiritual' (1955) 67 *Jur Rev* 129.

34 See further E Scobbie (ed), *Currie on Confirmation of Executors,* 9th edn (2011), paras 5-05–5-100; and Executors (Scotland) Act 1900, s 3.

35 See the discussion in A Barr, *Drafting Wills in Scotland,* 2nd edn (2009), paras 3.10–3.30.

36 That is to say someone over the age of 16, Age of Legal Capacity (Scotland) Act 1991, s 1(1) and s 9(f).

37 The advantages of which are discussed in A Barr, *Drafting Wills in Scotland,* 2nd edn (2009), paras 3.14–3.15.

duties.[38] Consequently, without express provision, the executor is not entitled to any renumeration.[39] It is possible that the executor is also a beneficiary or successor of the estate. Holding succession rights in respect of the estate is no bar to acting as executor,[40] provided the executor can observe their paramount duty to act in the best interests of all beneficiaries.

Acceptance of the nomination in a will is entirely within the discretion of the executor-designate. If they decline office, and there is no alternate nominee noted in the will, then the result may be that the beneficiary of a universal or general legacy,[41] or residuary legacy[42] in the will may seek constructive-appointment under s 3 of the Executors (Scotland) Act 1900.[43] That failing, an executor-dative may require appointment instead.

(2) Executors-dative

3.8 An executor-dative is one appointed by the court. In testamentary documents, the testator has nominated a person to act as executor. However, where there is no testamentary document, or no executor-nominate wishes to act, then an executor-dative may need to be appointed (or *decerned*) by the local sheriff court of the deceased's domicile. In totally intestate estates, an executor-dative will aways require appointment.

The process of appointment as executor-dative is separate from the process of confirmation, which is discussed below. The executor-dative first must have an appointment under the Confirmation of Executors (Scotland) Act 1858[44] before seeking confirmation of the estate. Who is entitled to appointment is governed by a rather ridiculous set of rules

38 *Inglis v Inglis* 1983 SC 8. On fiduciary duties generally, see G Gretton and A Steven, *Property, Trusts and Succession,* 5th edn (2024), paras 25.29–25.32.

39 W Wilson and A Duncan, *Trusts, Trustees and Executors,* 2nd edn (1995), para 31-16.

40 *Birnie v Christie* (1891) 19 R 334, per Lord McLaren at 338; *Smart v Smart* 1926 SC 32; and *Anderson v Hare* 1952 SLT (Sh Ct) 40.

41 This is where the entire estate is left to one legatee, for example a testator may leave their entire estate to their spouse.

42 See para **10.7.**

43 If the deceased had created a trust under their will, then any testamentary trustees may also seek appointment as executors-nominate instead, see para **7.3.**

44 1858 Act, s 2. See also Act of Sederunt (Edictal Citations, Commissary Petitions and Petitions of Service) 1971 SI 1971/1165 [as amended by Act of Sederunt (Intimation and Service) 2025 SSI 2025/301, reg 4].

deriving from instructions issued by the bishops in 1666 that have been subject to modification by statute over the years.[45] Those entitled to confirm include the universal legatee or residuary legatee (if there is a will), the next-of-kin, the creditors of the deceased, other legatees (if there is a will), the funerator, or the local procurator fiscal. Where the deceased's spouse or civil partner is to receive the entire estate, then the spouse has the exclusive right to be appointed as executor-dative.[46] It had been held competent for a guardian of the spouse to be confirmed as executor-dative,[47] as has an attorney *qua* incapax spouse of the deceased to be confirmed as executor-dative.[48] Consequently, the law seems to be moving further away from the traditional order of preference and it may be said that anyone with an interest in the estate may seek appointment.

Generally, the commissary jurisdiction to appoint executors-dative is often termed as 'administrative' in the sense that a sheriff *qua* commissary merely confirms those entitled in line with the order of preference. Disputes about the suitability of a party seeking confirmation, or regarding the validity of a testamentary document, or those entitled to succeed, are not ordinarily competent in commissary proceedings and must be litigated within the general civil jurisdiction of the sheriff rather than before sheriff *qua* commissary:[49]

> 'The duty of the Sheriff as Commissary is to determine who is entitled to the office of executor on the face either of the deeds which are put before the Court, or of the relation to the deceased which is set out as the title of the applicant.'

As Sheriff Principal Cox noted in *Russo v Russo*:[50]

> 'In none of these references [the sheriff looking at the *Currie on Confirmation* treatise], old or new, is there the slightest suggestion that a person entitled to the office of executor-dative can be denied appointment on the ground, for example, that he is corrupt or incapable of conducting

45 E Scobbie (ed), *Currie on Confirmation of Executors*, 9th edn (2011), Ch 6.

46 Succession (Scotland) Act 1964, s 9(4). See **Ch 6**.

47 *B's Guardian, Minuter* 2023 SCLR 601 (decided on 21 July 2010).

48 *Gordon, Ptr* (2023) SLT (Sh Ct) 187. See R MacLeod, 'The appointment of an attorney as an executor' (2023) (29) *SLT (News)* 135.

49 *Martin v Ferguson's Trs* (1892) 19 R 474, per Lord President Robertson at 478.

50 *Russo v Russo (No 1)* 1998 SLT (Sh Ct) 32, 35. See also *Ford v Campbell* 2015 SC GLA 28.

> business affairs. The whole emphasis is on entitlement to the office. Where there is a contest the contest concerns who has the greater right, i.e. who is the nearest in kin and therefore having, on intestacy at least, the better claim to the estate.'

Within contentious families, disputes about who should serve as executor are common.[51] The simplest solution where two parties are within the same branch of the order of preference, such as two children of the deceased, is to be confirmed as executor-dative is to conjoin them and appoint both. Otherwise, there is limited remedies to prevent the appointment of executors-dative. However, Macleod suggests that 'where there is a manifest conflict of interest and conduct which puts the executry estate in danger, an appropriate approach would be to refuse confirmation as opposed to granting it'.[52] There are few reported cases to put the matter totally beyond doubt. It should be noted that the Scottish Ministers were given the power to impose additional regulations requiring sheriffs to determine the suitability of the appointment of an executor-dative.[53] However, no such regulations have yet been made.

One additional requirement for executors-dative is to obtain a bond of caution (pr: *kay-shun*). This is a form of insurance policy obtained from specialist providers for the insurer to pay the estate's beneficiaries for any losses arising in the mismanagement of the estate by the executor. Caution is not required for executors-nominate,[54] or where the spouse or the civil partner of the deceased is serving as executor-dative by virtue of

51 *Russo v Russo (No 1)* 1998 SLT (Sh Ct) 32; *Russo v Russo (No 2)* Hamilton Sh Ct, 15 August 2005, unreported. See R MacLeod, 'Opposing the appointment of an executor dative' 2015 *SLT (News)* 103.

52 R Macleod, *Contentious Executries: Commissary and Executry Litigation in Scotland,* 2nd edn (2023), para 2-105.

53 Succession (Scotland) Act 2016, s 21. On the genesis of this power, see Report *on Succession* (SLC Report No 215, 2009), paras 7.13–7.16.

54 This is somewhat arbitrary given an executor-nominate may also mismanage the estate but the view is that 'people making wills select executors in whom they have confidence and usually appoint at least one person familiar with business or financial matters in order to ensure proper administration of the estate', Report *on Succession* (SLC Report No 124, 1990), para 8.35. See further discussion in the 1990 Report, paras 8.32–8.39; and the Report *on Succession* (SLC Report No 215, 2009), paras 7.6–7.12.

the spouse or civil partner having the right to the whole estate.[55] Caution is also not required where an estate has a value less than £36,000.[56]

(3) Executors-creditor

3.9 It should be noted that there is a third type of executor, an executor-creditor, who is a creditor of the estate that has sought appointment in order to realise all or part of the estate to pay off a debt that they are owed, albeit this practice is uncommon. Whilst a form of executor, in effect, appointment as executor-creditor is a matter of the law of diligence (debt recovery) and will not be considered here.[57]

CONFIRMATION

3.10 Whilst the executor-nominate or executor-dative has obtained an appointment for distributing the estate, they have no ownership of the deceased's property until they obtain confirmation. Section 14 of the Succession (Scotland) Act 1964 provides, in rather ambiguous terms, that:

> 'On the death of any person (whether testate or intestate) every part of his estate (whether consisting of moveable property or heritable property) falling to be administered under the law of Scotland shall, by virtue of confirmation thereto, vest for the purposes of administration in the executor thereby confirmed and shall be administered and disposed of according to law by such executor.'

Confirmation is thus what is termed a judicial conveyance.[58] The decree of confirmation conveys the estate and transmits ownership, or the ability to validly complete title in the case of land, to the executor. However, whilst transferring ownership, confirmation also transmits the deceased's debts

55 Confirmation of Executors (Scotland) 1823, s 2 [as amended by the Succession (Scotland) Act 2016, s 19].

56 Intestates Widows and Children (Scotland) Act 1875, s 3; The Confirmation to Small Estates (Scotland) Order 2011 SSI 435/2011, reg 3 [as amended by the Succession (Scotland) Act 2016, s 18].

57 See G Gretton (ed), 'Diligence', Volume 8 in *Laws of Scotland: Stair Memorial Encyclopaedia*, paras 350–59.

58 See K Reid, *The Law of Property in Scotland,* 2nd edn (2026), Ch 25(2).

and obligations to the executor.[59] By transmitting debts alongside property, confirmation is a case of universal succession.[60] Whilst in principle the executor may be the universal successor of the deceased, the executor's liability to the deceased's debts is actually limited to the value of the estate confirmed.[61]

Confirmation is, in strict legal theory, a necessary step to transfer ownership of any property not subject to a testamentary device. However, statistics seem to suggest that many families in Scotland are not attending to this process (one assumes due to the wish to avoid the cost of legal fees).[62] This presents a problem, in that the law of succession may be being entirely disregarded if there is no oversight or regulation by the judicial system. Where an executor fails to confirm, any property that needs to be disposed of by an executor remains in the *haereditas jacens* and neither the executor nor beneficiaries or anyone else in possession can be said to have a completed title to the property, conforming to what is believed to be the current legal rules for the transfer of ownership at death. An expedited process for confirmation does exist where the value of an estate is below £36,000, with the estate in these cases often being termed as a 'small estate'.[63] The sheriff-clerks will assist the family of the deceased to complete the necessary inventory in such cases.

Where a family member, or others, take possession of the deceased's property without confirmation, they may be liable to an action of 'vitious intromission' raised by the deceased's creditors under the Vitious Intromitters Act 1696.[64] At its extreme, the 'penal' consequence of vitious intromission is that the intromitter incurs universal liability (and that is to

59 *West Lothian Council v Clark's Trs* [2021] SAC (Civ) 11. See paras **4.28–4.33**.

60 On universal succession, see R Anderson, *Assignations* (2008), para 3-01; and K Reid, *The Law of Property in Scotland,* 2nd edn (2026), para 1077.

61 See **4.29.**

62 K Reid, 'Administration of Estates in Scotland' in K Reid et al (eds), *Comparative Succession Law: Volume 4: Administration of Estates* (2025), 438, and 455–56.

63 Intestates Widows and Children (Scotland) Act 1875, s 3; and Small Testate Estates (Scotland) Act 1876, s 3. The rate is currently set at £36,000 by the Confirmation to Small Estates (Scotland) Order 2011 SSI 2011/435. One would imagine this requires review in short course given inflation rates since 2011.

64 See further R Macleod, *Contentious Executries,* 2nd edn (2024), paras 2-123–2-130; and E Scobbie, (ed), *Currie on Confirmation of Executors,* 9th edn (2011), paras 1-54–1-58.

say, personal liability) for *all* of the deceased's debts without any limited liability as to the value of the deceased's estate.[65] Thus, in *Cunningham* v *McKirdy*,[66] the widow of the deceased was decerned as executrix-dative but failed to obtain confirmation and intermitted with the deceased's property. She was found universally liable.

THE INVENTORY

3.11 Deriving from the old requirements of an executor to provide a complete account of the deceased's estate to the local Church officials to allow calculation of the old quot,[67] an executor is required to provide an inventory as part of their petition for confirmation. [68] The inventory still serves a fiscal purpose today, as it must be sent to HMRC to enable the authority to determine whether inheritance tax is payable on the estate.[69]

The inventory must be a complete account of the deceased's estate, and the executor will give a declaration that the inventory is complete to the best of their knowledge and belief. It will include an estimated value of the deceased's property and liabilities. As noted above, the benefit of preparing the inventory is that an executor has their liability limited to the extent of the property listed on the inventory and later confirmed:[70]

> 'The limit of [the executor's] liability is the amount of the estate to which he has confirmed, and the inventory of the estate to which he has confirmed is conclusive on the subject, unless it is alleged that the executor either has concealed estate or has negligently failed to ingather it, and then his liability is personal.'

The executor is under a duty to ascertain all of the deceased's estate.[71] This includes an ancillary power to seek a court order to have the deceased's

65 Bell, *Prin*, § 1921.
66 (1827) 5 S 315.
67 A Anton, 'Medieval Scottish executors and the courts spiritual' (1955) 67 *Jur Rev* 129, 137–40.
68 Probate and Legacy Duties Act 1808, s 38.
69 To see the template Form C1, see https://www.gov.uk/government/publications/inheritance-tax-confirmation-c1. There is currently also a Form IHT400 which provides an account of the inheritance tax due for the estate.
70 *Macdonald Fraser & Co Ltd v Carins's Extrx* 1932 SC 699, per Lord Morison at 711.
71 *Pentland-Clark v Maclehose* [2012] CSIH 29, per Lord Carloway at para 41.

repositories and papers examined or sealed off from third parties.[72] If the executor has not included property on the inventory, then the executor has no title to it, and the grant of confirmation will not transfer ownership of that property to them.[73] Where the inventory is not a true reflection of the estate, the consequent grant of confirmation is open to reduction (alongside any penalties in the criminal law).[74]

PARTIAL CONFIRMATIONS AND OMITTED PROPERTY

3.12 Historically, in order to limit the amount of quot or composition dues payable to the commissaries, a practice arose whereby executors would only partially confirm to some of the property of the estate and not declare the full estate on the inventory.[75] This process was technically prohibited by the Probate and Legacy Duties Act 1808, though a loophole remained that whilst an inventory had to be complete to comply with the 1808 Act, the executor could still cherrypick which property on the inventory to confirm to.[76] This was later prohibited by the Confirmation of Executors (Scotland) Act 1823 by ending partial confirmations.[77] As such, an executor must confirm to the entire estate 'known at the time' to them.[78]

It may transpire that the inventory does not contain all the deceased's property, and consequently confirmation does not extend to that property, or the document has inaccurate information such as a valuation. In which cases, corrections may be required. A (humorously) named document, an eik, may be used to amend the original confirmation. This can only be used by the original executor confirmed to the estate. If the executor neglects to amend the original confirmation, then another interested party, provided they are also entitled to be decerned as an executor-dative, can seek to

72 See further E Scobbie (ed), *Currie on Confirmation of Executors,* 9th edn (2011), paras 19-68–19-75.

73 Probate and Legacy Duties Act 1808, s 42.

74 *Ahmed's Exr v Ahmed's Exr* [2026] CSOH 30, per Lord Colbeck at para 33.

75 See J Currie, *The Confirmation of Executors in Scotland,* 3rd edn (1902), 117–20.

76 ibid, 119.

77 1823 Act, s 3.

78 For a recent case in this area, see *Smith v Carnegie* [2020] SC LIV 26, where the executor was unaware of the existence of a bank account and other moveable goods.

confirm to the estate via confirmation *ad omissa vel male appretiata* with an amended inventory noting additional property or updated values.[79]

ACTIONS *COGNITIONIS CAUSA TANTUM*

3.13 Where an estate is *haereditas jacens* with no executor yet confirmed, there is a problem for creditors who wish to sue the estate in this period as there is no person to call as a defender in an action for payment. This frequently arises where there is a statutory time bar, such as the triennium for personal injury actions under the Prescription and Limitation (Scotland) Act 1973,[80] or the 12-month[81] period for cohabitant claims under s 29 of the Family Law (Scotland) Act 2006.[82] In such circumstances, the remedy for a creditor is to utilise the 'long-standing common-law remedy' [83] of raising an action *cognitionis causa tantum.*[84] This involves calling the next-of-kin as defenders, though they do not incur personal liability as the action is merely to constitute the debt judicially against the estate. In one case, an executor-nominate was held able to be sued before confirmation,[85] but the correctness of this decision is doubtful.[86]

DUTIES OF THE EXECUTOR

3.14 Once confirmed, the executor is subject to duties in the administration of the estate. As the executor is a form of trustee for the

79 Erskine, *Inst*, III.9.36. See *Mackay v Mackay* [2018] SC TAI 22.

80 1973 Act, s 17(2).

81 As amended by s 78 of the Trusts and Succession (Scotland) Act 2024.

82 See *X v A (No. 2)* 2016 SLT (Sh Ct) 411.

83 *Slight v Tait's Executor* 2021 SLT (Sh Ct) 495, per Sheriff McGowan at para 32.

84 *Stevens v Thomson* 1971 SLT 136; *Davidson, Pirie & Co. v Dihle* (1900) 2 F 640, per the Lord President at 642; *Smith v Tasker* 1955 SLT 347; *Watt v Assets Co Ltd* (1904) 6 F. 692, per the Lord President at 704, and Lord Kinnear at 792; *Turnbull v McNaughtan* (1850) 12 D 1097, per the Lord Justice-Clerk at 1100. See further, Sheriff Cubie (ed), *MacPhail's Sheriff Court Practice*, 4th edn, (2022), para 4.127.

85 *Emslie v Tognarelli's Executors (No. 1)* 1967 SLT (Notes) 66 per Lord Avonside at 67.

86 G Gretton (ed), 'Diligence and Enforcement of Judgments', Vol 8, in *The Laws of Scotland: Stair Memorial Encyclopaedia,* para 352.

beneficiaries of the estate,[87] the general principles and doctrine of trusts, such as breaches of trust, apply to executors as with other trustees.[88] Otherwise, the specific duties of an executor have been defined by the Inner House as follows:[89]

> 'The duty of an executor is one of factory. He requires to ingather the deceased's estate, to pay the debts due by the deceased and thereafter to distribute the ingathered estate to the beneficiaries in accordance with the wishes of the deceased as disclosed by any will. He represents the deceased; that is to say, in questions with third parties, he is the same person as the deceased (*eadem persona cum defuncto*). The title which he holds is subject to all pleas that could have been taken against the deceased.'

(1) Ingathering the estate

3.15 Whilst as owner the executor has 'all the powers of a natural person beneficially entitled to the property'[90] they are subject to an overriding duty 'to administer the estate with a view to immediate distribution'.[91] Consequently, absent any *mortis causa* trusts constituted by the deceased's will which may require an executor or testamentary trustee to hold property for a prolonged period of time, the executor must manage the estate and ingather assets to enable it to be transferred to the beneficiaries without undue delay. In practice, this involves the troublesome (and drawn out) process of contacting all the deceased's banks, pension and insurance providers, and other repositories to arrange

87 For history in the distinction between trustee and executor, see G Gretton, 'Trusts' in K Reid and R Zimmermann, *A History of Private Law in Scotland*, Vol 1 (2000), 514–16.

88 Trusts and Succession (Scotland) Act 2024, s 81(1). For the general rules on trust law, as updated by the 2024 Act, see G Gretton and A Steven, *Property, Trusts and Succession,* 5th edn (2024), Chs 24–26.

89 *Pentland-Clark v Maclehose* [2012] CSIH 29, per Lord Carloway at para 41.

90 Trusts and Succession (Scotland) Act 2024, s 15. This definition has not escaped criticism, see J Brown, 'Why use two words when just one would do? Some thoughts on Section 15 of the Trusts and Succession (Scotland) Act 2024' (2025) 29(3) *Edin LR* 302.

91 (1886) 14 R. 209, per Lord President Inglis at 211.

transfer and closure of accounts; taking possession of the deceased's home and other property; assuming control of the deceased's businesses to wind them down or prepare them for transfer as a going concern; selling any assets to realise their monetary value; and arranging the drawdown of funds to enable payment.

Where property is to be sold, the executor is 'to obtain the best possible price for an asset'.[92] In the case of incorporeal property, such as rights to repayment of a debt, the executor may sue the debtor for payment, raise actions for damages, or seek implementation of contracts that have passed to them by confirmation.[93] All is done to ensure that the best value of obligations owed to the deceased can be realised and the value transferred onwards to the beneficiaries.

Delays or failure to recover assets may lead to action against the executor taken by the beneficiaries.[94] The executor has some latitude in respect of the process of ingathering, for example, in determining if, how, or when to realise an asset. However, total failure may result in an action of accounting, and negligent management of the estate may lead to the executor being held liable for losses (as an *intra vires* breach of trust).[95]

(2) Paying the deceased's debts

3.16 As the deceased's debts and property have transmitted to the executor, from the perspective of third parties the executor is *eadem persona cum defuncto* (the same person as the deceased).[96] This maxim is found throughout executry law, alongside the phrase that the executor 'stands in the deceased's shoes', though one may argue that

92 *Inglis v Inglis* 1983 SC 8, per Lord Justice Clerk Wheatley at 15.

93 *Tait's Executrix v Arden Coal Co Ltd* 1947 SC 100; *Soutar's Exrs v James Murray & Co (Cupar) Ltd* [2002] IRLR 22; *Gardiners v Stewart's Trs* 1908 SC 985; *Cooper's Executors v Edinburgh District Council* 1991 SC (HL) 5.

94 See *Currie v Currie's Exr* 2023 SC 390 and the helpful review of the authorities canvassed by Lord Tyre at paras 15 to 19. For a hard case, see *Forman v Burns* (1853) 15 D 362 where the executor was held liable for the loss to the estate.

95 Trusts and Succession (Scotland) Act 2024, ss 31, 36, and 39.

96 *Stewart's Trustees v Stewart's Executor* (1896) 23 R 739; *Mitchell v Mackersy* (1905) 8 F 198; and *Tait's Executrix v Arden Coal Co* 1947 SC 100.

the widespread usage deviates from its original purpose, that is to allow creditors to recover their debts from the deceased's executor.[97] As Lord Brougham described:[98]

> 'It is a man's duty to pay his debts during his lifetime. He does a wrong if he spends the money wherewith he should satisfy all, in paying one, and leaving the others unpaid,—no question of that. Comes his decease; comes his executor in his shoes to represent him after his decease; and the executor has that very duty which the testator in his lifetime had, and which every honest man ought to perform,—the duty of paying his creditors equally.'

Just as an executor is able to demand or sue for payment where the deceased was a creditor, the deceased's own creditors are entitled to demand payment or commence proceedings against an executor for payment. The subject of debts is considered further below.[99]

(3) Distribution of the estate to beneficiaries

3.17 After payment of debts, the executor is able to distribute the estate to the beneficiaries. This distribution will be under the terms of the will,[100] or in satisfaction of legal rights,[101] or a under the rules of intestate succession.[102] The distribution itself is the subject of succession law and will be explored throughout this work. If the executor pays the wrong beneficiary, or makes over the wrong property, or the wrong amount of property to a beneficiary, then this is an *ultra vires* breach of trust which

97 See, eg, *Murray's Exr v Crofting Commission*, Scottish Land Court, 4 September 2023, where the executor was held able to submit applications as *eadem persona* as the deceased crofter, and *Cf* that decision with a recognition of the limits of the *eadem persona* maxim in *Santander UK Plc v Roofi's Executor* [2024] SAC (Civ) 44.

98 *Globe Insurance Company v Mackenzie* (1850) 7 *Bell's Apps* 296, per Lord Brougham at 319–20.

99 See paras **4.28ff**.

100 See **Parts 3 & 4**.

101 See **Ch 5**.

102 See **Part 2**.

will incur strict liability on the part of the executor.[103] The beneficiaries may recover any unjustified distribution from the recipient.[104]

TERMINATION OF OFFICE

(1) Resignation

3.18 By default, an executor-nominate has, or will shortly have, the power to resign office under s 5 of the Trusts and Succession (Scotland) Act 2024. In contrast, executors-dative cannot resign.[105] This relates to the fact that the executor-dative derives their appointment from the sheriff.

If the executor-nominate is the sole executor, or the only traceable and capax executor, then they are unable to resign until they have assumed another as executor or sought the appointment of a judicial factor for the estate.[106] Where the executor-nominate is incapacitated, the trustee's guardian or attorney may resign on their behalf.[107]

It may be the case that a will has expressly or implicitly prohibited resignation, in which case the executor cannot resign. In such cases, the executor will have to seek from the court the power to resign to override these express or implied terms.[108] Formerly, there was a restriction on resignation if an executor was renumerated or received an honorarium legacy.[109] However, this restriction has been removed by the 2024 Act.[110]

103 Trusts and Succession (Scotland) Act 2024, ss 33 and 37.

104 *Armour v Glasgow Royal Infirmary* 1909 SC 916; and *Grant v Grant's Exrs* 1994 SLT 163 (see the decision in *Grant* in light of the subsequent decision in *Morgan Guaranty Trust Company of New York v Lothian Regional Council* 1995 SC 151 which allows errors of law to be recoverable). Where the beneficiary has received property *ultra vires*, and thereafter sold the property to a purchaser in good faith and for value, s 24 of the Succession (Scotland) Act 2016 provides a protection for the purchaser that their title will be exempt from challenge.

105 Succession (Scotland) Act 1964, s 20 and Trusts and Succession (Scotland) Act 2024, s 81 (see the definition of trustee and exclusions for executors-dative).

106 2024 Act, s 5(2).

107 2024 Act, s 6.

108 2024 Act, s 16.

109 Trusts (Scotland) Act 1921, s 3(2).

110 2024 Act, *Explanatory Notes*, para 19.

(2) Removal

3.19 An executor may be removed by the court under s 7 of the 2024 Act on application of a co-executor, beneficiary or other person with an interest in the estate. This can be done on certain grounds.

The first ground is labelled opaquely as 'unfitness'.[111] This ground includes the involvement of the executor in the homicide of the deceased from whom they are serving as executor.[112] This can arise where the executor is being prosecuted, or has been convicted, of an offence relating to killing the deceased, including: (i) murder, (ii) culpable homicide, or (iii) an analogous offence outwith Scotland. Even if there is no prosecution or conviction for an offence, a court is still entitled to determine the executor was otherwise involved or contributed to the death. In such cases, the executor is deemed unfit and may be removed. Otherwise, 'unfitness' under the 2024 Act is sufficiently broad for the court to determine.

The second ground is where the executor has committed fiduciary breaches in their management of the estate or has acted in such a way as to give rise to a fiduciary breach. The third ground is where the executor has neglected their duties. The fourth ground is where the executor is incapax.[113] The fifth ground is where the executor is untraceable, that is to say, they cannot be traced and the court is satisfied that reasonable steps have been taken to trace them.[114]

An executor may also be removed extra-judicially. Co-executors may by majority vote to remove one of their number.[115] This includes where the executor has been incapacitated, convicted of an offence of dishonesty, or imprisoned for any offence, contempt of court, or failure to pay a fine. An additional ground is provided where the executor is a professional who has been appointed in the course of their business, such as a solicitor providing professional executry services. If the executor ceases to be a member of their profession or is no longer entitled to practise, then the other executors may remove the (former) professional executor.

111 2024 Act, s 7(1)(a).
112 2024 Act, s 8.
113 2024 Act, s 83.
114 2024 Act, s 84.
115 2024 Act, s 9.

A further process for removal is that the beneficiaries of the estate may unanimously agree to remove the executor provided they are 18, with capacity, and have a vested and non-contingent right to receive the estate property. This can only arise where there are no outstanding purposes for the executor to need to retain some or all of the estate, for example, to retain ownership of parts of the estate due to the currency of an improper liferent.

(3) Death

3.20 The office of executor will cease on the death of the executor. In the case where the deceased executor was the sole executor, then the executry will lapse as there is no officeholder. In such cases, there is a range of options for the administration to continue.

(a) Section 6 of the Executors (Scotland) Act 1900: Recovery or quasi-confirmation

3.21 Where the executor has died following confirmation, the executor's *own* executor can note the estate in the deceased executor's inventory to 'recover' it.[116] This allows the executor's executor to then transfer the property to the beneficiaries, another person entitled to carry on the executry, or to the beneficiaries' nominee for continued administration.

(b) Confirmation ad non executa

3.22 Where an executor has died, or if they are incapacitated, a person originally entitled to confirm to the estate as executor-dative can seek confirmation *ad non executa.*[117] This enables the person to be confirmed as executor and continue the administration of the estate.[118]

116 Executors (Scotland) Act 1900, s 6.
117 1900 Act, s 7.
118 See further, E Scobbie (ed), *Currie on Confirmation of Executors,* 9th edn (2011), paras 16-11–16-19.

(c) Appointment under the Trusts and Succession (Scotland) Act 2024

3.23 A court can appoint a fresh executor under s 1 of the 2024 Act on the petition by anyone with an interest in the estate.

(d) Warrant for completion of title by beneficiary

3.24 Under s 73 of the 2024 Act, a court may grant authority for a beneficiary to complete title to any heritable or incorporeal moveable property to any person 'absolutely entitled' to it but the executor died before issuing an assignation or conveyance. A similar rule exists for corporeal moveables under s 74 where the executor died before transferring possession to transfer ownership.

(4) Completion of distribution

3.25 Unlike the need for confirmation at the start of an executry, there is no formal judicial process for discharge or lodging of final accounts once an executry estate is exhausted and fully distributed,[119] though it is good practice to obtain written confirmation from each beneficiary of the estate.[120] Whilst it is generally considered that the office of executor terminates *de facto* once the distribution is complete, in some respects an executry never ceases. In *Forbes v McLean*,[121] a pursuer seeking damages sued an executor many years after the estate was considered to be distributed and settled. Lord Clark held that the action was competent.[122] Thus whilst the executor and beneficiaries may consider the estate as settled, and the executry complete, claims by creditors may still yet be raised.

119 *Johnston's Exr v Dobie* 1907 SC 31, per Lord McLaren at 34. However, see the process for court discharge under s 8 of the 2024 Act where an executor has died, resigned, or been removed from office.

120 See Law Society of Scotland, *Practice Rules 2011, Executry and Trust Accounting guidance*.

121 [2018] CSOH 88.

122 *Assets Co v Falla's Trustees* (1894) 22 R 178. See also *Kennedy v Bonnici* [2021] CSOH 106 and E Campbell, 'The Zombie Trust: Delictual liability and trustees' (2025) 29(1) *Edin LR* 148.

Chapter 4

Property and debts

INTRODUCTION

4.1 This chapter considers what property may be comprised in an estate and the particular rules that may apply in relation to succession to it. It considers aspects of both general property law and the law relating to family property which are both relevant in determining what forms part of a deceased person's estate. The final part of this chapter considers the deceased's liabilities and debts, and how debts transmit to the executor for them to meet the debts from the estate's assets.

PROPERTY *IN BONIS DEFUNCTI*

4.2 The Succession (Scotland) Act 1964, s 36(2) provides that any reference in the Act to the estate of a deceased person:[1]

> 'Shall, unless the context otherwise requires, be construed as a reference to whole estate, whether heritable or moveable, or partly heritable and partly moveable, belonging to the deceased at the time of his death or over which he had a power of appointment.'

In order for the estate to be administered by the executor, it is therefore necessary to first establish what property is within the estate. Essentially, the deceased person must have had rights in or over property which comprises his or her estate; that is, the property must have been *in bonis defuncti* (literally, in the goods of the deceased) at the date of death. From a property law perspective, it is what is within the deceased's patrimony at death that the executor is required to distribute to successors.

Moveable property which becomes payable on death, such as life insurance capital, and received by the executors of the deceased are deemed to form part of the moveable estate available for distribution to

1 1964 Act, s 36(2).

beneficiaries and in claims for legal rights.[2] The deceased may have had a right to certain property during life which right extinguishes or lapses on death; for example, a proper or improper liferent. By contrast, rights under a lease may or may not terminate on death.[3] The deceased may also have only had a possessory right in respect of certain property under a contract of hire such as motor vehicles or whitegoods; or ownership may have been shared with another person or persons and the deceased's share passes to the survivor automatically.[4] The deceased may have made a contract which was uncompleted at the time of death and which may alter the nature of the property from heritable to moveable or vice versa and thus the value of the estate which may be available for legal rights.[5] Additionally, the executor is under an obligation to pay all the debts of the deceased. The net value of the estate, less the value of any statutory or common law rights in succession, must be calculated before any provisions under a will can be given effect to.[6]

The sections that follow in this chapter focus on general issues of how property which belonged to the deceased is classified, and how this affects the composition of the deceased's estate. Special rules which apply to the devolution of certain types of property rights on death are also examined in order to consider what may be included as the subject of a right in succession.

Not all property which was *in bonis* of the deceased will necessarily form part of his or her executry estate since the 'estate' for the 1964 Act is only that property which falls to be administered by the executor. Property that does not vest in the executor and form part of the estate will be property destined to pass directly to a beneficiary on the death of the owner.[7] Since it will not form part of the estate, any such property will not be available for the payment of any statutory or common law rights or the payment of legacies bequeathed under the provisions of any testamentary document executed by the deceased.

2 *Beveridge v Beveridge's Exrx* 1938 SC 160.
3 See paras **4.15–4.26**.
4 See paras **7.18ff**.
5 See paras **4.11–4.14**.
6 See paras **4.28ff**.
7 See paras **7.18ff.**

VESTED RIGHTS OF SUCCESSION IN ANOTHER PERSON'S ESTATE

4.3 If the deceased acquired a vested right of succession to the estate of another person before his or her own death but had not received payment, the right will transmit to the deceased's executor.[8] Since the acquisition of a vested right and the date of payment or delivery of the property it concerns may be different, the right in succession may not be payable until some time after the deceased has died.[9] If the right has vested in the deceased before his or her death, the legacy will be payable to the deceased's executor when the date of payment becomes due and form part of the estate available to the beneficiaries.

As an example, if John dies and then Susan dies a day later, a legacy from John to Susan may have vested in Susan at the moment of John's prior death. If that is the case, Susan acquires a vested right which will pass to her executor and form part of her estate on death, provided that there was no clause requiring her to survive John for a specified period or, if there was, that she did in fact survive for that period.[10] Alternatively, the deceased may have acquired a vested right to a capital sum which is payable only at the end of a period of accumulation, or at the expiry of some other event.[11] Provided that the right had vested, the successor's executor will be entitled to payment of the fund or sum at the date when payment is due.

RIGHTS TO DAMAGES

4.4 The deceased person may have had a vested right to damages before his or her death and any such right, as incorporeal moveable property, will transmit to his or her executor. As a generality, the right to damages for breach of contract arises at common law and an action may either be brought by the executor, or continued if already brought

8 See para **1.13**; and *Mill's Trs v Mill's Trs* 1965 SC 384.

9 See paras **13.3–13.8**.

10 See paras **1.20**, **10.10–10.12**, **13.13**, and the Succession (Scotland) Act 2016, s 11.

11 See paras **13.13ff**.

by the deceased.[12] Rights of the executor in respect of damages arising in delict are more complex.[13] For personal or verbal injuries, including damages arising from harassment, the recovery of damages is regulated by the Damages (Scotland) Act 2011.[14]

(1) Personal injuries

4.5 The Damages (Scotland) Act 2011, s 2(1) provides that rights to damages for patrimonial or non-patrimonial loss in respect of personal injuries which have vested in the deceased immediately before his or her death transmit to the executor.[15]

Thus, if Cait is struck by a car and breaks her arm, she has accrued a right to *solatium* for pain and suffering for her broken arm, and a right to damages for any consequential patrimonial loss such as loss of earnings or physiotherapy costs. If she later dies, her executor can, within the period for limitation of actions,[16] commence proceedings against the driver of the car to recover those losses given the right to damages is an asset in her estate.[17]

Important limitations are put in place to this rule. An executor cannot recover patrimonial losses incurred after death.[18] In respect of non-

12 *Morrison v Morrison's Exrx* 1912 SC 892. For fuller discussion, see R Macleod, *Contentious Executries: Commissary and Executry Litigation in Scotland*, 2nd edn (2024), paras 1-025–1-051.

13 Significant reforms in this area have taken place over the years. The Scottish Law Commission has produced a number of reports in this area, see Report on *The Law Relating to Damages for Injuries Causing Death* (SLC Report No 31, 1973); Report on *Effect of Death on Damages* (SLC Report No 134, 1992); and Report on *Damages for Wrongful Death* (SLC Report No 213, 2008). These led to the Damages (Scotland) Act 1976; Damages (Scotland) Act 1992; and the present Damages (Scotland) Act 2011.

14 For a full treatment, see S Bogle and B Lindsay, *Thomson's Delictual Liability*, 9th edn (2025), paras 17.28ff; E Reid, *The Law of Delict in Scotland* (2022), paras 31.45–31.56; and A Paton (ed), *McEwan and Paton on Damages for Personal Injuries in Scotland* (looseleaf), Ch 13.

15 Damages (Scotland) Act 2011, s 2(1).

16 Prescription and Limitation (Scotland) Act 1973, Parts II and IIA.

17 2011 Act, s 10.

18 2011 Act, s 2(2).

patrimonial losses, such as a *solatium* claim, such damages can only be calculated until the point of death.[19]

(2) Fatal cases

4.6 Different rules apply where the personal injury causes death. The rules in this area depend on whether the death was instantly or subsequently caused.

In respect of instant death: If, in the above example, Cait were instantly killed when she was struck by the car, then the executor cannot claim for *solatium* or patrimonial losses. This is because the statute only provides for the transmission of rights vested in the deceased 'immediately before death'.[20] A patrimonial loss that happens *at* death would be irrecoverable, as would a claim for solatium arising from the injury. The right to damages would vest at the 'wrong moment' for the purposes of the 2011 Act in such cases.

In respect of subsequent deaths, ie, where an injury does cause death, but the deceased did not die instantly, then it is still possible for the executor to recover both patrimonial and non-patrimonial losses up to death itself.[21] This is because the right to damages had vested in the deceased, and thus recovery by the executor is possible.[22]

The reason for these restrictive rules is that relatives of the deceased can make claims for damages as 'dependant' claims instead.[23] In cases of instant death, this is the main remedy open to the family for recovery of losses as the executor has no claim to bring on behalf of the deceased. Such claims by relatives are possible insofar as the deceased did not (in their lifetime) discharge the defender's liability, or statute restricts such payments.[24]

The immediate[25] family of the deceased are allowed to make claims for damages for loss of support, personal services, reasonable funeral

19 2011 Act, s 2(2).
20 2011 Act, s 2(1).
21 2011 Act, s 10.
22 *Wells v Hay* 1999 Rep LR 44; and *Beggs v Motherwell Bridge Fabricators Ltd* 1998 SLT 1215.
23 2011 Act, s 3.
24 2011 Act, s 4(2).
25 See the definition in s 14(1)(a)–(d) of the 2011 Act.

expenses, and compensation for distress, anxiety, grief, sorrow, or other non-patrimonial benefits the relative could have received if the deceased had been alive.[26] Wider family members are entitled to make a claim for loss of support, services and reasonable funeral expenses.[27] Such claims can transmit to the family members' own executors should they die after the deceased.[28] Finally, it should be noted that special rules for compensation by relatives are in place for the difficult issue of asbestos exposure and mesothelioma.[29]

(3) Verbal injuries and harassment

4.7 Where the right to damages is in respect of a claim for defamation or any other verbal injury to reputation, the right can be transmitted to the executor *only* if the action was commenced by the deceased himself or herself and had not been concluded.[30] Once again, the executor who continues such an action is entitled to damages only for the period prior to the death of the deceased.[31]

In respect of damages for harassment, there is no qualification that litigation has been commenced by death, and such rights to damages for patrimonial or non-patrimonial losses owed by the harasser to the deceased up to death will transmit to the executor.

PROPERTY OWNED IN COMMON

4.8 Where property is owned in common by the deceased and another person or persons, the deceased's *pro indiviso* share of the property will ordinarily pass to the executor.[32] However, the deceased's home will often be the main thing owned in common with another person and title to it

26 2011 Act, s 4(1)(a), s 4(3), and s 6.
27 2011 Act, s 4(1)(b), and s 6.
28 2011 Act, s 9.
29 2011 Act, s 5.
30 2011 Act, s 4(3).
31 2011 Act, s 2(2).
32 On common ownership, see G Gretton and A Steven, *Property, Trusts and Succession*, 5th edn (2024), Ch 10; and K Reid, *The Law of Property in Scotland*, 2nd edn (2026), Ch 4(2).

may be subject to a survivorship destination in favour of the other co-owner(s). In this case, it will not form part of the deceased's estate but will pass directly to the co-owner(s).[33]

Where the property was in common ownership, it is important to understand how the rights of each owner may qualify the other's rights to the property. Where the deceased was survived by a spouse, civil partner or cohabitant, the question may arise as to whether a particular item of property belonged to the deceased individually or whether it was owned in common with the survivor of the relationship.

(1) The family home and household goods

(a) The home

4.9 Traditionally it was the case that the male spouse in a heterosexual marriage would be the sole owner of a couple's home. Inevitably, the monopoly that the husband had over this valuable asset could lead to issues regarding legal protections for the wife, which in turn led to the establishment of statutory occupancy rights under the Matrimonial Homes (Family Protection) (Scotland) Act 1981. The law of intestate succession under the Succession (Scotland) Act 1964 was also designed to try to ensure that a surviving spouse was not left homeless following the deceased's death, as will be discussed further below.[34]

It is an intrinsic aspect of ownership that there is a power of bequest over the thing owned and thus any owner is entitled to bequeath his or

33 See paras **7.21–7.25**.

34 See paras **6.16–6.18**. There is some research on the extent of knowledge on the part of the public in relation to the rights of spouses and cohabitants which supports the proposition that many believe that both partnerships gives rise to automatic rights in succession, regardless of whether any provisions to the contrary have been made by will or in whose name the title to the property is registered: see F Wasoff and C Martin, *Scottish Social Attitudes Survey 2004 Family Module Report*, available https://webarchive.nrscotland.gov.uk/3000/https://www.gov.scot/Publications/2005/08/02131208/12092 and Scottish Consumer Council, *Wills and Awareness of Inheritance Rights in Scotland* (2006).

her property (or *pro indiviso* share of ownership thereof)[35] by means of a testament to a third party, irrespective of whether the home is shared with another occupant. Where this does occur, a surviving partner, whether spouse, civil partner or cohabitant, may not challenge the bequest and has no legal entitlement to acquire the deceased's ownership in the home from their testate estate. Challenges to a will may be made only on the grounds of formal or essential invalidity,[36] and not simply because a surviving spouse has been disadvantaged.[37]

If the deceased partner was the sole proprietor, the statutory occupancy rights of spouses[38] and civil partners[39] (and the more limited occupancy rights of cohabitants)[40] enjoyed during the life of the non-entitled or non-owning partner will terminate on death. Additionally, neither the 1981 Act, nor the 2004 Act, has any application to the situation where one of the partners bequeaths his or her share of the property to a third party.[41]

It is more likely today that the two adults will co-own their home, often in equal *pro-indiviso* shares. Where the deceased and the surviving partner owned the home in common, a right to occupy the property does not derive from statutory occupancy rights, but solely from their right of ownership which will continue to apply after death.[42] However, the surviving co-owner, whatever their relationship status with the deceased, has no preferential right to buy-out the deceased partner's share from a third-party successor and the primary consideration which the executor is to

35 Unless title to the property has been taken in the names of both partners in common, subject to a survivorship destination and: (i) s 2 of the Succession (Scotland) Act 2016 has not operated; due to a formal termination in relationship; or (ii) the deceased had no power of evacuation or, if he or she did have the power, had not in fact evacuated it; see paras **7.23–7.24**. On common ownership generally, see G Gretton and A Steven, *Property, Trusts, and Succession* 5th edn (2024), Ch 10 and K Reid, *The Law of Property in Scotland,* 2nd edn (2026), Ch 4.

36 See **Chs 7 & 8**.

37 Though there is the ability to claim legal rights, see **Ch 5**.

38 Matrimonial Homes (Family Protection) (Scotland) Act 1981.

39 Civil Partnership Act 2004, ss 101–111.

40 Matrimonial Homes (Family Protection) (Scotland) Act 1981, s 18.

41 Though the definitions of 'dealing' under s 106(2) of the 2004 Act, and s 6(2) of the 1981 Act are rather vague.

42 See the simple yet effective discussion in G Gretton and K Reid, *Conveyancing,* 5th edn (2018), para 10-12.

have is whether the highest price could be obtained on the open market.[43] Where the deceased partner's share of ownership is bequeathed to a third party, the third party, as new co-owner, has the right to raise an action of division and sale.[44] Although s 19 of the 1981 Act and s 110 of the 2004 Act both contain an important restriction in relation to such actions by giving the court discretion to refuse or postpone decree, this restriction does not apply to actions raised by a third party after death.

As noted, where the deceased died intestate, the position regarding the home differs depending on whether the parties were spouses or civil partners, or cohabitants. Where they were spouses or civil partners, the surviving spouse or partner will be entitled to the deceased's interest in the family home, subject to certain limitations, under the Succession (Scotland) Act 1964, s 8.[45] Where the parties were cohabitants, the survivor may apply to the court for a property transfer order under s 29 of the Family Law (Scotland) Act 2006 to have the deceased's interest in the property transferred to him or her, but this will depend on the court considering a number of factors in exercising its discretion to make a transfer order.[46]

(b) The household goods

4.10 The ownership of things belonging to individual spouses, civil partners and cohabitants is a question to be determined by the ordinary rules of property law.

43 *Berry v Berry (No 2)* 1989 SLT 292 (*cf. Scrimgeour v Scrimgeour* 1988 SLT 590). This accords with the approach in lifetime and the limitations of the remedy of the action of division and sale, see K Reid, *The Law of Property in Scotland,* 2nd edn, (2026), para 103. At one point, the Scottish Law Commission recommended that a surviving spouse should have the option to acquire the deceased's share of the matrimonial home and its furnishings in satisfaction of his or her rights on intestacy or to purchase the share if the value exceeds the value of these rights and a similar option where these are part of the residue of the estate of which he or she is a beneficiary: *Report on Succession* (SLC Report No 124, 1990). This proposal was later reconsidered in light of amendments to the Commission's proposed reforms to the law of intestate succession, *Report on Succession* (SLC Report No 215, 2009), paras 2.17–2.18.

44 On actions of division and sale, see K Reid, *The Law of Property in Scotland,* 2nd edn (2026), paras 97–103.

45 See **Ch 6**.

46 See para **6.30**.

In relation to spouses and civil partners, the Family Law (Scotland) Act 1985, s 24 provides expressly that marriage or civil partnership shall not of itself affect the respective rights of the parties in relation to their property or the law of succession. Marriage or civil partnership does not, therefore, convert individual property to property held in common but it does have implications in relation to the distribution of certain items on termination of the relationship by death, divorce or dissolution. In particular, the 1985 Act establishes a rebuttable presumption that household goods kept or used at any time during the relationship within a family home are presumed to be co-owned by the spouses.[47] Such a presumption applies to any goods, including decorative or ornamental goods, other than money, securities, vehicles, or domestic animals.[48] Neither does the presumption apply to any goods acquired by way of gift or succession from a third party.[49]

In relation to cohabitants, the Family Law (Scotland) Act 2006 also provides the rebuttable presumption that each cohabitant has a right to an equal share in household goods acquired during the period of cohabitation, with household goods being defined in the same way as for spouses and civil partners.[50]

Clearly, items used for business purposes will be excluded, as will any items used by one partner alone (such as in pursuit of a sport or hobby). The operative word in each statute is 'used', which would seem to preclude any items which are merely collected. Yet, the fact that the decorative or ornamental aspects of any item are included in the presumption would appear to mean that antiques or works of art, for example, could be household goods provided that they are actually kept or used in the home for joint domestic purposes. Arguably, both parties simply enjoying looking at a painting hanging on the wall is a joint domestic purpose to some extent. In consequence, providing the relevant criteria are fulfilled, only a half-share of items comprising household goods will pass into the estate of the deceased partner, unless evidence is adduced to the contrary.

However, whilst the definitions are similar, the way in which the presumptions apply under the 1985 and 2006 Acts differs. In relation to spouses and civil partners, the Family Law (Scotland) Act 1985, s 25(1)

47 Family Law (Scotland) Act 1985, s 25(1).
48 1985 Act, s 25(3).
49 1985 Act, s 25(1).
50 2006 Act, s 26.

provides that the presumption applies 'unless the contrary is proved' and goes on in s 25(2) to provide that it will not be proved by reason only that the goods in question were purchased from a third party by either party alone or by both in unequal shares. In relation to cohabitants, the Family Law (Scotland) Act 2006, s 26(3) provides simply that the presumption of equal shares contained in s 26(2) 'shall be rebuttable'. This appears to imply that it will be rebutted if it is proved that one party alone paid for the goods and, accordingly, that the normal rules of property ownership are seemingly applied more strictly to cohabitants.[51]

CLASSIFYING THE DECEASED'S HERITABLE AND MOVEABLE PROPERTY

4.11 It has been explained in **Chapter 3** that Scots law has a distinction between heritable and moveable property, and that formerly this distinction meant that Scots law had separate intestate succession rules depending on the species of property. As a result of this distinction, which still has relevance today as will be explored in subsequent chapters,[52] it is necessary to classify the deceased's property into either being heritable or moveable property. In effect, one can think of a deceased's estate as having two parts or components. There is the heritable estate, and the moveable estate.

Example

Inventory	**Heritable Estate**	**Moveable Estate**
House	**£255,000.00**	
Car		**£12,650.00**
Tiffany bracelet		**£8,225.00**
Total	£255,000.00	£20,875.00

51 For further discussion, see E Sutherland, *Child and Family Law, Vol 2: Intimate Adult Relationships*, 3rd edn (2022), paras 3-069–3-075.

52 See **Ch 5** and **Ch 6**.

In most cases, classifying the deceased's property into either being heritable or moveable property will be straightforward using the ordinary rules of general property law.[53] However, some special rules are noted here.[54]

(1) Conversion

4.12 If the deceased had contracted to buy or sell property before their death and the contract had not been performed, it may result in the subject matter of the contract changing its character from heritable to moveable, or vice versa. Alternatively, there may be property which is deemed to have become acceded to the land which will convert it from moveable to heritable property.[55] In either case, this will have consequences for certain rights in succession, particularly legal rights which are payable from the moveable estate alone.

Conversion may be actual or constructive. Actual conversion occurs in two situations. First, if the property in question is the subject of a contract for the sale of heritage and at the date of death the deceased has not granted a disposition, the executor must complete the sale. In this case, the proceeds of the sale of the heritage become moveable.[56] Second, if the deceased contracted before death to buy heritage and at the date of death has not received a disposition, the executor must complete the purchase and the property becomes heritable.[57]

Constructive conversion occurs where the testator has given trustees express directions to sell heritable property and pay the proceeds to a

53 See para **3.2**.

54 For further discussion, see K Reid, *The Law of Property in Scotland,* 2nd edn (2026), paras 40–43.

55 See further G Gretton and A Steven, *Property, Trusts and Succession,* 5th edn (2024), paras 9.4–9.12.

56 *Chiesley v Chiesley* (1704) Mor 5531; *Heron v Espie* (1856) 18 D 917; *McArthur's Exrs v Guild* 1908 SC 743.

57 *Ramsay v Ramsay* (1887) 15 R 25; *Fairlie's Trs v Fairlie's Curator Bonis* 1932 SC 216 at 220 per LP Clyde. It should be noted that s 47(1) of the Land Registration (Scotland) Act 2012 prevents the deceased themselves from being entered as the proprietor in the Land Register as they are dead. The executor would have to take title in such cases, or remain as an unregistered holder (with the risks that this may bring), and dispone the land to successors as unregistered holder. On the conveyancing involved in an executry, see G Gretton and K Reid, *Conveyancing,* 5th edn (2018), Ch 26.

beneficiary or beneficiaries. The value of the heritable property is moveable, whether or not it is actually sold. This is because the truster's direction to sell heritage and pay a sum of money to a beneficiary indicates his or her intention that the legacy should be paid from moveable estate rather than indicating that any particular heritable property must be sold in order to pay the legacy at all. The significance of constructive conversion is that even where there has in fact been no sale of the heritable property, the value of the legacy will be included within the moveable estate and thus be available for claims to legal rights. Any claimants to legal rights will therefore be entitled to a share of the moveable estate including the value of the heritage which has been, or is to be, sold. Constructive conversion will not take place if the trustees have merely a power to sell heritage and it is sold either because it is necessary (for example, to pay debts) or there are no further trust purposes which require its retention.[58]

(2) Reconversion

4.13 Where there is an express direction to trustees to sell heritage and pay the proceeds to a beneficiary or an express direction to buy heritage for a beneficiary, it may be that the beneficiary chooses, in the first case, to take the heritage rather than its proceeds or, in the second case, to take a monetary sum rather than the heritage. This is known as reconversion. In *Bryson's Trustee v Bryson*,[59] it was held that reconversion could be express or implied. It can occur where there has been either a direct indication by the beneficiary of his intention to take the heritage or a lapse of time, together with relevant facts and circumstances, which shows an unequivocal determination on the part of the beneficiary to take the property as it stands. He or she may choose to take the heritage that forms the subject of the legacy rather than a payment representing its value. If, however, this is to the detriment of other beneficiaries, the trustees may refuse since they are under a duty to preserve the estate for the benefit of all beneficiaries.

58 *Buchanan v Angus* (1862) 4 Macq 374; *Sheppard's Trs v Sheppard* (1885) 12 R 1193; and *Taylor's Trs v Tailyour* 1927 SC 288.

59 *Bryson's Tr v Bryson* 1919 2 SLT 303 at 305, per Lord Sands. See also *Hogg v Hamilton* (1877) 4 R 845; McLaren I 237; *Grindlay v Grindlay's Trs* (1853) 16 D 27.

Alternatively, if the trustees have simply not acted on the truster's direction to sell, the beneficiary is entitled to intimate to them that he or she wishes to take the heritable property and not the proceeds of its sale. The same obtains if the direction has been to buy heritage for a beneficiary. The beneficiary is entitled to take the payment representing the value of the legacy and the direction will not reduce the value of the moveable estate available for legal rights.[60] The practical reason behind the rules is that if a beneficiary could not choose to take the monetary equivalent of the heritage he or she could simply sell it as soon as it was purchased and vice versa.

(3) Destination

4.14 In the context of succession law, moveable property can become heritable by destination as well as by conversion. The concept of destination is similar to that of accession in property law generally[61] but with one significant difference; rather than moveables becoming annexed to land and becoming heritable due to their affixture, moveable property that is heritable by destination are presumed to be separable but intended by the testator to be taken with the heritage as part of the subject of the legacy. This rule is rather limited in its usefulness in modern times given the assimilation of heritable and moveable property by the 1964 Act, but it remains a valid rule nevertheless and it is not unthinkable that a testator may wish to direct moveable property be distributed in such manner.

Whether destination occurs in a particular case depends on the express or presumed intention of the testator, depending on the facts and circumstances. Since heritable property was, historically, that property which descended to the heir-at-law,[62] a testator could indicate expressly or by implication what property he or she intended to pass with the heritage. Erskine states that the proprietor:[63]

60 *Lashley v Hog* (1804) 4 Pat 581. See paras **5.11–5.12**.

61 See G Gretton and A Steven, *Property, Trusts and Succession,* 5th edn (2024), paras 9.4.

62 See para **3.3.**

63 Erskine *Inst* II.2.14. Bell *Comm* II.2.3 states: 'by express destination a moveable subject may be declared heritable; a jewel or a picture, for example … and by tacit and implied destination, similar effect in questions of succession between heirs and executors may be produced'.

> 'Hath the right of settling any part of his estate in whatever manner he pleases, provided he shall properly discover his intention. He may therefore destine personal bonds due to himself, or his jewels, painting, plate, books, or even cash lying in his depositories, so as they may descend to his heir. The bare appointment of the proprietor to lay out his money on land, if it be clearly expressed, makes the sum heritable, though he should happen to die without taking any step to carry his appointment into execution.'

In *Johnston v Dobie*[64] a collection of building materials had been left lying on a piece of land. These were to be used in the process of constructing a building belonging to the deceased at the time of his death. The materials were held to be heritable on the ground that the fact that they were lying on the land showed evidence of his intention that they become heritable.[65] Similarly, where the deceased had started to erect a building but had not completed it, the funds required to do so were held also to be heritable.[66]

LEASES

4.15 Death does not necessarily terminate a lease. At common law, the doctrine of *delectus personae* applies to most leases, though a full account of its exact scope cannot be given here.[67] That doctrine operates to restrict the tenant's right to assign or transfer the lease *inter vivos* but, although a tenant may have no right to assign a lease where *delectus personae* applies, his or her heirs may still have a right to succeed to the lease irrespective of such restrictions.[68] The estate of a deceased person may therefore include

64 *Johnston v Dobie* (1783) Mor 5443.

65 Bell *Princ*, § 1475. Bell also states 'materials which … are deposited for the purpose of being built up, as part of a structure actually begun and proceeding, are heritable by destination', *Comm* II.2.3. Similarly, dung which was lying on the land before being applied to it was held to have become heritable by being dedicated to the land but not yet added: *Reids Exrs v Reid* (1890) 23 R 519.

66 *Bank of Scotland v White's Trs* (1891) 28 SLR 891; *Malloch v McLean* (1867) 5 M 335.

67 See C Anderson and L Richardson, *McAllister's Scottish Law of Leases,* 5th edn (2021), paras 7.19–7-21.

68 Bell *Prin,* § 1219; *Thomson v Watson* (1750) M 10337; and *Macalister v Macalister* (1859) 21 D 560.

a tenant's right of lease.[69] The Succession (Scotland) Act 1964, s 36(2) provides expressly that the estate of a deceased person includes a tenant's right of lease that was not expressed to expire on death[70] and, as part of that estate, will vest in the executor under s 14 on confirmation.

(1) General rules

4.16 Whilst the 1964 Act provides a general framework for the succession to leases, in recent years a great deal of legislation has focused on succession to particular types of leases, some of which has amended the 1964 Act in a significant way. The result is that the 1964 Act framework is now rather complex and, at the same time, set aside in many cases in favour of legislation discretely regulating succession to specific types of lease such as residential tenancies. Reforms aimed at simplifying the legislation as it relates to leases would be most welcome. In light of the statutory framework, this section considers the general framework of the 1964 Act before the subsequent sections consider special rules depending on the class of lease.

The following are the general rules, absent any special provisions for certain types of leases:

(a) No valid legacy

4.17 Where a tenant has not made a valid legacy of the lease, or a legacy has been made but has been refused by the legatee, the executor, under s 16 of the 1964 Act, is able to transfer the lease to another successor of the estate.[71] It would seem the case that s 16 would also be engaged in the cases of partial intestacy where there is no residuary legacy in the will (under which the lease may be validly bequeathed to the residuary

69 For wider discussion see R Rennie (ed), *Leases* (2015), paras 19-03–19-12; and C Anderson and L Richardson, *McAllister's Scottish Law of Leases*, 5th edn (2021), Ch 9.

70 This can occur with liferent leases, which terminate on the death of the tenant, see *Mountain's Trs v Mountain* 2013 SC 302. Otherwise it is common to encounter a term that the lease is irritated on the death of a tenant.

71 1964 Act, s 16(2).

legatee),[72] or in cases where a legacy of a lease has also lapsed such as due to a legatee's predecease.

The power of transfer under s 16 applies regardless of whether there is any express or implied[73] restriction on alienation. Recipients of the transfer can include any one of the persons entitled to succeed to the deceased's intestate free estate, or to claim legal rights, or claim prior rights. Such transfers are in satisfaction of the beneficiary's claim to the estate, and the landlord's consent is not required in such cases. It would seem likely that a cohabitant would not benefit from such a transfer given a cohabitant does not have a formal right of succession in intestacy as the spouse or civil partner enjoy. However, if the executor wishes to transfer the lease to a person who could not have succeeded the deceased under the rules of intestate succession, or indeed there is a transfer *not* in satisfaction of a person's claim in intestate succession, then this is permissible, but the landlord's consent will be required (except if the lease is an agricultural lease, which has a separate process noted below).[74]

There are time limits in place regarding the transfer process. If the lease is not transferred within one year from the date of death, then the executor or the landlord is entitled to terminate the lease upon notice.[75] The landlord and executor are free to come to an agreement to extend the date.[76] Such notices must be served within six months of the proposed termination date.[77] A curious provision provides that the six-month rule is without prejudice to any shorter period provided by another Act, thus meaning the notice may be shorter where another Act allows termination

72 See *Gardner v Curran* 2008 SLT (Sh Ct) 105, discussed in H Hiram, 'Bequests of residue and crofting tenancies: *Gardner v Curran*' (2009) 13(1) *Edin LR* 143. The point is not without difficulty due to inconsistent case law but whether the residue clause can be said to include the lease likely turns on construction of the will itself, see B Gill, *Agricultural Tenancies,* Vol 1, 4th edn (2017), para 52-05.

73 Such as where the lease is *delectus personae*.

74 1964 Act, s 16(2A). Rennie, *Leases,* para 19-08 suggests following the Scottish Land Court decision in *Budge v Budge (No.2)* 1993 SLCR 136, the executor does not have entirely free discretion to choose someone outwith the successors in intestacy. The provisions of the statute are not entirely clear, but one assumes Rennie to mean that the intestate successors are afforded preference before the lease is offered to another party, such as a cohabitant, wider family, or even a third party.

75 1964 Act, s 16(3)(b).

76 ibid.

77 1964 Act, s 16(4).

within an earlier time frame.[78] The executor may also determine that the lease cannot be disposed of, and so they may terminate the lease upon intimation to the landlord.[79] In the event that either party is aggrieved by a termination, the parties' right to compensation or damages is unaffected by these provisions.[80]

(a) Valid legacy

4.18 A tenant may make a legacy in their will for their lease to be bequeathed to another person. However, the express and implied terms of the lease will require analysis. If the lease prohibits assignation or alienation, then the tenant cannot *prima facie* make a valid legacy given they have a contractual obligation prohibiting them from doing so.[81] This exclusion is common in most well-drafted leases nowadays. However, it is here that the law is rather ridiculous and complex.

Where an *express* term of the lease prohibits assignation or alienation, and any legacy of the lease by the deceased is thus deemed invalid, s 16(2) of the 1964 Act may yet still operate so that the executor can still transfer the lease under the rules of intestate succession despite the prohibition on assignation. The comments above in respect of s 16 will apply in such situations.

In the case of an implied term restricting assignation, such as where the lease is *delectus personae,* then s 29 of the 1964 Act provides that a legacy may nonetheless still be valid – provided the legatee is a person who would have been able to succeed the deceased in intestacy. Where the legatee is not such a person, then the legacy will be invalid. However, s 16 also extends to cover implied restrictions too, and the executor may still be able to transfer the lease under the rules of intestate succession.

(2) Commercial leases

4.19 At common law, the lease of unfurnished urban subjects does not involve *delectus personae* and the tenant has the power to assign or

78 1964 Act, s 16(4).
79 1964 Act, s 16(3)(a).
80 1964 Act, s 16(5).
81 *Kennedy v Johnstone* 1956 SC 39.

bequeath it, but whether a lease is an urban lease actually has nothing to do with whether the subjects happen to be located in a town rather than the country. Rather, it depends on whether the main subject is buildings or land.[82] Since it is only in an agricultural lease that the main subject will be land itself, the subject of an urban lease will normally include all commercial and industrial premises regardless of where they are situated. In practice, most commercial leases exclude assignation or bequest or both as a term of the lease.[83] Accordingly, absent the application of s 16, the commercial lease will likely be terminated on death.

(3) Residential leases

4.20 Residential tenancies have their own legislation determining how the tenancy is to be distributed after death. The two current main tenancies, the Private Residential Tenancy (PRT), and the Scottish Secure Tenancy (SST) are noted here briefly.[84] PRTs are those used primarily in the private rental sector, whereas SSTs are those tenancies used in public and social housing.

(a) Private Residential Tenancies

4.21 Private Residential Tenancies are regulated by the Private Housing (Scotland) Act 2016. Part 6 of the 2016 Act deals with the death of a tenant and succession to the tenancy. An executor will not normally be involved in such cases as the succession is automatic.

If the tenant were co-tenanting with another, then the other person simply assumes the full tenancy.[85] Where the tenant was a sole-tenant, it is possible for others to inherit the tenancy rather than it being terminated

82 J Rankine, *A Treatise on the Law of Leases in Scotland,* 3rd edn, (1916) 174.

83 See the Property Standardisation Group's template commercial leases as an example, available https://psglegal.co.uk/leases-based-on-the-model-commercial-lease-mcl/.

84 For full discussion, including discussion of older types of tenancy, see M Combe and P Robson, *Residential Tenancies: Private and Social Renting in Scotland,* 4th edn (2019), Ch 12.

85 2016 Act, s 66.

altogether. A successor may be the tenant's romantic partner, relative, or carer.

Some preliminary points may be noted before considering the succession to a PRT by these parties. Firstly, the 2016 Act does not facilitate successive tenants inheriting a PRT and there is a general exclusion from succession to a PRT where the tenant had already succeeded to the tenancy. Additionally, the 2016 Act is primarily focused on preventing a harsh outcome where an occupant is evicted from their home after the sole tenant's death. As such only those who were using the property as their 'only or principal home'[86] are able to inherit. With these limitations in mind, the potential successors of a PRT are further explored below in the order of preference to inheriting a PRT that the Act provides.

The romantic partner of the tenant (as their spouse, civil partner or cohabitant) can inherit the tenancy.[87] This is provided certain conditions are met. Firstly, the tenancy cannot have been inherited by the tenant themselves.[88] Secondly, the landlord must have been informed by the tenant prior to death that their partner was residing in the property as their only or principal home.[89] Thirdly, and tied to the second, the partner must indeed have been using the property as their only or principal home at the tenant's death.[90] Finally, the partner must have been in marriage or civil partnership with the tenant, or had been living together as if married.[91] For cohabitants, an additional requirement is imposed. The cohabitant must have been living in the property as their only or principal home for at least six months up to the tenant's death.[92] Any period in which the landlord was unaware of such living arrangements will be discounted.[93]

Succession by another family member is possible where the tenant's romantic partner does not inherit the tenancy.[94] This is open to a wide

86 On this, see the discussion in *Roxburgh District Council v Collins* 1991 SLT (Sh Ct) 49.
87 2016 Act, s 67(1).
88 2016 Act, s 67(2)(a).
89 2016 Act, s 67(2)(b).
90 2016 Act, s 67(2)(d).
91 2016 Act, s 67(c); and s 70(1).
92 2016 Act, s 67(3) [as amended by the Housing (Scotland) Act 2025].
93 2016 Act, s 67(4).
94 2016 Act, s 68.

range of family members.[95] Certain conditions are again provided. Firstly, the tenancy cannot already have been inherited by the tenant.[96] Secondly, the relative must be at least 16 years old at the time the tenant died.[97] Thirdly, the relative must have been occupying the property as their only or principal home when the tenant died for at least six months up to the death.[98] The landlord again has to be aware of such living arrangements, and any period in which they were unaware is to be discounted.[99] If more than one relative meets these conditions, then the tenancy will be inherited in common.[100]

A final succession is possible where neither a partner nor an eligible relative is able to inherit. It is possible for a live-in or resident carer to acquire the PRT.[101] The carer is someone who was either providing care for the tenant or one of their family.[102] They do not need to be someone in paid employment for this role, and may well also be a family member.[103] For carers to inherit, the following conditions must be satisfied: Firstly, the carer has to be at least 16 years old at the time of death of the tenant;[104] Secondly, the carer had to be using the property as their only or principal home for at least 6 months up to death, which again the landlord was aware of;[105] and thirdly, the carer had given up their previous home when they took on caring responsibilities.[106] If there is more than one carer that meets these conditions, then the PRT will be inherited in common.[107]

Without succession by an eligible partner, relative, or carer to a sole PRT tenant, then the PRT will simply be terminated upon death.[108]

95 2016 Act, ss 70(1)(b)–70(3).
96 2016 Act, s 68(1)(b).
97 2016 Act, s 68(2)(a).
98 2016 Act, s 68(2)(b) [as amended by the Housing (Scotland) Act 2025].
99 2016 Act, s 68(3).
100 2016 Act, s 68(4).
101 2016 Act, s 69.
102 2016 Act, s 69(5).
103 M Combe and P Robson, *Residential Tenancies: Private and Social Renting in Scotland,* 4th edn (2019), para 12-29.
104 2016 Act, s 69(2)(a).
105 2016 Act, s 69(2)(b) and s 69(2) [as amended by the Housing (Scotland) Act 2025].
106 2016 Act, s 69(2)(c).
107 2016 Act, s 69(4).
108 2016 Act, s 65.

(b) Scottish Secure Tenancies

4.22 Scottish Secure Tenancies are regulated by the Housing (Scotland) Act 2001 as the standard form of tenancy for the social rented sector.[109] Under s 22, the tenancy passes to a 'qualified person' on the death of the tenant. The executor is not involved in this process as it passes to the qualified person by operation of law.

Schedule 3, paragraphs 2 to 4, of the 2001 Act provides the rules in defining the qualified person. Similar to PRTs, there is a ranking system for determining who is to be entitled to the tenanted property.[110] If a higher-ranking qualified person declines succeeding to the SST, then the landlord is to use best endeavours to notify the next in the order of succession.[111]

In the first instance, the SST can be transferred to: (1) the tenant's spouse or civil partner or a person living with the tenant as husband and wife or in a relationship which has the 'characteristics' of a relationship between civil partners;[112] or (2) the surviving tenant where the tenancy was held in common.[113] In the case of persons living with the tenant as husband and wife, or in a relationship as if civil partners, the qualified person must have been living in the house with the tenant for at least six months up to the tenant's death.[114]

In the second instance, Paragraph 3 provides that a qualified person can include a member of the tenant's family aged at least 16 years old and has lived in the property as the person's only or principal home within the six months prior to death.[115]

In the third instance, Paragraph 4 provides that a qualified person may be a carer providing care, or who has provided care for the tenant or a member of his or her family, providing that the carer is at least 16 years old, lived in the house as his or her principal home for at least six months

109 For further treatment, see M Combe and P Robson, *Residential Tenancies: Private and Social Renting in Scotland,* 4th edn (2019), para 23-35ff.

110 2001 Act, Sch 3, paras 6–8.

111 2001 Act, Sch 3, paras 10–12 [as amended by the Housing (Scotland) Act 2025].

112 2001 Act, Sch 3, para 2(a).

113 2001 Act, Sch 3, para 2(b).

114 2001 Act, Sch 3, para 2(2) [as amended by the Housing (Scotland) Act 2025].

115 2001 Act, Sch 3, para 3 [as amended by the Housing (Scotland) Act 2025]. For a recent example of this rule in action, see BBC News, 'Glasgow sisters to be evicted weeks after mother's death', 18 February 2022, available https://www.bbc.co.uk/news/uk-scotland-glasgow-west-60419890.

up to death, and had a principal home which was given up to live with the tenant.[116]

In all cases, the tenant or the qualified person must have informed the landlord that the tenanted property was their only or principal home.[117] Additionally, where the property had special accommodations, such as wheelchair accessible design or other modifications, then a person will only qualify for succession if they have needs suitable for those accommodations.[118] In the event that there is more than one qualified person falling within one of the paragraphs above, then the parties must agree on whether there will be a sole or joint tenancy, that failing then the landlord will decide.[119]

Section 22(2) provides that on the death of a qualified person who succeeded to the tenancy under s 22(1), the tenancy passes by operation of law to a second qualified person. Thus, unlike PRTs, there can be a second successive inheritance of an SST. On the death of the second qualified person, the tenancy is terminated.[120] Any potential qualified person as successor to the second qualified person is granted a grace period of six months to remain in the property.[121]

If there are no qualified persons either in the first succession or in the second succession, or every qualified person declines the tenancy, the tenancy is simply terminated upon death.[122]

(4) Agricultural leases

4.23 Agricultural leases have very complex underlying law. Where there is an agricultural lease in which the deceased had some form of interest, specialist advice from an agricultural or rural lawyer is invariably needed as the margin for error is often high.[123] In light of this, this section touches upon them only in the highest possible terms.[124]

116 2001 Act, Sch 3, para 4 [as amended by the Housing (Scotland) Act 2025].
117 2001 Act, Sch 3, para 4A.
118 2001 Act, Sch 3, para 5.
119 2001 Act, Sch 3, para 9.
120 2001 Act, s 22(4).
121 2001 Act, s 22(9).
122 2001 Act, s 22(3).
123 As a cautionary tale, see *Paul v Ogilvy* 2001 SLT 171.
124 The law is always subject to change and reform, indeed significant reforms were made by the Land Reform (Scotland) Act 2025, but for the latest treatment see L Fotheringham, *A Practical Introduction to Scottish Agricultural Law*, 2nd edn (2025), Ch 14.

In practice, despite the detailed provisions of relevant legislation, succession to agricultural tenancies may be relatively uncommon. There are several reasons for this view. First, there may not be a lease at all or, if there is a lease, it may be outwith the scope of the Agricultural Holdings Acts.[125] Secondly, succession to the lease may be the subject of a special destination inserted into the lease.[126] If the special destination is valid and has not been evacuated, s 18(2) of the 1964 Act excludes confirmation to the lease by the executor. The effect of a special destination inserted into a lease is thus that the succession by a particular individual to the tenancy is approved by the landlord in advance of the tenant's death. The tenancy continues uninterrupted without the need for involvement by the executor and any delays caused by identifying the transferee are avoided.

Thirdly, and common today, the tenant may be a juristic person in which the deceased had a controlling interest in the juristic person, rather than the deceased holding the right of lease personally. In such circumstances, it is the juristic person that is the tenant rather than the deceased. Whilst the deceased may make direction for the transfer of shares in the juristic person, or these shares are distributed under the rules of intestate succession, the tenant will continue to hold the lease notwithstanding changes in its controlling personnel. Yet, in the case of partnerships the result may be different. It is common that an agricultural tenant may be a partnership, but a partnership will ordinarily terminate on the death of any one of the partners. As such, without a tenant under the lease, the tenancy could be at an end.[127]

The following sections discuss the types of agricultural lease upon which a tenanted farm will operate under. It may also be possible that the tenant is a small landholder, of which the Land Reform (Scotland)

125 B Gill, *Agricultural Tenancies,* Vol 1, 4th edn (2017), para 1-16ff.

126 See R Rennie, *Leases* (2015), para 19-13.

127 *IRC* v *Graham's Trustees* 1970 SLT 149 but see *Lujo Properties Ltd v Green* 1997 SLT 225 where an assignable lease was able to continue to exist. It may be possible that the lease was 'with the house' upon which a change in partners does not necessarily mean the end of the tenancy, see *Moray Estates Development Co v Butler* 1999 SLT 1388. This area is fraught with difficulty and could be the subject of a treatise on its own right. A limited remedy for 'farming partnerships' where the landlord (or their associate) is a partner of the firm is available under Part 6 of the Agricultural Holdings (Scotland) Act 2003.

Act 2025 introduces clearer provisions for succession.[128] Only a handful of small landholdings remain in Scotland, so they are not discussed here.[129]

(a) 1991 Act Tenancies

4.24 As the name suggests, these tenancies are regulated by the Agricultural Holdings (Scotland) Act 1991.

A tenant has the power to make a legacy of their tenancy to their family members.[130] The 1991 Act sets out who these family members may be, which includes those who may be able to succeed in intestate succession under the Succession (Scotland) Act 1964.[131] Of these family members, there is a special class of 'near relative' who have special rights that are noted below.[132]

Where the legatee accepts the bequest, then the legatee must give notice to the landlord.[133] The giving of the notice will be treated as an acceptance of the lease (unless the landlord serves a counter-notice, see below) and be binding from the date of death.[134] If the legatee declines the bequest, the lease falls to be distributed by the rules of intestate succession under s 16 of the 1964 Act.

If the landlord is unhappy with the proposed new tenant under the legacy, then after receipt of the notice from the prospective tenant, the landlord can serve a counter-notice objecting to the transfer. Where the legatee is a near relative, the objection has to be under one of the specified grounds under s 12A of the 1991 Act.[135] After that counter-notice has been served, and the notice *induciae* has elapsed, the landlord is entitled to apply to the Scottish Land Court to have the transfer to the legatee declared null and void.[136]

128 Land Reform (Scotland) Act 2025, Sch 2, Part 5, Ch 3.

129 The Scottish Agricultural Census (2021) records only 59 small landholdings are left in Scotland.

130 1991 Act, s 11 [references in section are to the 1991 Act as amended by the Land Reform (Scotland) Act 2025].

131 1991 Act, ss 11(1A)–(1B).

132 1991 Act, s 10A(6).

133 1991 Act, s 11(2).

134 1991 Act, ss 11(3) and s 12A.

135 1991 Act, ss 12A(2)–12(4).

136 1991 Act, ss 12A(5)–12A(8).

In the case of the landlord objecting to any other person other than a near relative being the new tenant, the roles reverse under s 12B. In these situations, the counter-notice served by the landlord will declare the legacy as null and void.[137] The legatee is then free to appeal to the Scottish Land Court to have this nullification overturned.

If a legacy is declared null and void by the landlord or the Land Court, the story does not end there. The distribution of the lease can be attempted under intestate succession instead.[138] Section 16(2) provides that if a legacy is declared null and void, or any legacy was declined, then the executor can still attempt to transfer the lease again to one of the beneficiaries in the intestate estate in the same manner as if no legacy had been made.[139]

For intestate succession, s 16(2) of the 1964 Act is engaged because at common law all agricultural leases have an implied condition that the lease cannot be transferred.[140]

Where a transfer is made by s 16 of the 1964 Act, the new tenant must give notice to the landlord under the 1991 Act.[141] Again, the landlord may be unhappy with the proposed new tenant and serve a counter-notice. The transferee must again be categorised as either being a 'near relative' or wider family member as the 1991 Act is re-engaged. If the new tenant is a 'near relative', the notice allows the landlord to obtain an order from the Land Court to have the lease terminated.[142] If the Land Court determine the lease should be terminated, then it can so order termination.

If the prospective tenant is a wider family member, the notice itself can terminate the lease entirely unless the tenant applies to the Land Court to have this decision quashed.[143] Otherwise, or if the court fails to overturn the counter-notice, the lease will be treated as terminated from Whitsunday or Martinmas at least one year from the date of the counter-notice.

As with the general framework, there are set time periods in which the executor must perform the transfer. Ordinarily this is one year from the

137 1991 Act, s 12B.
138 1991 Act, s 12C(3).
139 1964 Act, s 16(2)(b).
140 Bell, *Prin*, § 1214–1216.
141 1991 Act, s 12.
142 1991 Act, s 12A.
143 1991 Act, s 12B.

date of death, though the time limit may be extended until any Land Court litigation is determined (including any appeals thereof).[144] If no transfer is made then the landlord may terminate the lease with at least one year's notice.[145] If the executor believes that no transfer is possible, then they may inform the landlord of that fact to bring about termination.[146]

(b) Short Limited Duration Tenancy (SLDTs), Limited Duration Tenancies (LDTs), and Modern Limited Duration Tenancy (MLDTs)

4.25 These tenancies are regulated by the Agricultural Holdings (Scotland) Act 2003. Again, the tenant has a power to leave a legacy of their tenancy to their family.[147] The objection and Land Court mechanisms under the 1991 Act are again available in the event of a dispute regarding the proposed legatee.[148] If the legacy is declared null and void, or if the legatee declines the tenancy, then the rules of intestate succession under s 16 of the 1964 Act apply.[149]

Under s 16(4A) of the 1964 Act, the executor can transfer these leases in intestacy to any person entitled to succeed under intestate succession, or to any other person without the consent of the landlord.[150] An interesting requirement, different from other transfers under s 16, is that the transfer can only be made if it is in the best interests of the deceased's estate.[151]

The person whom the executor has transferred the lease must give notice to the landlord.[152] The landlord again may wish to object to the proposed succession and objection by counter-notice and recourse to the Land Court under the 1991 Act are available.[153]

144 1964 Act, s 16(3)(b)(i).
145 1964 Act, s 16(4)(a).
146 1964 Act, s 16(3)(a).
147 2003 Act, s 21 [references to the 2003 Act are as amended by the Land Reform (Scotland) Act 2025].
148 2003 Act, s 21(2).
149 2003 Act, s 21(3).
150 1964 Act, s 16(4A)–(4E).
151 1964 Act, s 16(4E).
152 2003 Act, s 22(1).
153 2003 Act, s 22(2).

Unlike with 1991 Act tenancies, a further option is that the landlord may wish to obtain the lease themselves, in which case *confusio* would presumably operate to terminate the lease.[154] This is designed to provide a mechanism for the landlord to pay value for the acquisition in order for the lease to be terminated. Instead of sending a counter-notice objecting to the transfer to the intestate successor, the landlord must serve an acquisition notice. The landlord must take the lease on reasonable terms no less favourable than the potential new tenant.

Similar to 1991 Act tenancies, the transfer must ordinarily be made within one year from the date of death, subject to adjustment where Land Court litigation is underway.[155] Where no transfer is likely, then termination by the executor is possible provided it is in the best interests of the deceased's estate.[156]

(5) Crofts

4.26 Succession of tenancies for crofts are another area of notorious difficulty.[157] They are regulated by the Crofters (Scotland) Act 1993, ss 10 and 11. Under s 10(1) of the 1993 Act a crofter has the right to bequeath the tenancy to any natural person.[158] A legatee, if accepting the croft, must give notice to the landlord, and thereafter send a copy to the Crofting Commission, within 12 months of the death of the former crofter.[159] If no notice is sent, or no copy is lodged, within the time frame then the legacy will be null and void.[160] When the copy is sent to the Crofting Commission, the Commission will then pass this to the Keeper to update the Crofting Register. Upon registration of the legatee's details in the Crofting Register, the legatee will retroactively become the crofter from the date of death.[161] All liabilities for the croft will pass to the new crofter

154 2003 Act, s 22(3).
155 1964 Act, s 16(4C) and s 16(4D).
156 1964 Act, s 16(4E)(b).
157 See D Flynn and K Graham, *Crofting Law* (2017).
158 1993 Act, s 10(1) [references to the 1993 Act are as amended by the Crofting and Scottish Land Court Bill as passed by the Scottish Parliament on 24 March 2026].
159 1993 Act, s 10(2).
160 1993 Act, s 10(3).
161 1993 Act, s 10(4), 10(7); and Crofting Reform (Scotland) Act 2010, s 8(5).

and the executor may require them to pay any expenses they have incurred in the interim management of the croft.[162] Special rules are in place when the testator wished to leave the croft to more than one person, and the croft is to be subdivided.[163] In such cases, the consent of the Commission will be required for the legacy to have effect.

Where the crofter has died intestate, or an attempted legacy is null and void,[164], the executor has the right to transfer the tenancy under s 11 of the 1993 Act. This is to be distributed under the provisions of the Succession (Scotland) Act 1964, s 16(2) and will include any person with the right to succeed to the intestate estate in satisfaction of their claim. As one difference from other transfers, a cohabitant is entitled to the transfer of the tenancy provided they had been living as if married or in a civil partnership of the deceased for at least two years.[165] Such transfers must ordinarily be made within 24 months from the death of the deceased.[166] Where a transfer is made, the executor must inform the landlord and the Commission.[167] The Commission will then pass the details to the Keeper for the successor to be entered into the Crofting Register as the new crofter.[168] The date of registration will be the date of transfer of the croft to the new crofter.

If no notice is given within 24 months, then the landlord is entitled to then terminate the croft.[169] However, the landlord must notify the Commission that no transfer has been notified to them.[170] This enables the Commission to take steps to declare the croft vacant.[171]

162 1993 Act, s 10(4E).
163 1993 Act, s 10(4A).
164 1993 Act, s 10(5).
165 1964 Act, s 8(2A); and s 8(6)(za).
166 1964 Act, s 16(3A).
167 1993 Act, s 11(1).
168 1993 Act, s 11(1A).
169 1964 Act, s 16(3). See *Pattinson v Matheson* [2022] CSIH 43 and Y Evans and D Adam, 'Succession: Crofting tenancy transfers in intestacy' (2022) 67(12) *JLSS* online edition, available https://www.lawscot.org.uk/members/journal/issues/vol-67-issue-12/succession-crofting-tenancy-transfers-in-intestacy/.
170 1993 Act, s 11(2).
171 1993 Act, s 11(4).

MONEY AND BANK ACCOUNTS

4.27 Where the deceased had money in a bank held in his or her own name, the money will form part of his or her moveable estate. Significant misunderstandings arise when money is kept in a 'joint bank account'.

Money in a joint bank account does not come into the category of joint property such that the monies automatically pass to the surviving account holder(s).[172] This is a common misunderstanding, and an 'area where the conception of the ordinary man in the street is quite at odds with the true legal position'.[173]

Where there is more than one signatory to an account, the account holders are entitled to withdraw the funds available in the account as they are empowered to do so under their contract with the bank. However, this is not any determinative proof of ownership of the monies. When monies have been contributed by both parties, the proportion of ownership that each joint account holder holds, in every case, will be a matter of fact.[174] Where it is not possible to prove ownership of the fund, it will be presumed to have been owned in equal shares.[175] If the other account holder wishes to claim that all or part of the fund in the account was a gift from the deceased, the onus will be on them to provide evidence of this.[176] Thus, if the survivor after death simply withdraws the whole sum from the account and cannot show that he or she had the right to ownership of it all, then he or she will be liable to account for it.[177]

A bank account in the name of 'A and B and the survivor' will also be ineffective to convey ownership of the whole fund to the survivor at

172 If it were, the funds would revert to the survivor because each party would be a kind of trustee for the other: *Banff Magistrates v Ruthin Castle Ltd* 1944 SLT 373. A bank account (whatever its type) is not a deed of trust and no rights of ownership can be conferred by it: *Cairns v Davidson* 1913 SC 1054.

173 J Kerrigan, 'Special destinations – survivorship and bank accounts revisited' 2011 *SLT (News)* 5, 6.

174 There is a presumption established for cohabitants under s 27 in respect of monies held in a bank account for joint household expenses are to be in equal shares. Additionally, s 26 of the Family Law (Scotland) Act 1985 makes similar provision for civil partners or spouses. These are rather limited provisions as the account would have to be shown to be for household expenses or housekeeping allowances.

175 *McArthy's Executors v McCafferty* 2000 GWD 14-549.

176 *Forrest–Hamilton's v Forrest–Hamilton* 1970 SLT 338.

177 *Dinwoodie's Exrx v Carruthers' Exr* (1895) 23 R 234.

death since money in bank accounts cannot be the subject of a special destination. Special destinations are contained in written titles to property, and most frequently to be found in titles to heritable property. They can be used in relation to moveables but the moveable property must be the subject of a document of title.[178] As such, wording in a bank account cannot be taken to have testamentary effect to transfer ownership of the money to the surviving account holder on death.

Since a bank account is essentially a contract between customer and bank[179] neither a deposit receipt (or its more modern equivalent, the deposit account) nor a promissory note is constituent of a title giving ownership of the property[180] and the bank, despite what that institution may believe, has no right to determine the ownership of any funds of the account holders held by it.[181] The particular arrangements between the account holders in relation to the operation of the account are a matter for them; the bank's obligation is simply to honour the terms of the contract made between itself and the account holder(s).[182]

DEBTS

4.28 Debts of any sort, whether heritable or moveable, are payable from the deceased's estate before distribution of any legacies or other claims can be made.[183] Prior to the Succession (Scotland) Act 1964, heritable debts were payable by the heir and not the executor since only the moveable estate vested in the latter. A creditor could sue either the

178 The type of moveable property which can be subject to special destination was limited by the effect of the Blank Bonds and Trusts Act 1696 and is now limited by the Requirements of Writing (Scotland) Act 1995, under which only writing can establish a truster-as-trustee trust. On special destinations, see paras **7.19–7.25.**

179 See M Meston 'Survivorship Destinations and Bank Accounts' [1995] *SLPQ* 315; and J Kerrigan, 'Special destinations – survivorship and bank accounts revisited' (2011) (2) *SLT (News)* 5.

180 *Cuthill v Burns* (1862) 24 D 849.

181 *Anderson v North of Scotland Bank* (1901) 4 F 49; *Crosbie's Trs v Wright* (1880) 7 R 823; *Macdonald v Macdonald* (1889) 16 R 758.

182 Meston, 'Survivorship destinations', 319, does suggest that a survivorship clause in an account may be given effect to as a matter of contractual obligation. However, this may well still be defeated should the deceased have made express provision in their will to the contrary as to the bequest of *ownership* of the money.

183 *Heritable Securities Investment Association Ltd v Miller's Trs* (1892) 20 R 675.

heir or the executor for payment of a debt[184] and each had rights of relief against the other.[185]

Although the whole of the deceased's estate now vests in the executor for the purposes of administration,[186] the distinction between heritable and moveable debts remains significant. The value of a surviving spouse's or civil partner's prior right to the dwelling house on intestacy, and claims for legal rights by the surviving spouse, civil partner and children will be affected by the relative values of the debts to be paid out of the heritable and moveable estate respectively.

Section 14(3) of the Succession (Scotland) Act 1964 retains the rule that debts must be paid from the part of the estate to which they relate by providing that:

> 'Nothing in this section [assimilation of heritage to moveables for the purposes of administration] shall be taken to alter any rule of law whereby any particular debt of a deceased person falls to be paid out of any particular part of his estate.'

Since the whole of the deceased's estate vests in the executor for the purposes of administration, it follows that the executor will be liable to pay all of the debts due by the deceased. For this reason, no legacies can be paid until at least six months but no more than a year[187] has elapsed from the date of confirmation of the executor, in order to allow sufficient time for creditors to present their claims for payment. The executor is also liable to pay claims for legal rights before payment of other beneficiaries.[188]

(1) The executor's liability

4.29 The executor is liable for the deceased's debts only to the limit of the value of the confirmed estate as listed under the inventory. The term

184 *British Linen Co v Lord Reay* (1890) 12 D 949; *Carnoustie v Meldrum* (1630) Mor 5204.

185 Erskine *Inst* III.9.48.

186 1964 Act, s 14.

187 All ordinary creditors rank equally if their claims are intimated to the executor within six months of the death of the deceased: Act of Sederunt, 28 February 1662.

188 *Naismith v Boyes* (1899) 1 F (HL) 79 at 81.

used to describe the executor's limited liability is liability *secundum vires inventariis.*[189]

If the estate appears to be solvent after six months, the executor can pay the beneficiaries once debts are satisfied. If it appears to be insolvent, it is the responsibility of the executor to comply with the terms of the Bankruptcy (Scotland) Act 2016 and arrange for the estate to be sequestrated.[190] Before that point, however, the executor must not have paid any of the creditors since creditors cannot be paid in the order that they make their claims – rather on the basis of equality of their entitlement. If, however, a creditor does not make a claim within the six-month period and the executor, without knowledge of the existence of the debt, distributes the estate to the beneficiaries, the executor is not liable for the debt personally.[191] Beneficiaries are, in theory, liable for the payment of any debts to the extent of the value of any legacy or legacies paid to them. They are not, however, liable for any debts unpaid by the executor while the estate was in his or her hands if in fact there were sufficient funds in the estate to have paid the debt and, in this case, the executor is personally liable.[192]

(2) Order of payment of debts

4.30 The order in which debts must be paid by the executor is in convention with the relevant parts of the Bankruptcy (Scotland) Act 2016, s 129: (1) deathbed and funeral expenses (reasonably incurred); (2) reasonable expenses in administering the estate; (3) secured debts; (4) preferred debts; and (5) ordinary debts.[193]

189 Stair, *Inst*, III.8.64.

190 Bankruptcy (Scotland) Act 2016, s 5.

191 *Stewart's Trs v Evans* (1871) 9 M 810; and *Beith v Mackenzie* (1875) 3 R 185.

192 J McLaren, *The Law of Wills and Succession,* 3rd edn (1894), para 2395: 'Heirs of provision succeeding under a deed of simple destination incur a passive liability, but only to the extent of the value of the succession.' See W Wilson and A Duncan *Trusts, Trustees and Executors,* 2nd edn (1995), paras 34-05–34-25.

193 On what constitutes secured debts, preferred debts and ordinary debts, see F McCarthy, 'Insolvency: Bankruptcy' in R Anderson (ed), *Scots Commercial Law,* 2nd edn (2022), para 13.61ff.

Funeral expenses include the reasonable costs of the burial or cremation, a headstone[194] and refreshments for mourners following the disposal of the body.[195] The person who has arranged the funeral ('the funerator') and paid for it has a right of relief against the executor, provided that the expenses have been reasonable. He or she is also entitled to be confirmed as an executor-creditor if no one else applies for the office, in order to ensure payment.[196] Separately, a funerator can be confirmed as executor-dative if no one else comes forward.[197] Although on some views they should be considered as a debt, claims for legal rights are not counted as debts in the sense of having any priority over creditors.[198]

(3) Heritable and moveable debts

4.31 The deceased person's debts are likely to be moveable, with one important exception. Where the deceased has owned heritable property, usually his or her home, and has taken a secured loan to pay for it, the loan will usually have been secured against the heritable property in the form of a standard security under the Conveyancing and Feudal Reform (Scotland) Act 1970.

Example

Inventory	Heritable Estate	Moveable Estate
House	**£255,000.00**	
Car		**£12,650.00**
Tiffany bracelet		**£8,225.00**
Gross value	£255,000.00	£20,875.00

194 *Moncrieff v Monypenny* (1713) Mor 3945. See also Bell *Prin* § 1402–03.

195 *Glass v Weir* (1821) 1 S 163.

196 On the procedure for appointment, see Wilson and Duncan *Trusts, Trustees and Executors,* 2nd edn, (1995) ch 35; and E Scobbie (ed), *Currie on Confirmation of Executors in Scotland,* 9th edn, (2011), paras 6-76ff.

197 E Scobbie (ed), *Currie on Confirmation of Executors in Scotland,* 9th edn, (2011), paras 6-115ff.

198 *Naismith v Boyes* (1899) 1 F (HL) 79. See para **5.2** on legal rights as debts.

Debts		
Funeral expenses		(£5,000)
Secured loan on house	(£100,000)	
Credit card debt		(£3,000)
Net value	£155,000.00	£12,875.00

If the deceased dies testate and has bequeathed the house subject to a secured loan to a beneficiary, the beneficiary must take it *cum onere* and thus is liable for any heritable debt secured against it.[199] The debt must also be entered in the inventory of the estate to which the executor confirms,[200] as a burden on the security subject. If the house is worth less than the loan, it must be sold and the debt paid from the general estate of the deceased, including the moveable estate.[201] Where the property is a dwelling house within the definition of the Succession (Scotland) Act 1964, s 8(1) and is the subject of a claim for prior rights by the surviving spouse or civil partner, the value of the survivor's right is subject to deduction of any debt secured over it.[202]

(4) Heritable debts and life insurance

4.32 In many cases of a secured loan, the contract of loan will have been secured in two ways: first, by the granting of a standard security in favour of the lender; and secondly, by an assignation of a life insurance policy to the lender too.[203] In such cases, the proceeds of any insurance policy are

199 *Douglas's Trs v Douglas* (1864) 2 M 1379. This is in accordance with the general rules that a beneficiary who takes a bequest is liable for any debt secured on it; see *Stewart v Stewart* (1891) 19 R 310.

200 E Scobbie (ed), *Currie on Confirmation of Executors in Scotland,* 9th edn, (2011), para 10-80.

201 See D Cusine, *Standard Securities* (1991), para 6.14; J Halliday, *Conveyancing Law and Practice in Scotland,* 2nd edn, Vol 2 (1997), para 55–94.

202 Succession (Scotland) Act 1964, s 8(6)(d). See para **6.10**.

203 Conform to s 1(4) of the Moveable Transactions (Scotland) Act 2023.

moveable and the debt must be paid *pro rata*, between the heritable and moveable securities respectively, according to the proportions of the total value of the security which they represent.[204] In such situations, there is one contract of loan but two secured assets: (i) the house; and (ii) the life insurance policy. Each secured asset must contribute to the payment of the debt.

Example

D bought a house. He took out a secured loan of £400,000 to help him to purchase the property. At the time, his financial advisor encouraged him to take out a life insurance policy to allow his family to pay off the loan at his death. He arranged a policy of £400,000 and assigned the benefit of the capital sum to the lender. D dies sometime later. The house has a market value of £550,000 at his death, and the security has £340,000 outstanding.

The payment of the debt, as apportioned, would be:

House	£550,000	
Life Insurance		£400,000
Secured Loan	(£196,842.11)	(£143,157.89)
Net Values		
House	£353,157.89	
Life Insurance		£256, 842.11

Following *Graham v Graham,* both secured assets must be used *pro rata* to pay off the loan. Thus, to pay off the £340,000 secured debt, £143,157.89 must be paid from the capital sum paid from the life insurance, and £196,842.11 must be paid from the sale proceeds of the house.

In practice, the executor and beneficiaries may negotiate in such a way to avoid the house being sold, but under a strict application of the rule in *Graham* then the distribution would be as above.

(5) Debt, co-owned property and recompense

4.33 Where the house was owned in common with a partner and a life insurance policy taken out jointly by them, the consequences will depend

204 *Graham v Graham* (1898) 5 SLT 319.

on the terms of the policy. A joint life policy can take one of two main forms, each having different consequences in relation to the estate of the first of the joint policyholders to die.[205]

With the first type, the proceeds of the policy are payable to the estate of the first deceased. If the executor pays the outstanding debt over the house in full, using the proceeds of the life policy to do so, the deceased partner has effectively paid the whole of the debt notwithstanding that each partner is notionally liable for only half of the debt. Consequently, the surviving partner is liable to the estate for half the sum, in order that the total value of the estate is not diminished.

With the second type, the proceeds are payable to the survivor. This time, the position is reversed and the estate will be liable to the surviving partner for half the proceeds. This sum will be a debt on the estate and payable before any right in succession. If the policy has been assigned and the insurance company pays the proceeds secured against the loan directly to the lender, the executor acquires a right of relief against the survivor for a one-half share of the proceeds on the basis of recompense. However, it arises only if there was no intention of donation by the deceased given this would provide a *causa* or basis for the transfer to the survivor.

In *Christie's Executor v Armstrong*[206] the deceased and his partner had obtained a loan from a building society to re-mortgage their home. Title to the house was in their joint names and subject to a survivorship destination. They granted a standard security in favour of the building society and assigned to it an endowment policy on the life of the deceased.

When he died, the deceased's share of the house passed to his partner under the survivorship destination. The insurance company paid the whole of the debt to the building society directly to it. His partner therefore took sole ownership of the house, free of debt.

The deceased had died intestate, survived by a wife and children from whom he had been separated for several years. One of the children was appointed executor of the deceased and raised an action against her father's partner for recompense, on the ground that the deceased was liable for

205 See G Gretton, 'Endowment Mortgages and the Law of Succession' (1987) 32 *JLSS* 303; A Dalgliesh, 'Insurance policies, securities and claims to legal rights' (1987) 32 *JLSS* 423; and G Gretton 'Life Policies and the law of succession' (1988) 33 *JLSS* 141.

206 1996 SC 295.

only a one-half share of the debt and the remaining value in the insurance policy should belong to his moveable estate. If the executor succeeded, the value of her father's moveable estate, and thus the value available for claims for legitim by her and her siblings, would be enlarged. The court held that actual payment by the deceased or his estate to the defender was not necessary in order to entitle the pursuer to obtain relief:[207]

> 'In our opinion the fact that the policy was assigned to the building society in security for the loan made by them to the deceased and the defender did not prevent the defender from obtaining benefit, in that the arrangements which the deceased had made enabled the building society to use the proceeds of the policy assigned to them to extinguish not only the deceased's half share of the debt to the building society but the defender's half share as well.'

Where a claim for recompense is made, the success of the claim will depend on satisfying three tests: loss by the pursuer; *lucratus* on the part of the defender; and no intention of donation on the part of the pursuer, as well as general equitable principles.[208] In *Christie's Exr,* it appeared that there may have been an intention of donation on the part of the deceased and the court allowed proof before answer.

207 1996 SC 295, per Lord Ross at 298.

208 Bell, *Prin* § 538: 'Where one has gained by the lawful act of another, done without any intention of donation, he is bound to recompense or indemnify that other to the extent of the gain.' See *Varney (Scotland) Ltd v Burgh of Lanark* 1976 SLT 46; *Lawrence Building Co Ltd v Lanark County Council* 1978 SC 30, 1979 SLT 2; *Royal Bank of Scotland plc v Watt* 1991 SLT 138; *Morgan Guaranty Trust Co of New York v Lothian Regional Council* 1995 SLT 299.

Chapter 5

Legal rights and aliment

INTRODUCTION

5.1 It is not possible for a person to entirely disinherit their spouse, civil partner, or issue in Scots law, whether in testate or intestate succession. There can be a misconception amongst the general public that Scots law permits total freedom of testation, in which a person can simply make a will which disregards their family. This is far from the truth. Scots law, like many civil law legal systems, employs a principle of 'forced heirship', though this terminology is not routinely used in Scotland.[1] A surviving spouse or civil partner, and any children of a deceased person, each have an automatic entitlement in Scots law to claim a share of the deceased's moveable estate, regardless of whether the deceased died testate or intestate.

This automatic entitlement is known in Scotland as 'legal rights'.[2] Although the extent of entitlement is identical, the sources of the right differ as between surviving spouses, children and civil partners. In relation to a surviving spouse and issue, entitlement to legal rights arises at common law. The particular rights of each class of person in legal rights are known as *jus relicti* (or the male widower's right), *jus relictae* (or female widow's right), and legitim (the children's right, or 'bairn's part'). In relation to civil partners, legal rights were introduced expressly by the Civil Partnership Act 2004[3] and mirrors the position of spouses at common law. Cohabitants have no entitlement to legal rights, but they may have a claim to a share of the deceased partner's intestate estate under s 29 of the Family Law (Scotland) Act 2006.

1 For an overview of mandatory family protection in different jurisdictions, see K Reid et al (eds), *Comparative Succession Law, Volume III: Mandatory Family Protection* (2020).

2 See the definition of legal rights in the 1964 Act, s 36(1).

3 2004 Act, s 131(5).

Legal rights are fixed and determinate entitlements that arise *a priori* to any judicial declaration of their existence and apply to all cases. Entitlement takes the form of a right to a capital payment of a one-third or a one-half share of the moveable estate of the deceased, with the share depending on whether both a spouse or civil partner and children survive. In valuing and satisfying claims for legal rights, the distinction between heritage and moveables in succession law remains important.[4]

Though less discussed, there is a second, more limited form of protection for the deceased's family through maintenance in the form of aliment. This is rather limited in its use and has been the subject of calls for reform though, as will be seen, recent attempts at reform of legal rights has been abandoned, and reform to aliment is, at the time of writing, still unimplemented.

THE NATURE OF LEGAL RIGHTS

5.2 The origins of legal rights are obscure, seemingly dating back to (at least) the early medieval period in the times of King David I.[5] Their origins may never be conclusively ascertained, and they are often referred to as having existed since time immemorial. Whilst ancient rights, and notwithstanding refinements at the level of detail brought about by statutory amendments,[6] the fundamental principles of legal rights have largely remained unchanged throughout history.

4 It also remains important in calculating a surviving spouse or civil partner's monetary right under the Succession (Scotland) Act 1964, s 9; see para **6.23**.

5 On the history, see K Reid, 'Legal Rights in Scotland' in *Comparative Succession Law, Volume III: Mandatory Family Protection* (2020). A version of legal rights is described in the *Regiam Magestatam* and the *Leges Burgorum*. The origin of the right has been attributed variously to Roman law, English law, French law, Norman law and the law of Germanic tribes. Gardner, however, in his treatise on the history of legal rights concludes that it dates from the reign of David I: see J C Gardner, *The Origin and Nature of the Legal Rights of Spouses and Children in the Scottish Law of Succession* (1928).

6 The Married Women's Property (Scotland) Act 1881, the Intestate Moveable Succession (Scotland) Act 1855, the Succession (Scotland) Act 1964, the Law Reform (Miscellaneous Provisions) (Scotland) Act 1966, the Adoption (Scotland) Act 1978 the Law Reform (Parent and Child) (Scotland) Act 1986 have all altered the common law. The Civil Partnership Act 2004, s 131 assimilates the position of civil partners to that of spouses. On the pre-1964 law see J Walker, *Law of Intestate Succession in Scotland* (1927) and for a historical outline of the most important statutory amendments see D Bartos and M Meston, *Bartos and Meston on the Succession (Scotland) Act 1964,* 6th edn (2015).

Legal rights have been defined as 'a species of family protection for the benefit of a surviving spouse and the deceased's children'[7] and reflect the view that a person ought not to be able to dispose of his or her estate entirely according to individual preferences but ought to be bound to leave something to those with whom he or she had the closest ties. Lord Salvesen in *Hutton's Trustees v Hutton's Trustees* summed this up in giving his view of the justification for the right:[8]

> 'I regard the right which our law gives to children in their father's estate, in common with the laws of most civilised countries except England, as a very important check on capricious or unjust testaments, which not merely inflict injustice on individuals but are often contrary to the public interest.'

Following from the idea that the deceased is under a duty to make such provision, the nature of legal rights may be understood as being that of a debt on the estate, albeit one which is deferred to the claims of creditors.[9] In *Naismith v Boyes* Lord Watson explained that:[10]

> 'The legal claims of the widow and children are not, strictly speaking, rights of succession … They are in the nature of debts which attach to the free succession after the claims of onerous creditors have been satisfied. Hence, it has frequently been said judicially that, in respect of their legal claims, the widow and children are heirs in competition with onerous creditors, and are creditors in competition with heirs.'

7 'Will and Succession', Vol 25, in *The Laws of Scotland: Stair Memorial Encyclopaedia,* para 772.

8 The Married Women's Property (Scotland) Act 1881, ss 6 and 7, had extended the right of legitim and *jus relicti* to a woman's moveable estate. In English law, surviving spouses and children have had a discretionary right to challenge the will of the deceased since 1938 and current provisions are contained in the Inheritance (Provision for Family and Dependants) Act 1975: see A Learmonth, *Williams, Mortimer & Sunnucks on Executors, Administrators and Probate,* 22nd edn (2023), Part 6; S Ross, *Inheritance Act Claims: Law and Practice*, 4th edn (2017); and A Francis, *Inheritance Act Claims: Law, Practice and Procedure* (looseleaf).

9 *Inglis v Inglis* (1860) 7 M 435. On the taxation consequences of legal rights, detailed treatment in respect of inheritance tax can be found in HMRC's *Inheritance Tax Manual,* sections IHTM12201 to IHTM12253, available https://www.gov.uk/hmrc-internal-manuals/inheritance-tax-manual/ihtm12201.

10 (1899) 1 F (HL) 79 at 81. See also *Russel v Attorney General* 1917 SC 28.

This view has been borne out by judicial decisions and observation in a number of subsequent cases and appears to represent the current position.[11]

LEGAL RIGHTS CLAIMED FROM THE MOVEABLE ESTATE ALONE

5.3 One of the most important points to understand is that legal rights are only payable from the *moveable* estate of the deceased. This point is always a common pitfall for students new to the area. Legal rights can never be claimed from the heritable part of an estate. The reason for this goes back to the historical distinction between heritable and moveable property and the old and different rules of succession for each.[12]

Formerly, Scots law did have a form of legal rights in the heritable estate, only for spouses, which was known as 'terce' and 'courtesy', whereas the *jus relicti, jus relictae* and legitim came from the moveable estate. A terce was the right of a female widow to a liferent of a third of the deceased's heritable property, whereas the more generous courtesy for male widows was a liferent of the entire heritable estate. Terce and courtesy were abolished by the Succession (Scotland) Act 1964.[13] However, the relict's rights and right to legitim from the moveable estate were not affected by the 1964 Act's reforms, leaving them to continue to be claimed from the moveable estate alone.[14] These developments are why legal rights are only ever claimable from the moveable estate alone.

The entitlement of surviving spouses, civil partners and children to legal rights from the deceased's moveable estate means that where a person is survived by one or both, only one-third or one-half of the moveable estate remains available for payment of legacies. This remaining portion is known as the *dead's part* and, strictly, speaking, is the only part of the moveable estate over which the deceased has the absolute or free power

11 See *Sanderson v Lockhart–Mure* 1946 SC 298 at 299 where a claim for legitim was defined as 'simply a claim of debt exigible from the deceased's estate and bearing interest from the date of the ancestor's death'; and *Duncan v Duncan* 2000 GWD 26–1012.

12 See **3.2**.

13 1964 Act, s 10.

14 1964 Act, s 10(2).

of testation.[15] The dead's part will comprise a third of the moveable estate alongside the heritable estate of the deceased (which, for the reasons noted above, remains untouched by legal rights).

In a number of cases, owing to a lack of awareness of legal rights, the deceased may in fact have tested over the whole moveable estate. However, if legal rights are claimed, these will defeat up to two-thirds of the entitlement of any beneficiaries to whom legacies of moveable property have been bequeathed. Strictly speaking, legal rights are not claims; rather, they are rights that arise *ex lege* and must be discharged by the person entitled if he or she chooses to renounce the rights. If he or she has been given a legacy by the deceased, an entitled person must choose whether to take the legacy and discharge legal rights or claim payment of them.

There are therefore three situations in which legal rights may be claimed. First, where a testator has left nothing to a surviving spouse, civil partner or children by testament. Second, where the value of any legacy or legacies given a spouse, civil partner or children is less than the value of the legal rights to which they are entitled. Third, where a person has died intestate and moveable estate remains after payment of prior rights to the surviving spouse.[16] In testate succession, this means that if children have been given nothing by way of legacies from the deceased, they can claim a proportion of the value of the moveable estate in competition with any testamentary provisions to which the surviving spouse or civil partner is entitled and vice versa.

In some cases, however, the statement that legal rights are absolute entitlements may be somewhat hollow. Indeed, there are significant criticisms of the current system.[17] The reasons for such criticism include:

(1) In both testate and intestate succession, legal rights may be defeated if the deceased has left no moveable estate from which

15 It has been argued by Gardner, *The Origin and Nature of the Legal Rights* (1928), 75, that this is to put the cart before the horse and that 'the more correct view is to realise that in Scotland the power of testing has, from its introduction, never been extended to more than one-third of a man's whole estate, where he had both a wife and children, and not to regard the indefeasible portions or the wife and children as having been created to limit the power of testing'.

16 See para **6.25**.

17 Report *on Succession* (SLC No 215, 2009), para 3.3.

to claim them. In many estates, heritable property forms the most valuable asset, yet legal rights have no application as they are limited to the moveable estate alone. Where an estate is 'heritable heavy', there may be little that passes to a claimant of legal rights.

(2) The use of *quasi*-wills or testamentary devices may defeat legal rights since this form of conveyancing removes property from the deceased's patrimony at death.[18] A claimant of legal rights will have no claim to any moveable property subject to these controls, as they are not part of the deceased's estate.

(3) In intestate succession, legal rights are postponed to and may be defeated by claims for prior rights by a surviving spouse or civil partner under the Succession (Scotland) Act 1964 if these claims totally or in large part exhaust the moveable estate. Additionally, the right to legitim may be defeated by a surviving spouse or civil partner renouncing his or her legacy to create an artificial intestacy for this purpose.[19]

(4) Similarly, the right of children of the deceased to legitim may be defeated by a surviving cohabitant's right to claim under s 29 of the Family Law (Scotland) Act 2006.

(5) Legal rights may not be the fairest way to determine mandatory protection for spouses and issue as it is based on status rather than familial relationship. The Scottish Law Commission give a useful example demonstrating the problem:[20]

> 'A man of 70 who is a self-made millionaire and has not visited his aged mother for twenty years is entitled to legitim from her estate in exactly the same way as his impoverished unmarried sister who nursed their mother during her last illness: and he remains entitled to legitim even if his mother has bequeathed all her property to her daughter in recognition of the care she has received from her.'

In light of these criticisms, and others, legal rights have been the subject of attempted reform over the years.

18 See para **7.18**.

19 See para **6.46**.

20 Discussion Paper *on Succession* (SLC DP No 136, 2007), para 3.92.

REFORM AND THE LONG ROAD BACK TO THE STATUS QUO

5.4 The Scottish Law Commission took the view that while a system of fixed shares has advantages over a discretionary system of entitlement, in which a court awards provision from the estate at its discretion,[21] there was little justification for children to have an automatic right to a share in their parent's estate and that their entitlement should be abolished. However, the Commission acknowledged that this view was controversial.

Ultimately, in its 1990 report, the Commission recommended that a new system of entitlement for spouses and children be introduced, in the form of fixed shares from the whole estate, both heritable and moveable,[22] and that a complicated 'slice' system should be introduced. This would mean a surviving spouse receiving 30% of the first £200,000 of the net estate plus 10% of any excess over that sum. The issue's share should be 15% of the first £200,000 plus 5% of any excess over that sum but the estate subject to the issue's legal share should not include the first £100,000 of any net estate to the fee of which the surviving spouse succeeds. Where there is no surviving spouse, the issue should receive the same provision as that of a surviving spouse where there are no issue.[23] In every case where an estate was sufficiently large to make any payments of legal shares possible after satisfaction of the surviving spouse's right to a fixed sum plus a 'slice' of any excess remaining, children would have the right to a legal share from their parent's estate.[24]

The Commission took the view that the distinction between heritage and moveables is arbitrary and unprincipled, with the consequence that the estate available for legal share is dependent on factors relative to every individual case. It recommended, therefore, that in relation to the legal

21 This reflects the views of some commentators, see M Meston, 'Succession – Rights or discretion?' (1987) *Jur Rev* 1, and N MacCormick, 'Discretion and Rights' (1989) 8 *Law and Philosophy* 23. For a more positive outlook on a discretionary scheme, see H Hiram, 'Reforming Succession Law: Legal Rights' (2008) 12 *Edin LR* 81.

22 Report *on Succession* (SLC Report No 124, 1990), Pt III.

23 Report *on Succession* (1990), recommendation 8. See also D R MacDonald, 'Reforming the Law of Succession' (1990) *JLSS* 270.

24 Scottish Law Commission *Report on Succession* (Scot Law Com No 124) 1990 Pts II and III.

shares available to the spouse and issue, heritable and moveable property should be completely assimilated.[25]

The Commission later undertook a further project on succession law and produced a second report in 2009.[26] At that time, the Commission again considered reform of legal rights and attempted to provide a simpler model than what was proposed in 1990. Amongst this was a clear resolution to end the restriction towards claiming legal rights from heritable property:[27]

> 'It is a fundamental tenet of our proposals that legal share for both the deceased's surviving spouse or civil partner and the deceased's issue should be exigible from the whole of the deceased's estate, heritable as well as moveable property. This has been done not only to simplify the law but also to reflect the increase in value of heritable property so that in many cases it is by far the most valuable part of the deceased's estate.'

In respect of spouses and civil partners, the Commission considered that they should be given a legal share, which would amount to 25% of what the spouse could have received if the deceased had died intestate.[28] This would apply to the entire estate, rather than just moveable property alone as is currently the case. In respect of children and issue, difficulties with reforming legitim arose. The Commission had considered abolishing legitim and replacing it with an alimentary scheme whereby dependent children, such as young children, could receive financial provision.[29] However, in respect of adult non-dependent children the Commission proposed removing protection from disinheritance entirely.[30] These proposals were strongly criticised, notably by Professor Dot Reid.[31]

In its final recommendations, the Commission could not reach a clear decision on the reform to legitim – viewing fixed protection for children as a question of social policy and a political issue which needed to be decided by the Scottish Parliament.[32] Instead, the Commission, unusually,

25 Report on *Succession* (SLC Report No 124, 1990) Recommendation 7.

26 Report *on Succession* (SLC Report No 215, 2009).

27 ibid, para 3.61.

28 ibid, para 3.6.

29 Discussion Paper *on Succession* (SLC DP No 136, 2007), para 3.91.

30 ibid, para 3.101.

31 D Reid, 'From the Cradle to the Grave: Politics, Families and Inheritance Law' (2008) 12(3) *Edin LR* 343.

32 Report *on Succession* (SLC Report No 215, 2009), para 3.35.

gave two options. One was that all children and issue should have a fixed share of 25%, calculated in the same manner as proposed for spouses and civil partners, and the other was that only dependent children should be entitled to claim a capital sum as awarded by a court.[33]

After the Commission published its report, the Scottish Government wished to undertake further consultation.[34] At the same time, the Land Reform Review Group undertook a review of Scotland's land laws and methods to improve ownership concentrations. Part of the Review Group's examination involved succession law. The Review Group considered that the distinction between heritable and moveable property should be removed and that legal rights should be claimed from the estate irrespective of the species of property:[35]

> 'The Group considers that, while this issue involves land, the driving need for removing the remaining distinction between heritable and moveable property, should be a straightforward matter of social justice based on the current disadvantaged position of spouses and children.'

With this impetus, the Government announced in 2014 to look at implementing the Commission's recommendations and to:[36]

> 'Introduce a Succession Bill to ensure that the law in this area is fairer, clearer and more consistent. We also plan to consult in the coming year on further legislation on succession which will aim to radically overhaul the current law in this area. As part of this modernisation the distinction between movable and immovable property would be removed to give children, spouses and civil partners appropriate legal rights over both forms of property. This should ensure a just distribution of assets among a deceased's close family to reflect both societal change and expectations. These changes will be an important aspect of our series of measures in respect of Land Reform.'

Thereafter, in 2015, the Scottish Government launched a consultation on widescale reforms to succession law, including legal rights.[37] It is here

33 Report *on Succession* (SLC Report No 215, 2009), Part 3.

34 *Letter from Minister of Community Safety to Scottish Law Commission* dated 13 July 2009.

35 Land Reform Review Group, *The Land of Scotland and the Common Good* (2014), s 6, para 16.

36 *One Scotland: The Government's Programme for Scotland 2014-15* (2014), 12.

37 A separate consultation on the 'technical' aspects of the Commission's report was carried out which led to the Succession (Scotland) Act 2016.

that events took a rather unfortunate turn, with the effect of the proposed reforms on agricultural land playing a significant part.

In 2009, the Commission had considered the risk of whether a farm's or landed estate's ownership or tenancy could be fragmented by the new fixed shares scheme for children such that operation of a farm could prove unworkable if the owners or tenants were more than one. Ultimately the Commission considered that such concerns raised by the agricultural sector were 'largely misplaced'.[38] However, the agricultural sector in 2015 still had concerns regarding abolishing the distinction between heritable and moveable property and opening up legal rights or legal shares to heritable property.[39] In the Government's consultation responses, it seemed that consultees did not favour either reforming legal rights or abolishing the distinction between heritable and moveable property. Accordingly, in 2018, the Government concluded:[40]

> 'The current scheme of legal rights attracts criticism but it does have the benefit of striking a balance between testamentary freedom and limited protections for spouses/civil partners and children.
>
> Further encroachment on the autonomy of individuals would undermine their ability to manage their affairs as they wish. The alternative consulted on would attract a greater degree of criticism than the current system given the lack of consensus about children's rights and because of the viability concerns about the impact of the removal of the distinction between heritable and moveable estate on certain land based businesses. On that basis we do not intend to bring forward reforms in this area.'

As such, there are no plans to reform legal rights in Scots law for the foreseeable future (at least in the case of testate succession as a protection from total disinheritance).[41] The present situation that Scots law finds itself in is aptly summarised Professor Kenneth Reid:[42]

> 'Faced, finally, with an open choice on the issues, Scotland seemed unwilling or unable to decide as to the proper balance between freedom

38 Report *on Succession* (SLC Report No 215, 2009), para 3.64.

39 *Consultation on the Law of Succession* (2015), para 3A.13.

40 *Scottish Government response to the Consultation on the Law of Succession* (2018), 11.

41 On the position for intestate succession, see para **6.3**.

42 K Reid, 'Legal Rights in Scotland' in *Comparative Succession Law, Volume III: Mandatory Family Protection* (2020), 449.

of testation and family protection. Uncertain as to the future, she chose to stick with the past.'

ENTITLEMENT TO LEGAL RIGHTS

5.5 Where a person entitled to claim legal rights instead claims payment of any legacy bequeathed to him or her by the deceased, his or her entitlement to legal rights will be discharged, expressly or by implication. If, however, a benefit is acquired by a person entitled to legal rights by means of a testamentary device,[43] so that the subject of the benefit does not form part of the deceased's estate, and the property is payable directly to the beneficiary, that person remains entitled to claim legal rights over the moveable estate.

In addition, if a person entitled to legal rights elects to take their 'conventional provisions' (that is, legacies bequeathed by the deceased in their will) or any entitlements under a will substitute, the legatee remains entitled to legal rights in relation to any part of the estate which is intestate. Thus, where any portion of the moveable estate is undisposed of by testament or where part of the estate becomes artificially intestate, claims by entitled persons may be made in respect of that estate, provided that it is not exhausted claims for prior rights.

If a person to whom a legacy has been given is also entitled to claim legal rights and they elects to do so, the value of other legacies payable under the will may abate in order to satisfy the claim.[44] A person who claims legal rights cannot insist on delivery of any particular item of moveable property since the right is a personal right against the executor to a share in the value of the whole moveable estate and not a real right in the property itself.[45]

Where the deceased is survived by either a spouse or civil partner and by children, the value of the moveable estate after payment of debts is divided into three, with the spouse or civil partner receiving a one-third share and the children a one-third share equally between them. This

43 See para **7.18**.

44 See paras **10.13–10.14**.

45 *Tait's Trs v Lees* (1886) 13 R 1104; *Inglis v Inglis* (1860) 7 M 435; and *Cameron's Trs v Mclean* 1917 SC 416.

division of the estate is known as the 'tripartition', in which there is the relict's part, the bairn's part and the dead's part. This can be shown in the following example:

Example

X dies survived by her husband, A, and two children, B and C. Her moveable estate is worth £30,000. In calculating the value of A, B and C's claims for legal rights, the moveable estate is divisible into three parts. A is entitled to £10,000 and B and C to £10,000 between them.

Where the deceased is survived only by a spouse or civil partner or by children (or more remote descendants), instead of a tripartition, there is a 'bipartition'. The net moveable estate is divided into two, and the claimants receives half:

Example

X dies childless, survived by her husband A. Her net moveable estate is worth £30,000. In calculating the value of the husband's claim for legal rights, the net moveable estate is divisible into two parts. A is entitled to £15,000.

The right of the surviving spouse is known as '*jus relicti*' or '*jus relictae*'; the right of a civil partner is known as rights under s 131 of the Civil Partnership Act 2004 (though they often are just termed the same as the spousal rights) and the right of the children is known as 'legitim' or the 'bairn's part'. The remaining third or half which is left after these claims have been satisfied is the 'dead's part'. If a spouse or civil partner has predeceased the deceased, the claim which he or she would have had is extinguished since there is no representation in *jus relicti*, *jus relictae* or civil partner rights under s 131 of the 2004 Act.

In testate succession, the rights of a surviving spouse, civil partner or children are payable *before* any legacies can be distributed to beneficiaries under the terms of the will. Claims for legal rights are deducted from the value of the net moveable estate and the balance, the dead's part, then becomes available for the payment of legacies.

Example

X is survived by her civil partner A and two children B and C. X has bequeathed her whole estate to charity. The moveable estate is valued at £30,000. A claims her right to a one-third share under s 131 of the Civil Partnership Act 2004 and B and C claim legitim of a one-third share between them. The balance of £10,000 is payable to the charity.

LEGITIM

5.6 While the entitlement of spouses and civil partners to legal rights lapses on termination of the relationship (whether by death, divorce or dissolution) and no other person is entitled to claim in his or her place, the position of predeceasing children is rather different. Whereas legal rights are personal to spouses and civil partners, the deceased person's whole line of descent retains entitlement to legitim. Thus, where a child has predeceased the deceased and he or she is survived by children, these grandchildren (or remoter issue if they have also predeceased) are entitled to represent their ancestor and claim legitim by way of representation in his or her place.[46]

The second rule which applies to legitim, but not to the spousal rights or rights under s 131 of the Civil Partnership Act 2004, is that where one or more children have received an advance from the estate of the deceased during his or her lifetime, the value of their claim may be reduced accordingly under a doctrine known as collation.

(1) Representation in legitim

5.7 The Succession (Scotland) Act 1964, s 11 provides for representation in legitim;[47] that is, it enables the claim of child who

46 Succession (Scotland) Act 1964, s 11.

47 At common law there was no right of representation by children in the moveable estate, although the principle of primogeniture meant that there was selective representation, in the heritable estate, in order to identify the heir where no children of the deceased survived. One of the recommendations of the Mackintosh Committee was to introduce infinite representation and this has been introduced in the Succession (Scotland) Act 1964, ss 5 and 11 in relation to the intestate estate and legal rights respectively, *Law of Succession in Scotland: Report of the Committee of Inquiry* (Cmd 8144, 1951), para 13.

predeceased the deceased and who would have been entitled to legitim had he or she survived, to transmit to his or her issue:

> 'In circumstances where a child who has failed to survive the deceased has left issue who survive the deceased, and the child would, if he had survived the deceased, have been entitled. . . to legitim out of the deceased's estate, such issue shall have the like right to legitim as the child would have had if he had survived the deceased.'

'Issue' includes all descendants, however remote.[48] Thus, not only grandchildren but also great-grandchildren or even great-great-grandchildren have the right to claim legitim from the deceased's moveable estate if no nearer descendant survives.

Example

X dies survived by two children A and B and predeceased by a third child C. C is survived by a child D. D, X's grandchild, is entitled to legitim from X's estate in place of C.

The rule that infinite representation applies to legitim does not mean that the share of any issue representing their parent will necessarily be the same as the share which may be claimed by any surviving children of the deceased. Different rules of entitlement apply where the claimants are of different degrees of relationship to the deceased. The division of the legitim fund depends essentially on whether at least one child, as well as remoter issue, has survived the deceased. There are two ways in which legitim can be divided: *per capita* and *per stirpes*.

(2) Per capita division

5.8 Section 11(2)(a) of the Succession (Scotland) Act 1964 provides that where two or more persons have a right to legitim by way of representation, the legitim fund shall be divided equally, provided that all claimants are of the same degree of relationship to the deceased. Clearly, there has to be more than one claimant before the question of division

48 *Turner's Trs v Turner* (1897) 24 R 619. See also paras **11.7–11.8.**

arises but where the claimants are all of the same degree of relationship the division will be *per capita*. If, for example, the deceased is survived only by grandchildren, the division will be *per capita* since they will be all of the same degree of relationship to the deceased.

Example

X is survived by her three grandchildren C, D and E, the children of her predeceasing daughters A and B.

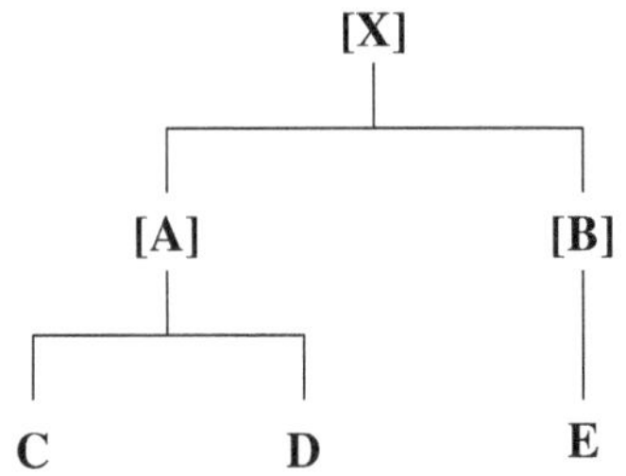

The legitim fund is £30,000. C, D and E each receive £10,000 as a one-third share of the legitim fund.

(3) Per stirpes division

5.9 Section 11(2)(b) provides for a *per stirpes* scheme of division where the claimants are of different degrees of relationship to the deceased. In this case, the legitim fund is to be divided equally into a number of parts equal to the aggregate of:

(i) those of the said persons who are nearest in degree of relationship to the deceased (in this paragraph referred to as the nearest surviving relatives); and

(ii) any other persons who were related to the deceased in that degree and who (if they had survived him) would have been entitled to legitim out of his estate, but who have predeceased him leaving issue who survive him, and are entitled to legitim out of his estate; and, of those parts, one shall be taken by each of the nearest surviving relatives, and one shall be taken *per stirpes* by the issue

> of each of the said predeceased persons, being issue who are entitled as aforesaid.

Children of predeceasing siblings share the same portion that their parent would have received, had he or she survived the deceased. This contrasts with his or her right to share the legitim equally if no member of the previous generation has survived.[49]

Example

X is survived by her son A and her three grandchildren D, E and F, the children of her predeceasing daughters B and C.

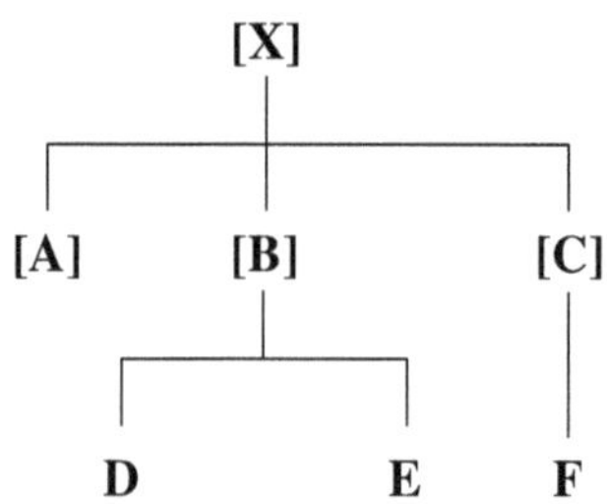

The legitim fund is £30,000. A is of a nearer degree of relationship to X than D, E and F and the fund is divided *per stirpes*. A receives £10,000 as a one-third share; D and E receive £10,000 between them as a one-sixth share each; and F receives £10,000 as a one-third share.

The division is based on there being three survivors of X, with two of them being represented by their children. The surviving grandchildren of each branch receive the same as their parent would have done. B would have received a one-third share, so her children therefore receive her one-third share between them. F has no siblings and receives the whole one-third share that C would have been entitled to had she survived.

(4) Collation inter liberos

5.10 Collation *inter liberos* (collation amongst the children) is the equitable principle at common law that it would be unfair if a child were

49 See M Meston, 'Representation in succession' (1995) 1 *SLPQ* 83.

to receive the same share of the legitim fund as other claimants if he or she has already received certain types of donations during the deceased's lifetime. The effect is that, nominally at least, the value of any such donations is added back to the legitim fund available at the time of the deceased's death. Based on the presumption that a parent would not wish to treat his or her children differently, the purpose of the principle is to equalise the shares of legitim and thus the total legitim fund available on death.[50] As Lord McLaren puts it:[51]

> 'The principle is, that the value of such advances or provisions is to be added to the legitim fund, out of which the donee is then to receive such a sum as, when added to the advances already received, will place him on a footing of equality with the other children.'

Provided that the payment made to the claimant is of a qualifying type, advances can be seen as a partial payment to account of a claim for legitim since, theoretically at least, payments made during the deceased's lifetime reduce the value of the legitim fund at death. Only certain types of payment are considered as advances which the claimant may be required to collate. Lifetime gifts to a person eligible to claim legitim which qualify as collatable advances may be considered as representing total or partial satisfaction of a claim for legitim on death. This, however, is based on a double fiction:[52]

> 'It assumes that the father has paid a part or whole of his indebtedness at a time when no relationship of debtor and creditor existed between the father and the child. It further assumes that the payment is made out of the legitim fund although confessedly the legitim fund is at the time non-existent.'

A child who has received a collatable advance needs to collate only if two conditions are met: first, if he or she does not discharge his or her claim to legitim; and second, if another claimant for legitim requests that the advance be collated. Since the purpose of the doctrine is to 'secure equality in the distribution of the legitim fund among the children who

50 Erskine, *Inst*, III.9.24; Bell *Prin*, § 1588.

51 J McLaren, *The Law of Wills and Succession as Administered in Scotland*, 3rd edn (1894), para 316.

52 *Coats' Trs v Coats* 1914 SC 744, per Lord President Strathclyde at 748.

are actual claimants on the fund',[53] it follows that if only one person out of several who are entitled to claim legitim actually does so, the sole claimant cannot call on the others to collate. Collation arises only where there is a competition between claimants who are each claiming shares of the legitim fund. If a person entitled to legitim has received a collatable advance and discharges his or her right to legitim, a claimant for legitim who has either received no advance or a smaller advance cannot require the non-claimant to collate.

Collation does not apply to payments made to spouses or civil partners, even though the consequence of any such gifts is that the total moveable estate and, consequently, the legitim fund, is reduced. The deceased can make gifts of unlimited value to his or her spouse or civil partner without claims for *jus relicti*, *jus relictae* or rights under s 131 of the Civil Partnership Act 2004 being affected or any requirement to collate the value of the gift arising.

(5) Collatable advances

5.11 For a payment to be considered as collatable, it must be clear that the deceased intended the sum to be an 'advance' out of the estate rather than simply an outright gift[54] or a payment made in the normal course of carrying out parental duties and responsibilities. Such payments would include, for example, payment for the child's maintenance and education. Loans, which the child is under an obligation to repay, cannot be collatable since the payment was never a gift to begin with.[55] Testamentary provisions in favour of a person entitled to claim legitim are not collatable; for example, if one child is entitled to a legacy from the deceased's estate, its value is

53 ibid.

54 Distinguishing between an advanceable gift and a simple gift can be difficult. A modest gift for a birthday or religious holiday, or even a present for a new home, would likely not be collatable. The more substantial the gift the more it is likely to be collatable. Even where the deceased uses the word 'free gift', it may yet still be deemed as a collatable advance, *Douglas v Douglas* (1876) 4 R 105.

55 Construction of such payments as either gift or loan can be difficult in a family context, see *Russell's Executor v Russell's Executrix* [2025] SC GLA 19 and S MacDonald-Mulvihill, 'A twenty-first century prodigal son: Donation between family members' (2025) 29(3) *Edin LR* 476.

not collatable even if the subject of the legacy is moveable property.[56] And, since legitim is payable from the moveable estate only, gifts of heritable property to a child are not collatable. In addition, a testator may provide expressly that collation is not to apply to the child's claim for legitim.

Advances that can be considered as collatable are those kinds of payments that go beyond the normal discharge of parental responsibilities, such as setting a child up in business or furnishing his or her home. The onus of proving that a gift made during the deceased's lifetime to a person entitled to claim legal rights was in fact an advance of legitim, rather than a gift, lies on the executor.[57] Regardless of how long before death the advance or advances were made, no interest between the date of the advance and the date of payment of the claim is chargeable.

The doctrine of collation is preserved expressly in the Succession (Scotland) Act 1964, s 11(3), which provides that nothing in s 11 of the 1964 Act is to be construed as altering the rules relating to collation. Further, where a person is entitled to legitim by virtue of representation, s 11(3) of the 1964 Act provides that he or she is also under a duty to collate. Thus, where an advance has been made to a predeceasing child, the share of any descendant of that child claiming legitim is subject to collation of the advance made to his or her ancestor. Collation, therefore, applies not only to the immediate descendants of the deceased but also to remoter issue claiming legitim by way of representation. Such a descendant will receive his or her share subject to collation of 'the proportion appropriate to him of any advances made' to the ancestor. However, because of the rules as to *per stirpes* division, it is possible that the share of legitim to which the claimant is entitled is of a different proportion to that to which his or her ancestor would have been entitled. The way in which s 11(3) of the 1964 Act is to be construed and, consequently, how the appropriate proportion of the collatable advance is to be determined is therefore highly ambiguous.[58]

56 If, however, all persons entitled to the payment of legacies from the moveable estate were to renounce them and claim legal rights instead, this would in effect amount to collation of the value of the legacies.

57 Where the advance was made to the claimant's ancestor, proving the advance will be particularly difficult but the burden of proof is not as stringent as that required to prove a debt: *Welsh v Welsh's Trs* (1878) 5 R 542.

58 See M Meston 'Collation of advances to ancestors' 1967 *SLT (News)* 195. For an alternative view, see a letter from A Johnston in 1967 *SLT (News)* 224 and Meston's reply 1967 *SLT (News)* 247.

(6) Calculating the collated fund

5.12 If a payment to a person entitled to legitim is considered to be a collatable advance, the amount of the advance is (notionally) added to the legitim fund in order to enlarge the amount available to other claimants and reduce the share available to the child who received the advance.

Example

X dies survived by three children A, B and C. The legitim fund on X's death is worth £10,000. A has received a collatable advance of £2,000. All three children claim legitim. B and C call on A to collate the advance so that the notional collated legitim fund is now £12,000. It is divided *per capita* with A's advance then being deducted from his share of the collated fund:

Collation:			
A	**B**	**C**	**Total**
4,000	**4,000**	**4,000**	**12,000**
(2,000)	______	______	**(2,000)**
2,000	**4,000**	**4,000**	**10,000**

The fund to be divided is the fund on death, so that the £10,000 available for satisfying claims for legitim is divided between the three claimants, with the claimant who has received the advance receiving a reduced share of the fund (£2,000). The effect is that the children who have not received a collatable advance are entitled to a greater share of the actual legitim fund available on death.

DISCHARGING LEGAL RIGHTS

5.13 A beneficiary under a will cannot take legal rights as well as a legacy from the estate of the deceased. Instead, they must make an election and choose which to claim. Since legal rights vest in persons entitled to them on the death of the deceased and a right under a will may vest at the same time,[59] it follows that one of them must be discharged.

59 See **Ch 13**.

Discharge of legal rights does not result necessarily in the share of the person discharging accrescing to any of the other claimants and enlarging the total legitim fund. Rather, the discharged share may remain available for the payment of legacies (if the estate is testate) or forms part of the intestate free estate available to those entitled to take it. In most cases, an election to take a legacy will result in the forfeiture of legal rights but, exceptionally, this may not always be the case if the doctrine of equitable compensation applies. In those cases, a person electing to take 'conventional provisions', such as a legacy, remains entitled to legal rights from any moveable estate that is, or becomes, intestate.

(1) Election

5.14 The requirement that a beneficiary who is entitled to claim them must choose between legal rights and conventional provisions is known as the doctrine of approbate and reprobate; that is, to claim both is a contradiction since it would be simultaneously to accept and reject the same instrument. If a will provides for payment of a legacy to a person entitled to legal rights, that person must, therefore, elect which to claim. The question of how a beneficiary under a testament should exercise his or her capacity to elect for legal rights in lieu of a legacy may depend on several factors: for example, whether the beneficiary wishes to accept the intention of the testator; whether a legacy is more valuable; or whether, where it is difficult to value, a cash payment is preferable. Beneficiaries entitled to legal rights should always be advised of their options and given full information on which election to make, since the validity of a discharge may depend on this. Only an express discharge can extinguish a claim for legal rights in any estate which falls into intestacy.

No express discharge of the right to *jus relicti*, *jus relictae*, rights under s 131 of the Civil Partnership Act 2004 or legitim is required where the beneficiary has accepted a legacy or legacies which are clearly of greater value. Although an election may, therefore, be implied from conduct (under the doctrine of homologation), all beneficiaries entitled to claim legal rights should nonetheless be advised of their rights and, in practice, the executor usually obtains a formal discharge from the potential claimant. However, where a person has neither been bequeathed a legacy out of a testate estate nor claimed legal rights, this will not be construed as an implied discharge, provided that the prescriptive period has not elapsed. Further, even where it is quite clear that an election must be made, there is no requirement that it be made within any particular period of time, unless there is evidence that other beneficiaries have an interest in there being an early election.[60]

If a person entitled to claim legal rights dies before making an election, the executors of his or her estate have the right to make an election and to claim legal rights on his or her behalf.[61] If no election has been made before death, the power to elect transmits to the executors since mere delay in making an election does not bar a valid claim, provided that it is made within the prescriptive period.[62] An averment of mora, taciturnity and acquiescence may succeed in barring a claim for legal rights. For example, in *Pringle's Exrs v Pringle*,[63] a widow survived her husband for 10 years without making an election. She had been asked to do so on several occasions and, as part of an action of multiplepoinding, her husband's trustees had consigned the amount of her conventional provisions. The fact that she had made no election and raised no objection to her husband's trustees was construed as acquiescence. A claim may also be barred by a failure to elect if other beneficiaries have suffered financial prejudice as a result.[64]

(2) Capacity to elect

5.15 An election, whether express or implied, may be invalid and therefore reducible if the person making the election has no capacity to make it, inadequate information on which to base the decision has been provided or no independent legal advice has been received.

(a) Children

5.16 The Age of Legal Capacity (Scotland) Act 1991, s 1(1) provides that a person over the age of 16 has legal capacity to enter into any

60 *Watson's Trs v Watson* 1958 SLT 63.

61 *Mill's Trs* 1965 SC 384; and *Campbell's Trs v Campbell's Trs* 1950 SC 48.

62 *Mackenzie v Mackenzie* (1873) 11 M 681

63 *Pringle's Exs v Pringle* (1870) 8 M 622. See also *Neave's JF v Neave's Tr* 1928 SLT 411; and *McMurray v McMurray's Trs* (1852) 14 D 1048.

64 *Robinson v Robinson's Trs* 1934 SLT 183.

transaction, a 'transaction' including any unilateral transaction under s 9 of the 1991 Act. However, in certain circumstances, any such transaction may be set aside under s 3(1) of the 1991 Act:

> 'A person under the age of 21 years … may make application to the court to set aside a transaction which he entered into when he was of or over the age of 16 but under the age of 18 years and which is a prejudicial transaction.'

Under s 3(2) of the 1991 Act a 'prejudicial transaction' is a transaction:

(a) which an adult, exercising reasonable prudence, would not have entered into in the circumstances of the applicant at the time of entering the transaction; and

(b) has caused or is likely to cause substantial prejudice to the applicant.

Accordingly, while persons over the age of 16 have the capacity to elect whether to take their conventional provisions or claim legitim, any such election may be liable to being set aside if prejudicial to their interests.[65] Where the beneficiary is a child, an election made without legal advice may be revoked at any time prior to the right prescribing.[66] The older cases emphasise that the important issue in relation to the validity of an election is whether the child was not only given sufficient information on which to base the decision, but also whether independent legal advice was given. In *Walker v Orr's Trustees*[67] the children of the deceased elected for legitim instead of a legacy. They were shown neither a copy of the will, told the value of the estate nor encouraged to obtain independent legal advice. Thirteen years after electing, they revoked the election and claimed their legacies instead. Since the children had been minors at the time of making the election, the court upheld the revocation. An election made by a child

65 For the purposes of liability to inheritance tax, a provisional election must be made by the executor within two years of the death of the child's parent but if, before reaching the age of 20, the child makes an election different from that of the executor, liability may be recalculated: Inheritance Tax Act 1984, s 147. See J Kessler and W Grant, *Drafting Trusts and Will Trusts in Scotland*, 2nd edn (2018), para 17.9.

66 *Walker v Orr's Trs* 1958 SLT 220. Legal rights prescribe in 20 years: Prescription and Limitation (Scotland) Act 1973, ss 6–7, and Sch 1.

67 *Walker v Orr's Trustees* 1958 SLT 220.

under 16 is, accordingly, void. A person who has parental responsibility for a child under the age of 16 can make an election on his or her behalf but, if the election has been prejudicial to the child's interests, the child can sue the person who made the election once he or she reaches the age of 16.

(b) Adults

5.17 Prior to the Succession (Scotland) Act 1964, parents could discharge the right of any of their prospective children by ante-nuptial contract. Under s 12 of the 1964 Act, such a discharge is ineffective 'unless such child or issue shall elect to accept in lieu of legitim the provision made in his favour under the contract' where the contract post-dates the coming into force of the 1964 Act. Spouses or civil partners may contract to exclude each other from claiming legal rights but cannot exclude their children or remoter issue. All potential claimants to legal rights must, therefore, consent personally to their discharge.

Where the person making the election is an adult, an election may also be revoked. In *Dawson's Trustees v Dawson*[68] a widow's revocation of her previous election was upheld where it was shown that she had been under a false impression as to the relative value of her legal rights and her testamentary provisions. It was undoubtedly significant in this case, however, that 'nothing [had] followed on her election which might not easily be undone, so as to restore all parties to the same situation as if no benefit had been accepted under the will'.[69] Similarly, in *Stewart v Bruce's Trustees*,[70] an election by a widow who had been unduly pressed to make an election, with inadequate information as to their value and without legal advice was reduced. An absence of independent advice that would have enabled the claimant to make a fully informed decision is also likely to mean that a revocation will be upheld.

Where an election is implied from conduct, the test of a binding election is whether or not it is injurious to the financial interests of the person electing, a test applied quite independently of whether or not that person

68 (1896) 23 R 1006.

69 ibid, per Lord Kinnear at 1008.

70 (1898) 25 R 965.

has received full information or independent advice.[71] Even where advice has been given, a revocation of an election may be valid if the information has been inadequate or the time of the election is considered to have been premature.[72]

(c) Adults with incapacity

5.18 Where a person suffers a mental incapacity, the court may make the decision to discharge entitlement to legal rights on that person's behalf under the Adults with Incapacity (Scotland) Act 2000, s 53. In *M, Applicant*[73] a widower suffering from Alzheimer's Disease was unable to make an election to discharge his entitlement to *jus relicti*. His three adult children, under a power of attorney, applied to the court to make an intervention order discharging the claim on his behalf. The court held that, notwithstanding the benefit to the applicants, the crucial test in making an order is whether there would be a benefit to the adult. In this case, he had no need of the money from his deceased wife's estate and it had been his express wish when he had capacity, as well as that of his wife, that her estate should pass directly to their children. In the circumstances, the court held that it was appropriate to authorise the applicants to execute a renunciation of their father's claim to legal rights. There has been discussion of whether it is appropriate for the 2000 Act to be utilised in such a manner, though the decision in *M* has proved influential elsewhere.[74]

(3) Revocation of an election

5.19 An election to renounce entitlement to legal rights may be made provisionally. The person entitled may elect to accept testamentary provisions but reserve the right to claim legal rights at a later stage.[75] Although the power to elect transmits to the executors of an entitled person

71 *Donaldson v Tainsh's Trs* (1886) 13 R 967.
72 *Stewart v Bruce's Trs* (1898) 25 R 965.
73 2007 SLT (Sh Ct) 24.
74 See A Barr, 'The Will To Make A Will' in A Steven et al (eds), *Nothing So Practical As A Good Theory: Festschrift for George Gretton* (2017).
75 *Watson's Trustees v Watson* 1910 SC 975.

who has died before making it, the power to revoke an election which has been made by an entitled person does not.[76] Accordingly, in *Harvie's Executors v Harvie's Trustees,*[77] the executors of a widow who had died before receiving independent information or advice sought declarator that no election had been made by her. Her solicitor had informed her that an election had to be made and he arranged to have the executry accounts made available to help her make the decision. She continued to live on the farm that had been bequeathed to her by her husband but died before the accounts became available. Her executors raised an action of declarator that she had not renounced her right to *jus relictae*, on the ground that a course of actings do not amount to an election unless in full knowledge of the relative values of legal rights as against the conventional provision. The court held that there was no absolute rule that a widow must have independent legal advice before making a binding election and since there was no evidence that the lack of independent advice had been injurious to her pecuniary interests, it could not hold that no election had been made.

TIMING AND THE EFFECT OF DISCHARGE

(1) Pre-death discharges

5.20 If a person entitled to claim legal rights renounces expressly his or her right prior to the death of the person from whose estate it could have been claimed, the right does not vest in the potential claimant's patrimony at the death of the deceased. In consequence, the distribution of the estate is, at least potentially, altered.

The effect of a pre-death renunciation is the same as that of predecease, in that the renouncer is treated as having died when calculating the shares available to those who have not discharged their entitlement. The difference from predecease, however, is that renunciation by an entitled person precludes the possibility of representation by their children. In *Hog v Hog*[78] the testator was predeceased by his wife and survived by six children, five of whom had given lifetime discharges of their claims to legitim. The question arose as to whether the one child who had not

76 *Edward v Cheyne* (1888) 15 R 33.

77 *Harvie's Exrs v Harvie's Trs* 1981 SLT (Notes) 126.

78 *Hog v Hog* (1791) Mor 8193.

renounced her right was entitled to half the moveable estate, with the shares the other five would have had accrescing to her by virtue of their discharges. The court held that:[79]

> 'The effect of renunciation of legitim is … the same as that of the death of the renouncer; so that if the children renounce, the whole goods in communion become the dead's part, or fall also under the *ius relictae*; and if only some of the children be thus forisfamiliated, the whole legitim may be drawn by such as remain *in familia*. In the same manner, when a wife renounces her *ius relictae*, this, instead of increasing solely the powers of the husband, renders the subject of it liable to the legal division between father and children.'

Thus, where any claimant (whether to legitim or *jus relicti*, *jus relictae* or rights under s 131) discharges his or her claim to legal rights before the testator's death, the share or shares will accresce to those who elect to claim.[80]

Example

X has four children, one of whom renounces her right to legitim during X's life. When X dies, the legitim fund is divided between the three children who have not renounced their claims.

If the right to *jus relicti*, *jus relictae* or a right under s 131 is renounced by a surviving spouse or civil partner prior to the death of the deceased, and the deceased is survived by children, the moveable estate will be divided into two parts, the legitim fund and the dead's part, as if the renouncing spouse or civil partner had not survived the deceased.

Example

X is survived by her husband A and four children. A renounces his right to *jus relicti* during X's life. When X dies, A is treated as having predeceased X and the moveable estate is divided into two parts, the legitim and the dead's part. The four children receive half the moveable estate between them *per capita*.

79 *Hog v Hog* (1791) Mor 8193.
80 See also *Panmure v Crokat* (1856) 18 D 703.

The effect is, clearly, the same if all potential claimants to legitim discharge their claims.[81]

Example

X dies survived by his wife A, and two children B and C. The children renounce their claims to legitim prior to X's death. When X dies, B and C are treated as having predeceased X and the moveable estate is divided into two parts, *jus relictae* and the dead's part. A receives half the moveable estate under her *jus relictae*.

(2) Post-death discharge

5.21 Where a person entitled to legal rights renounces his or her claim after the death of the deceased, the discharge will not be effective in enlarging the share of the moveable estate available to any other claimants to it. Instead, it will fall to the residue (in testate succession) or the intestate free estate (in intestate succession).[82] The rationale for that rule is that legal rights vest *a morte*; that is, on the death of the deceased. Unlike a discharge made during the life of the deceased, a renunciation by an entitled person after the death of the deceased amounts to the renouncing of a right which the entitled person has already acquired. The same right cannot vest twice; the rights of those who have not renounced their claims have vested on death, and it is, accordingly, impossible that the share of the person who has renounced can enlarge the share of those who have not.[83]

Example

X dies survived by a spouse A and three children B, C and D. After X's death, A claims his relict right whilst B discharges her claim to legitim by electing to claim a legacy given to her under X's will. The legitim fund is valued at £12,000.

81 See *Campbell's Trs v Campbell* (1862) 24 D 1321.
82 See paras **6.34–6.43** and para **10.7**.
83 *Fisher v Dixon* (1840) 2 D 1121, (1843) 2 Bell's App 63.

B's (discharged) share of the legitim (£4,000) does not accresce to the other children, C and D. The legitim is still divided into three *per capita*, with C and D receiving £4,000 each. The final one-third share of the legitim (£4,000) renounced by B falls to the residue of the estate.

ELECTION AND PARTIAL INTESTACY

5.22 While the doctrine of approbate and reprobate prevents a surviving spouse, civil partner or child from claiming legal rights in addition to a legacy in testate succession, it does not preclude a claim for legal rights out of any part of the estate which is intestate.[84] This holds true, however, only where an express discharge does not discharge legal rights entirely, or discharges legal rights from the testate estate only.

In *Petrie's Trustees v Mander's Trustees*,[85] the testator had bequeathed a legacy of the residue of his estate to his widow in liferent and his children in fee. The deed contained a provision that the legacies were in full satisfaction of legal rights. The widow elected to claim the legacy and she executed a formal acceptance of it, reserving her right and the right of her executors to *jus relictae* if any of the estate fell into intestacy. The testator's children had already predeceased him, and the fee consequently had fallen into intestacy at the date of the deed. The court held that the reservation of the right in intestacy was effective and that the claim for *jus relictae* from the intestate estate passed to the widow's executors.

FORFEITURE AND EQUITABLE COMPENSATION

5.23 The doctrine of approbate and reprobate that prevents someone from accepting and rejecting the same document requires that a beneficiary entitled to both legal rights and to testamentary provisions must elect which of them to claim. If he or she accepts payment of the testamentary provision, entitlement to legal rights is discharged unless expressly reserved.

84 *Naismith v Boyes* (1899) 1 F (HL) 79.
85 *Petrie's Trs v Mander's Trs* 1954 SC 430.

This position, however, is absolute only in relation to wills made after the coming into force of the Succession (Scotland) Act 1964 on 10 September 1964. Prior to this date, there was an exception to the general rule against approbate and reprobate. A legatee under a will could, at common law, claim legal rights without necessarily forfeiting his or her legacy. The principles of equitable compensation were applied, whereby compensation could be due to other legatees disadvantaged by a claim for legal rights being paid out of the estate and the value of their legacies restored. However, not only could the value of the original gift to a disadvantaged legatee be restored; the doctrine also permitted payment to the claimant for legal rights of any surplus capital that remained after compensation to the legatees had been made. A claimant to legal rights could, therefore, be entitled to the portion of the estate remaining after payment of compensation to legatees *in addition* to the payment of legal rights.

The usual means of achieving restoration of the original legacy or legacies was to invest and accumulate income from the capital value of the estate; hence the doctrine usually applied only when the subject of the legacy forfeited was a right to income. The person electing to take legal rights and, therefore, a cash lump sum, instead of the legacy was paid their legal rights, and then the income, the subject of the legacy, was accumulated in order to build up funds with which to compensate legatees who have been disadvantaged.

This issue was particularly complex in the case of an improper liferent. An improper liferent is a tripartite relationship involving trustee, liferenter and fiar.[86] The trustee, such as an executor, will hold ownership of the property or fund and ordinarily makes decisions on investments and management of the same. The liferenter is then entitled to the income, or fruit, of the invested fund or property. The fiar, the person intended to inherit the property or fund, holds a right to demand payment upon satisfaction of the liferent (which ordinarily terminates on the death of the liferenter).

If the claimant of legal rights was bequeathed a right of liferent, a problem arose that the renunciation of the liferent did not normally accelerate vesting of the fee in the fiar, and therefore payment of the fund, if payment

86 For further analysis, see G Gretton and A Steven, *Property, Trusts and Succession,* 5th edn (2024), para 23.14.

of the fee was expressly postponed to the date of payment, such as the death of the liferenter.[87] As a consequence, there was no one entitled to the income from the property.[88] This so-called 'shadow liferent'[89] continued to accumulate income for the duration of the liferent and once the fund had accumulated sufficiently to compensate the legatees, the income once again became available to the liferenter who had claimed legal rights under the doctrine of equitable compensation.

For example, in *Macfarlane's Trustees v Oliver*[90] a testator granted alimentary liferents of the residue of his estate for the benefit of his children, A and B. There was no clause declaring that the legacies were in full satisfaction of legitim or expressly excluding a claim for legitim. On the testator's death, B elected to claim legitim. The testator's trustees accumulated the income of half of the residue until they had restored to the estate the amount withdrawn to pay legitim to B in order to compensate A for the loss of income which had resulted from B's claim. After restitution to A, there was a competition for the remaining half of the income from the residue. The court held that complete compensation to those who had suffered by the payment of the legitim was all that was necessary both in terms of the will and equitable considerations. B was therefore entitled to the income of the share of the residue that the testator had given for the remainder of her life.

(1) Section 13 of the 1964 Act

5.24 The Mackintosh Report recommended abolition of the doctrine of equitable compensation due to its complications[91] but instead, s 13 of the Succession (Scotland) 1964 Act was enacted. Its effect was not to

87 However, in a simple improper liferent 'to A in liferent and B in fee', then B would become the fiar in principle from death, *Carleton v Thomson* (1867) 5 M (HL) 151, though payment of the funds would have to await the extinction of the liferent.

88 *Muirhead v Muirhead* (1890) 17 R (HL) 45.

89 See G Gretton 'Vesting, Equitable Compensation and the Mysteries of the Shadow Liferent' 1988 *SLT (News)* 149.

90 (1882) 9 R 1138.

91 *Law of Succession in Scotland: Report of the Committee of Inquiry* (Cmd 8144, 1951) para 19.

abolish equitable compensation but to introduce the presumption that a final satisfaction clause will be implied into every will unless a contrary provision is expressly included:

> 'Every testamentary disposition executed after the commencement of this Act by which provision is made in favour of the spouse or any issue of the testator and which does not contain a declaration that the provision so made is in full and final satisfaction of the right to any share in the testator's estate to which the spouse or the issue, as the case may be, is entitled by virtue of *ius relicti, ius relictae* or legitim, shall (unless the disposition contains a provision to the contrary) have effect as if it contained such a declaration.'[92]

Thus, under s 13, a beneficiary cannot claim a share of a testator's estate and, at the same time, claim legal rights. Prior to the introduction of s 13, a testator may or may not have included a clause stating expressly either that acceptance of a legacy was in full and final satisfaction of a claim for legal rights or that a claim for legal rights would result in forfeiture of a legacy. The insertion of the clause was entirely at the discretion of the testator and an election, in the absence of such a clause, was not mandatory.

In certain circumstances, the doctrine of equitable compensation still applies. The old law may still arise in wills executed before 10 September 1964[93] and while the effect of s 13 of the 1964 Act and s 131(4) of the Civil Partnership Act 2004 is to require an election between legal rights and conventional provisions, it does not necessarily preclude equitable compensation being made to those beneficiaries who have been disadvantaged in post-1964 deeds by a claim for legal rights.

Additionally, although the effect of s 13 of the 1964 Act is that a binding election must always be made between legal rights and conventional provisions or a legacy, a person who claims a legacy remains entitled to also claim legal rights in relation to any portion of the estate which is or becomes intestate.[94]

92 The Civil Partnership Act, s 131(4) replicates the provision in relation to civil partners.
93 See further J Murray, 'Some of the problems of equitable compensation' 1995 *SLT (News)* 59.
94 *Naismith v Boyes* (1899) 1 F (HL) 79.

(2) Equitable compensation post-1964

5.25 Though there is now statutory provision limiting the occurrence of shadow liferents, discussed below, the case of *Munro's Trustees v Munro*[95] serves as an illustration of how a claim for equitable compensation may have arisen. The testatrix had provided a liferent to her husband for her residue of the estate. The fee of three-fifths of the residue was to pass to her son, and a fee of two-fifths was to pass to her daughter, whom failing the children's own issue were entitled to the fee instead.

The son, the daughter and the husband, claimed legal rights in place of accepting these legacies. The testator had included an express clause of satisfaction. Lord Fraser noted that the claim of legal rights had the effect that the spouse and children 'have finally and completely forfeited their conventional provisions under the settlement'.[96] However, as termination of the liferent was dependent on the spouse's death, the court held that this did not necessarily preclude compensation being paid to other beneficiaries who were adversely affected by a claim for legal rights. In particular, the son's claim for legitim did not carry with it forfeiture by his issue, since their right was not dependent on his and compensation could still be made to them.[97] As such, the court held that equitable compensation to the issue of the children should be possible and that:[98]

> 'In my opinion the appropriate method of making equitable compensation, in the circumstances of the present case, is for the trustees to accumulate the income of the remaining one-third of residue until the death of [the spouse], or until accumulation becomes illegal, or until provision has been made for full equitable compensation, whichever of these events occurs first...The trustees should hold the accumulations along with the remaining one-third of residue and divide the whole fund between [the children's issue], in the event of the conditional institution in their favour taking effect, in the proportions of two-fifths and three-fifths respectively.'

Thus, despite s 13 of the 1964 Act, it may well still be possible for equitable compensation to apply. However, the question of how, exactly,

95 *Munro's Trs v Munro* 1971 SC 280.

96 1971 SC 280, at 288.

97 See now s 8 of the Succession (Scotland) Act 2016 and whether the result in *Munro's Trs* would be the same in present times.

98 1971 SC 280, at 290–91.

the doctrine is or can be applied in any given case remains obscure. There is no general formula that can be applied; rather, it is applied as 'may be most reasonable in the circumstances of each case'.[99]

Application of equitable compensation is largely limited by the removal of shadow liferents by the Succession (Scotland) Act 2016.[100] If a legacy of an improper liferent is renounced, such as by a claimant of legal rights, then s 7 of the 2016 Act provides that the fee is to vest in the fiar at that point unless the deed provides otherwise. Thus, there cannot be an implied 'shadow liferent' to accumulate income for payment to legatees when a claimant elects to claim legal rights after 1 November 2016, unless the testator expressly provided otherwise.

(3) What is left of equitable compensation?

5.26 As result of s 7 of the 2016 Act, the main area in which equitable compensation historically applied is now limited. However, the wider doctrine remains unrepealed. The necessary question is when can equitable compensation apply outwith liferents, annuities or payments of income? The Scottish Government has asked this question in determining whether repeal of the doctrine entirely is required.[101] Ultimately the Scottish Government concluded:[102]

> 'In light of the fact that whatever mischief arose from the continued existence of the doctrine has now been largely removed we do not intend to legislate in this area.'

One might be quick to think that with the removal of shadow liferents by the 2016 Act, then the entire doctrine of equitable compensation is banished into history. However, Professor George Gretton provides one interesting example:[103]

99 *Rose's Trs v Rose* 1916 SC 827, per Lord Johnson at 849.

100 Scottish Law Commission, Report on *Succession* (SLC Report No 124, 1990), paras 3.45ff, and Report on *Succession* (SLC Report No 215, 2009), paras 6.44ff.

101 Consultation *on the Law of Succession* (February 2019).

102 Consultation *on the Law of Succession* (February 2019), para 4.2.5.

103 G Gretton, 'Vesting, equitable compensation and the mysteries of the shadow liferent' 1988 *SLT (News)* 149, 151.

'A testator's estate is £30,000 heritage and £90,000 moveables. He leaves one child and no widow. The will leaves the heritage to the child and the moveables to a cousin, The son claims legal rights (£45,000). Does this mean that the cousin gets only the balance of the moveables while the child takes the heritage as the heir in intestacy? Such a result seems very odd: one would have thought that the heritage falling into intestacy would be used as a fund wherewith to make equitable compensation to the cousin.'

There may be a role for a rule akin to equitable compensation in such cases as Gretton's example above.[104] Equitable compensation is an area which would benefit from further research and study.

DEFEATING LEGAL RIGHTS

5.27 Although legal rights arise automatically by operation of law in persons entitled to claim them, there are, nonetheless, various means by which a potential claim for legal rights may be defeated. If a testator wishes to exclude a spouse, civil partner or child from taking a share of his or her estate, certain steps, made before death, can make this possible.

First, it follows from the fact that legal rights are exigible from the moveable estate that it is only if the estate includes moveable property can a claim arise. If all the deceased's moveable property has been sold, given away or made the subject of an *inter vivos* donation prior to death, any claims for legal rights will be defeated. Such transfers do not constitute a fraudulent frustration of legal rights;[105] even where the donor has reserved a liferent for themselves.[106] The fact that the moveable property is the subject of an *inter vivos* donation which is revocable is also irrelevant; the determining fact is whether the donation has actually been revoked[107]

104 Consider for example the outcome in *Kerr, Petitioner* 1968 SLT (Sh Ct) 61 and whether some form of equitable compensation should have been available to the disadvantaged child by the wife's renunciation of the legacy of the entire estate. There is something to be said for some form of discretionary power of a court to prevent unjust outcomes for a beneficiary of an estate, whether under the doctrine of equitable compensation, or otherwise.

105 *Allan v Stark* (1901) 8 SLT 468.

106 *Agnew v Agnew* (1775) Mor 8210.

107 *Hutton's Trs v Hutton's Trs* 1916 SC 860.

since if a gift has not been delivered or a gift has in fact been revoked, the deed in which the gift is made will be ineffective. The gift must have been an actual gift and simply writing an IOU to the donee without conveyance or delivery is ineffective in transferring ownership of the property out of the donor's patrimony.[108]

Legal rights may also be defeated because the testator has invested his or her moveable property in the purchase of heritage, although this option is not necessarily a practicable one. Directions to trustees to buy heritage after the testator's death (and therefore to convert moveable estate to heritable estate) do not exclude a claim to legal rights[109] since legal rights vest immediately on the testator's death. The deceased may, however, defeat legal rights by means of will substitutes disposing of all or most of his or her moveable property on death. He or she may nominate a beneficiary to take the proceeds of a life insurance policy or pension and these will be payable directly to the person nominated rather than forming part of the executry estate.[110] Such benefits can form a very significant part of deceased's assets but a nomination will, in many cases, have been made in favour of a spouse, civil partner or children. There may be nominations to categories of beneficiary other than a spouse, civil partner or children but, again, the question of whether legal rights will be excluded or not will depend on their terms.

Lastly, if the deceased wished a spouse or civil partner to succeed to his or her whole estate to the exclusion of any children, he or she could achieve this simply by dying intestate, providing that the value of his or her estate is no greater that the aggregate value of the prior rights available to surviving spouses and civil partners on intestacy. In this case, a claim for prior rights would exhaust the estate and thus exclude any claims for legitim. If the estate were of an appropriate size, the same objective could be achieved by a testator bequeathing his or her entire estate to a spouse or civil partner, the spouse or civil partner renouncing the legacy so that the estate becomes artificially intestate, and then claiming prior rights in order to exhaust the estate and defeat claims for legitim.[111]

108 See further S Macdonald-Mulvihill, *Scots Law of Donation,* thesis, University of Edinburgh (2024), paras 2.16–2.20.

109 *Lashley v Hog* (1804) 4 Pat 581. See also para **4.12**.

110 See paras **7.18ff**.

111 *Kerr, Petr* 1968 SLT (Sh Ct) 61. See also para **6.46.**

VALUING CLAIMS FOR LEGAL RIGHTS

5.28 The value of the property which comprises the moveable estate is clearly a question of particular importance in relation to claims to legal rights. In order to make an informed election between a legacy and a claim for legal rights, the beneficiary should know their relative values. It is also of importance in relation to taxation, and it is in the process of completing an inventory of the estate, required for these purposes, that a valuation of the total estate – and, in consequence, the moveable estate – will be obtained.[112]

Taxation is not dealt with in this book since it is a specialist matter outwith its scope but, briefly, for the purposes of valuing a claim to legal rights, the general rule is that the value of the property is that which obtains at the date of death; this will normally be the same value as the moveable estate entered on the inventory (and thus the value that will be taxed upon). Yet, the inventoried value may only be an estimate alone,[113] and indeed the executor may not include all items in the inventory.[114] A claimant need not accept this notional inventoried value as the value of the claim but may insist on waiting until the property is realised (if such is to happen) before accepting a valuation and electing whether to claim.[115]

It is the actual, realised value which represents the value of the moveable estate and a share of that value to which a claimant is entitled[116] and this is the case whether the realised value is higher or lower than the estimated

112 For the purposes of calculating liability to inheritance tax, the inventory to which the executor confirms includes the whole of the deceased's estate (heritable and moveable) including any property which the deceased had either a beneficial interest or a power of disposal before his or her death: Inheritance Tax Act 1984, ss 5 and 49(1). The value is the price which the property might reasonably be expected to have fetched if sold on the open market immediately prior to death: ss 4(1) and 160 of the 1984 Act.

113 *Harley v Harley's Executrix* 2022 SCLR 263.

114 *Smith v Carnegie* [2020] SC Liv 26, though as a matter of executry law partial confirmations should not be possible under s 3 of the Confirmation of Executors (Scotland) Act 1823 as the executor must make a declaration as to that effect and if other property is discovered then an eik must be lodged. See **Ch 3**.

115 *Watson's Trs v Watson* 1910 SC 975; and *Mackenzie v Mackenzie's Trs* (1873) 11 M 681.

116 *Alexander v Alexander's Trs* 1954 SC 436.

value.[117] Where the property is to be realised, the executor is under a duty to realise it without undue delay.[118]

Where the deceased was domiciled in Scotland, the moveable estate includes any moveable property situated abroad.[119] Interest on claims runs from the date of death[120] and is payable at a rate determined as reasonable by the court in all the circumstances, although the same rate as prescribed for payments of prior rights (7%) is often applied.[121] Interest will not normally be payable where there has been an undue delay in making the claim.[122] Legal rights prescribe after 20 years under the Prescription and Limitation (Scotland) Act 1973 with the prescriptive period running from the date of death.[123]

ALIMENT

(1) The obligation of aliment

5.29 The right to aliment from the deceased's estate has nothing to do with succession law as such but relates solely to the continuing right of certain dependants of the deceased to be maintained by him or her, on either a temporary or permanent basis. The right to aliment is a right which certain relatives may have – at least, in theory – in addition to rights of succession and legal rights, although claims for aliment on death are made rarely. Under the law prior to the coming into force of the Succession (Scotland) Act 1964, the right to aliment was a corrective to the fact that widows and younger children could be considerably worse off financially on the death of the husband and father than they were during his life. The obligation to aliment arises at common law, and the Family Law (Scotland)

117 *Milne v Milne's Trs* 1931 SLT 336; and *Warrack v Warrack's Trs* 1934 SLT 301.

118 *Gilchrist v Gilchrist's Trs* (1889) 16 R 1118; *Russel v A-G* 1917 SC 28, 1916 2 SLT 207.

119 See further E Crawford and J Carruthers, *International Private Law: A Scots Perspective,* 4th edn (2015), Ch 18.

120 *Gilchrist v Gilchrist's Trustees* (1889) 16 R 1118; *Russel v Lord Advocate* 1917 SC 28; *Sanderson v Lockhart-Mure* 1946 SC 198; and *Kearon v Thomson's Trs* 1949 SC 287.

121 Interest on Prior Rights (Scotland) Order 1981 SI 1981/805, Art 2.

122 *Wick v Wick* (1898) 1 F 199; *Young v Young* 1965 SLT (Notes) 95, OH.

123 1973 Act, ss 6–7, and Sch 1.

Act 1985 defines what it is and to whom it is owed. Section 1(2) defines what as:

> 'An obligation to provide such support as is reasonable in the circumstances, having regard to the matters to which a court is required or entitled to have regard under section 4 of this Act in determining the amount of aliment to award in an action for aliment.'

Section 1(1) of the 1985 Act provides that aliment is owed by spouses and civil partners to each other, by a father or mother to his or her child and by a person to a child who has been accepted by him or her as a child of his or her family. A 'child' is defined in s 1(5) of the 1985 Act as a person under the age of 18 or a person under the age of 25 who is undergoing 'instruction at an educational establishment, or training for employment or for a trade, profession or vocation'.

Section 1(4) makes clear that the obligation of aliment may subsist after the person who owes it has died. It provides that:

> 'Nothing in this section shall affect … any rule of law by which a person who is owed an obligation of aliment may claim aliment from the executor of a deceased person or from any person enriched by the succession to the estate of a deceased person.'

Section 1(4) of the 1985 Act preserves the rule at common law that a person who is owed an obligation of aliment may claim it from the executor of the deceased or from any person enriched by the succession to the estate of a deceased person.

Under s 4(1), the amount of any aliment awarded will depend on the needs and resources of the parties, the earning capacities of the parties; and all the circumstances of the case. Under s 4(2), where two or more parties owe an obligation of aliment to another person, there shall be no order of liability, but the court, in deciding how much, if any, aliment to award against any of those persons, shall have regard, among the other circumstances of the case, to the obligation of aliment owed by any other person. This highlights the reasons why aliment on death is uncommon. First, surviving spouses and civil partners are likely to be provided for by the deceased's will or entitled to legal rights or entitled to prior rights on intestacy;[124] second, in

124 See *Russell v Wood's Trs* 1987 SLT 503 at 506 where Lord Cullen held that having regard to a child's potential claim to legal rights, it was not appropriate to grant decree for payment of aliment.

relation to children, it is unlikely to be due because a second person also owes an obligation of aliment to them, most likely the surviving parent or step-parent. Under s 4(3), one of the circumstances that may be taken into account in deciding whether or in what amount aliment is due is whether the person from whom it is being claimed is giving support, whether financial or otherwise, to anyone else as a dependant in his or her household, regardless of whether or not an obligation of aliments is due to them.[125]

(2) Temporary aliment

5.30 If the deceased had owed the obligation of aliment to an eligible person or persons, it may be that temporary aliment may be payable by the deceased's executor. The maximum period during which aliment may be payable by the executor will be from the date of death until any legacies to which the claimant is entitled or claims on intestacy or legal rights become payable. This is usually after at least six months have elapsed, in order for claims by creditors of the deceased to be received by the executor.

Aliment ranks as an ordinary debt, and any payments by way of temporary aliment must be deducted from the gross value of the estate in order to calculate the net value available for distribution to beneficiaries, heirs in intestacy or in satisfaction of claims for legal rights. Claims for payment of aliment do not, however, have a preference over the rights of ordinary creditors and are not payable if the estate is manifestly insolvent[126] but if the executor does make payments of aliment and the estate later turns out to be insolvent, he or she will not be liable.[127] If payment of arrears

125 The right to aliment on death in relation to surviving spouses is also preserved expressly in the Succession (Scotland) Act 1964, s 37(1)(c). On the face of things, it seems anomalous that only the right of a surviving spouse is referred to when aliment may be payable to children as well (*Beaton v Beaton's Trs* 1935 SC 187) and, unlike other provisions of the 1964 Act, s 37(1)(c) has not been amended by the Civil Partnership Act 2004 so as to apply it to civil partners as well as spouses. However, the provisions of s 37(1)(c) seem unnecessary in light of the provisions of the Family Law (Scotland) Act 1985 s 1(4) which preserves the right to aliment and which has been amended by the 2004 Act.

126 *Lindsay's Creditors v His Relict* (1714) Mor 11847; and *Buchanan v Ferrier* (1822) 1 S 323; but *cf Barlass v Barlass's Trs* 1916 SC 741 at 748.

127 *Barlass v Barlass's Trs* 1916 SC 741; and *MacCullum v MacLean* 1923 SLT (Sh Ct) 117.

of aliment is due by a deceased person who had been sequestrated before his or her death and the arrears arose prior to the date of sequestration, these are not payable unless the amount had been quantified by a court decree or was the subject of a binding obligation which could be proved by writing.[128] A payment of aliment is not a payment to account which falls to be deducted from any legacies payable to the claimant at a later date but is payable pending payment of any such legacies.[129]

The Scottish Law Commission has concluded that temporary aliment should be abolished.[130] However, on consultation in 2015, a large body of respondents (39%) still maintained that it should be retained. As such, the Scottish Government formed the view that 'on the basis that the right has some practical utility it would not be abolished'.[131] The latest position appears to be that temporary aliment will be retained, though a new time limit will be introduced for such claims.[132]

(3) Aliment de iure representationis

(a) Persons entitled to claim

5.31 A claim for aliment *de iure representationis* is a claim at common law against either trustees under a continuing trust[133] or the beneficiaries of the deceased's estate to the extent that they are enriched by the succession. It is a continuing obligation which may arise if certain persons to whom the deceased owed an obligation of aliment during life do not receive a

128 Bankruptcy (Scotland) Act 2016, Sch 2, para 2.

129 *Breadalbane's Trs v Breadalbane* (1843) 15 SJ 389; *Baroness de Blonay v Oswald's Reps* (1863) 1 M 1147; and *McIntyre v McIntyre's Trs* (1865) 3 M 1074.

130 Scottish Law Commission, Report on *Succession* (SLC Report No 124, 1990), paras 9.6ff; and Report on *Succession* (SLC Report No 215, 2009), paras 7.36ff.

131 *Scottish Government Response to the Consultation on the Law of Succession* (2018), para 57; and *Law of Succession: Consultation* (2019), para 4.1.

132 *Scottish Government Response to Consultation on the Law of Succession* (2020).

133 Provided that the trustees are liable for the deceased's debts: *Riddell's Trs v Riddell* (1802) Mor App voce Aliment p 5; *Ormiston v Ormiston's Trs* (1838) 11 SJ 232; *Spalding v Spalding's Trs* (1874) 2 R 237; *Baillie's Trs Ptrs* (1896) 33 SLR 589; and *Stevenson v McDonald's Trs* 1923 SLT 451.

fair and reasonable share of the estate or if their share of the estate is insufficient for their support.[134]

If adequate testamentary provision for those to whom the obligation is owed has been made, the obligation does not transmit to the deceased's representatives and, if a claimant has received a reasonable share of the estate but has spent it and become impoverished as a result, his or her claim does not revive.[135]

A claim for aliment *de iure representationis* may be made only by surviving spouses and any children of the deceased and not by surviving civil partners or children accepted by the deceased as a child of the family. Although he or she may have owed the obligation of aliment to children whom he or she had accepted as a child of his or her family and to a civil partner under the Family Law (Scotland) Act 1985, s 1(4) restricts the scope of the obligation *iure representationis* to those to whom the obligation is owed at common law. Since the 1985 Act did not introduce any new representative liability, an obligation to aliment any person during life terminates on the death of the person by whom the obligation was owed. Ancestors and more remote descendants are also excluded, because the deceased did not owe the obligation of aliment to them during his or her life; accordingly, there can be no obligation to transmit to his or her representatives on death.[136]

(b) The nature of the obligation

5.32 Aliment *iure representationis* is not an ordinary debt since it is not one for which the executor is liable. A claim for aliment to be paid over the medium to long term, indeed for any period beyond six months,

134 *Thomson v McCulloch* (1778) Mor 434; *Lowther v McLaine* (1786) Mor 435; *Ferguson v Logan* (1809) *Hume* 5; *Smith v Smith* 11 Mar 1812 FC; *McGregor v Ballantyne* (1818) 6 S 1144; *McConochy v McConochy* (1830) 8 S 604; and *Hobbs v Baird* (1845) 7 D 492.

135 *Strathmore v Strathmore's Trs* (1825) 1 W & S 402; *Stuart v Court* (1848) 10 D 1275; and *Gay's Tutrix v Gay's Tr* 1953 SLT 278.

136 Prior to the Family Law (Scotland) Act 1985, a person had in some circumstances an obligation to aliment grandchildren and parents: see *Younger Children of Seaton v Weir* (1764) Mor 431; *Dalziel v Dalziel* (1768) Mor 450; *Parish Council of Leslie v Gibson's Trs* (1889) 1 F 601; and *Buchanan v Morrison* 21 Jan 1813 FC.

will not, accordingly, delay distribution of the estate;[137] the estate will be distributed to the beneficiaries or trustees and a claim for aliment may be made against them.[138] If the surviving spouse or children claim legal rights, it would seem at first sight that there can be no obligation of aliment *iure representationis*. If, however, the estate comprises very little moveable estate, so that the value of a claim for legal rights cannot be considered a fair and reasonable provision, a claim may arise against the beneficiaries since a claim for legal rights does not bar a claim for aliment *iure representationis*.[139]

The right continues as long as support is needed but lapses if it is discharged.[140] Discharge may be implied if a fair and reasonable share of the estate is received; implied discharge is, therefore, a ground for raising an equitable defence against a claim for aliment. If, however, the estate comprises mainly heritage and, accordingly, is unavailable for legal rights, the right of aliment *iure representationis* may be important. Despite its potential efficacy, modern case law is scarce. The Scottish Law Commission had considered it for abolition.[141] On consultation in 2015, respondents agreed.[142] As such, the Scottish Government has committed to its abolition, unlike temporary aliment which will continue. The date of such reform remains unseen.

137 *Beaton v Beaton's Trs* 1935 SC 187; and *Hutchison v Hutchison's Trs* 1951 SC 108.

138 *Davidson's Trustees v Davidson* 1907 SC 16; *Beaton v Beaton's Trs* 1935 SC 187; and *Hutchison v Hutchison's Trs* 1951 SC 108.

139 *Thomson v Hood* (1898) 6 SLT 258; and *Anderson v Grant* (1899) 1 F 484.

140 Family Law (Scotland) Act 1985, s 5.

141 Scottish Law Commission, Report on *Succession* (SLC Report No 124, 1990), paras 9.4ff; and Report on *Succession* (SLC Report No 215, 2009), paras 7.36ff.

142 *Scottish Government response to the Consultation on the Law of Succession* (2018), para 56.

Part 2:

Intestate succession

Chapter 6

Intestate succession

INTRODUCTION

6.1 If a person dies without disposing of all or any of his or her property by way of a will or testamentary document, he or she dies intestate[1] and as long as any property that belonged to the deceased is undisposed of on death, that property will comprise the intestate estate of the deceased.[2] Intestate succession is regulated by statute, principally by the Succession (Scotland) Act 1964, and the whole of a deceased person's intestate estate will be distributed in accordance with its rules – which this chapter explores.

Intestate succession is by far the most common form of succession in Scotland, with testate succession being the minority. Surveys consistently show that many people in Scotland fail to execute wills or testamentary documents, leading to a distribution of their estate largely by way of intestate succession.[3] The way in which property is distributed under the rules on intestacy is therefore important for a significant proportion of

1 The main form of testamentary disposition or testamentary document is a will, but property may also be transmitted by legal devices having the same or similar effect: see paras **7.18ff**.

2 This includes all property that was *in bonis* of the deceased at the time of his or her death; see **Ch 4**.

3 Empirical data differs but broadly it is accepted that a majority of people in Scotland do not have a will. See National Will Register's *National Wills Report* (2025), available https://www.nationalwillregister.co.uk/app/uploads/2025/09/The-National-Wills-Report-2025.pdf; Brodies LLP, *The Future of Wealth Transfer* report (2025), available https://brodies.com/assets/uploads/files/downloads/yougov-report-web.pdf; and Scottish Legal News, 'Over two-thirds of Scottish adults lack up to date will', Tuesday 3 September 2024, available https://www.scottishlegal.com/articles/over-two-thirds-of-scottish-adults-lack-up-to-date-will. For older government studies see, Scottish Consumer Council, *Wills and Awareness of Inheritance Rights in Scotland* (2006); and Scottish Office Central Research Unit, *Succession Law* (1990).

the population. In framing the rules of intestate succession, it is generally regarded that the law should impute to the deceased such intentions for the transmission of his or her property as he or she would have had if a will had actually been made. However, it has become quite clear that the rules contained in the 1964 Act do not reflect either the assumptions or the preferences of those dying intestate in Scotland in modern times.[4]

THE 1964 ACT

6.2 The current law of intestate succession is contained in the Succession (Scotland) Act 1964.[5] The Act consolidated and amended some of the previous common law and statutory rules but also introduced wholly new concepts to the law of intestate succession. Before the passing of the Act, and as noted in **Chapter 3**, different rules had applied to the heritable and moveable parts of the intestate estate, with the heir-at-law (under the system of primogeniture) taking the heritage and the next-of-kin the moveables.[6] The 1964 Act abolished primogeniture and the preference for males and assimilated heritage and moveables for the purposes of succession to the intestate estate so that persons became entitled to succeed without distinction in terms of their gender and, to the type of property to which they were entitled to succeed.

Whereas at common law spouses had been regarded as 'strangers' to the deceased and only blood relatives could be classed as heirs or kin, one of the major reforms of the 1964 Act was to add spouses to the persons entitled to succeed to the intestate estate. Of greater significance, socially as well as doctrinally, the old rights of terce and courtesy, which gave a surviving widow or widower a right to, respectively, a liferent of one-third or the whole of the heritage owned by the deceased at the time of his or her death, were abolished.

4 See D Reid, 'Why is it so difficult to reform the law of intestate succession?' (2020) 24(1) *Edin LR* 111.

5 On the history of the passage of the 1964 Act, see K Reid, 'Intestate succession in Scotland' in K Reid et al (eds), *Comparative Succession Law: Volume II: Intestate Succession* (2015).

6 On the pre-1964 law see: J McLaren, *The Law of Wills and Succession as Administered in Scotland.* 3rd edn, Vol 1 (1894) Pt II; J Walker, *The Law of Intestate Succession in Scotland* (1927); and K Reid, 'Intestate Succession in Scotland' in K Reid et al (eds), *Comparative Succession Law: Volume II: Intestate Succession* (2015).

In their place, the surviving spouse's 'prior right' to fixed entitlements from the estate was introduced. These rights are 'prior' in that claims to them must be paid before legal rights and before any distribution of the intestate free estate under s 2 of the 1964 Act. Prior rights are not, strictly speaking, rights of succession as such, but are preferential entitlements payable before the intestate estate may be distributed. Following the introduction of civil partnerships, Schedule 28, Part 1, of the Civil Partnership Act 2004 has amended the 1964 Act to allow civil partners to claim prior rights too.

The distinction between heritable and moveable property remains important in relation to the computation of prior rights as will be explored in further detail below. The distinction between heritable and moveable property also remains important in order to calculate the value of claims to legal rights, since these are payable in intestate as well as testate succession, and payable only from the moveable part of the estate.

The rules set out in the Succession (Scotland) Act 1964, Pts I and II, which regulate the distribution of a wholly or partially intestate estate, are relatively straightforward and apply whenever a person has died wholly or partly intestate, by leaving the whole or part of his or her property undisposed of by testamentary disposition. An intestate estate will ordinarily be distributed, *after* payment of debts, in the following order:

(1) Prior rights.

(2) Legal rights.

(3) Intestate free estate.

Where a cohabitant makes a claim under s 29 of the Family Law (Scotland) Act 2006, the rules as to when a cohabitant's award is to be paid out from the estate can result in a very awkward 'sandwiching' of deduction of the value of the award between the computation of the relict's right and legitim if there is also a spouse, civil partner, and issue present in the succession alongside the cohabitant.[7]

It should be noted that the provisions of the 1964 Act do not apply to hereditary titles and coats of arms and these continue to devolve according

7 See below at paras **6.32–6.33**.

to the common law of heritable succession.[8] The rules of the 1964 Act will be explored fully, but it is worth first noting the attempts at reform of the 1964 Act, as this is an omnipresent issue throughout this chapter.

REFORM AND THE 'FRESH APPROACH'

6.3 The law of intestate succession is currently the focus of attempts at reform and, like legal rights,[9] has also been subject to aborted reform. As early as 1990, it had become clear that the 1964 Act was unsatisfactory in many regards, and the Scottish Law Commission embarked on a project to recommend a new set of rules for intestate succession.[10] For the Commission, some of the criticisms of the 1964 Act included:[11]

(1) The system is complex, with different rights and rules at different stages of the transfer. This will be illustrated in this chapter for readers to make their own decision on.

(2) The rules can provide unfair results.

(3) The 1964 Act has not kept pace with changes in society such as cohabitating unmarried couples, blended families, accepted children, and stepchildren.

(4) People are living much longer, leading to many children only inheriting property when they themselves are middle-aged or older.

(5) The most valuable part of most estates is now heritable property, principally the deceased's home, and this trend was not envisaged by the drafters of the 1964 Act.

In 1990, the Commission had proposed a new system to reconcile the different issues at play. When the issue was revisited in 2009, the

8 1964 Act, s 37(1)(a). This is justified on the basis that these, by their nature, must devolve on one person: *Law of Succession in Scotland: Report of the Committee of Inquiry* (Cmd 8144, 1951), para 8.

9 See para **5.3**.

10 Report *on Succession* (SLC report No 124, 1990), Part II.

11 Discussion Paper *on Succession* (SLC DP No 136, 2009), Part 2; Report *on Succession* (SLC Report No 215, 2009), para 1.3.

Commission recommended a simplified system to what was proposed previously.[12] Broadly the 2009 recommendations involved a threshold sum in which the spouse was entitled to the entire estate up to a set figure (£300,000) and any residue above this figure should be divided between the spouse and issue. Where there was no issue, then the spouse would inherit the entire estate, and conversely, where there was no spouse, then the issue would inherit the entire estate. The Commission did not propose that accepted children or stepchildren should be entitled to have a right in succession under the rules of intestate succession.[13] Neither did they wish to give a cohabitant a fixed right in succession, though they did recommend an improved discretionary scheme for a cohabitant to apply to court.[14]

In 2015, on consultation for the proposed implementation of the Commission's 2009 recommendations, responses did not show consensus to the proposed reforms to intestate succession (alongside the proposed reforms to legal rights).[15] Particular issues raised included:

- Whether it was entirely fair that spouses should be afforded preference over the deceased's descendants in inheriting the majority of an intestate estate.
- Where the deceased died within a 'second family', whereby the deceased had remarried to a new spouse who was not the biological parent of the deceased's children, whether it was entirely fair that the new spouse should inherit the majority of an estate to the detriment of the deceased's blood relations, such as children and other descendants.
- The position of unmarried couples and the suitability of s 29 of the 2006 Act as a limited remedy for cohabitants.
- The position of stepchildren and accepted children.

Given the lack of overall support for the Commission's proposals, the Scottish Government committed to 'a fresh approach to reform in this area to determine if it is possible to identify intestacy reform which would

12 Report *on Succession* (SLC Report No 215, 2009), Part 2.

13 See para **2.14**.

14 Report *on Succession* (2009) Part 4.

15 *Scottish Government response to the Consultation on the Law of Succession* (2018).

deliver outcomes which would be more in line with the expectations of modern-day Scots and their families'.[16]

Subsequent consultation was carried out in 2019 involving a comparative exercise looking at other jurisdictions' approaches to intestate succession.[17] Once again no overall consensus could be identified.[18] Owing to this dissensus, there is currently an inertia to reform. The Scottish Government wishes that intestate succession 'should reflect and deliver the outcomes that individuals and their families would expect and on which there should be consensus'.[19] Whether this can be achieved where there are such diverse views on who people consider to be family, and who they should like to inherit from, remains to be seen.

DEFINING INTESTACY AND THE INTESTATE ESTATE

(1) Intestacy

6.4 In slightly muddled wording,[20] the Succession (Scotland) Act 1964, s 36(1) provides that:

> 'An intestate is a person who has died leaving undisposed of by testamentary disposition the whole or any part of his estate, and 'intestate' shall be construed accordingly.'

Thus, any property which belonged to the deceased person ('the intestate') during life that is undisposed of by testamentary disposition or document such as a will, or any device having testamentary effect, will fall into the intestate estate and be distributed according to the provisions of Part I of the 1964 Act. The meaning of a 'testamentary disposition' is defined in s 36(1):

> '"Testamentary disposition" in relation to a deceased, includes any deed taking effect on his death whereby any part of his estate is disposed of or under which a succession thereto arises.'

16 ibid para 27.

17 *Consultation on the Law of Succession* (2019).

18 *Scottish Government Response to the Consultation on the Law of Succession* (2020).

19 *Scottish Government Response to the Consultation on the Law of Succession* (2018), para 23.

20 It is common to refer to an estate as intestate, but it is odd to refer to a person as 'an intestate' in the way the 1964 Act (and older legislation) does. This edition dispenses with that terminology in relevant places.

Property disposed of by devices other than a will or testament will not form part of the deceased's estate and will not, therefore, be available for legal rights[21] or form part of the intestate estate. For example, a special destination inserted into a title to property is not a form of testamentary disposition as such, but it does have testamentary effect. Accordingly, s 36(2)(a) of the Succession (Scotland) Act 1964 provides that if the deceased owned heritable property which was subject to a special destination in favour of another person, the property is not to be treated for the purposes of the 1964 Act as part of the estate of the deceased. If the special destination could be, and in fact was, evacuated, by a testament or otherwise, the property is to be treated as part of the deceased's estate on which he or she has tested.[22]

A testament may dispose of only part of the estate, so that the estate is 'partially intestate'. Whether intestacy is total or partial, s 1(1) provides that the whole of the intestate estate shall devolve, without distinction as between heritable and moveable property, in accordance with the provisions of Part I of the 1964 Act. The terms of s 1(1) are underscored by the definition of an estate in s 36(2). It is:

> 'The whole estate, whether heritable or moveable, or partly heritable and partly moveable, belonging to the deceased at the time of his death or over which he had a power of appointment.'

No category of property, therefore, is exempt from forming part of the intestate estate and may be distributed only in the manner provided in ss 1–7 of the Act.

(2) The intestate estate

6.5 The most confusing aspect of the 1964 Act is that the definition of 'intestate estate' changes according to the context in which it is being referred to. Although the confusion is of little practical significance, it makes it difficult to conceptualise what comprises the intestate estate. Is

21 See **Ch 4**.

22 On special destinations and their evacuation see para **7.22**. The provisions of s 36(2) are a re-statement of the pre-1964 position: see *Connell's Trs v Connell's Trs* (1886) 13 R 1175 and *Hare* (1889) 17 R 105, where destinations to third parties prevented the property forming part of the estate available to the heirs on intestacy.

it the whole estate undisposed of by a will? Or is it only the estate which remains after payment of debts and claims for prior and legal rights?

The interpretation section of the Act provides under s 36(1) that the intestate estate is, in relation to the deceased, simply 'so much of his estate as is undisposed of by testamentary disposition'. It then defines the terms 'net estate' and 'net intestate estate'. They:

> 'Mean respectively so much of an estate or intestate estate as remains after satisfaction of estate duty,[23] and other liabilities of the estate having priority over legal rights, the prior rights of a surviving spouse and rights of succession, or, as the case may be the proportion thereof properly attributable to the intestate estate.'[24]

Under s 36(1), therefore, the net intestate estate is the estate remaining after payment of debts to the deceased's creditors[25] but before deduction of any claims for prior and legal rights.

Part I of the Act deals with rights in succession to the intestate estate. They are rights independent of the entitlements conferred on surviving spouses and civil partners as prior rights, and rights which surviving spouses, civil partners and children are entitled to as legal rights. This is emphasised by s 1(2) which provides that 'nothing in this Part of the Act shall affect legal rights or the prior rights of a surviving spouse or civil partner', with the result that rights to the intestate estate that arise under Part I are rights to the intestate estate that remains after claims for prior and legal rights have been satisfied, and not the totality of the estate falling into intestacy on death after deduction of any debts of the deceased.

Thus, the provisions in Part I come into effect only after the satisfaction of any claims to entitlements for prior and legal rights set out in Part II. If the intestate estate were not defined as being the estate remaining after payment of prior and legal rights provided for in Part II, then the prior relatives listed in s 2 of the 1964 Act would be entitled to every part of the estate undisposed of by testamentary disposition and prior and legal rights would, effectively, be defeated. If, however, the deceased is survived by neither a spouse or civil partner or by children, so that no claims for prior

23 Today, inheritance tax.

24 This part of s 36 has not been amended by the Civil Partnership Act 2004 but in defining prior rights, s 36 refers to them as the rights conferred under ss 8–9 on a surviving spouse or civil partner.

25 See paras **4.28ff**.

or legal rights arise, the intestate estate is simply that estate which is available to relatives as rights in succession to the intestate estate under s 2. If any property which belonged to the deceased person during life is undisposed of by any form of testamentary disposition or device having testamentary effect, it will fall into the intestate estate and be distributed according to the provisions of Part I of the 1964 Act.

The net intestate estate has a different meaning in relation to the right of cohabitants under the Family Law (Scotland) Act 2006 to claim a discretionary share in the intestate estate of a deceased cohabitant. Under s 29(2), any order for payment to the surviving cohabitant is to be made out of the net intestate estate. Section 29(10) of the 2006 Act defines the net intestate estate as:

> 'So much of the intestate estate as remains after provision for the satisfaction of inheritance tax, debts and the legal rights and prior rights of any surviving spouse or surviving civil partner.'

No reference is made to the deduction of the legal rights of children, with the result that the intestate estate available for a claim by a cohabitant is the estate remaining after deduction of any claims for prior rights and legal rights of a surviving spouse or civil partner but before satisfaction of any claims for legitim.

Terminological confusion also arises because, in computing claims for legal rights, the portion of the moveable estate traditionally known as 'the dead's part' over which the deceased had total freedom of testation forms all or part of the free estate in intestate succession. The term 'free estate' is not used in the 1964 Act but is used to describe the remaining estate after claims for prior and legal rights have been satisfied.[26] Clearly, since the deceased has not tested at all, there can be no dead's part in intestate succession; thus, the one third or one half of the moveable estate remaining after satisfaction of legal rights that would fall into the dead's part in testate succession to pay legacies is allocated to the free estate in intestate succession. The 'intestate free estate' will therefore comprise (i) this remaining share of the moveable estate, together with (ii) any remaining heritable estate after payment of prior rights.

26 See D Bartos (ed), *Bartos and Meston on the Succession (Scotland) Act 1964*, 6th edn (2015), paras S2-01ff.

THE PRIOR RIGHTS OF THE SURVIVING SPOUSE AND CIVIL PARTNER

6.6 Prior rights are the statutory entitlements of the surviving spouse or civil partner of the deceased to payment of certain specified assets, including money, from the intestate estate. Claims for prior rights must be satisfied before legal rights[27] and the rights of any persons entitled to succeed to the free intestate estate under the Succession (Scotland) Act 1964, s 2.[28] Whereas claimants for legal rights are entitled to a fixed proportion of the moveable estate only, prior rights are payable from the heritable as well as the moveable estate. Three types of prior rights are set out in ss 8–9 of the 1964 Act; the housing right, the right to furniture and plenishings, and the monetary right.

The maximum value of each right is revised from time to time by the Scottish Ministers and the current values are:

- £473,000 for the dwellinghouse or housing right;
- £29,000 for the plenishings or furnishings right; and
- £50,000 or £89,000 as financial provision (the value that can be claimed depends on whether issue also survive the deceased).[29]

The value of the £473,000 housing right is controversial and has been the subject of criticism.[30] The reason for this is that the current figure, and

27 Section 10(2).

28 Section 1(2).

29 The Succession (Scotland) Act 1964, ss 8(1) and 8(3) and 9(1) gives power to the Secretary of State (now the Scottish Ministers due to s 53 of the Scotland Act 1998) to make order fixing the maximum values of prior rights from time to time. The current values are fixed by the Prior Rights of Surviving Spouse (Scotland) Order 2011, SSI 2011/436 and the rate of interest set by the Interest on Prior Rights (Scotland) Order 1981, SI 1981/805.

30 D Reid, 'Why is it so difficult to reform the law of intestate succession?' (2020) 24(1) *Edin LR* 111; D Reid and N Sweeney, 'Land reform, inheritance rights and unintended consequences' (2015) 27(4) *Child and Family Law Quarterly* 403; D Reid, 'Inheritance rights of children' (2010) 14(2) *Edin LR* 318; and D Reid 'From the cradle to the grave: Politics, families and inheritance law' (2008) 12(3) *Edin LR* 391. It is also worth noting that Professor George Gretton, then as a commissioner in the Scottish Law Commission, dissented in the Scottish Law Commission's *Report on Succession* (SLC Report No 215, 2009) on the proposed 'threshold sum' for spouses being set at £300,000, see para 2.15 of the 2009 Report.

the preceding £300,000 figure in 2005, represented a dramatic increase in the value in comparison to threshold figures set previously in the twentieth century.[31] Its effect is that in most cases of total intestacy, the dwellinghouse (often the most valuable asset in the estate) is claimable solely by the spouse or civil partner, which means that its value, or sale proceeds, cannot pass to the deceased's children.

Indeed, the value of all three prior rights means that the payment of prior rights is likely to exhaust, or virtually exhaust, the entire estate in most cases of intestacy. In consequence, it is unlikely that there will be much, if any, property remaining in the estate with which to pay legal rights or any free estate to distribute to the relatives listed in s 2.[32] Whether these rules are fair is open to debate; on one view, it provides the spouse with a comfortable entitlement to prevent them from being destitute, homeless, or forced to move after their spouse's death, which is one of the policy aims of the 1964 Act.[33] On another view, the current scheme in many cases disinherits the blood family, notably the deceased's children, and prevents 'dynastic succession'[34] in which wealth can be redistributed to descendants to allow them to utilise these assets for their own benefit. As such it can be argued, that the current system disadvantages descendants and stifles socioeconomic progression amongst young generations of Scots, particularly at a time when the older generations are the wealthiest in our society. Horizontal succession, and the passage of wealth between spouses, does not assist in eliminating the financial disparity that exists

31 Prior Rights of Surviving Spouse (Scotland) Order 1999 SI 1999/445. As Bartos and Meston note, the original figure in 1964 was a substantial sum and to some extent the 2005 and 2011 figures have merely returned the prior right to its initial aim, D Bartos (ed), *Bartos and Meston on the Succession (Scotland) Act 1964,* 5th edn (2015), para S8-05.

32 For this reason, the computation and examples given below illustrating the distribution of an intestate estate, whereby the estate is sufficiently large to enable all types of possible claim to be made is unusual. The Mackintosh Report, which recommended the changes which subsequently became enacted in the Succession (Scotland) Act 1964, recognised that the rules were devised mainly with small- and medium-sized estates in mind: see *Law of Succession in Scotland: Report of the Committee of Inquiry* (Cmd 8144, 1951), para 6.

33 D Bartos (ed), *Bartos and Meston on the Succession (Scotland) Act 1964,* 6th edn (2015), para S8-01.

34 K Reid, 'Intestate Succession in Scotland', in K Reid et al, *Comparative Succession Law: Volume II: Intestate Succession* (2015), 395.

between the generations in our society. However, the debate about whether the spouse or issue should have priority in intestacy, referred to by Barr as the 'bed vs blood' debate can, and will, continue in respect of any reform to the current scheme.[35]

Three important rules in respect of prior rights should be recognised from the outset:

(1) Firstly, it must be emphasised that if a person has died wholly testate and left no provision for a surviving spouse or civil partner, the only claim on the estate that can be brought by the spouse or civil partner is for legal rights.[36] Financial dependency of the surviving spouse or civil partner on the deceased during life is irrelevant to his or her entitlement to prior rights.

(2) Secondly, prior rights on intestacy are available only to surviving spouses and civil partners; cohabitants have no entitlement to prior rights, except in the case of a transfer of a croft tenancy, although payment from the intestate estate may be ordered by the court under s 29 of the Family Law (Scotland) Act 2006 at its discretion.

(3) Thirdly, it should be remembered that representation does not apply to prior rights, so that the descendants of the predeceasing spouse or civil partner alone, ie: the deceased's stepchildren, have no entitlement to claim prior rights on behalf of their parent.

(1) The structure of prior rights

6.7 Part II ss 8–9 of the 1964 Act set out the three types of prior right available to a surviving spouse or civil partner of the deceased. If the deceased died partially intestate, a surviving spouse or civil partner retains a right to some or all of the prior rights set out in ss 8–9, depending

35 A Barr, 'Death the leveller–Happy and unhappy family succession' (2020) 24(1) *Edin LR* 143. See also, K Reid, 'Mixing without matching: Fractions, slabs, and the succession rights of the surviving spouse and children' (2020) 24 *Edin LR* 118 and J Schmidt, 'Trying to square the circle: Comparative remarks on the rights of the surviving spouse on intestacy' (2020) 24 *Edin LR* 123.

36 See **Ch 4**.

on the circumstances and certain conditions being met. Section 8 gives a right in the deceased's interest in a dwellinghouse and a right to their plenishings or household goods.[37] Section 9 gives a right to a monetary sum as financial provision for the deceased.

Each of the three types of prior right may be claimed independently of the other. For example, the deceased may not have had a dwellinghouse which the surviving spouse has a right to claim but he or she may have owned the furniture and other household goods. A claim for the latter is not dependent on a claim for the former being available.

Example

X and Y live in a tied house, the tenancy of which forms part of the remuneration for X's job, and Y has no right of succession to the tenancy. The furniture and household goods belong to X and Y equally. X dies intestate. Y cannot claim the housing right under s 8(1) but can claim X's share of the furniture and plenishings under s 8(3) and for financial provision under s 9.

Although each prior right is available independently of the other(s), each is payable according to the order set out in ss 8 and 9 of the 1964 Act so that the monetary right under s 9 is postponed to the rights to housing and household goods under s 8.[38] This means that, for example, the value of the monetary right cannot be paid until or unless the rights under s 8 has first been satisfied. This is in accordance with the main aim of the 1964 Act that the housing needs of a surviving spouse or civil partner are met adequately, while balancing his or her interests with those of blood relatives.

Additionally, prior rights can be claimed only if there are sufficient assets in the estate with which to pay them.

37 The 1964 Act, s 8(3), gives a right to 'furniture and plenishings' rather than 'household goods' as used in the Family Law (Scotland) Act 1985, s 25 but on the assumption that their definitions are identical, the latter terminology is used throughout this text; see paras **6.18–6.21**.

38 1964 Act, s 9(6)(a).

Example

X dies intestate, survived by a spouse and child. His estate comprises solely household goods worth less than the maximum value prescribed under the Succession (Scotland) Act 1964, s 8(3). The surviving spouse can claim the furniture and plenishings but there can be no claim for money under s 9 as the claims under s 8 have exhausted the estate. There can be no claims for legal rights, nor any distribution of intestate free estate, and the value of the intestate estate is nil following the spouse's claim under s 8(3).

Prior rights prescribe after 20 years[39] and the value of prior rights applicable in any particular case is the statutory value which was in force at the date of the deceased's death.[40] Interest on the financial provision prior right under s 9(1) of the Succession (Scotland) Act 1964, is payable at the rate of 7% between the date of death and the date of payment to the surviving spouse.[41]

(2) The dwellinghouse right

6.8 Under the Succession (Scotland) Act 1964, s 8(1), the first prior right of a surviving spouse or civil partner (or a cohabitant in the case of a croft)[42] is to the relevant interest in a dwellinghouse included in the intestate estate. The purpose of s 8 is to facilitate the retention by the surviving partner of the family home and to enable them to continue living in it. Alternatively, it provides, in certain circumstances, for the payment of a capital sum sufficient to acquire alternative accommodation. This aim is offset somewhat by a maximum value being placed on the right in order to prevent the possibility of very valuable heritable property passing entirely to the family of either spouse or civil partner to the exclusion of the deceased's blood relatives or, in such a case, exhausting entirely the heritable estate available for claims by prior relatives to the intestate free estate. In an attempt to minimise conflict between these competing aims

39 Prescription and Limitation (Scotland) Act 1973, s 7 and Sch 1, para 2.
40 Succession (Scotland) Act 1964, s 9A.
41 1964 Act s 9(1); and Interest on Prior Rights (Scotland) Order SI 1981/805.
42 1964 Act, s 8(6)(2A).

and interests, the housing right is payable in two different ways but, in all cases, its value is limited to £473,000.

Where the house was owned in common by both spouses or both civil partners, the survivor will have a prior right in respect to the deceased's *pro indiviso* share,[43] provided that the other general tests of eligibility are satisfied. Firstly, the dwelling must come within the definition set out in s 8(6)(a). Secondly, the deceased must have had a relevant interest in it under s 8(6)(d). Thirdly, s 8(4) provides that the surviving spouse or civil partner must have been ordinarily resident in the dwellinghouse at the date of the deceased's death. Although the provisions of s 8 of the 1964 Act in relation to the dwellinghouse right must be read as a whole, their separate aspects will be considered in turn.

(a) Definition of 'dwellinghouse'

6.9 Section 8(6)(a) sets out a fairly broad definition of a 'dwelling house' for the purposes of satisfying a claim under s 8(1). It provides that a dwellinghouse includes 'a part of a building occupied at the date of death of the [deceased] as a separate dwelling'. It also includes:

> 'Any garden or portion of ground attached to, and usually occupied with, the dwelling house or otherwise required for the amenity or convenience of the dwelling house.'

For example, if a barn or outhouse is occupied as a dwellinghouse, then that part will come within the meaning of s 8 and so be available for prior rights. 'Garden' and 'portion of ground' are to be understood in the ordinary sense. If, for example, the house is set in several acres of land, the land will not be construed as 'ground occupied with' the house even if the house and the land are the subjects of the same title in the Land Register. At first sight, this would appear problematic. How much land would have to be attached before it ceased to be possible to describe it as 'attached to, and usually occupied with, the dwelling house' for its 'amenity or convenience'? Although two or three-acre gardens are not uncommon in the country, the question of whether 10 or 20 acres would be included as

43 If title has been taken in the names with a survivorship destination of both co-proprietors and the survivor, it will not form part of the intestate estate; see para **7.21.**

ground occupied with the house is likely to be merely theoretical. It is unlikely, in fact, either that a house with many acres attached would be valued at no more than the maximum value prescribed under s 8 of the 1964 Act or that subjects of this sort are not used for carrying out a trade, profession or occupation such as agricultural land so that the house itself will not be transferred to the surviving spouse or civil partner.[44]

(b) Definition of 'relevant interest'

6.10 A surviving spouse or civil partner is entitled to the deceased's 'relevant interest' in a house but not necessarily to ownership of the house itself. A relevant interest is not limited to the right of ownership but includes an interest as a tenant as well. However, the right to a tenant's interest is severely circumscribed by other legislation. Although there has been no amendment to s 8(8)(d) of the 1964 Act, succession to Private Residential Tenancies under the Private Housing (Tenancies) (Scotland) Act 2016 and Scottish Secure Tenancies under the Housing (Scotland) Act 2001 is excluded since these Acts both regulate succession to the tenancies to which they apply, and these include most current tenancies in the rental market.[45] A question of prior rights should not arise in a succession to residential tenancies as a result. Succession to agricultural leases also have their own statutory provision, though there is some relevance to prior rights under the statutory provisions for the relevant tenancy. Thus, while the provisions of s 8(8)(d) of the 1964 Act do, in theory, apply to leases, there are very few (if any) residential tenancies to which they will in fact apply.

Section 8(6)(d) provides that the relevant interest of the deceased is the interest subject to any heritable debt secured by it. This will usually be in the form of a secured loan, with the deceased having granted a standard security in favour of the lender. The debt must therefore be deducted from the value of the house in computing the value of the relevant interest. If the deceased had a life policy (often a 'mortgage protection' or endowment policy) as an additional security for the secured debt, it is not always the case that the proceeds of the policy will pay off the debt directly to the

44 See paras **6.15–6.17**.
45 See paras **4.20–4.22**.

lender. If not, the net value remains the same as the value of the relevant interest, but this will depend on the terms of the particular policy and whether or not it has been assigned to the lender.[46]

Where there is any dispute over the value of the house, s 8(5) of the 1964 Act provides that the question of the value is to be determined by an arbiter. If the parties fail to agree on the appointment of the arbiter, then the sheriff in the deceased's domicile will appoint one.[47] If the deceased's domicile is uncertain or the deceased was not domiciled in Scotland, the arbiter will be appointed by Edinburgh sheriff court.

(c) Elections where two or more houses

6.11 If the estate comprises a relevant interest in two or more dwellinghouses, s 8(1) provides that a surviving spouse or civil partner must, within six months of the date of death, elect which of these several interests is to be the subject of the claim. If the deceased had a relevant interest in more than one house but title to any of them was subject to a survivorship destination in favour of the surviving spouse, only the house or houses which were not subject to such a destination or otherwise disposed of will form part of the intestate estate.[48] In this case, the surviving spouse is entitled to claim the dwellinghouse right under s 8 in relation to the house or houses which do form part of the intestate estate, subject to the criteria of entitlement and the requirement to make an election between them.

Example

X and Y owned a house in common, with title taken in both their names and the survivor of them. X also had relevant interests in two other houses in which Y was ordinarily resident.

X dies intestate. The house passes to Y under the destination, and Y is also entitled to claim the interest in one of X's other houses under s 8(1).

46 See paras **4.31–4.33**.
47 See ss 3(5) and 134(2) of the Courts Reform (Scotland) Act 2014.
48 See paras **7.19–7.20**.

(d) Ordinarily resident

6.12 Section 8(4) provides that the prior right to the dwellinghouse applies only where the surviving spouse has been 'ordinarily resident' in the house at the death of the deceased. Thus, if the deceased owned any house in which the surviving spouse was not living within at the relevant time, then prior rights may not be claimed in relation to that house. A surviving spouse or civil partner would not be entitled to the interest in a house used only for business purposes, and he or she may or may not be entitled to claim the housing right in respect of, for example, a holiday cottage or country house unless the test of ordinary residence is satisfied.

The spouses or civil partners need not have been living together at the date of death for the test to be satisfied; it is necessary only that the surviving spouse or civil partner has been ordinarily resident in any dwellinghouse in which the deceased had a relevant interest prior to his or her death. If, for example, spouses had become estranged and the surviving spouse had moved into a separate house in which the deceased had a relevant interest, the spouse may nonetheless satisfy the criteria of ordinary residence in the house owned by the deceased.

Example

X and Y are married and live together in a house owned by X. X also owned a cottage which was let to tourists in the summer months. Some time before X's death, X and Y became estranged, and Y moved into the cottage.

X had a relevant interest in both the house and the cottage, and it may be that Y can be considered either as having been (i) ordinarily resident in both the house and the cottage, (ii) ordinarily resident in the house only or (iii) ordinarily resident in the cottage only. Y is entitled to claim the housing right under s 8 of the 1964 Act although she will be put to an election if she was ordinarily resident in both.

(e) Satisfaction of the right: Payment or transfer

6.13 Providing that the relevant criteria necessary to establish the entitlement of a surviving spouse or civil partner have been met, the form in which the right is payable then falls to be determined according to the value of the house and the nature of the deceased's interest. The right will be paid either as a transfer of the deceased's interest in the house (in effect, transfer of the house itself) or as a capital sum.

The primary purpose of the prior right to the dwellinghouse under s 8(1)(b) is to prevent a surviving spouse or civil partner from becoming homeless, but whereas the exceptions to the right to the interest contained in s 8(2) can be understood within a context of maximising the capital value of the estate, the same cannot be said for exceptions applying where the value of the house exceeds the statutory maximum value of the right. It is obvious that where a surviving spouse or civil partner takes the whole interest in the dwellinghouse under s 8(1)(a)(i) he or she is free to realise its value once the interest has been transferred simply by selling it. The manner in which he or she ultimately deals in the property is of no relevance to the design of the provision since he or she has the same freedom as anyone else to enjoy all the usual incidents of ownership. But the question arises as to why it should be that satisfaction of the prior right under s 8(1)(b) should be separated entirely from the house in question. In effect, it is not a dwellinghouse to which the surviving spouse or civil partner has a right; rather, it is a right to money, which may or may not entail the house being sold in order to satisfy it.

Example

X dies intestate, having a relevant interest in a house worth £500,000. The surviving spouse, Y, has no right to the house itself but is instead entitled to claim a capital payment of £473,000 from the heritable part of the intestate estate. Y must therefore vacate the house in which he was ordinarily resident for the house to be sold.

A surviving spouse or civil partner has no automatic right to pay to the estate the difference between the value of the right and the value of the deceased's interest in the house where it is used for carrying out a trade, profession or occupation, or is worth more than £473,000, in order that he or she may purchase the outstanding balance on the deceased's interest in the house.

Although a surviving spouse or civil partner has no right to demand it, in practice, some other arrangement may be negotiated depending on the attitude of the executor. The surviving spouse may be in a position to pay the difference between the value of the house and the value of the right under s 8(1) but whether he or she is able to do so will depend on the executor making no objection to the purchase.

(f) Transfer of the relevant interest

6.14 If the house is worth no more than £473,000 and does not form part of subjects used for carrying out a trade, profession or occupation, s 8(1)(a)(i) applies and the surviving spouse or civil partner may claim the whole of the deceased's relevant interest in the house. In this case, the executor will transfer the interest directly to them.

Example

X dies intestate survived by his wife, Y. X had a relevant interest in a house in which Y was ordinarily resident at the time of his death. The value of the house is £250,000. X's interest is transferred to Y by the executor.

Where s 8(1)(a)(i) applies, the surviving spouse or civil partner becomes the owner of the house upon transfer by the executor, and he or she does not have the right to claim a monetary equivalent.

(g) Payment as a capital sum

6.15 There are two situations where the housing rights will not take the form of a transfer of the deceased's relevant interest in the house to the surviving spouse or civil partner but will, instead, be payable as a capital sum.

(i) Trade, Profession or Occupation Property

6.16 Where the house forms part of the subjects of a tenancy or lease under which the deceased was the tenant or the house forms the whole or part of subjects that were used by the deceased for carrying out a trade, profession or occupation, s 8(1)(a)(ii) applies. To some extent, s 8(2)(a) and (b) of the 1964 Act overlap. Although s 8(2)(a) of the 1964 Act applies solely to leases and tenancies, s 8(2)(b) applies to any type of interest, whether held as proprietor or tenant. Thus, a tenant under a lease could also have used the subjects for the carrying out of a trade, profession or occupation. Section 8(2)(a) will, however, apply in very few cases since succession to most residential leases and tenancies are regulated by separate statutory regimes.

Where one or both of the circumstances referred to in s 8(2), the surviving spouse or civil partner is not entitled to the relevant interest itself but is instead entitled to a sum equal to the value of that interest, provided it is not worth more than £300,000. In the case of a house forming the whole or part of a subject used for carrying on a trade, profession or occupation, however, s 8(2)(b) is subject to the caveat that s 8(1)(a)(ii) will apply *only* if the value of the estate as a whole 'would be likely to be substantially diminished' if the dwellinghouse were to be disposed of separately. If the dwellinghouse is attached to larger subjects such as, for example, a farm, a shop or a GP's surgery, then the transfer of the dwellinghouse is likely to reduce the overall value of the estate and thus reduce the estate available to persons entitled to succeed to the intestate estate.

Example

X owns a farm and dies intestate. The farmhouse forms only part of the subjects used for carrying on a trade, profession or occupation. The value of the estate would be substantially diminished if the farm could not be disposed of as a whole. Under s 8(1)(a)(ii) the surviving spouse, Y, is entitled to a sum of money equal to the value of the relevant interest in the dwellinghouse, provided it is worth no more than £473,000.

(ii) Value greater than £473,000

6.17 As already noted, if the value of the relevant interest is greater than £473,000, s 8(1)(b) provides that the surviving spouse or civil partner is entitled to receive the maximum sum of £473,000.

Whether the payment is to be made from the heritable or the moveable estate is somewhat unclear.[49] The better view seems to be that it should

49 Bartos and Meston suggests that the right to money be considered as a right in lieu of the interest. It should thus be seen as an integral part of the house and the sum taken from heritage, D Bartos (ed), *Bartos and Meston on the Succession (Scotland) Act 1964*, 6th edn (2015), para S8-06.

be deducted from the heritable estate. Unless the deceased had an interest in heritable property other than the dwellinghouse, this will mean that the dwellinghouse will clearly have to be sold and £473,000 of the sale proceeds be made over to the spouse or civil partner by the executor.

The surviving spouse or civil partner also has a claim to money under s 9 of the 1964 Act, the payment apportioned rateably between the heritable estate and moveable estate. Any remaining balance in the heritable estate after such deduction under s 9 will be unavailable for legal rights, given legal rights cannot be paid from the heritable estate, and so will be distributed to the person or persons entitled to succeed to the intestate estate under s 2 of the 1964 Act.

(3) The plenishings right

6.18 Just as the aim of the Succession (Scotland) Act 1964, s 8(1) is to enable a surviving spouse or civil partner to stay in the family home or to provide sufficient capital to acquire alternative accommodation, so the aim of s 8(3) is to ensure that he or she can continue to furnish that home. It would be rather silly to give a spouse or civil partner the home under the s 8(1) dwellinghouse right for removal men to turn up and remove the entire contents from it at the instruction of the executor. Section 8(3) addresses that issue by giving the spouse the right to claim plenishings too.

Section 8(3) provides that the surviving spouse or civil partner of the deceased has the right to the furniture and plenishings of a dwellinghouse, up to a maximum statutory value of £29,000. As detailed further below, the definition of 'furniture and plenishings' in the 1964 Act is almost identical with the definition of 'household goods' under the Family Law (Scotland) Act 1985 and the latter. More contemporary terminology in place of 'plenishings' is adopted here, except where otherwise demanded.

A surviving spouse or civil partner may claim the household goods whether or not the deceased had a relevant interest in the house from which they are claimed so that if the deceased had no relevant interest in a house or a house does not form part of the intestate estate – because, perhaps, title to it is subject to a special destination or, if it is a tenancy, the surviving spouse or civil partner will either succeed to it directly under separate statutory provision or have no entitlement to succeed to it at all – the household goods may still be claimed under s 8(3).

Example

X and Y are married and live in private rented accommodation. X dies intestate has no right to acquire X's interest in the dwellinghouse under the 1964 Act.[50] However, Y was ordinarily resident in the house and has a prior right under s 8(3) of the 1964 Act to X's share of the furniture and plenishings up to £29,000.

As with the housing right, a surviving spouse or civil partner must have been ordinarily resident in the house in which the household goods are located. There is no monetary alternative to the right; the actual items of furniture or other prescribed articles in the house are taken, up to the value of the statutory maximum, or the right will lapse. The right exists only if the household goods do in fact form part of the intestate estate so that any item that is the subject of a hire-purchase agreement is excluded but not any item which is the subject of a credit agreement, subject to any outstanding debt to the seller being paid for ownership to have passed to the deceased.

Many items in a home are purchased by both parties to the relationship, and it may well be that the surviving spouse or civil partner already holds a *pro indiviso* share in some or all of the household goods that form part of the intestate estate and which may be claimed under s 8(3). The Family Law (Scotland) Act 1985, s 25(3) provides that household goods, including decorative and ornamental goods, which are kept or used at any time during the marriage or civil partnership in any family home for the joint domestic purposes of the parties, are presumed to be owned in equal shares unless the contrary is proved.[51] This means that a claim by a surviving spouse or civil partner for household goods under s 8(3) of the 1964 Act will relate to the deceased's half share only.

(a) Definition of furniture and plenishings

6.19 Furniture and plenishings are defined under s 8(6)(b) to include:

50 Though see s 67 of the Private Housing (Tenancies) (Scotland) Act 2016 which will transfer the tenancy.

51 See para **4.10**.

> 'Garden effects, domestic animals, plate, plated articles, linen, china, glass, books, pictures, prints, articles of household use and consumable stores; *but does not include* any article or animal used at the date of death of the [deceased] for business purposes, or money or securities for money, or any heirloom [emphasis added].'

The items listed within the definition in s 8(6)(b) of the 1964 Act are not exhaustive; rather, the provision states merely that furniture and plenishings include the specified items. It is silent on the question of whether cars or other vehicles, excluded under s 25 of the Family Law (Scotland) Act 1985, and s 26 of the Family Law (Scotland) Act 2006, are included as furniture and plenishings. Clearly, vehicles other than cars (such as tractors, vans etc) would normally be used for business purposes and thus be excluded, but it seems unlikely that ordinary cars are to be considered part of furniture and plenishings.[52]

A notable exception is that heirlooms are excluded expressly by the 1964 Act, but the definition of heirloom is somewhat vague, being stated in s 8(6)(c) as:

> 'Any article which has associations with the [deceased]'s family of such nature and extent that it ought to pass to some member of that family other than the surviving spouse of the [deceased].'

The exclusion from the meaning of household goods under s 25(3) of the 1985 Act, items acquired by gift or succession from a third party, may be more definite to explain what heirlooms are under the 1964 Act. However, that is of no assistance in determining the point at which a thing becomes an heirloom since it may be that items purchased by the deceased in their lifetime are considered as such by members of their family.[53] The

52 Bartos and Meston suggest that these may be included if they can reasonably be seen as an appurtenance of the house: D Bartos (ed), *Bartos and Meston on The Succession (Scotland) Act 1964,* 6th edn (2015), para S8-30.

53 Neither is it clear who is entitled to receive any heirlooms. They are excluded from prior rights, but legal rights are claimed from the whole moveable estate and there is no rule to exclude them from the share of the moveable property which can be claimed by a surviving spouse. If legal rights are not claimed, it will be the person or persons entitled to the intestate estate net of prior rights who will receive an heirloom or heirlooms. In general, however, it appears that disputes over the acquisition of any particular items considered as heirlooms by members of the deceased's family are a matter for them to resolve between themselves.

engraved pocket watch of the deceased's grandfather would likely be an heirloom and excluded from the spouse, but would the cheap painted vase that the deceased's grandmother bought at a jumble sale fifty years ago be so excluded too? It is a difficult issue to which there appears to be no judicial interpretation and will likely turn on matters of fact.[54]

(b) The value of the right

6.20 Section 8(3)(a) provides that where the intestate estate includes furniture and plenishings, the surviving spouse or civil partner is entitled to the whole of them where they are worth no more than £29,000.[55] Section 8(3)(b) provides that, where they are worth more than £29,000, the surviving spouse or civil partner is entitled to choose which items to take up to that value. Thus, if the household goods forming part of the intestate estate are worth more than £29,000 he or she can choose freely whichever particular items he or she wishes to take.

Example

X dies intestate, owning furniture and plenishings worth £40,000. Her surviving spouse is entitled to choose items up to the value of £29,000, provided that they do not fall outwith the definition set out in s 8(6)(b) of the 1964 Act.

Where there is a dispute as to the value of any furniture and plenishings, s 8(5) provides that an arbiter is to be appointed in the same manner as to disputes over the value of a dwellinghouse.

(c) Election

6.21 Where the deceased had a relevant interest in more than one house, s 8(3) provides that the right shall have effect 'only in relation to

54 See Bartos and Meston's humorous discussion of grandmother's 'best tea dishes', *Bartos and Meston,* para S8-31.

55 While the value of the dwellinghouse right increased from £130,000 to £300,000 between 1999 and 2005, and then from £300,000 to £473,000, the increase in the value of the right to household goods during the same periods was a more modest increase from £22,000 to £24,000, and then £24,000 to £29,000 respectively.

the furniture and plenishings of such one of them as the surviving spouse or civil partner may elect' and that an election must be made within six months of the date of death. The furniture and plenishings do not, therefore, have to be taken from the same house whose interest the surviving spouse claims under s 8(1).

Example

X dies intestate, survived by her spouse, Y. Y was ordinarily resident in two houses in which X had a relevant interest. Y elects to take X's interest in House 1 under s 8(1) but the furniture in House 2 under s 8(3).

The surviving spouse or civil partner must choose, therefore, from which house the right is to be claimed. He or she can select which items to take from any one house (provided that their total value is within the statutory limit) but the effect of the election is that it is not possible to cherry-pick by selecting some goods from one house, and some from another.

(4) Financial provision: the monetary right

6.22 Section 9 of the 1964 Act provides that the surviving spouse or civil partner of the deceased is entitled to a right to money from the intestate estate. The value of the right depends on whether or not the deceased was survived (1) only by a spouse or civil partner or (2) by a spouse or civil partner and issue (children or remoter descendants). Where he or she is survived by a spouse or civil partner alone, s 9(1)(b) provides that the maximum sum is currently £89,000.[56] Where both classes of person survive the deceased, s 9(1)(a) provides that the maximum sum that may be claimed by the surviving spouse or civil partner is currently £50,000.

Clearly, the monetary right can be satisfied only if there are sufficient funds to pay it, either in full or in part. If not, it is paid up to the extent that a fund exists. Section 9(2) provides that where the intestate estate is less than the sum which the surviving spouse is entitled to claim under s 9(1),

56 The current values are fixed by the Prior Rights of Surviving Spouse (Scotland) Order 2011, SSI 2011/436.

his or her right will be 'satisfied by the transfer to him or her of the whole of the intestate estate'.

'Intestate estate' has a particular definition in relation to calculating the monetary right, and s 9(6)(a) provides that 'intestate estate' in this context means 'so much of the net intestate estate as remains after the satisfaction of any claims under the last foregoing section'. It is, in other words, the estate which remains after satisfaction of the right to housing and household goods under s 8 and underlines the point that the monetary right is postponed to the rights available under s 8. Section 9(6)(a) also leaves no room for doubt that, even though payment of prior rights, including the monetary right, may exhaust the estate, the sums stipulated are payable to the surviving spouse to the exclusion of any other claims on intestacy.

(a) Apportionment between heritable and moveable estate

6.23 It follows that where only heritage or only moveables remain in the intestate estate, the whole of the right under s 9(1) will be payable from whichever of the funds remain after payment of the rights under s 8.

If both remain after payment of rights under s 8, s 9(3) provides that the monetary right under s 9(1) is to be 'borne by, and paid out of, the parts of the intestate estate consisting of heritable and moveable property respectively in proportion to the respective amounts of those parts'. In other words, the payment is to be apportioned between the heritable estate and the moveable estate. This provision helps mitigate against the possibility that a claim for each prior right by the surviving spouse or civil partner will exhaust either the heritable or moveable property to the detriment of either heirs entitled to the intestate free estate or claimants for legal rights (including the surviving spouse or civil partner him or herself). It aims to balance the estate by not prejudicing the entitlement of one or other class (who may in fact be one and the same) so that legal rights (payable only from the moveable estate) or claims to the free intestate estate (in which heritage and moveables are assimilated) may not be excluded arbitrarily by a surviving spouse or civil partner choosing to take the value of the right from one fund rather than the other.

The following example shows what would happen without the provision of s 9(3):

Example

Y, a surviving civil partner, claims the housing right under s 8(1) and household goods under s 8(3). The deceased, X, was also survived by children, and the value of the prior right under s 9 is thus £50,000. After Y's rights under s 8 have been satisfied, £40,000 and £20,000 of moveable and heritable property, respectively, remain in the intestate estate.

If the monetary right could be paid from the moveable estate alone, Y could only claim the £40,000 in the moveable estate and exhaust the moveable estate entirely. No claims for legitim or rights under s 131 of the Civil Partnership Act 2004 could then be made by X's children or Y.

If the right under s 9(1) were payable from the heritable property only, B could claim only £20,000 and the value of the heritable estate available to X's children under s 2 of the 1964 Act would be nil.

In order to avoid either outcome, s 9(3) provides that where both heritable and moveable property remain in the intestate estate after satisfaction of claims under s 8, ie, the dwellinghouse right and the plenishings right, the right to money must be satisfied from each fund in proportion to the value of the whole estate. The net capital value of both the heritable and moveable estate must be calculated as a ratio or proportion of the net capital value of the intestate estate after satisfaction of any rights payable under s 8.

The provisions of s 9 thus give a preferential right to a surviving spouse whilst, at the same time, hedging it around with provisions aimed at minimising the exclusion of children from the succession. Balanced against this, it should be remembered that it is children and not spouses or civil partners who have the prior claim to the intestate free estate. The result is that if only heritable property remained after payment of the right to money, the surviving spouse or civil partner can have no claim for the relict's right, and the remaining heritable property will devolve under s 2 of the 1964 Act.

Example

X dies intestate, survived by a spouse and two children. The maximum value of the monetary right which can be claimed by the spouse is £50,000. Assuming that the value of the intestate estate is more than sufficient to satisfy all three prior rights in full, the monetary right will be apportioned between the heritable and moveable estate as follows:

	Heritable Estate	**Moveable Estate**	**Total**
X's estate after debts satisfied.	**£550,000**	**£60,000**	**£610,000**
Prior rights			
Housing Right S 8(1)	(£473,000)		
	£77,000		
Furnishings Right S 8(3)		(£29,000)	
	£77,000	*£31,000*	*£108,000*
Financial Provision S 9(1)	(£35,648.15)	(£14,351.85)	
Remaining estate	**£41,351.85**	**£16,648.15**	**£58,000**

How, then, were the figures reached to pay the £50,000 in s 9 financial provision here? An apportionment was carried out using the following formulas:

(1) To calculate the amount of the financial provision from the remaining heritable estate after deduction of the s 8 rights:

$$\frac{\textit{Remaining heritable estate}}{\textit{Remaining total estate}} \times \textit{Financial Provision}$$

$$\frac{£77{,}000}{(£77{,}000 + £31{,}000)} \times £50{,}000 = £35{,}648.15 \ (\textit{rounded to 2dp})$$

(2) To calculate the amount of the financial provision from the remaining moveable estate after deduction of the s 8 rights:

$$\frac{\textit{Remaining moveable estate}}{\textit{Remaining total estate}} \times \textit{Financial Provision}$$

$$\frac{£31{,}000}{(£77{,}000 + £31{,}000)} \times £50{,}000 = 14{,}351.85 \ (\textit{rounded to 2dp})$$

It may be remarked upon just how much the fictional spouse has received out of the estate in prior rights before account is taken of any claim they may have under legal rights, ie: the *jus relictae, jus relicti,* or s 131 of the 2004 Act. Under prior rights, in a net estate of £610,000, the spouse has received:

Prior Rights	Value
S 8(1) Dwellinghouse Right	£473,000
S 8(3) Furnishings Right	£29,000
S 9(1) Financial Provision	£50,000
Total	**£552,000**

For a spouse to receive nearly all of a relatively high-value estate such as in this example is why, for many, it is felt that current prior-right figures are perhaps too generous to a spouse or civil partner.

The remaining £58,000 in the estate will then pass to be distributed under the relict's right, payment of s 29 claims (if any), legitim, and then finally distribution of the remaining free estate under s 2 of the 1964 Act. By the time it reaches the legitim and the free estate, very little of the estate may actually be left for the children to claim.

(b) Interaction of financial provision with 'legacies'

6.24 In cases of partial intestacy, where only some of the deceased person's estate is undisposed of by testamentary disposition, and the surviving spouse or civil partner is entitled to receive a legacy from the deceased's testate estate, the value of that legacy must be offset against the value of the monetary right. Section 9(1) provides that entitlement to the monetary right is subject to the *proviso* that, unless the legacy is renounced, a surviving spouse or civil partner will be entitled to receive only the sum which remains after deduction of its value or amount. A legacy for these purposes is defined in s 9(6)(b) as including:

> 'Any payment or benefit to which a surviving spouse or civil partner becomes entitled by virtue of any testamentary disposition; and the amount or value of any legacy shall be ascertained as at the date of the [deceased]'s death.'

At first sight, this would seem to include only property which is disposed of by a will and exclude rights to which the surviving spouse becomes entitled by other means[57] but the meaning of s 9(6)(b) is clarified by s 36(1) which states that for the purposes of the 1964 Act a 'testamentary disposition' includes

> 'Any deed taking effect on [the testator's] death whereby any part of his estate is disposed of or under which a succession thereto arises.'

A 'legacy' is therefore any gift given under a deed that has testamentary effect and includes, for example, any heritable property that is not the subject of the dwellinghouse right or, for example, the proceeds from an insurance policy or a pension scheme. It will also include rights conferred under a special destination[58] so that where a house is the subject of a survivorship destination, the deceased's one-half *pro indiviso* share which passes to the surviving spouse will count as a legacy for the purposes of s 9.[59] Therefore, as long as 'legacies' thus defined are payable to the surviving spouse (or indeed to anyone else), the estate will be only partially intestate.

Example

X dies intestate, survived by a spouse, Y, and son. Y is entitled to receive the proceeds of X's life insurance policy worth £20,000 under a nomination in her favour. Y must offset her rights to the proceeds against her entitlement to £50,000 under s 9 and Y is therefore only entitled to claim the reduced sum of £30,000 under s 9.

Where, however, the legacy is of a type to which s 8 applies, the value of any legacy or legacies of this type will not be deducted. Because each prior right is an independent entitlement, there is no requirement to offset legacies of a house or household goods, regardless of their value. Accordingly, where any house or household goods bequeathed to a surviving spouse or civil partner, he or she will be entitled to claim the monetary right in full, to the extent that it can be satisfied from that estate.

57 Eg, a nomination under a life insurance policy or a special destination: see para **7.26**.
58 It should be noted that this definition applies only in relation to claims for prior rights and not to claims for legal rights from an intestate estate.
59 See para **7.20**.

Example

X's estate is partially intestate. She is survived by a spouse, Y, and one child. The total value of the intestate estate is £20,000. X has given a legacy to Y of his interest in the dwellinghouse worth £100,000 and his share of the household goods worth £20,000. Y is not required to deduct the value of either legacy from her entitlement to £50,000 under s 9. The intestate estate is worth less than her entitlement under s 9, and Y is therefore entitled to the whole £20,000.

The corollary of the proviso is that if the deceased had a relevant interest in more than one house, the surviving spouse or civil partner cannot claim both the dwellinghouse right under s 8(1) in respect of any house included in the intestate estate *and* accept a legacy of another dwellinghouse from the testate estate while claiming the full value of the monetary right under s 9(1). The same principle applies to household goods. Thus, exempting a dwellinghouse or plenishings from the set-off requirement does not mean that a surviving spouse can benefit twice. It means simply that where a dwellinghouse or furniture and plenishings are the subject of a legacy from the testate estate, the surviving spouse or civil partner will not be barred from claiming the monetary right and be consigned to a worse position than if the deceased spouse or civil partner had died intestate.

LEGAL RIGHTS

6.25 The nature and extent of legal rights are discussed in **Chapter 5** and all that needs to be said here is that legal rights may be claimed by a surviving spouse, civil partner, and children (or their descendants by way of representation) in intestate as well as testate succession. The Succession (Scotland) Act 1964, s 1(2) defines the 'intestate estate' as 'so much of the net intestate estate as remains' after satisfaction of prior and legal rights'.

Since an intestate estate is comprised of any property which is undisposed of by testamentary disposition, it follows that once any claims to prior rights have been satisfied, legal rights may also be claimed. This applies in partial as well as total intestacy. Before considering the distribution of the free intestate estate, the effect of legal rights on the distribution of an intestate estate is illustrated below.

Example

X dies intestate, survived by a spouse, Y, and a child, A. X's estate comprises a relevant interest in the family home worth £200,000 in which Y was also ordinarily resident. The household goods in the home are worth £20,000. X also had moveable property worth £60,000. X died with no debts. Y claims his full prior rights.

	Heritable Estate	**Moveable Estate**	
Family Home	£200,000		
Household goods		£20,000	
Other moveable property		£60,000	
	£200,000	£80,000	
Prior rights			
Housing Right S 8(1)	(£200,000)		To Y
Furnishings Right S 8(3)		(£20,000)	To Y
Financial Provision S 9(1) *NB: There is no apportionment here as the heritable estate has been exhausted by s 8(1).*		(£50,000)	To Y
	£0.00	£10,000	
Legal rights			
Jus relicti		(£3,333.33)	To Y
Legitim		(£3,333.33)	To A
Intestate free estate	£0.00	£3,333.33	

COHABITANTS' SECTION 29 CLAIMS

6.26 Section 29 of the Family Law (Scotland) Act 2006 confers on surviving cohabitants the right to apply to the court for an order for payment out of a deceased cohabitant's intestate estate.[60] This provision implements in part the recommendations made by the Scottish Law Commission in respect of family law reforms in 1992[61] but the Act does not implement its recommendation that the right to claim in testate succession should also be introduced. Introducing cohabitant protection from disinheritance in testate succession has been consistently raised in the ongoing reforms to succession law.[62] The Scottish Law Commission has taken the view that claims to testate succession should be possible.[63] However, respondents to Scottish Government consultations on reform have not shown consensus on extending claims where the deceased has made a will.[64]

The thorn of cohabitant claims in testate succession aside, there is an ongoing wider call for repeal and replacement of s 29 with an improved statutory definition of cohabitants and refined factors for the court to consider in making awards. As of the time of writing of this edition, the Scottish Government is gathering views on cohabitants' experiences of making s 29 claims as part of wider reforms to cohabitant rights, both in lifetime and on death.[65] This follows on from the Scottish Law Commission's examination of the current operation of s 28 claims where a cohabitation terminates otherwise than on death.[66]

(1) A claim for provision not a right of succession

6.27 A common misunderstanding is that cohabitants enjoy the same rights as other relatives by virtue of s 29 of the 2006 Act. However, s 29

60 The definition of cohabitant is contained in s 25 of the Family Law (Scotland) Act 2006; see also para **2.25**.

61 Report on *Family Law* (Scot Law Com No 135, 1992), paras 16.31–16.37.

62 See para **6.3**.

63 Report *on Succession* (SLC Report No 215, 2009), Part 4. For an interesting analysis of how cohabitants are treated in other jurisdictions, and what can be learned for Scots law, see G Christandl, 'Succession rights for cohabitants' (2020) 24(1) *Edin LR* 138.

64 *Scottish Government Response to the Consultation on the Law of Succession* (2018), para 52.

65 *A Scottish Government Consultation on Family Law* (2025), paras 1.71–1.77.

66 Report on *Cohabitation* (SLC Report No 261, 2022).

of the 2006 Act does not give a cohabitant a fixed right of succession as they would have enjoyed had they been married or in a civil partnership. Instead, s 29 empowers the court, at its discretion, to order a payment to a surviving cohabitant from their deceased partner's intestate estate.[67] The advantages and disadvantages of the court discretionary-based scheme in place of a fixed right of succession has been summarised by the Commission as follows:[68]

> 'We pointed out that the system had the advantage of flexibility. The court can take into account the circumstances of each individual case and make an appropriate order. This in turn makes it easier to extend the system to a wider range of people than surviving spouses and children. We pointed out, however, that the system also had disadvantages. A court application is necessary and the applicant is dependent on the court's discretion. The embarrassment and inconvenience of having to assert a claim may deter many claimants, particularly the less aggressive. There is great room for differences of opinion between judges and for uncertainty about the outcome of an application. The proceedings may involve a distasteful and distressing disclosure of details of the relationship between the deceased and the applicant. The proceedings may be costly and productive of delay in winding up estates.'

The provisions of the 2006 Act in relation to cohabitants do not alter the current law of intestate succession under the Succession (Scotland) Act 1964. Instead, it sets up a parallel framework of provision. The effect of this overlap means that where the deceased is survived by both a spouse or civil partner and a cohabitant, as well as, or instead of, other relatives, the provisions of s 29 of the 2006 Act and the provisions of the Succession (Scotland) Act 1964 will come into operation simultaneously. It may be that, in certain cases, the provisions of the 2006 Act will override rights to legitim and to the intestate free estate, and that an award under s 29 may have the effect of reducing or excluding any such claims entirely.

(2) Eligibility

6.28 Section 29(1) provides that the deceased must have died intestate within the meaning of the 1964 Act,[69] and this means that an order may

67 For an overview of the underlying principles and operation of s 29, see *Kerr v Mangan* [2014] CSIH 69, per Lady Smith at paras 6–20.

68 Report *on Succession* (SLC Report No 124, 1990), para 3.4.

69 1964 Act, s 31(1), see paras **6.4–6.5**.

be made only in relation to the deceased cohabitant's intestate estate.[70] In order to be eligible to apply, the applicant must have been domiciled in Scotland and cohabiting with the deceased immediately before his or her death.[71] For the 2006 Act, as amended by the 2014 Act, a cohabitant means two people of the same or different sex living together as if married.[72] Further factors are to be considered by the court in determining whether the couple are indeed cohabitants, this includes:[73]

(a) the length of the period during which the couple have been living together (or lived together);

(b) the nature of their relationship during that period; and

(c) the nature and extent of any financial arrangements subsisting, or which subsisted, during that period.

Despite the term cohabitant implying 'living together' as a necessary condition for a claim to be made, the courts seem to take a wider view on this point, and provided the relationship subsists and other factors are present such as joint-financial arrangements then the test for cohabitation may well still be satisfied.[74]

An application by a surviving cohabitant for an order under s 29 must currently be made within six months, though soon to be twelve months, of the day on which the deceased died.[75] Application may be made to the

70 2006 Act, s 29(1)(a); the provisions of s 29 will also apply if the deceased died partially intestate; see para **6.45.**

71 2006 Act, s 29(1)(b). For the meaning of cohabitation, see **2.25.**

72 2006 Act, s 25(1), [as amended by the Marriage and Civil Partnership (Scotland) Act 2014, ss 4(3) and 4(4)].

73 2006 Act, s 25(2).

74 *B v B* 2014 GWD 30-593, per Sheriff Principal Stephen at para 3; and Scottish Law Commission, *Report on Cohabitation* (SLC Report No 261, 2022), para 3.8. See further, K Macfarlane, *Thomson's Family Law in Scotland,* 8th edn (2022), para 8.2; F McCarthy, 'Defining cohabitation' 2014 *SLT (News)* 143; and E Sutherland, *Child and Family Law, Vol 2: Intimate Adult Relationships,* 3rd edn (2022), paras 6-445ff.

75 2006 Act, s 29(6) [as amended by the Trusts and Succession (Scotland) Act 2024, s 76]. Formerly the period for claim was a rather curt six months, which could cause problems if no executor had yet confirmed to the estate within that time, see *X v A (No 1)* 2016 SLT (Sh Ct) 404 and *X v A (No 2)* 2016 SLT (SH Ct) 411. See also *Simpson v Downie* [2012] CSIH 74; *Pert v McCafferty* [2020] CSIH 5; and *Knight v Henderson* [2023] SAC (Civ) 2. It is presumed that as the extension of the time limit is relatively uncontroversial, this part of the 2024 Act will be brought into force in relatively short course.

Court of Session, a sheriff in the sheriffdom in which the deceased was habitually resident at the date of death or, if that is uncertain, Edinburgh Sheriff Court.[76]

(3) The nature and extent of a section 29 order

6.29 Section 29 of the 2006 Act permits the surviving cohabitant of the deceased the right to apply to the court for payment of a capital sum out of the deceased's net intestate estate[77] or the transfer of property (heritable or moveable) from the net intestate estate.[78] The court may also make such interim orders as it thinks fit.[79]

The extent of any s 29 order is subject to an overall cap. The cohabitant cannot receive more than what they could have received had they been married to or in a civil partnership with the deceased.[80] An artificial exercise has to be conducted by the court to determine what a spouse or civil partner could have received from the estate out of prior rights, legal rights and any distribution of the intestate free estate under s 2 of the 1964 Act. Arrival at this total figure or transfer value provides the maximum ceiling with which a cohabitant could receive under a s 29 order. However, the court has discretion in determining the transfer value for any order.

Example

X dies survived by a cohabitant Y and their child. X died solely owning their family house worth £450,000 and furnishings worth £40,000. Otherwise, X had moveable estate worth £300,000. Y makes a claim under s 29 of the 2006 Act. To compute the maximum figure that can be awarded, the following notional calculation is required:

76 2006 Act, s 29(5).

77 2006 Act, s 29(2)(a)(i).

78 2006 Act, s 29(2)(a)(ii). See *Kerr v Mangan* [2014] CSIH 69, per Lady Smith at para 10.

79 2006 Act, s 29(2)(b).

80 2006 Act, s 29(4).

	Heritable Estate	**Moveable Estate**	
House	£450,000		
Furnishings		£20,000	*Household goods presumed co-owned under s 26 of the 2006 Act.*[81]
Moveables		£300,000	
Total Estate:	£450,000	£320,000	
Notional Prior Rights			
Dwellinghouse Rights S 8(1)	(£450,000)		
Plenishings Rights S 8(3)		(£20,000)	
	£0.00	*£300,000*	
Financial Provision S 9(1)		(£50,000)	
Remaining estate after notional prior rights		*£250,000*	
Notional Legal Rights			
Jus relictae		(£83,333.33)	

Total distribution if married	
Dwellinghouse right	£450,000
Plenishings right	£20,000
Financial Provision	£50,000
Jus relictae	£83,333.33
Total	**£603,333.33**

The court cannot award more than £603,333.33 in making a s 29 order.

81 See para **4.10**.

(4) The exercise of the court's direction

6.30 How a solicitor advises their client on how or what the court will consider the appropriate award to make under a s 29 order is a matter of notorious difficulty.[82] As Lady Smith noted in *Kerr v Managan*:[83]

> 'The court's discretion is so unfettered as to make it extraordinarily difficult, if not impossible, to predict accurately what may be the outcome, at first instance, of an application under section 29.'

The making of any such order is at the discretion of the court, having regard to matters including those set out in s 29(3). These are:

(a) the size and nature of the deceased's net intestate estate;

(b) any benefit received, or to be received, by the survivor: (i) on, or in consequence of, the deceased's death; and (ii) from somewhere other than the deceased's net intestate estate;

(c) the nature and extent of any other rights against, or claims on, the deceased's net intestate estate; and

(d) any other matter the court considers appropriate.

Guidance on how these factors are to be weighed is absent, and the courts seem to undertake a very contextual analysis in making their decision on the appropriate award. As Sheriff Miller commented:[84]

> 'Subsection (3) is extremely wide in its scope. Its precise and unequivocal terminology brings within its ambit the opportunity to present an exceedingly broad range of facts and circumstances that might be deemed appropriate in the particular circumstances of any given case.'

Additionally, there is little reported case law that makes it hard to determine any definitive conclusions on the factors a court will have

82 See F McCarthy, 'Rights in succession for cohabitants: *Savage v Purches*' (2009) 13(2) *Edin LR* 325; and J Kerrigan, 'Section 29 of the Family Law (Scotland) Act 2006 – the case for reform?' (2008) (26) *SLT (News)* 175.

83 [2014] CSIH 69, at para 18.

84 *Fulwood v O'Halloran*, 6 January 2014, Glasgow Sheriff Court (unreported).

particular regard to.[85] However, it is worth noting that the Inner House has considered fairness itself is not an issue in determining the award to make.[86]

In *Savage v Purches*,[87] the deceased and the cohabitant had been cohabiting for nearly three years. The cohabitant sought a s 29 order. The court did note the lack of joint-financial arrangements that the couple had, and the relatively short nature of the cohabitation. Further, the sheriff noted that the deceased had received a substantial capital sum from the deceased's pension and, *inter alia*, decided to make a nil (£0.00) award.[88]

In *Windram, Applicant*,[89] the couple had cohabitated for over two decades and had two children. In light of the relative dependency that the cohabitant had on the deceased, as she worked part-time and attended to the housework and upbringing of the children, the court made a substantial award, including the transfer of the family home and a capital sum. In *JH v LM*[90] the couple had been in a happy relationship for nearly 40 years, and the court was minded making 'an award near the maximum possible'.[91]

As 'each case will turn on its own facts',[92] the subjectivity employed by the courts presents difficulties from the viewpoint of a bereaved cohabitant and their certainty for financial security after death. A court-based discretionary scheme invariably carries this risk, as the Scottish Law Commission recognised in the 1990s.[93] Both Kerrigan and Macfarlane suggest that the lack of certainty leads to a lack of reported case law, as many cohabitants may consider accepting a settlement from the executor

85 Research by Centre for Research on Families and Relationships in 2010 showed relatively few s 29 claims are actually made which likely has an impact on why there is little reported caselaw in the law reports, Briefing 51 'No longer living together: how does Scots cohabitation law work in practice?' (2010), quoted and discussed further in A Griffiths et al, *Family Law,* 4th edn (2015), para 10-69.

86 [2014] CSIH 69, per Lady Smith at para 41.

87 (2009) SLT (Sh Ct) 36.

88 See further F McCarthy, 'Rights in succession for cohabitants: *Savage v Purches*' (2009) 13(2) *Edin LR* 325.

89 2009 Fam LR 157.

90 2024 Fam LR 19.

91 2024 Fam LR 19, per Sheriff Flinn at para 36.

92 *JH v LM* 2024 Fam LR 19, per Sheriff Flinn at para 33, quoting Sheriff Scott in *Windram, Applicant* 2009 Fam LR 157.

93 See para **6.27**.

rather than run the risk of costly litigation for a s 29 order.[94] Respondents to the Scottish Government's consultations on reforms do not show a majority view in favour in giving a cohabitant a fixed right of succession, though there seems to be consensus on improving the criteria on which a s 29 claim is quantified at the least.[95] Whether this will improve uptake remains to be seen.[96]

(5) The date and method of payment

6.31 Where an order is made for payment of a capital sum under s 29(2)(a)(i), the court may specify that it shall be payable either on a date specified or be payable in instalments.[97] If an order is made by the court under s 29, the date and method of payment may be varied on application by any party having an interest.[98] Where an order is made for the transfer of specific property to the applicant under s 29(2)(a)(ii), the court may specify the date on which the transfer shall be effective.[99]

These provisions differ markedly from the provisions relating to the prior rights of a surviving spouse or civil partner under ss 8–9 of the Succession (Scotland) Act 1964 and underline not only the discretionary but also the secondary nature of the provisions of s 29. Prior rights must be satisfied in full before any other part of the intestate estate is distributed; there is no scope for payment in instalments; and the interests of any other person in the estate, whether claimants for legal rights or persons entitled to the free intestate estate, are irrelevant. In addition, no specific provision is made under the Act for the payment of interest if there is a delay between the date of the order and the date of payment or where payments are made by instalment.

94 K Macfarlane, *Thomson's Family Law in Scotland,* 8th edn (2022), para 8.7; and J Kerrigan, 'Section 29 of the Family Law (Scotland) Act 2006 – the case for reform?' 2008 *SLT (News)* 175, 176.

95 *Response to the Consultation on the law of succession* (2020), 3.

96 A Barr, 'A view from practice' (2010) 14(2) *Edin LR* 313, 317.

97 2006 Act, s 29(7).

98 2006 Act, s 29(9).

99 2006 Act, s 29(8).

(6) Interaction with other relatives' rights of succession

(a) Interaction with spousal or civil partner rights

6.32 Section 29(10) defines the net intestate estate from which payments or transfers to a surviving cohabitant may be made as:

> 'So much of the intestate estate as remains after provision for the satisfaction of:
>
> (a) inheritance tax;
>
> (b) other liabilities of the estate having priority over legal rights and the prior rights of a surviving spouse or surviving civil partner; and
>
> (c) the legal rights, and the prior rights, of any surviving spouse or surviving civil partner.'

This subsection makes clear that it is entirely possible that the deceased will be survived by a spouse or civil partner, as well as by a cohabitant. Where this is the case, claims by a cohabitant are deferred to claims for prior rights and legal rights by a surviving spouse or civil partner.

(b) Interaction with legitim

6.33 The definition of net intestate estate under s 29(10) also makes clear that where the deceased is survived by children, claims by a surviving cohabitant may be preferred to claims for legitim and the intestate free estate. However, this is somewhat at odds with the normal understanding of the order of distribution in intestate succession and a complication arises for the calculation and payment of legitim.

Since legal rights vest *a morte testatoris*, the calculation of legitim is already somewhat pre-determined before the cohabitant makes a s 29 claim. Since a claim by a cohabitant does not vest at death but is awarded by the court at a later date, it is difficult to see how an award under s 29 could then defeat the issue's already vested right.

However, for the purposes of s 29 of the 2006 Act, the net intestate is the estate remaining before payment of any claims for legitim by the deceased's children or claims for payment of the free intestate estate. Thus, cohabitants may be awarded all or part of an estate that would, in the absence of a s 29 claim, have been payable to the deceased's children or other issue after satisfaction of any claims for prior rights, legal rights or rights under s 131 of the 2004 Act. An example can illustrate the conceptual difficulty:

Example

X dies, survived by a spouse, Y. X has been separated from Y for many years and has been in a cohabiting relationship with Z for some years. X and Y had two children, A and B.

X died intestate. He solely-owned the home worth £500,000 where he and Z lived, with furnishings in the home amounting to £60,000. Otherwise, X had moveable estate worth £200,000. On X's death, Z makes a claim under s 29 of the 2006 Act and the sheriff, considering the short-term nature of the cohabitation, is awarded a capital payment of £100,000.

	Heritable Estate	**Moveable Estate**	
House	£500,000		
Furnishings		£30,000	*Household goods presumed co-owned under s 26 of the 2006 Act.*[100]
Moveables		£200,000	
	£500,000	*£230,000*	*£730,000*

Y's prior rights			
Dwellinghouse Right S 8(1)	N/A		*Not ordinarily resident.*
Plenishings Right S 8(3)		N/A	*Not ordinarily resident.*
Financial Provision S 9(1)	(£34,246.58)	(£15,753.42)	*To Y.*
	£465,753.42	£214,246.58	

100 See para **4.10**.

Y's legal rights			
Jus relictae		(£74,415.53)	*To Y.*
		£139,831.05	
Z's s 29 Order			
S 29 Order		(£100,000)	*To Z.*
	£465,753.42	£39,831.05	

How then is the legitim to be distributed? The children should have been entitled to receive the same value as the spouse, £74,415.53, from the moveable estate. However, this is now impossible because of Z's s 29 court order and there are insufficient funds in the estate. Two theories emerge as a potential solution. The first is that the legitim will need recalculated on the basis of the remaining moveable estate:

Legitim Theory 1:		£39,831.05	
Legitim		(£13,277.02)	*To A and B.*
Intestate Free Estate	£465,753.42	£26,554.03	

The alternative theory is there is no recalculation of the legitim but a partial abatement must take place.[101] The legitim is paid out on the basis of what remains with a partial abatement, and the intestate free estate must fully abate in this case.

Legitim Theory 2:		£39,831.05	
Legitim		(£39,831.05)	*To A and B.*
Intestate Free Estate	£465,753.42	£0.00	

In most cases the end result of the distribution to the issue may be the same given, for the reasons noted below, the intestate free estate would ordinarily pass to any issue present in the succession too. However, given legitim has its own rules of distribution, such as discharges and collation *inter liberos*, the effect of a s 29 claim has to be reconciled with the order of distribution under the 1964 Act in some way to ensure the wider rules of succession law are respected.

101 On abatement, see paras **10.13–10.14**.

ENTITLEMENT TO THE INTESTATE FREE ESTATE

6.34 Section 2 of the Succession (Scotland) Act 1964 sets out the rights in succession of different classes of person to the intestate free estate, ranked in order of preference.

As rights of succession to the free estate are postponed to prior rights and legal rights, s 2 of the 1964 Act comes into effect only where there is free estate remaining after satisfaction of claims by creditors, claims for prior, legal rights, and any s 29 claim. The right in s 2(1) gives preference to the deceased's line of descent and only when the possibility of finding a descendant has been exhausted does the succession open to the spouse, then collaterals and ascendants.

Under s 2(2) the right of each category of person ranked in s 2(1) is a hierarchy deferred to claims by a 'prior relative', with the children of the deceased ranking first. A prior relative is 'a person of any other class who, if he had survived the [deceased], would have had right to the intestate estate or any of it'. The phrase 'any of it' refers to the possibility that the intestate estate may be shared between several people. Only if there is no claimant in a class ranked higher in the list will the succession open to a claimant in the next category.

This means that as long as any member or members of a higher-ranked class survive and claim the free estate, a claim by a member or members of the next class is precluded. The classes of heirs enumerated in s 2(1) form a hierarchy, with the persons described at s 2(1)(a) having rights to the entire intestate estate before the succession opens to the class of relatives in the following subsection, and so on. The only exception in s 2(1) to a single class of persons having the right to the whole free estate is where the deceased is not survived by any direct descendants or a spouse but is survived by both parents and collaterals.

(1) Representation in the intestate free estate

6.35 Section 5(1) provides that representation applies to succession to the free intestate estate. The children or remoter issue of a predeceasing member of a class are entitled to the like right as their ancestor to the whole or part of the intestate estate as that person had he or she survived the deceased. Scots law has infinite representation, so grandchildren, great-grandchildren or great-great-grandchildren (as representatives of children) and so on would be preferred to spouse, collaterals or parents as the next ranking classes under s 2.[102]

Excepted from this rule are the issue of parents (since their issue are the deceased's collaterals and rank alongside them where both survive and after children where the parents have predeceased) and the issue of a surviving spouse or civil partner (since if any of the latter's children survived, they would either rank first, or be step-children with no entitlement to succeed).

Example

X dies intestate. He is survived by his father and his brother's daughter. Under s 2(1)(b), surviving parents and siblings rank equally. Representation applies to the issue of collaterals. X's father and X's niece (by representation under s 5) are entitled to claim equally under s 2(1)(b).

(a) Per stirpes and per capita distribution of the intestate free estate

6.36 Section 6 provides for the division of the intestate estate between claimants of the same class but of different degrees of relationship to the deceased. Under s 6(a) the intestate estate is to be divided equally between all persons of the same degree of relationship to the deceased (*per capita* division). Under s 6(b) the intestate estate is to be divided equally into a number of parts equal to the aggregate of: (i) those persons nearest in degree of relationship to the deceased; and (ii) any other persons related to the deceased in that degree but who have predeceased leaving surviving issue (*per stirpes* division). Surviving children take the whole intestate estate as head of the *stirps*, to the exclusion of their issue and the issue of any predeceasing children take the share that their parent would have had equally between them. *Per stirpes* division, therefore, involves division *per capita* at the level of the individual members of the *stirps*.[103]

102 On infinite representation, see K Anderson, 'Intestacy in Scotland: The Laughing Heir' (2011) 2 *Aberdeen Student Law Review* 52.
103 See paras **5.7–5.9**.

Example

X dies intestate, survived by a child B and two grandchildren C and D, the children of his predeceasing child A.

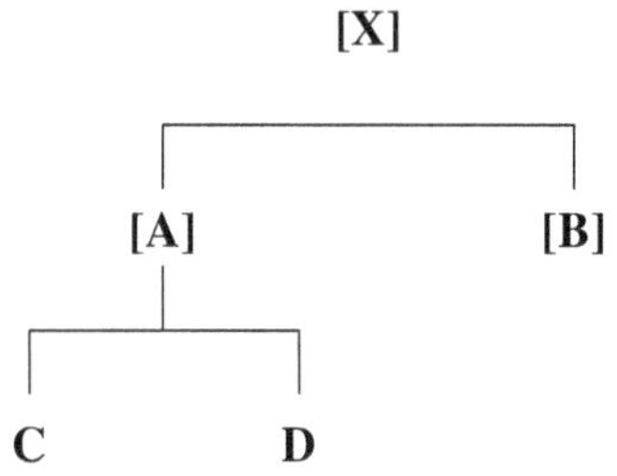

The intestate estate will be divided between B, C and D under s 2(1)(a) and the division will be *per stirpes* under s 6(b), with C and D representing A. B is entitled to a one-half share of the net intestate estate, and C and D to a one-half share equally between them.

(2) The order of succession

(a) Descendants

6.37 Section 2(1)(a) provides that where the deceased is survived by children, the children shall have the right to the whole of the intestate estate. Section 5 provides that representation applies and division is according to the scheme in s 6. Consequently, children and more remote descendants, or both, have the first claim to the whole intestate estate. If there are issues to take the intestate estate, any claim for legitim will be largely notional since they will be entitled to the whole moveable and heritable estate remaining after claims by the surviving spouse or civil partner – though where there is a collatable advance or discharge of legitim, computation of the legitim fund may still be relevant. **Chapter 2** sets out in detail which persons may be considered to be 'children' but, in brief, they include posthumous children, adopted children and children of unmarried parents – but not stepchildren.

Example

X is survived by a spouse and two children, A and B. After payment of prior rights, £30,000 of moveable estate remains. X's surviving spouse receives £10,000 as *ius relicti*, leaving a balance of £20,000. £10,000 will be divided between A and B *per capita* as legitim. The final £10,000 is also divided between A and B *per capita* under Section 2.

(b) Surviving spouse or civil partner

6.38 If no descendants survive, s 2(1)(ab)[104] provides that where a spouse or civil partner survives the deceased, he or she shall have the right to the whole intestate estate.

Under the pre-1964 law, a surviving husband or wife of the deceased did not have a right to succeed beyond claims for legal rights. It was only with the introduction of the 1964 Act that they were given the right to succeed to the intestate estate – which was one of the more radical departures from the common law. However, their ranking was formerly much lower in the order of succession, coming after collaterals and parents, until they were 'promoted' by the Trusts and Succession (Scotland) Act 2024. This promotion was brought about by the agreed consensus on giving the surviving spouse or civil partner the entire estate where the deceased died with no descendants.[105] Representation does not apply to the spouse's or civil partner's rights, thus excluding stepchildren.

(c) Collaterals and parents

6.39 If no descendants, spouse, or civil partner survive the deceased, s 2(1)(b) provides that where brothers and sisters and one or both parents survive, the surviving brothers and sisters will take half the intestate estate between them and the surviving parent or parents the other.

104 As introduced by s 77 of the Trusts and Succession (Scotland) Act 2024.

105 *Scottish Government Response to the Consultation on the Law of Succession* (2018), para 17.

Example

X is survived by both of her parents, A and B, and by two brothers C and D. A, B, C and D each take one quarter of the intestate estate *per capita*.

Representation under s 5(1) applies to the collaterals and the scheme of division under s 6 will apply if any of the collaterals have predeceased but are survived by children.[106]

Example

X is survived by her mother, A, her sister, B, and her nephew, D, the son of her predeceasing brother, C.

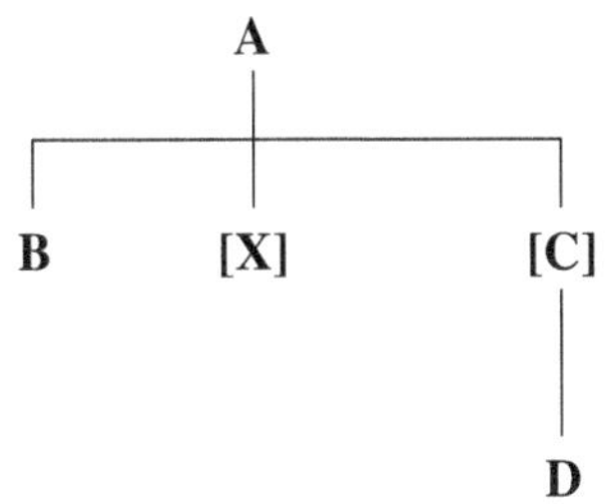

A takes a one-half share of X's intestate estate. B and D take the other half, with D representing C.

The provisions of s 2(1)(b) are subject to the rule that the right of collaterals of the half blood is postponed to the right of collaterals of the full blood.[107]

(d) Collaterals

6.40 If the deceased has no surviving children, spouse, civil partner, or parents but is survived only by brothers and sisters (or their descendants), s 2(1)(c) provides that they will succeed to the whole intestate estate.

106 See paras **6.35–6.36**.
107 See para **6.40**.

Example

X dies intestate, survived by her sisters, A and B. They are entitled to the whole intestate estate.

Section 3 of the 1964 Act provides that references in s 2(1) to brothers and sisters are to include brothers and sisters of the half-blood as well as brothers and sisters of the whole blood. This means that collaterals sharing only one parent with the deceased are included within the class of persons with rights to succeed under s 2(1)(b) and (c).

However, a rather arcane rule is engaged with half-siblings. The rights of half-brothers and half-sisters are restricted by the provisions of s 3, which provides that in succession to the intestate estate:

> 'The collaterals of the whole blood shall be entitled to succeed thereto in preference to the collaterals of the half blood.'

This means that where collaterals of both the whole-blood and the half-blood survive the deceased, only the collaterals of the whole blood are entitled to succeed to the intestate estate. Half-brothers and half-sisters have no rights in succession unless no collaterals of the full blood survive the deceased.

Example

X dies intestate. Her parents, A and B have both predeceased her, but A had married for a second time to C and had another child, D. X is survived by her sisters, Y and Z and by her half-sister, D.

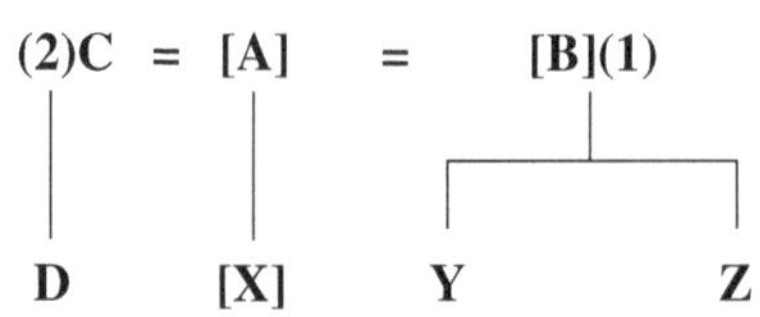

As Y and Z are collaterals of the whole blood to X, and their claims rank in preference to D's. D has no entitlement to a share in X's intestate estate.

Descendants of collaterals of the whole blood will take by representation under s 5(1) in preference to any surviving siblings of the half blood and division will be *per stirpes* where claimants are of different degrees of relationship to the deceased.[108]

Example

X dies intestate, survived by his half-brother A, and his nephew C, the son of his predeceasing sister, B.

A — [X] — [B]

|

C

C takes the whole intestate estate by way of representation under s 2(1)(c) and s 6(a). Only if B had not been survived by issue would A have taken the whole intestate estate.

An adopted child of the deceased person will be considered a collateral of the full blood to any natural children of that person if, and only if, he or she was adopted by both parents (together as spouses) of that natural child.[109] If only one of the natural child's or children's parents adopted him or her, he or she will be considered as being of the half blood. As in the case of half-brothers and half-sisters, a child adopted by one parent only will have no right of succession where any children of the full blood or their representatives survive.

Where only collaterals of the half blood or their representatives survive the deceased, they are entitled to succeed on the same basis as collaterals of the full blood if any had survived. Section 3 provides that where collaterals of the half blood have the right to succeed, the members of the class shall rank equally between themselves, regardless of whether their relationship to the deceased (or their ancestor if he or she takes by representation) is through the mother or through the father. To the modern reader, this would hardly appear worthy of note until it is remembered that, before the 1964 Act, the law made a distinction between persons related by the half-blood consanguinean (through the father) and those related through the half-blood uterine (through the mother). Rights of succession derived

108 See para **6.36**.
109 Succession (Scotland) Act 1964, s 24(1). See also para **2.8**.

through the former category were more favourable than those derived through the latter.[110] The distinction derives from the fact that at common law a person's mother did not count as next of kin. The result was that brothers and sisters of the half-blood uterine could not, accordingly, have any rights of succession rights at all to the intestate estate of a half-brother or half-sister where the shared parent was their mother.[111]

Example

A dies intestate, survived by his half-brothers, B and C.

[A] — B — C

B and C are entitled to the whole intestate estate.

(e) Parents

6.41 If no prior relatives (namely, children, collaterals, and spouses or civil partners) survive the deceased, s 2(1)(d) provides that the surviving parent or parents of the deceased have the right to the whole intestate estate. This means that it is only if no collaterals or descendants of collaterals survive (whether of the whole or the half blood) that parents have the right to succeed to the whole estate. Representation does not apply as the issue of parents would be the deceased's collaterals. Since both parents are in the same degree of relationship to the deceased, the division of the estate is *per capita* where both survive.

(f) Other heirs

6.42 If the possibility of finding an heir to the intestate estate from among the prior classes has been exhausted, the provisions of s 2(1)(f) to

110 Under the pre-1964 law, not only were rights of the half blood postponed to those of the full blood, but rights of the half blood uterine were postponed both to collaterals of the half blood consanguinean *and* parents.

111 Succession rights of collaterals of the half blood uterine were introduced by the Intestate Moveable Succession (Scotland) Act 1855, s 1 to include rights both as collaterals of the deceased and as representatives of their parent. Even so, their right extended only to a one-half share of the moveable estate, so that where there was no other class of person entitled to succeed, the other one-half share fell to the Crown as *ultimus haeres*.

s 2(1)(i) open the succession to ancestors. Beginning with uncles and aunts, the remaining subsections of s 2(1) include the relatives of either parent of the deceased, thus again departing from the pre-1964 law by admitting to the succession relatives on the maternal as well as the paternal side of the deceased's family. Section 2(1)(f) opens the succession to uncles and aunts; (collaterals of parents); s 2(1)(g) to grandparents; s 2(1)(h) to great-uncles and great-aunts (collaterals of grandparents); and s 2(1)(i) to very remote ancestors, generation by generation. This latter class thus includes great-great-grandparents.

Representation under s 5(1) applies to these classes of relatives with representation of spouses, civil partners and parents excluded. Thus, where predeceasing uncles and aunts are survived by children (the deceased's cousins) they will be entitled to succeed before the succession opens to the next class, grandparents. The division will be *per capita* under s 6(a) so that the intestate estate will be divided equally between all persons in the same degree of relationship to the deceased regardless of which side of the deceased's family they belong to. Under s 6(b), it will be divided *per stirpes* where those entitled to succeed are in a different degree of relationship as a consequence of representation.[112]

Example

X dies unmarried, predeceased by his parents, A and B. He is survived by his aunt, C, his uncle, D and his cousins, F and G, the children of his predeceasing uncle, E.

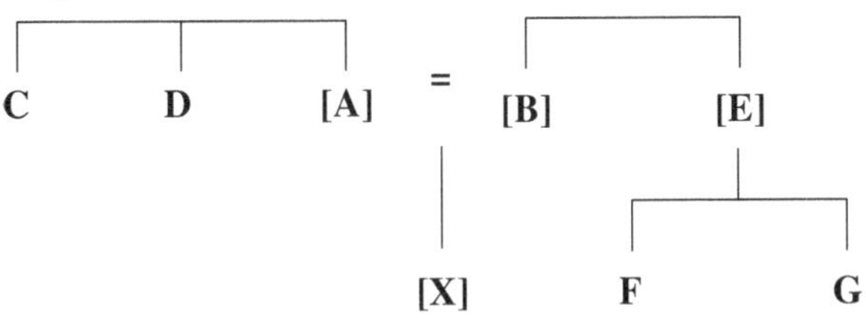

The division is *per stirpes* under s 6(b). C and D each take a one-third share. F and G represent E and take a one-third share equally between them.

Where an executor has to search for an heir through an ancestor more remote than a parent, the procedure may become somewhat complex. For

112 See para **6.36**.

example, second cousins, second cousins once removed and third cousins may be entitled to succeed. When it is considered that the class entitled to succeed may also include relatives of the half blood, the complexities can become enormous. Genealogical researchers or 'heir hunters' are typically employed to trace the family using public records.

This is the consequence (and, possibly, the cost) of infinite representation in succession. Even though the expenses of attempting to trace any living relative of the deceased may exhaust the estate, the executor is under a duty to keep searching until an eligible person is found, if not all eligible persons.

(g) The Crown as ultimus haeres

6.43 If the deceased's blood line is exhausted, or if it cannot be ascertained following inquiry, then the Crown claims the estate as *ultimus haeres* (last heir). The right of the Crown at common law to take the intestate estate where no other entitled person survives is retained in the Succession (Scotland) Act 1964, s 7. The origin of the right is ancient, and similar provision exists in other western legal systems.[113]

The King's and Lord Treasurer's Remembrancer (KLTR) is tasked with receiving such estates, which has a dedicated office called the National *Ultimus Haeres* Unit (NUHU).[114] The NUHU will attempt to trace the family of the deceased before realising the estate, retaining the funds, and then, once 20 years' negative prescription has passed to extinguish all immediate rights of succession, the proceeds are paid to the Scottish Consolidated Fund.[115] The KLTR website displays such estates available for claim.[116]

113 For a recent scandal in England & Wales, see M McClenaghan et al, 'Revealed: King Charles secretly profiting from the assets of dead citizens', *The Guardian,* 23 November 2023, available https://www.theguardian.com/uk-news/2023/nov/23/revealed-king-charles-secretly-profiting-from-the-assets-of-dead-citizens.

114 See https://www.kltr.gov.uk/ultimus-haeres/national-ultimus-haeres-unit/.

115 KLTR Office, *Ultimus Haeres policy,* policy UH6, available https://www.kltr.gov.uk/about/our-policies/#uh6-claiming-uh-estates---time-limit. See also BBC News, 'The people who die alone with no one to mourn them', 6 September 2020, available https://www.bbc.co.uk/news/uk-scotland-53805937.

116 See https://www.kltr.gov.uk/ultimus-haeres/deaths-being-investigated/.

In practice, the Crown has discretion to make grants from the estate to persons who have a moral claim on the deceased's estate, or to a person for whom the deceased might reasonably have been expected to make provision. Applicants might include the deceased's long-term friends, carers, stepfamily, or accepted family.

EXAMPLE DISTRIBUTION OF WHOLLY INTESTATE ESTATE

6.44 The purpose of the following example is to illustrate how a wholly intestate estate may be distributed with all rights on intestacy being claimed. In this example, it is assumed that X owns the family home as sole proprietor. In reality, however, the family home is more likely to be co-owned by two spouses or civil partners and a person owning property to such a value is more likely to have died testate as it is often an incident of a house purchase transaction that the buyer makes a will directing the distribution of ownership of the home on their death.

Example

Larry dies intestate, survived by a spouse Olivia and two children, Frances and Romy.

Larry owned the family home in Dowanhill worth £500,000, with no secured loan. The household goods are worth £40,000. Larry had a new car worth £12,000. Larry also owned a collection of watches inherited from his father worth £10,000. Larry had a series of stocks on the market worth £100,000.

Larry died with a credit card with £4,000 outstanding. His funeral and cremation costs £12,000.

	Heritable Estate	**Moveable Estate**	**Notes**
Inventory			
Home	£500,000		
Household goods		£20,000	*Presumed co-owned under s 25 of the Family Law (Scotland) Act 1985.*
Car		£12,000	
Watches		£10,000	
Investments		£100,000	
Funerary costs		(£12,000)	
Credit Card debt		(£4,000)	
Net Values	**£500,000**	**£126,000**	**£626,000**
Prior Rights			
S 8(1) Dwellinghouse Right	(£473,000)		To Olivia
S 8(3) Plenishings Right		(£20,000)	To Olivia
	£27,000	*£106,000*	*£133,000*
S 9(1) Financial Provision	(£10,150.38)	(£39,849.62)	Apportioned under s 9(3).
	£16,849.62	£66,150.38	
Legal Rights			
Jus relictae		(£22,050.13)	To Olivia
Legitim		(£22,050.13)	To Frances and Romy (£11,025.07 each)
Intestate Free Estate	£16,849.62	£22,050.13	
	£38,899.75		
	(£38,899.75)		To Frances and Romy. (£19,449.87 each)
	£0.00		

Each successor receives:

Olivia	£565,050.13
Frances	£30,474.94
Romy	£30,474.94
Total	**£626,000.00**

PARTIAL INTESTACY

6.45 The rules on intestacy in the Succession (Scotland) Act 1964 apply to 'so much of an estate which is undisposed of by testamentary disposition'[117] and will thus apply on partial intestacy. Partial intestacy will arise where, despite a testator having executed a valid testamentary document, parts of its provisions are ineffective or do not provide a complete distribution of the estate.[118] The deceased may not have disposed of all of his or her property by testament or a partial intestacy may arise because they have omitted to include a residuary legatee, who will take any part of the remaining estate not bequeathed specifically to any beneficiary.

A surviving spouse or civil partner has the same rights on partial as in total intestacy. Providing that any property is undisposed of by testamentary disposition, prior rights can be claimed in respect of the dwellinghouse, the furniture and plenishings and money. Since each prior right is independent of the other, the surviving spouse will have a right to any or all prior rights, depending on the circumstances.

Example

X dies survived by her civil partner, A. She has bequeathed her share of the family home to A, but a provision in her will giving a legacy of £10,000 to her sister B is ineffective, and it falls into intestacy. A is entitled to claim the whole £10,000 under Section 9 since she has received no legacies from X other than one which relates to prior rights under s 8.

117 1964 Act, s 36(1).
118 See **Part 4** below. See also G L Gretton, 'Partial intestacy' 1986 *SLT (News)* 201–02.

Under s 9(1), the value of any legacy to the surviving spouse must be deducted from the value of his or her entitlement unless the legacy is of a type that can be claimed under s 8.

If proper consideration is given to the drafting of the deed, no part of the estate should be intestate. Appropriate solutions should be contained within the deed to avoid, as far as possible, intestacy occurring. Inserting destinations-over and providing for a residuary legatee should prevent partial intestacy resulting but, if it does, and there is a surviving spouse or civil partner, claims for prior rights must be satisfied from the intestate part of the estate.[119] If there is no surviving spouse or civil partner, the intestate estate will be distributed to those persons entitled to succeed to the deceased under s 2 of the 1964 Act.

ARTIFICIAL INTESTACY

6.46 An estate may become artificially or partially artificially intestate in two circumstances. Firstly, if a will has been made by the deceased but it is reduced, the estate will fall to intestacy and be distributed according to the provisions of the Succession (Scotland) Act 1964, Pt I.[120] Secondly, a surviving spouse or civil partner who is a universal legatee may renounce his or her legacy, with the effect that the whole estate falls into intestacy and becomes available for prior and legal rights. Partial artificial intestacy may also result where a beneficiary renounces a legacy in order to claim legal rights.[121]

Renunciation by a universal legatee to create a partial intestacy involves a rational calculation on the part of the surviving spouse or civil partner who wishes to exclude claims for legitim by the deceased's issue. For intestacy to be total, the beneficiary must be a universal legatee so that the only possible outcome of renunciation can be total, artificial intestacy. This possibility and its consequences were made apparent in *Kerr, Petitioner*.[122]

119 On the drafting of wills generally, see A Barr, *Drafting Wills in Scotland*, 2nd edn (2009).

120 It may be reduced on the grounds of formal invalidity (see **Ch 7**) or essential invalidity (see **Ch 8**) or because a child of the deceased has invoked the *conditio si testator sine liberis decesserit* (see para **7.16**).

121 Unless there is a residuary legatee, see para **10.7**.

122 *Kerr Ptr* 1968 SLT (Sh Ct) 61.

A widow was the universal legatee of her husband. A daughter from a previous marriage had also survived him, and her entitlement to legitim would have reduced the estate available for payment of the legacy to the widow. To prevent any moveable estate being available to satisfy the daughter's claim, the widow renounced her legacy of the whole of her husband's estate and the question for the court was whether intestacy was the invariable outcome of the renouncing of a universal settlement. The court answered in the affirmative, with the result being that the widow could claim prior rights and exhaust the entire (now intestate) estate, thus excluding her stepdaughter's claim to legitim. Clearly, it is only possible to exclude entirely claims by children if the total value of the estate is less than the maximum prior rights values under ss 8–9 of the 1964 Act at the relevant time.

Part 3:

Testaments and testators

Chapter 7

Testaments and testamentary devices

INTRODUCTION

7.1 In intestate succession, the deceased had not expressed how they wish their estate to be disposed of on death. In testate succession, the deceased person has clearly expressed their intentions for distribution of their estate in the form of a testamentary document.[1] A 'testament' is a document of such nature that constitutes and gives effect to a person's intentions as to the disposal of his or her property after death. The principle underlying the whole law of testate succession is that of 'testamentary freedom';[2] a testator is free to dispose of his or her property in such manner as he or she wishes, subject to claims for legal rights[3] and certain constraints of law and policy.[4]

For the document as a whole[5] to be valid and have binding effect as a testamentary document, it must: (i) conform to the basic rules of capacity and be free from wrongful third-party interference, (ii) conform to the rules for the execution of testamentary documents; and (iii) clearly demonstrate an *animus testandi* (an intention to test) on the part of the testator.[6] This chapter considers the rules relating to identifying an intention to test in

1 For a historical account of the law relating to the making of wills, alongside useful commentary of the current law, see K Reid, 'Testamentary formalities in Scotland' in K Reid et al (eds), *Comparative Succession Law: Volume I: Testamentary Formalities* (2011).

2 For an interesting exposition of this principle, see A Braun, 'Testamentary responsibility' (2024) 28(3) *Edin LR* 325 and the collection of chapters in M Anderson and E Arroyo i Amayuelas, *The Law of Succession: Testamentary Freedom: European Perspectives* (2011).

3 See **Ch 5**.

4 See **Ch 12**.

5 On the validity of legacies in the document, see **Part 4**.

6 To 'test' means to witness or verify, from the Latin *testare*, and a person who executes a testament is known as a 'testator' or 'testatrix' depending on their gender. For convenience, testator is used in this chapter.

documents executed by the deceased, alongside the requirements of formal validity. **Chapter 8** explores the effect of incapacity and wrongful third-party interference which may further affect the testamentary document from being considered as valid and binding.

Where there is a deficiency or invalidity in a testamentary document such that no *animus testandi* can be validly demonstrated, the outcome may be that the law treats the document as simply having no effect.[7] In these cases, the result is that the estate will be intestate and fall to be distributed in accordance with the rules of intestate succession provided in the Succession (Scotland) Act 1964 and set out in **Chapter 6**.

TESTAMENTARY DOCUMENTS

7.2 In testate succession, the deceased has executed a document of testamentary nature in which they have set out the intended distribution of all or part of their estate after death.[8] Testamentary documents must conform to particular legal forms if they are to function as a means of instructions for the executor in distributing property to nominated beneficiaries or legatees. Clearly, a person cannot test over property to which they had no right at the time of their death and the property that forms the subjects of legacies given by testament must, therefore, have been *in bonis defuncti* of the testator and they must have had the power of testation in relation to it.[9] Only writings which dispose of property that the deceased already has a right to, or in, at death can be classified as testamentary writings 'proper'. By contrast, rights relating to property that are contingent on the deceased's death (such as nominations specifying the beneficiary of the proceeds of an insurance policy) do not derive from testamentary writings but from other deeds which have testamentary effect. These types of devices may dispose of a large proportion of the deceased's property but property disposed of in this way will not vest in the executor and will not, accordingly, form part of the deceased's estate and will not be available for legal rights.

7 Of course, in a voidable deed, it takes effect until reduced by the court.

8 Though no single definition exists, see the definition in s 28(3) of the Succession (Scotland) Act 2016.

9 A bequest of property that is not *in bonis* of the deceased at the time of his or her death is *legatum rei alienae* but not necessarily void; see paras **4.2**, and **10.19.**

Clark's Executor v Clark[10] illustrates the importance of distinguishing between different types of writing. The testator had written to M, stating 'in the event of my death I do hereby leave and bequeath to M the whole of my collection of postage stamps'. Two years later, he executed a will in which he bequeathed the whole of his estate to the Pathologist Society of Edinburgh for the purposes of cancer research. His will contained a clause stating that he cancelled all previous wills made by him. After the testator's death, the Pathologist Society agreed to pay the testator's sister a liferent of the income from her brother's estate and averred that his estate included the stamp collection. It argued that the will was a universal settlement: it disposed of the entire estate to one beneficiary and it therefore revoked automatically all previous and inconsistent bequests. M averred that the will did not revoke the earlier donation: the revocation clause in the will referred only to wills and not to all of the deceased's testamentary writings. In any case, the term 'will' had no technical meaning. The court held that the revocation clause was to be construed narrowly to apply only to previous wills and not to all testamentary writings. The letter granting the legacy of the stamp collection was not a 'will' and if the testator had really intended that the collection should pass to the Pathologist Society, the revocation clause would have referred to all testamentary writings.

MAKING A WILL AND OTHER TESTAMENTARY DOCUMENTS

7.3 There are three key types of writing that typically form a testamentary document. These are wills, trust dispositions and settlements, and codicils. Not all three are employed in every case, and a will is the most usual way in which a person expresses his or her testamentary intention.[11] As well as making provisions for the disposal of the estate, wills also nominate an executor in whom the property will vest at confirmation for the purposes of ingathering and distributing the estate.[12]

10 *Clark's Executor v Clark* 1943 SC 216.

11 See M Meston, 'The power of the will' 1982 *Jur Rev* 172.

12 Indeed, the appointment of an executor was the most fundamental point of making a will in early medieval Scotland, see A Anton, 'Medieval Scottish executors and the courts spiritual' (1955) 67 *Jur Rev* 129.

A trust disposition and settlement (often abbreviated as a TDS) is similar to a will, except that rather than the deceased's property transmitting to an executor, it transmits to testamentary trustees (of which executors are a species),[13] and is administered for the trust purposes, such as the maintenance of children or the administration of a liferent. The trustees are empowered not simply to pay debts and convey legacies to beneficiaries but also to hold the property for the benefit of the beneficiaries, possibly over a long period of time.[14]

A will or a TDS is often a single, discrete document, drawn up by a solicitor, under which the deceased person's entire estate will be passed to various beneficiaries in terms of the provisions which he or she has expressed in the deed. A testator may execute a will or TDS and, at a later date, execute one or more codicils that may amend or alter the original document. Codicils typically serve to merely amend or alter an existing document, rather than revoke it entirely and make new provisions *in toto*.

Whilst these are the common ways in which a person makes testamentary provisions, there is no prescribed format as to what constitutes a will or other testamentary document. Testamentary documents may also comprise more informal letters written by the testator which set out his or her wishes and intentions as to the legacies to be bequeathed to beneficiaries. Whether such informal writings are to be construed as having testamentary effect must be ascertained from the context in which the apparent expression of testamentary intention appears. Such writings must be distinguished between (a) writings that demonstrate a definite and final intention on the part of the deceased for the disposal of his or her estate from (b) other writings which appear merely to be the deceased's musings or half-complete changes of mind as to the possible destination of his or her property after death.

13 Trusts and Succession (Scotland) Act 2024, s 81(1) for the meaning of trustee.

14 The law of trusts is beyond the scope of this book but for a treatment of trusts in light of the Trusts and Succession (Scotland) Act 2024, see G Gretton and A Steven, *Property, Trusts and Succession,* 5th edn (2024), Chs 24–26. An older but more extensive treatment, though soon to be out of date, can be found in W Wilson and A Duncan *Trusts, Trustees and Executors,* 2nd edn (1995).

INTENTION TO TEST (*ANIMUS TESTANDI*)

7.4 The fundamental requirement of a testamentary document is that the testator actually intended it to have testamentary effect. In other words, the writing must show the deceased had an intention to test, or *animus testandi,* when executing the document. In a professionally drafted document, this will be simple enough, and the preamble to a will typically contains wording clearly indicating the document is to have testamentary effect, such as:[15]

> 'I, Ephesia Jolly, residing at 12 University Gardens, Glasgow G12 8QQ, in order to settle the succession to my estate after my death provide as follows…'

This can seem entirely straightforward. However, difficulties can arise where the document is not altogether clear as to whether it was intended to have testamentary effect. A significant volume of case law has been generated where informal writings such as letters, diaries and notes have been found indicating some form of discussion about the distribution of property after the deceased's death, and whether such informal writings were intended to have testamentary effect.[16]

Where there is doubt as to whether the document is testamentary, the decisive factor for a court in assessing the document is whether or not it can be established that the testator meant it to represent his or her concluded testamentary intention. It is therefore vital to ascertain whether a document was in fact intended to be a clear and final intention to bequeath property, as Lord President Emslie noted in *Jamieson's Exrs and Fyvie*:[17]

> 'What we have to decide is whether the holograph writing, properly construed in the light of the agreed circumstances only, evinces a present concluded testamentary intention.'

15 Taken from A Barr, *Drafting Wills in Scotland,* 2nd edn (2009), appendix.

16 As some examples of such documents that have kept the courts busy in this area in in recent years, see *Carswell v Skelton* [2025] SC HAM 54; *Downey's Exrs, Applicants* [2021] SC EDIN 60; *Gray's Exr v Manson* [2017] CSOH 25; *Fulton v Muir* [2017] CSOH 25; and *Hamilton, Ptr* 2015 SLT (Sh Ct) 176. It is a fruitful area for litigation, see further R MacLeod, *Contentious Executries: Commissary and Executry Litigation in Scotland,* 2nd edn (2023), paras 2-50–2-054.

17 1981 SC 1, per Lord President Emslie at 3.

Much can turn on the reading of the document itself and its context rather than on a matter of strictly following precedent from other cases before the courts:[18]

> 'Construction of the holograph writing against this background is not assisted by consideration of decisions in other cases which proceed upon their own facts and circumstances. We must do the best we can with the particular language of this holograph writing itself and the background peculiar to this case.'

Evidence that a person intended merely to make testamentary provision at some future date is insufficient to show that he or she conclusively carried out such an intention. Precursory documents falling short of evidencing completed testamentary intent might be said to show only mere aspirations, wishes or thoughts. For example, a note as to what the deceased thought his or her intentions might be in future[19] or an instruction to a solicitor to draw up a will in particular terms may not evidence completed testamentary intent. Generally, a letter to a solicitor from a person stating his or her testamentary intentions and requesting that the solicitor draft a will to that effect is not capable of constituting the testator's final intention or, therefore, having binding effect.[20]

Whether instructions alone are testamentary depends, therefore, on the manner and form in which the instructions have been given, although even apparently informal instructions may be declared valid, depending on all the surrounding facts and circumstances.[21]

The court has shown flexibility in cases where documents have been more informal than what is expected of a traditional will, although it remains the case that testaments must always be constituted in traditional writing and subscribed to be formally valid.[22] This seems to derive from the courts' reluctance against creating an intestacy, in that if the deceased

18 1981 SC 1, per Lord President Emslie at 4.

19 *Jamieson's Exrs and Fyvie* 1981 SC 1.

20 *Munro v Coutts* (1813) 1 Dow 437; *Colvin v Hutchison* (1885) 12 R 947; *Stuart v Stuart* 1942 SC 510; and *Cameron's Trs v Mackenzie* 1915 SC 313 (*cf MacLaren's Trustees v Mitchell and Brattan* 1959 SLT 290 and *Barker's Executors v Scottish Rights of Way Society Ltd* 1996 SC 396).

21 *MacLaren's Trustees v Roberts* 1959 SC 359. On the use of extrinsic evidence, see *Munro v Coutts* (1813) 1 Dow 437 and *Stuart v Stuart* 1942 SC 510.

22 Requirements of Writing (Scotland) Act 1995, s 2(1).

has executed a document in such a manner that indicates a concluded testamentary effect, then the courts will try to give it effect to honour the deceased's intentions and avoid at least some of the estate being distributed by the rules of intestate succession. As Lord President Inglis stated in *Colvin v Hutchison*:[23]

> 'I do not think it matters how inelegant, or how imperfect grammatically a testator's language may be, if it can fairly be construed to mean that he bequeaths certain sums of money to certain individuals, sufficiently designed in the writing itself.'

There are many examples in this area, but a few cases of note are offered here. In *Rhodes v Peterson*[24] a woman wrote a letter to her daughter, stating *inter alia* 'I want you to have the house and contents.' She stated that she intended to make a formal will but 'just in case anything happens to me in the meantime this letter will establish your formal claim'. She signed the letter 'Mum'. The letter was held to be a valid testament.[25]

In *Davidson v Convy*[26] the deceased had written the words 'my will' on an envelope and signed her name beneath the words. The envelope was unsealed and contained a single sheet of paper with her testamentary instructions written in her own handwriting. The court held that the use of the signature evinced the necessary finality of intention and that the words 'my will' were 'clearly adoptive in character'.[27] Although the contents of the envelope may have changed over time so that the signature and the content of the envelope may not have been unequivocally linked, it held that the deceased would have recognised the adoptive force of what was written on the envelope and it was 'inconceivable that she should leave within it a testamentary writing other than one to which she intended effect to be given'.[28]

23 (1855) 12 R 947, per Lord President Inglis at 955.

24 1971 SC 56.

25 The signature 'mum' is troublesome for probativity under the 1995 Act. However, it is capable of being valid (though improbative) under s 7(2)(c) as a description provided that it is their intended or normal method of signature for the type of document.

26 2003 SC 420. The case was distinguished, on the facts, from the previous cases of *Taylor's Executrices v Thom* 1914 SC 79 (where the testator had not signed either the envelope nor the sheet of paper) and *Stenhouse v Stenhouse* 1922 SC 370 (where the deceased had failed to sign the outside of the envelope).

27 2003 SC 420, per Lord Marnoch at para 6.

28 2003 SC 420, per Lord Marnoch at para 7.

In *Barker's Executors v Scottish Rights of Way Society Ltd*[29] the testator had executed a formal will in 1985. Shortly before her death in 1991, she wrote to her solicitors, enclosing an earlier will dated from 1983 on which she had made various handwritten additions and alterations, as well as other writings. In the letter she referred to what she had sent as an 'extra ordinary document'[30] and stated that she had signed it for it to be adopted as a will in case things did not go well for her, given her ongoing health problems. The pursuers argued that the letter and enclosed documents amounted only to instructions to her solicitor to alter her will. The court held *inter alia* that while the testatrix was giving her solicitor instructions to change her will, it was also plain from the letter that, given the state of her health, she intended that the document should constitute an immediate testamentary document. The court held that the documents in question constituted a single instrument and should be looked at as a whole, since the testatrix had attempted to link the numbered list of legacies in the altered 1983 copy will with the subsequent bequests contained in the other writings. When she sent the 1991 package to her solicitor, she regarded herself as settling her affairs on a complete basis.

FORMAL VALIDITY

(1) Testamentary documents executed before 1 August 1995

7.5 Whilst it is advisable to update a will regularly, a will or testamentary document executed before the Requirements of Writing (Scotland) Act 1995 came into force on 1 August 1995 may still require analysis today under the old law as to whether it is a formally valid testament.

Generally, testamentary writings executed before the coming into force of the 1995 Act may be in one of two forms; attested wills or privileged writings.[31] Each has separate requirements for validity but only a formally attested deed will be considered probative; that is self-proving, so that

29 1996 SC 396.

30 1996 SC 396, per Lord Johnston at 399.

31 For a fuller account of the execution of deeds under the old law, see R Rennie and D Cusine, *The Requirements of Writing* (1995), Ch 2.

no further evidence is required to fulfil the requirements of validity. By contrast, privileged writings are not probative in the full sense of the word, in that further evidence as to their authenticity is required, but they may be considered probative for the purpose of satisfying requirements as to their constitution.

The most basic requirement of validity of testamentary writing in any form before the passage of the 1995 Act was the subscription of the deed by the granter. For further examination of the substantive rules for deeds executed before the commencement of the 1995 Act, readers are directed to the previous edition of this work.[32]

(2) Testamentary documents executed after 1 August 1995

7.6 The Requirements of Writing (Scotland) Act 1995, which came into force on 1 August 1995, simplified the law relating to the constitution of deeds in comparison to the complex old law.[33] Whether the 1995 Act is simple to understand in modern times is a different question that may have to be answered in the negative. Successive statutory reforms have unfortunately made the 1995 Act an unwieldy piece of legislation. The Scottish Law Commission is currently reviewing the law relating to the execution of documents to see whether improvements can be made.[34]

(a) Writing and subscription

7.7 The 1995 Act provides that writing is required for the making of any will, testamentary trust disposition and settlement or codicil.[35]

To be formally valid, s 2 provides that the only requirement for the formal validity of a testamentary document is that it must be subscribed

32 See H Hiram, *Scots Law of Succession,* 2nd edn (2007), paras 5.5–5.12. See also 'Wills and Succession', Vol 25, in *The Laws of Scotland: Stair Memorial Encyclopaedia,* Ch 5(2).

33 See the work of the Scottish Law Commission in their recommendations which led to the 1995 Act, Report *on Requirements of Writing* (SLC Report No 112, 1988).

34 See https://www.scotlawcom.gov.uk/execution-documents.

35 1995 Act, s 1(2)(c). A useful discussion of the interaction of the 1995 Act with the execution of testamentary documents can be found in E Scobbie (ed), *Currie on Confirmation of Executors,* 9th edn (2011), Ch 3.

by the granter.[36] Like the old law, subscription is an absolutely essential requirement for formal validity, as the classic statement by Lord Trayner in *Foley v Costello* sets out:[37]

> 'I think the law of Scotland requires subscription as the essential and only admissible evidence of a concluded expression of will on the part of a testator. … In my opinion the rule is inflexible — no subscription, no will — and to admit the consideration of facts and circumstances to modify that rule would be very inexpedient and dangerous.'

Section 7 provides the rules of subscription. Subscription must be signed by the testator 'at the end of the last page' of the document.[38] In *Weatheritt's Exrs, Applicants*,[39] the deceased had made a homemade will running to three pages, but the deceased had signed the will on the first page alone which the sheriff held to be invalid. Affixing a signature at the bottom of the last page of the document after the document's operative parts is of paramount importance.

For what constitutes an acceptable signature, a natural person may sign by:[40]

(a) their full name (eg: 'Elizabeth Mary Clark');[41]

(b) their surname and at least one forename, or an initial or abbreviation or familiar form of a forename (eg: 'Elizabeth Clark', 'E Clark', 'EM Clark', 'Lizzie Clark');[42] or

(c) any other name, description, initials or mark provided this is a usual method of signing a testamentary document, or it was intended to be their signature for the testamentary document in question (eg: 'Mum', 'Your loving sister', 'Liz', 'Lizzie', 'Elizabeth', 'EMC' etc).[43]

36 1995 Act, s 2(1).

37 (1904) 6 F 365, 369-370. See also *Taylor's Exrs v Thom* 1914 SC 79; and *Robbie v Carr* 1959 SLT (Notes) 16.

38 1995 Act, s 7(1).

39 [2024] SC JED 3.

40 1995 Act, s 7(2). For further analysis and discussion, see A Barr, *Drafting Wills in Scotland,* 2nd edn (2009), para 2.38.

41 1995 Act, s 7(2)(a).

42 1995 Act, s 7(2)(b).

43 1995 Act, s 7(2)(c).

The third category can cause problems in respect of achieving probative status for the document, as noted below. However, provided it can be shown that they are their usual or intended method of signature, the testamentary document can still be valid.[44] Finally, it should be noted that special rules are made for signatures for the Royal Family and the nobility.[45]

In the event that the testator is blind or unable to physically sign a document, such as due to medical impairment, special provision is made for certain individuals to sign on their behalf.[46] This is commonly referred to in the legal profession as 'notarial execution', albeit the 1995 Act does not require a sworn notary public. Instead, a solicitor, advocate, justice of the peace, or sheriff clerk may execute documents on behalf of the unable testator.[47] There are special restrictions in the event that the signatory or their immediate family are in line to benefit from the document, such that they are disqualified from receiving such benefits.[48] Before the signatory executes the document, the testator must make a declaration that they are indeed blind or unable to write, and the signatory must have read, or offered to read, the document to the testator so they are satisfied with its contents.[49] In the event that a blind person still wishes to sign the document, they can still do so.[50]

It should be noted that, unlike the position with other documents which require being in writing under the 1995 Act, it is not currently possible to constitute a formally valid testamentary document with authentication by electronic signature. A testamentary document must be in traditional paper format that is physically subscribed by the testator.[51] The lack of

44 As an example of this in the old law, in *Draper v Thomason* 1954 SC 136, the deceased had signed a letter subscribed with 'Connie' alone, yet Lord Patrick could 'see no valid objection to the letter in point of form' given this was her usual method of signing letters to relatives, see the judgment at 143.

45 1995 Act, s 7(6). Only the sovereign is permitted to superscribe the top of a deed, on the basis that he or she does not have time to read everything put in front of him or her for signature, Stair, *Inst,* IV.42.3 and 1995 Act, s 13.

46 1995 Act, s 9 and Sch 3. See also s 10A which permits the authorised signatory to not have to be physically present with the testator when the execution takes place.

47 1995 Act, s 9(6).

48 1995 Act, s 9(4).

49 1995 Act, s 9(1).

50 1995 Act, s 9(7).

51 The Land Registration etc. (Scotland) Act 2012 (Commencement No. 2 and Transitional Provisions) Order 2014 Sch, Part 2.

electronically signed wills has been described as a 'a deep hole in Scots succession law'.[52]

(b) Probativity

7.8 Whilst achieving validity of the document is important, there is a further standard that a testamentary document must obtain known as probative (or self-proving) status. Probative status gives a document a hallmark, and indeed can be thought of as a 'gold standard' for deeds, in that the document is presumed to be validly executed.[53] Thus, a court can look at a probative deed and can be satisfied from the face of the deed that the testator in question was indeed the person who subscribed the document. This is a presumption alone and may be overturned on an evidential hearing as to the actual execution of a document. However, it is a worthwhile presumption to have with a document as the onus is placed on a party challenging the document to overturn the presumption and show that it was not validly executed.

Achieving probative status is necessary in testate succession because an executor-nominate can only obtain confirmation with a probative document. Under s 21A of the Succession (Scotland) Act 1964, an executor-nominate cannot obtain confirmation with an improbative testamentary document.[54] Therefore, it is somewhat necessary for the document to achieve probative status alongside being formally valid in order to allow the testate estate to be distributed. After confirmation is obtained, s 32 of the 1964 Act treats the grant of confirmation as a judicial endorsement that the testamentary document is formally valid.[55]

To achieve probative status, the requirements of s 3 of the 1995 Act must be satisfied. Section 3 provides that a document is probative if:

52 L Wright, 'Cases of the paperless will' (2019) 64(4) *JLSS*, online edition, available https://www.lawscot.org.uk/members/journal/issues/vol-64-issue-04/cases-of-the-paperless-will/. The Law Commission of England & Wales has recommended the introduction of electronic wills into English law, Report on *Modernising Wills*, Vol I (LC Report No 419, 2025), Ch 8.

53 1995 Act, s 3(1).

54 1964 Act, s 21A(a).

55 1964 Act, s 32.

(a) it bears to have been subscribed by the testator using either their full name, or their surname with at least one forename or initial;[56]

(b) it bears to have been signed by a witness with a signature in the manner consistent with the above, and the witness includes their details on the document;[57]

(c) There is nothing in the document to indicate that it was not validly witnessed or not validly signed by the testator;[58] and

(d) The document has been signed on every 'sheet'[59] by the testator. The reason for this requirement is to safeguard against fraud, whereby a person may swap the sheets of the document with a legacy or other wording that benefits them after the will has been executed by the testator.

Attestation by a witness is perhaps the most important requirement for probative status, though the others are necessary too. Having a witness sign is the witness attesting that the testator signed the document. Attestation provides a person other than the testator (who in most cases will be dead by the point that any questions arise as to their subscription of the document) to evidence that it was the testator who signed the document in question, and the witness can then be called upon in court to recount this if need be.

The witness must know the granter,[60] and be at least 16 years old and have capacity.[61] The witness must either see the testator subscribe to the

56 1995 Act, s 3(1)(a); and see the wording in s 7(2)(c) that 'except for the purposes of section 3(1) to (7) of this Act…'.

57 1995 Act, s 3(1)(b).

58 1995 Act, s 3(1)(c). This is a negative requirement that nothing in subsections s 3(4)(a)–(e) is shown in the deed.

59 Note the use of the word 'sheet' rather than 'page' in this part of the 1995 Act. If a will is printed double-sided, does the testator have to sign each sheet of paper once, or do they have to sign each side of the sheet as each side is a page? The view taken has been that only signing one side is permissible as the wording of s 3(2) uses the term 'sheet', not page. See Report *on Requirements of Writing* (SLC Report No 112, 1988), paras 5.5–5.7.

60 1995 Act, s 3(4)(c)(i) and s 3(5). See *Brock v Brock* 1908 SC 964.

61 1995 Act, s 3(4)(c).

document,[62] or observe the testator acknowledging his subscription to the witness as one 'continuous process' after the testator signed the document.[63] What this means is that a testator could later show the signed document to a witness and then ask the witness to sign the document to attest to the testator's execution. In respect of the testator's acknowledgement:[64]

> 'It must be an acknowledgment which leaves no doubt in the mind of the witness. It may either be in words, which leave less room for ambiguity, or by acts, which must be very precise, and will be carefully scanned.'

The circumstances may be such that the silence of the granter may suffice as an acknowledgement to the witness.[65] However, a witness must sign as soon as the acknowledgement is performed to them because the witness's signature must be added in a 'continuous process' following the acknowledgement. As long as, in any reasonable sense, this is the case, the witness need not subscribe in the presence of the testator immediately – though too long a period after acknowledgement may prove troublesome.[66]

(c) *Probativity via court docquet*

7.9 In the event that probative status cannot be achieved from the face of the document itself, it is possible to apply to court for a docquet or short certificate that can allow the document to achieve probative status instead. There are various phrases for this mechanism, but it is often termed as 'setting up',[67] in that the court sets up the deed as probative.[68]

Section 4 of the 1995 Act allows an application to be made to the court to confer probative status provided the document is at least formally

62 1995 Act, s 3(4)(d).

63 1995 Act, s 3(4)(e).

64 *Cumming v Skeoch's Trs* (1879) 6 R 963, per Lord Justice Clerk Moncrieff at para 967.

65 *Cumming*, per Lord Justice Clerk Moncrieff at para 967. See Lord Cameron's summary of the requirements in *MacDougall v MacDougall's Executors* 1994 SLT 1178.

66 See *Thomson v Clarkson's Trustees* (1892) 20 R 59.

67 See E Scobbie, *Currie on Confirmation*, 9th edn (2011), Ch 19.

68 By obtaining the docquet, it will also be deemed formally valid given probative status is self-proving status. A s 4 endorsement would establish a presumption that is has been validly signed.

valid.[69] Thus, if a letter with concluded testamentary effect is found but is only signed 'Your loving sister, Julie' with no witness, it is possible to apply to court for a s 4 endorsement that the letter is probative given the subscription at least achieves formal validity. That is provided evidence can be shown that the signature was the deceased's normal way of executing documents of that type, or their intention for that document in question.

Evidence of the signing of the document can be resolved by way of a witness affidavits, though it can be the case that sometimes hearings are required. An Act of Sederunt[70] provides the form of application, and affidavits to be completed by witnesses. Affidavits can be, for example, by a person confirming the signature is indeed the testator's own, or even that the person was a witness to the testator's signature, albeit they did not sign the document at the material time.[71]

This process can be utilised as part of other court proceedings, such as where the validity of the document is being challenged or even as part of the grant of confirmation. In more contentious areas where more than one challenge is being advanced in respect of the document, then the matter is likely to be resolved by way of a proof in a wider court action.[72]

(d) Alterations

7.10 It is not uncommon to find a testamentary document where there is a defined text but then the document bears amendments such as scored-out lines or handwritten changes. For the 1995 Act, alterations include any:[73]

> 'Interlineation, marginal addition, deletion, substitution, erasure or anything written on erasure ['erasure' nowadays is colloquially known as tippex after the brand name.]'

69 Without subscription with a signature conform to s 7(2), then s 4 is of no assistance, see *Weatheritt's Exrs, Applicants* [2024] SC JED 3.

70 Act of Sederunt (Requirements of Writing) 1996 SI 1996/1534.

71 Act of Sederunt, para 7.

72 See as examples, *Boyd v Boyd* [2025] SC FAL 102; and *Carswell v Carswell* [2025] SC HAM 54.

73 1995 Act, s 12(1).

It can be a source of difficulty to work out whether these alterations, deletions or amendments are part of the document. Naturally, the law is suspicious of such alterations, given it can be hard to determine who exactly made the changes, whether they were made by the testator or by someone else such as a disappointed beneficiary trying to improve their inheritance.

The 1995 Act breaks down alterations into two types depending on the timing of the alteration. If the alteration was made before the testator subscribed the document, then it is deemed to be part of the document and thus will have testamentary effect.[74] If the alteration was made after the testator subscribed the document, then it will only be incorporated into the document provided the alterations have been signed by the testator.[75] Naturally, it may be quite hard to prove when the document was altered and whether this was pre- or post-subscription. In a dispute, the timing of the alteration may be determined by evidence.[76]

Alterations can also achieve probative status.[77] However, that presumption can be disapplied if the court hears evidence to the contrary. For pre-subscription alterations, provided the document is otherwise probative and has a testing clause narrating when the alteration was made, then this narration is taken at face value as a presumption as to the timing of the alteration and that the testator made the alteration.[78] If these requirements cannot be met, then a court can set-up the alterations as probative instead.[79]

For post-subscription alterations, achieving probative status is more cumbersome.[80] Each alteration must be signed and witnessed with the witness signature affixed to the document too.[81] In the event an alteration involves more than one sheet, each sheet must be signed by the testator.[82] Given how hard it may be to have each alteration signed by both testator

74 1995 Act, s 5(1)(a).
75 1995 Act, s 5(1)(b).
76 1995 Act, s 5(3).
77 1995 Act, s 5(4).
78 1995 Act, s 5(5).
79 1995 Act, s 5(6).
80 1995 Act, Sch 1.
81 1995 Act, Sch 1(1)(1).
82 1995 Act, Sch 1(1)(2).

and witness on a page, an alternative system allows a court to set-up the alterations as probative instead.[83]

It should be noted that alterations interact with the law in relation to revocations, and therefore the law of revocations of testamentary documents has to be considered too in determining the validity of an alteration to an existing document.[84]

REVOCATION OF WILLS

7.11 A will may be changed at any point during the testator's life, but just as he or she must have the intention and the capacity to make a will, he or she must also have the power and capacity to revoke one.[85] Equally, it may be important to prove that a will has not been revoked and that the testator did not in fact change his or her testamentary intentions. Accordingly, it is vital that the testator should have made his or her intention to revoke the will sufficiently clear. One method of revocation is to destroy the document, but this may lead to issues about whether it has instead been lost or misplaced. Revocation can be implied as well as express, and a simple form of implied revocation is simply to execute a new testamentary document in terms incompatible with the old one. Unless the two documents can be read together as a coherent whole, the new document will supersede the old.[86]

POWER TO REVOKE AND SUCCESSION AGREEMENTS

7.12 It would be an obvious absurdity if a testator were simply unable to change his or her testamentary intentions after a will had been made[87] and

83 1995 Act, Sch 1(2)(1).

84 1995 Act, s 5(2)(a).

85 *Sivewright v Sivewright's Trs* 1920 SC (HL) 63; Stair *Inst* II.8.37; Erskine *Institute* I.7.33; and M Meston 'Wills and the testator's *animus revocandi*' 1984 *SLT (News)* 90. On capacity, see **Ch 8**.

86 See para **7.15**.

87 'All is ambulatory during the defunct's life, and may be taken away expressly or implicitly, by posterior or derogatory deeds, unless the defunct be obliged by *inter vivos* deed not to alter the same' Stair *Inst* III.8.33.

any clause in a will stating that it is irrevocable is therefore ineffective.[88] However, it is common for a testator to have entered into an agreement in their lifetime, known variously as 'succession agreements', 'contracts to test' or 'agreements to test'.[89] In these agreements, the testator will have contractually agreed with, or promised to, a beneficiary to settle their estate in that beneficiary's favour. A common example is where the testator agrees or promises to bequeath their house to a beneficiary, or otherwise to leave them a substantial legacy. This may arise as a simple promise out of love, favour or affection for the legatee, or it may reflect the fact that the legatee has given the testator financial assistance during their lifetime such that the legatee would like an agreement that these monies are to be recouped after the testator's death.

Where it has been agreed that the deceased is to make an 'irrevocable' will under these agreements, the power of a testator to validly revoke the will, and make fresh provision, will be waived or limited due to the prior contractual agreement. As such, a disappointed legatee under the agreement can seek reduction of the subsequent will. Whilst it is possible for such contracts to affect the power to revoke, the law is rather complex in this area, and there are initial hurdles to consider.

Firstly, any agreement of this kind between testator and beneficiary must be made according to the normal legal rules regulating the constitution of promises or contracts. In *McEleveen v McQuillan's Executrix*,[90] the testator's daughter averred that she and her husband had provided the funds for her father to purchase a house. Her father had agreed that she would inherit the property on his death and had executed a will directing his executor to make the house over to her on his death. He then revoked that will and executed another in which he directed that the residue of his estate, including the house, be divided between another daughter and a third person. The court held that the agreement had to be in writing, and

88 *Dougall's Trustees v Dougall* (1789) Mor 15949.

89 See D Hutchison, 'Succession Agreements in South African and Scots Law' in K Reid et al (eds), *Exploring the Law of Succession: Studies National, Historical and Comparative* (2007); D Carr, 'Will-Substitutes in Scotland' in A Braun and A Röthel (eds), *Passing Wealth on Death: Will-Substitutes in Comparative Perspective* (2016), Part VIII; and R Macleod 'Death and the transfer of heritable property' (2016) (1) *Jur Rev* 19.

90 1997 SLT (Sh Ct) 46.

conform to the 1995 Act,[91] and that a bare verbal agreement in respect of heritable property could not defeat the terms of a will. In *Khosprowpour v Mackay*,[92] a similar issue arose once again. The deceased had borrowed monies from the pursuer to enable her to purchase her flat from the local authority. In turn, it was averred that the deceased undertook orally to make provision in her will to transfer the flat to the pursuer on her death. Such a will was averred to be executed, but then in 2003 the deceased made another will leaving the flat to her children instead. Lord Turnbull considered Sheriff Principal Macleod's decision in *McEleveen* as on point and that, as the agreement related to heritable property, then it required it to be in writing.[93] In *Davies v Cassie,*[94] a similar issue arose but in respect of a promise. The deceased died intestate but had for several years, it was averred, promised to leave his estate to his daughter. No such promise had been executed in writing.[95] Lord Colbeck considered that even if there had been formal validity, the expressions by the deceased could not be considered as a legally binding promise in any event.[96]

Secondly, where the agreement or promise is constituted correctly, which will depend on its nature and the property agreed to be bequeathed, such contracts or promises to test do not give rise to a right to the legatee to demand a conveyance of property in the event that the testator has failed to honour their agreement. In *Da Lathouwer v Anderson*[97] a husband and wife had obtained monies from the pursuer to purchase a home. They had agreed to repay the loan over a period of time and then agreed to bequeath the house via an 'irrevocable' bequest.[98] Such agreement was made in writing and was formally valid. After both of the couple had died, it transpired that neither party had made such a bequest in their wills. Lord Emslie considered that the initial written agreement, in which the undertaking to make the bequest was agreed, was not in itself a testamentary writing such that a conveyance could be demanded

91 1995 Act, s 1(2)(a)(i).

92 [2014] CSOH 175.

93 [2014] CSOH 175, per Lord Turnbull at paras 21–22.

94 [2025] CSOH 36.

95 As would be required by s 1(2)(a)(ii) of the 1995 Act.

96 See further, M Hogg, 'Where there is not a will, is there a way? *Davies v Cassie*' (2025) (2) *Jur Rev* 97.

97 [2007] CSOH 437.

98 [2007] CSOH 437, per Lord Emslie at para 1.

by the pursuer.[99] However, as a binding contract, his lordship accepted that a claim for damages could be possible as a contractual remedy against the executor instead.

Thirdly, the availability of alternative remedies under the agreement may allow the testator to revoke any will made under the agreement. In *Hutchsion v Graham's Executor*,[100] the testator's granddaughter had guaranteed the loan on her grandmother's house and paid all the loan instalments. In return, the grandmother made a will in which she bequeathed her house to her granddaughter, and she also signed a minute of agreement in which she bound herself not to dispose of the property by either *inter vivos* or *mortis causa* deed to anyone but her. The agreement also stated that, if she did, she would be liable to her granddaughter for all the sums she had expended in relation to the house. She then executed a new will in which she left her whole estate to her daughter, who was by then living with her. The court held that the agreement did not render the provision in favour of the granddaughter in the first will irrevocable but anticipated revocability and provided for what would happen in the event of a breach. In consequence, the granddaughter was precluded from seeking reduction of the new will.

Where there is no issue with the validity of the agreement or alternative remedies, then it is possible for the disappointed legatee to seek an action of reduction of a will in breach of the agreement. As an example, in *Paterson v Paterson*[101] a mother undertook to bequeath her whole estate to her son in return for various payments that he had made to her and signed a minute of agreement to the effect that the new will 'was to be regarded as irrevocable'. She subsequently made a new will, revoking her previous will and disposing of her estate to a third party. The son was successful in his action of reduction.

EXPRESS REVOCATION

7.13 The clearest evidence that a testator intended to revoke a will is that he or she has made a new will and inserted a clause that states that the

99 [2007] CSOH 437, per Lord Emslie at para 7.

100 [2006] SCLR 587.

101 *Paterson v Paterson* (1893) 20 R 484. See also *Napier v Orr* (1864) 3 M 57; and *McLachlan v Seton's Trustees* 1937 SC 206; and *Wheeldon's Executor Nominate v Spence's Executrix Nominate* [2014] CSOH 69.

testator revokes all previous wills or other testamentary writings. It is not necessary that new provisions be made, providing that the revocation is executed according to the same formalities as are required for the formal validity of a will.[102] If he or she intended to revoke testamentary writings other than a will, or more than one will, this must be stated expressly in the revocation clause[103] or be stated in clear words that leave no room for doubt as to the testator's intention.[104]

Intention to revoke is also clear if the testator physically destroys the will. In that case, there is revocation *animo et facto*, since both the intention and the physical act of destruction are present. It follows that accidental destruction does not revoke a will and neither does destruction whilst insane or in a fit of rage or a state of drunkenness since, in these circumstances, the testator lacks the necessary capacity. For example, in *Laing v Bruce*,[105] the testator's will had disappeared. The pursuers averred that when the testator died she had been insane and that she had destroyed the will while lacking the necessary capacity to revoke it. This was held to be a possible ground for ignoring an apparent revocation and letting the original will stand. In this particular case, however, it was not proved that the testator had in fact been insane.[106]

Destruction may also be symbolic. In *Nasmyth v Hare*[107] the testator had executed a will and sealed it. The sealing was an idiosyncratic solemnity of execution that he had prescribed for himself, and it had no legal effect. He later cut off the seal. Since the testator had himself considered the sealing to indicate finality of execution, the act of cutting it off was held to have been an act amounting to revocation of the deed.

Destruction of the deed may have been carried out by the testator personally but may also have been carried out by someone else under their specific authority.[108] If a testator instructs a solicitor to draw up a new

102 *Kirkpatrick's Trustees v Kirkpatrick* (1874) 1 R (HL) 37; and *Stirling Stuart v Stirling Crawfurd's Trustees and Executrix* (1885) 12 R 610.

103 *Clark's Executors v Clark* 1943 SC 216.

104 *Ballantine v Ayr Magistrates* (1836) 16 S 325; *Allan v Glasgow* (1846) 5 Bell App 379, HL; *Tait's Trustees v Chiene* 1911 SC 743; *Hannay's Trustees v Keith* 1913 SC 482; *Stewart v Campbell's Trustees* (1917) 2 SLT 259, OH.

105 *Laing v Bruce* (also known as *Norman v Dick)* (1838) 1 D 59.

106 See **Ch 8**.

107 *Nasmyth v Hare* (1821) 1 Sh App 114.

108 *Bonthrone v Ireland* (1883) 10 R 779 at 790.

will, this does not authorise the destruction of the old one[109] but if he or she instructs the solicitor expressly to destroy it and the solicitor does not do so, the testator is nonetheless held to have revoked it since he or she did everything in his or her power to do so.[110]

The testator may also amend, rather than destroy, the original will in such a way as to indicate a partial or total revocation of it. Such amendments, and it should be stressed that they should be deletions or erasures – rather than additions or substitutions – do not require the testator's signature under the 1995 Act.[111] In *Cruickshank's Trustees v Glasgow Magistrates*[112] the testator had shown his intention to revoke his will simply by scoring over the deed with a pencil, although evidence was required to prove that it had been the testator himself who had done this. In *Thomson's Trustees v Bowhill Baptist Church*[113] the testatrix had cut out sections of a copy of the deed, signed near the gaps and written an explanation of what she had done on it. The destruction, together with the signatures and written explanation, was held to have revoked it. Similarly, in *Crosbie v Wilson*[114] a copy of the testator's will was found cut into three pieces after her death. This would have amounted to revocation but for the fact that there was no proof that it had been the testator herself who had destroyed it.

MISSING WILLS

7.14 Notwithstanding the fact that a testator is entitled to revoke a will by destroying it, difficulties may arise where it is known that the testator had one in his or her possession during life, but it cannot be found

109 *Bruce's JF v Lord Advocate* 1969 SC 296.

110 J McLaren, *The Law of Wills and Succession as Administered in Scotland,* 3rd edn (1894), para 745; and W Dickson, *The Law of Evidence in Scotland,* 2nd edn (1887), para 905.

111 1995 Act, s 5(2)(a). See *Pattison's Trs v University of Edinburgh* (1888) 16 R 73; and K Reid, 'Execution or revocation' (1986) *SLT (News)* 129.

112 *Cruickshank's Trs v Glasgow Mags* (1887) 14 R 603.

113 *Thomson's Trs v Bowhill Baptist Church* 1956 SLT 302. See also *Pettigrew's Trustees v Pettigrew* (1884) 12 R 249; *Manson v Edinburgh Royal Institution for the Education of Deaf and Dumb Children* 1948 SLT 196, OH.

114 *Crosbie v Wilson* (1865) 3 M 870.

after his or her death. In *Crosbie v Wilson*[115] it was held that there was no presumption in Scots law that the testator must have destroyed a will where one is missing but that view seems now to have been reversed.[116] In *Bonthrone v Ireland* Lord Young stated:[117]

> 'For as a man may effectually cancel or revoke his will by destroying it, when it is shown that a man duly executed a will and had it at one time in his custody, and it is not forthcoming at his death, the legal presumption, in the absence of evidence to the contrary is that he destroyed it *animo revocandi* … If the law were otherwise, a man plainly could not cancel his will by merely destroying it.'

This view was reinforced by Lord McLaren, who stated in his treatise that 'where a will known to have been in existence is not forthcoming after the testator's death, it is necessarily presumed to be non-existent'[118] although in *Young v Anderson*, he pointed out that presuming a will to have been revoked unless it is proved that it was not revoked involves the difficult task of proving a negative.[119]

If a person wishes to found on a missing deed, he or she may raise an action of proving the tenor, providing that what its terms were can be proved.[120] The onus is on that person to prove the *casus amissionis,* or the circumstances of the loss. It will need to be shown that the document was not destroyed by the testator, perhaps because it was actually lost or destroyed by a third party,[121] and thus not revoked by the testator themselves. The person will also need to prove: (i) the substance (ie: the terms, or 'tenor') of the missing deed, and (ii) that it was executed by the testator as a formally valid testamentary document.[122]

115 *Crosbie v Wilson* (1865) 3 M 870, per Lord Justice-Clerk Ormidale at 877.

116 *Lauder v Briggs* 1999 SC 453; *Clyde v Clyde* 1958 SC 343; *Bruce's JF v Lord Advocate* 1969 SC 296; *Laing v Bruce* (1838) 1 D 59; and *Winchester v Smith* (1863) 1 M 685; *Young v Anderson* (1904) 7 F 128.

117 *Bonthrone v Ireland* (1883) 10 R 779 at 790.

118 J McLaren, *The Law of Wills and Succession* 3rd edn (1894), para 746.

119 *Young v Anderson* (1904) 7 F 128 at 135.

120 See 'Proving the tenor of lost testamentary documents – a guide' (2024) 88 *SPCLR* 5.

121 *Walker v Brock* (1852) 1 D 362.

122 See *Dow v Dow* (1848) 10 D 1465; *Young v Anderson* (1904) 7 F 128; *Clyde v Clyde* 1958 SC 343;and *McLernan v McLernan* (6 March 2001, unreported), OH.

IMPLIED REVOCATION

(1) Subsequent wills

7.15 Where the testator had executed more than one will or codicil to a will, the court will attempt to read them together in order to produce a coherent whole from which to ascertain his or her completed testamentary intention.[123] If, however, the provisions in a later deed are inconsistent with the provisions of a previous deed, the later deed may impliedly revoke all or part of the earlier. Implied revocation is clearest where the later will makes a universal settlement, where the entire estate is transferred to trustees or a single beneficiary; in this case, the earlier will is revoked in its entirety.[124] Alternatively, only certain provisions of the earlier will may be revoked.[125] The provisions of the previous will are also revoked if different or additional beneficiaries are named or the terms of the later will contradict those of the earlier.[126]

(2) Revocation by the conditio si testator sine liberis decesserit

7.16 The *conditio si testator sine liberis decesserit* is the rebuttable presumption that a testator would not intend to omit making testamentary provision for his or her own child or children.[127] If invoked, the doctrine will revoke entirely all testamentary writings of the parent. The original purpose of the doctrine was to allow provision to be made for a posthumous child of the testator, but its scope has been extended to include children born after the date on which the will was executed. The birth of any children may be presumed to have revoked all testamentary writings executed prior to their birth, and the effect of the doctrine is that the estate

123 See para **7.3**.

124 *Cadger v Ronald's Trustees* 1946 SLT (Notes) 24. See also *Grant v Stoddart* (1849) 11 D 860; *Sibbald's Trustees v Greig* (1871) 9 M 399; *Bertram's Trustees v Matheson's Trustee* (1888) 15 R 582; *Rutherford's Trustees v Dickie* 1907 SC 1280.

125 *Park's Trustees v Park* (1890) 27 SLR 528.

126 See further KGC Reid 'Execution or revocation?' 1986 *SLT (News)* 129.

127 For a further analysis, see R Paisley, 'The Roman and Civilian origins of the *conditio si testator sine liberis decesserit* in Scots' law' (2015) 19(1) *Edin LR* 1.

falls into intestacy.[128] There are, however, two important conditions that must be satisfied before the presumption can be applied.

Firstly, the presumption is rebuttable on evidence that the testator intended to exclude the child. It will not be rebutted simply because he or she had ample time and opportunity before death to make a new will making provision for the child. In *Milligan's Judicial Factor v Milligan*,[129] 10 years elapsed between the birth of the testator's child and his, the testator's, death and the court held that the mere lapse of time was insufficient to rebut the presumption that the testator would not intend to omit to make provision for the child. On the contrary, there must be clear evidence that the testator did wish his or her will to remain effective and did not intend to make provision for the child. In *Stuart-Gordon v Stuart-Gordon*,[130] the testatrix was aware of her poor health and had been considering her will at about the same time as her child was born. She died shortly after the birth. It was shown that she knew that the child would be well provided for from other sources and, because of this, had deliberately decided to omit her from her will. In this case, her will was given effect as if the child had not been born.

Secondly, the *conditio* does not arise automatically. The onus is on the child to invoke the *conditio* and it must be in the child's best interests to apply it. Since the effect of revoking the will is that the estate will fall into intestacy, the child's claim to legal rights or the intestate estate may be defeated if claims for prior rights by a surviving spouse or civil partner will exhaust the estate.[131] If that is likely to be the case, the better solution may simply be for the child to claim legitim out of the testate estate.

The existence of the *conditio si testator* also raises a problem in the case of unmarried parents. If one partner has made a will bequeathing the whole estate to the other and the *conditio si testator* is invoked, the deceased's partner will not be entitled to receive anything from the resulting intestate estate bar making a claim under s 29 of the Family Law (Scotland) Act 2006.[132] Previously, the Scottish Law Commission

128 See M Meston 'The *conditiones si sine liberis*' (1981) *JLSS* (Workshop).

129 *Milligan's JF v Milligan* 1910 SC 58.

130 *Stuart-Gordon v Stuart-Gordon* (1899) 1 F 1005.

131 See *Greenan v Courtney* [2007] CSOH 58 and H Hiram, 'The *conditio si testator* as family policy: *Greenan v Courtney*' (2007) 11 *Edin LR* 431.

132 See paras **6.26ff**.

had recommended the abolition of the *conditio si testator.*[133] However, a sizeable number of respondents to the Scottish Government's consultation advocated its retention. As such, the Scottish Government concluded that it will not seek its abolition.[134]

REVIVAL OF REVOKED WILL

7.17 Until the Succession (Scotland) Act 2016, a rule existed that if a subsequent will was revoked, an earlier will may be revived as the effective testamentary document on death. In *Bruce's Judicial Factor v Lord Advocate*[135] the testator executed a will in which he expressly revoked all previous wills, but he did not instruct his solicitor to destroy his previous will. When he died, the later will could not be found, and it was presumed that he must have destroyed it. In consequence, the earlier will was effective.

As the Scottish Law Commission noted,[136] it was unlikely that any testator imagined that the previous will had been retained by his or her solicitors, was to remain 'in a state of suspended animation ready to spring into life at any time'.[137] Accordingly, it recommended reform.

As such, s 5 of the 2016 Act contains a provision that if a will, or part, is expressly or implicitly revoked by a subsequent will, the revocation of the subsequent will does not bring back the earlier will into operation on death.[138] The result of the revocation of all or part of the second will, with no other testamentary document in place, may result in the estate becoming partially or totally intestate. As this part of the 2016 Act is not retrospective, any revocations of a subsequent will must have been made

133 Report *on Succession* (SLC Report No 215, 2009), paras 6.18–6.21.
134 *Scottish Government response to the Consultation on the Law of Succession* (2018), para 55.
135 *Bruce's JF v Lord Advocate* 1969 SC 296. See also *Scott's JF v Johnston* 1971 SLT (Notes) 41.
136 Report on *Succession* (SLC Report No 124, 1990), paras 4.67–4.76. See also M Meston 'Revival by revocation of the revoking will' 1974 *SLT (News)* 153.
137 Report on *Succession* (SLC Report No 124, 1990), para 4.68.
138 2016 Act, s 5(2).

after 1 November 2016 for s 5 to apply.[139] For earlier revocations, the old law pre-2016 Act applies.

TESTAMENTARY DEVICES

7.18 If a person does not make a will, this does not necessarily mean that all of his or her estate on death will fall into intestacy. Testamentary devices, also known as will substitutes or *quasi*-wills, enable a person's property to pass directly to another person after the deceased's death without falling into the estate available for distribution to beneficiaries under a will or to the prescribed classes of person entitled to legal rights or the intestate estate.[140] The use of will substitutes may, in some cases, avoid entirely the necessity to make a will at all. They are commonly found in some form in many estates.[141]

None of the various forms of will substitutes can be defined as testamentary writings or testamentary documents *per se* but they have a testamentary character and are deemed to be testamentary in effect in that they provide for the absolute disposal of property after death. This means that where a person dies intestate but has disposed of some property by a will substitute, none of the property so disposed of will be available for distribution under the Succession (Scotland) Act 1964 although benefits obtained under a will substitute count as legacies for the purposes of s 9.[142] Neither can it form part of the estate available for claims to legal rights. The concept of 'estate' relates only to that property which vests

139 Succession (Scotland) Act 2016 (Commencement, Transitional and Saving Provisions) Regulations 2016, SSI 2016/210.

140 Section 36 of the Succession (Scotland) Act 1964 provides that only property which is undisposed of by testamentary disposition can form the intestate estate. The section further provides that a testamentary disposition includes any deed taking effect on death, whereby any part of the deceased's estate is disposed of or under which a succession thereto arises. Accordingly, an 'intestate' is a person who has died leaving undisposed of by testamentary disposition the whole or any part of his or her estate and intestate shall be construed accordingly: see paras **6.4–6.5**.

141 See D Carr, 'Will-Substitutes in Scotland' in A Braun and A Röthel (eds), *Passing Wealth on Death: Will-Substitutes in Comparative Perspective* (2016). Other chapters in this monograph are worthwhile to read, particularly Braun's chapter on England & Wales.

142 See para **6.24**.

in the deceased's executors for the purposes of administration and the disposition of property on death by means of will substitutes is, therefore, one method by which a testator may defeat the possibility of claims for legal rights.[143] Common forms that will substitutes can take are described in the following paragraphs.

(1) Special destinations

(a) Definition of special destinations

7.19 A destination is simply a direction contained within a document of title that the property is to be transmitted to a specified person on the death of the proprietor and it is *special* when it relates only to the specific item of property that forms the subject of the destination rather than regulating the transmission of a general category of property.[144] Its function is to regulate succession to the subject without it forming part of the deceased's estate.

Designed originally to circumvent the devolution of property according to the old rules of property and succession,[145] it has given rise to a number of practical and theoretical problems, with the consequence that special destinations have had a 'fiercely litigious' history'.[146] As such, they are controversial, and much has been written on them.[147] Meston, the

143 See para **5.3**.

144 For example, such as may be referred to in a general legacy where the individual items of property which comprise the legacy are indistinguishable from each other: see para **10.4**.

145 See para **3.3**.

146 J Halliday 'What makes a destination special?' (1977) 22 *JLSS* 16.

147 See G Gretton, 'Survivorship destinations' 1977 *SLT (News)* 197; J Halliday, 'What makes a destination special?' (1977) 22 *JLSS* 16; M Morton, 'Special destinations as testamentary instructions' 1984 *SLT (News)* 133; J Halliday, 'Special destinations' 1984 *SLT (News)* 180; G Gretton, 'Death and debt' 1984 *SLT (News)* 299; G Gretton, 'Destinations' (1989) 34 *JLSS* 299; M Meston 'Survivorship destinations and bank accounts' (1995) 1 *SLPQ* 315; D Brand, 'Time for special destinations to die?' 2000 *SLT (News)* 203; K Swinton, 'And to the survivor of them?' (2006) 74 *Scots Law Gazette* 12; J Kerrigan, 'Separation agreements, survivorship destinations & succession' 2010 *SLT (News)* 25; J Kerrigan, 'Survivorship destinations – The debate continues' 2014 *SLT (News)* 175; K Reid and G L Gretton, *Conveyancing 2014* (2015), 169–74; G Junor, 'Surviving special destinations: *Hill v Hill*' (2016) 84(1) *Scots Law Gazette* 14; K Reid and G Gretton, *Conveyancing 2016* (2017), 203–10; and J Kerrigan, 'Survivorship destinations – Yet more developments' 2017 *SLT (News)* 125.

eminent succession lawyer, goes so far as to call special destinations an 'abomination' and argued for their total abolition.[148]

The origins of special destinations are because, that prior to the Titles to Land Consolidation (Scotland) Act 1868, heritage could not be bequeathed but transmitted automatically to the deceased person's heir-at-law. The special destination was invented as a conveyancing device that could circumvent the bar on testamentary dispositions of heritable property and thus could effectively defeat the heir-at-law's claim.[149] Title to the property is taken in the name of the grantee and his or her specified successor and, because the destination is specified in the disposition of the property itself, the gift is not considered as a legacy despite its testamentary effect.

Because a special destination is contained in a written title to property rather than being created by a separate deed (and thus regulated by the law of obligations), it follows that it is most frequently to be found in titles to heritable property, specifically they are inserted into the disposition at the time a grantee(s) purchases the property. They can also be used in relation to moveable property, provided that it is the subject of a document of title or written conveyance but the types of moveable property which can be subject to special destination were limited by the Blank Bonds and Trusts Act 1696, and now the Requirements of Writing (Scotland) Act 1995, under which only writing can establish a trust.

Money in a joint bank account does not fall within this category since a bank account, no matter of what type, is not of itself a deed of trust and, accordingly, no rights of ownership can be conferred by it.[150] Bonds, shares[151] and policies of assurance[152] may contain a special destination since these forms of moveable property must conform to the statutory requirements for documents of title.

148 M Meston 'Survivorship destinations and bank 'accounts' (1995) 1 *SLPQ* 315.

149 Prior to the Titles to Land Consolidation (Scotland) Act 1868, such destinations were not termed 'special' by virtue of the fact that it was impossible to alter succession to heritage by testamentary disposition. Rather, they were termed 'destinations' or 'simple destinations' to distinguish them from entails and destinations-over. See J Halliday 'What makes a destination special?' (1977) 22 *JLSS* 16.

150 That a deposit receipt is not a deed of trust was established in *Cairns v Davidson* 1913 SC 1054. See also para **4.27**.

151 *Buchan v Porteous* (1874) 7 R 211; *Connells's Trs v Connell's Trs* (1886) 13 R 1175; *Fraser v McKillican* (1905) 13 SLT 81; *Colenson's Exor v Davidson* 1930 SLT 359.

152 *Milne v Grant's Exrs* (1884) 11 R 887.

(b) Effect of special destinations

7.20 The Succession (Scotland) Act 1964, s 36(2)(a), provides that where any heritable property is subject to a special destination in favour of any person and has not been evacuated[153] 'the property shall not be treated for the purposes of the Act as part of the estate of the deceased'.

There are three exceptions to s 36(2)(a). Firstly, where the destination is 'one which could competently be, and has in fact been, evacuated by testamentary disposition or otherwise'.[154] Secondly, where 'any heritable property over which a deceased had a power of appointment has not been disposed of in exercise of that power and is in those circumstances subject to a power of appointment by some other person'.[155] This means that property subject to these exceptions is not available for legal rights or prior rights or distribution to heirs in intestate succession. The effect of a special destination is therefore testamentary but the document in which it is inserted is not a testamentary deed.

The third and very limited exception is contained in section 18 of the 1964 Act. Although property subject to a special destination does not normally form part of the deceased's estate, it may vest in the executor only for the purpose of conveying the property to the person entitled to it under the destination, if such conveyance is necessary.[156] This will not be necessary where the special destination is a survivorship destination. This is because a survivorship destination will only be contained within the title where both the deceased and the person entitled to the property under the destination were co-owners of the property, so that the survivor has an existing title through his or her own *pro indiviso* share.

(c) Survivorship destinations

7.21 The most commonly used type of special destination is a survivorship destination. This arises where title to property is taken in common by one or more parties and destined to whichever of the

153 This term means 'cancelled'.

154 1964 Act, s 36(2)(a).

155 1964 Act, s 36(2)(b).

156 Succession (Scotland) Act 1964, s 18. This restates the previous law; see *Bisset v Walker* 26 November 1799, FC.

parties survives the other. It is a form of special destination in that it is incorporated into a disposition (the deed which transfers ownership of heritable property) and specifies who is to take each party's share on either of the grantees predeceasing the other.

A typical form of wording is 'to A and B equally between them and the survivor'. As an example, Mary and Harold McMillan are a young couple who are purchasing a property from Brian. Their solicitor tells them a survivorship destination would be a worthwhile mechanism to have in the disposition.[157] They agree. The solicitor inserts survivorship wording into the draft disposition to reflect this. At settlement of the purchase, the signed disposition from Brian will read:

> I, Brian Carrick...HEREBY DISPONE to the said Mary McMillan and Harold McMillan, equally between them and the survivor...

What this means is that both Mary and Harold each acquire a 50% *pro indiviso* share of ownership in the property from Brian. This is the position in lifetime until one of them dies, at which point the survivor will acquire the deceased's *pro indiviso* share and become the full owner of the property. Thus, if Mary dies 20 years after the purchase of the property, Harold becomes the full owner of the property at the moment of Mary's death. There is no need for Mary's executor to transfer her *pro indiviso* share to Harold as her share of ownership has automatically accresced to Harold at death through the wording in the disposition executed many years ago.

Co-owners who employ survivorship destinations are usually spouses, civil partners or cohabitants, but they may equally be siblings or friends.[158] In the lifetime of each owner, each owner has a separate *pro indiviso share*, neither party has a right of ownership in the other party's share until or unless the destination comes into effect. The property is owned in common, with each party owning a one-half *pro indiviso* share of the property during life with the predecessor's share accrescing to the

157 Many professional negligence claims arise if the solicitor fails to discuss the effect of a special destination, see A Kentish and C Finnieston, 'Risk: Death and taxes – the perils of survivorships' (2023) 68(5) *JLSS* online edition, available https://www.lawscot.org.uk/members/journal/issues/vol-68-issue-05/risk-death-and-taxes-the-perils-of-survivorships/.

158 For the detailed results of a survey carried out in 1985 for the Scottish Law Commission see D Nichols 'Special Destinations in Scotland' (1990) 35 *JLSS* 189.

survivor on death.[159] The only right that is conveyed by one party to the other during life is the right to be the successor to that other person's share, and it follows that each party has an independent right to dispose of his or her share of the property *inter vivos,* whether onerously[160] or gratuitously.[161] The effect is the same as if there had been a mutual will; A's share is destined to B, and B's to A. The survivorship destination regulates ownership of the property during life but it also operates as a destination-over; title is taken by A and B and the share of each will transmit to the other should either predecease.

(d) Evacuation of survivorship destination

7.22 The simplicity of using a survivorship destination also carries risks. It may be the case that one of the owners thinks the destination is now not helpful, such as where a couple have become estranged or where siblings have fallen out, and they no longer wish the survivor to inherit their share of ownership. As such, they may seek to cancel, or 'evacuate', the survivorship destination. The general rule is that a survivorship destination may always be evacuated *inter vivos* but *mortis causa* evacuation, where the deceased tries to cancel out the survivorship destination through their will, is more problematic and is discussed here at length.[162]

The cardinal principle of a testamentary document is that it expresses a completed testamentary intention. As a corollary, a testator may change that intention at their will, and the granter of a testamentary deed can revoke it in whole or in part at any time prior to death.[163] A special destination, by contrast, is not a testamentary deed and the presumption of the grantee's general power to evacuate it by *mortis causa* deed is rebuttable. This is

159 In *Munro v Munro* 1972 SLT (Sh Ct) 6 it was held that the effect of a survivorship destination was to convert common property to joint property so that neither party was entitled to convey his or her share to a third party. This decision is generally agreed to have been wrongly decided: see G Gretton 'Destinations' 1989 *JLSS* 302; and K Reid 'Common property: Clarification and confusion' 1985 *SLT (News)* 57.

160 *Steele v Caldwell* 1979 SLT 228.

161 *Smith v MacIntosh* 1989 SLT 148.

162 For *inter vivos* evacuations, see G Gretton and K Reid, *Conveyancing,* 5th edn (2018), paras 27-19ff.

163 See paras **7.13** and **7.24**.

the case both where the terms of the will purport to revoke expressly the destination and where a will purports to revoke all previous testamentary writings.[164] Because a special destination is not a testamentary writing, the doctrine of implied revocation which applies to testaments does not apply to destinations even if the testator has the power to evacuate.

When a special destination can be evacuated by means of a *mortis causa* testamentary disposition, the will must contain an express reference to the destination and an express intention that it be evacuated. The Succession (Scotland) Act 1964, s 30, consolidates the common law position and provides an explicit statement of the rule:

> 'A testamentary disposition executed after the commencement of the Act shall not have effect so as to evacuate a special destination (being a destination which could competently be evacuated by the testamentary disposition) unless it contains a specific reference to the destination and a declared intention on the part of the testator to evacuate it.'

A general provision in a will revoking previous testamentary writings or provisions inconsistent with the destination will *not* therefore be an effective means of evacuation. In *Marshall v Marshall's* Executor[165] a husband and wife took title to a house in common with a survivorship destination attached. Each party had contributed to the price. The husband then made a will in which he left his share of the house to his daughter but made no specific reference to the special destination. Apart from the husband being in any case barred from evacuating the destination, this was contrary to s 30 of the Succession (Scotland) Act 1964.

As an important prior condition of the application of s 30, the destination must be one that can competently be evacuated by a testamentary disposition. In other words, there must be a *power to evacuate* in addition to complying with s 30 of the 1964 Act.

(e) The power to evacuate mortis causa

7.23 Evacuation *mortis causa* by a party who has paid the whole purchase price of the property is always valid, but in other situations there

164 On the basis that a special destination is not a testamentary writing: *Connell's Trs v Connell's Trs* (1886) 13 R 1175; and *Murray's Exrs v Geekie* 1929 SLT 524.

165 *Marshall v Marshall's Exor* 1987 SLT 49. See also *Stirling's Trs v Stirling* 1977 SLT 229, 1977 SC 139.

is no absolute rule that will provide a solution in every case where the question of the power to evacuate is in doubt. Rather, in the absence of evidence to the contrary, the presence of certain facts may point to the application of legal presumptions.

Where the property subject to the survivorship destination is owned in common by the deceased and the survivor but only one of the parties has paid the whole purchase price of the property, only the party who has paid the price has the power to evacuate the destination *mortis causa*, by will or otherwise, without the consent of the other.[166] In the absence of any contrary evidence, it will be presumed that the party who has paid is the donor of a one-half share of the property to the other party, the donee. The donee is deemed to have accepted the gift subject to the condition that the gift will revert to the donor if he or she survives the donee. He or she is free to evacuate the destination only during life, whether gratuitously[167] or for consideration,[168] but has no power to evacuate by testamentary disposition.[169] The donor, by contrast, has an unfettered right to dispose of his or her share both *inter vivos* and *mortis* causa.[170]

(f) Bars to evacuation

7.24 There are four situations in which evacuation by one or both (or all) of the parties may be barred from doing so *mortis causa* but only one of the four is of sufficient importance to be dealt with in detail here. The first is where there is a clause of return attached to property which, in effect, grants only a conditional right to the grantee so that he or she has no right to test over the property.[171] The second is where the parties make an agreement that all rights of succession in each other's property

166 *Brown's Tr v Brown* 1943 SC 488; and *Hay's Tr v Hay's Trs* 1951 SC 329.

167 *Smith v MacKintosh* 1989 SLT 228.

168 *Steele v Caldwell* 1979 SLT 228.

169 *Renouf's Trs v Haining* 1919 SC 497; *Taylor's Exrs v Brunton* 1939 SLT 281. On the question of the apparent unfairness to the non-contributing party, see M Morton 'Special destinations as testamentary instructions' 1984 *SLT (News)* 133.

170 *Brown's Tr v Brown* 1943 SC 488.

171 The granter provides that the title shall revert to himself or his heirs, rather than to a third party if a particular event occurs or fails to occur. Examples would be where the grantee predeceases the granter or fails to produce issue: Erskine *Inst* III.8.45.

are renounced so that the power to evacuate the destination is expressly reserved to the grantee or to both co-owners,[172] although in practice this is rare.[173] The third is where the property was a gift from a third party and the destination is construed as an implied condition of the gift that neither party has the power to evacuate it.[174] These, however, are either practically extinct or turn on their own, rather unusual, facts. The fourth, and most important, is where the power to evacuate is contractually excluded, either expressly or by implication, since a contract made during life will override what would otherwise have been an unfettered right of testation.[175]

Where both parties have contributed to the price, they may have made an express contract that the destination is not to be evacuated by one or both of them and, in this case, the situation is clear. Where they have not made an express contract, an obligation not to evacuate *mortis causa* may be implied, and evacuation by either party will be incompetent. It is in these types of cases that difficulties have arisen. The leading case is *Perret's Trustees v Perret*.[176] Here, the parties had taken title to the matrimonial home equally between them and to the survivor. Each had contributed equally to the price of the house, and it was held that this fact constituted an implied contract not to revoke the destination *mortis causa*. Lord President Dunedin stated:[177]

> 'I think [there] was a contractual arrangement where each took the chance of getting the half of the other, and accordingly I think the property stands upon its own destination and is not carried, and could not be carried, by any testament whatsoever. The moment that disposition was actually

172 *Redfern's Exrs v Redfern* 1996 SLT 900.

173 Gretton suggests a form of words whereby the express power to evacuate is reserved. After the destination itself, the following words or similar words could be inserted to make this power explicit: 'but expressly declaring that the said grantees and each of them shall have full right and power to evacuate the foregoing destination both *inter vivos* and *mortis causa*': see G Gretton 'Destinations' (1989) 34 *JLSS* 299, 302.

174 *Brown's Tr v Brown* 1943 SC 488.

175 'Legacies may be left whether there be testaments or not, and either in the testament, codicils, or apart; but all is ambulatory during the defunct's life, and may be taken away expressly or impliedly, by posterior or derogatory deeds, unless the defunct be obliged by contract *inter vivos*, not to alter the same; in which case contract and paction doth so far overrule the power of testing, that posterior deeds, whether expressly or impliedly altering, would be ineffectual': Stair *Inst* III.8.33.

176 1909 SC 522.

177 1909 SC 522, at 528.

> delivered, as it was by the mere fact of taking the destination as between these two people, I do not think this destination could have been altered except by joint consent of the spouses.'

The principle that equal contribution to the price constitutes a contract that bars evacuation by either party remains established law despite attempts to overturn it.[178] It also makes clear that the question of whether an implied contract exists is a matter of fact in relation to the contributions actually made and a question of construction as to whether the deed itself contains intrinsic provisions excluding the right of evacuation. The presumption is confined to those cases where one party has attempted to dispose of his or her share by testamentary disposition and has no application to dispositions *inter vivos*.[179] Whether or not there is an implied contract is a matter to be construed solely from the narrative contained in the deed. The actual wording used cannot be contradicted by admitting extrinsic evidence to show that the true position is otherwise. The parties are deemed to have formed a contract by consenting to the insertion of words in the narrative clause referring to the contributions of the parties, as evidenced by the title having been registered in those terms.[180] However, if the parties agree that the narrative is incorrect and that in fact no such contract barring evacuation exists, the true position can be declared.[181]

Problems could have arisen in the past where married co-owners divorced and one party bequeathed his or her interest in the house without evacuating the destination. In consequence, a bequest of the house by testament to a third party would be invalid and the former spouse would take the whole interest if he or she survived the testator.[182] This point often came as a shock to many former couples, who attended to divorce and changed their will but did not think to check the title deeds to their property too. The issue no longer arises since the Succession (Scotland) Act 2016 provides that divorce or annulment of a marriage, or dissolution or annulment of a civil partnership revokes, an unevacuated survivorship destination by deeming each party to have predeceased the other.[183]

178 *Shand's Trs v Shand's Trs* 1966 SC 178; and *Marshall v Marshall's Exr* 1987 SLT 49.
179 *Steele v Caldwell* 1979 SLT 228, per Lord Allanbridge at 231.
180 *Gordon-Rogers v Thomson's Exrs* 1988 SC 145.
181 *Hay's Tr v Hay's Trs* 1951 SLT 170.
182 *Gardner's Exrs v Raeburn* 1996 SLT 745.
183 2016 Act, s 2(2). See para **2.2**.

However, the risk of a 'surprise' transfer under a survivorship destination to the surviving co-owner remains where a couple have become estranged or separated without having attended to divorce or termination of the civil partnership, or the couple are unmarried cohabitants. Even if a contrary provision is made in the will, these co-owners may not have power to evacuate the special destination.

(g) Rights of creditors

7.25 Notwithstanding that property subject to a survivorship destination will normally pass directly to the survivor without vesting in the executor and thus being available to the deceased's creditors, the right of the survivor may be postponed to the right of the deceased's creditors. Institutional authority is clear on the point. Bell states that where there is a survivorship destination:[184]

> 'Each has a fee which his debts will affect: the survivor becomes sole fiar; but the right thus bestowed seems to be of the nature of a mere destination. Either of the parties may dispose of, or grant securities over, the subject, which will be effectual notwithstanding the destination to the other; or his creditors may adjudge it, and so defeat the right of the associate.'

Erskine states that where there is a survivorship destination and one of the parties dies:[185]

> 'The survivor has the fee of the whole, exclusive of the heirs of the deceased – not only the fee of his original share, but that of the share belonging to the predeceased, in so far as it is not exhausted by his debts.'

Despite institutional authority, it was held in *Barclay's Bank v McGreish*[186] that creditors had no claim to property which passed under a survivorship destination to the debtor's spouse, but his view was reversed in *Fleming's*

184 *Comm* (7th edn) i, 62; see also Bell, *Prin,* § 1922.

185 *Inst* III.8.35). See also Burns, *Conveyancing Practice,* 4th edn (1957), 370–71 where it is stated that the predeceasing proprietor's share is subject to his or her debts.

186 1983 SLT 344. See D J Cusine 'Of debts and destinations' (1984) 29 *JLSS* 154; M Morton 'Special Destinations as Testamentary Instructions' 1984 *SLT (News)* 133; G Gretton 'Death and debt' 1984 *SLT (News)* 299. For a contrary view see J M Halliday 'Special destinations' 1984 *SLT (News)* 180 (later retracted in Halliday's *Conveyancing Law and Practice in Scotland* (1985), para 22.18).

Trustees v Fleming,[187] with the result that notwithstanding the fact that property subject to a survivorship destination does not form part of the deceased's estate but passes directly to the person nominated under it, it will remain available for the claims of creditors. The facts of the case were that a husband and wife had taken title to property equally between them and the survivor. The husband was sequestrated and died five years later. The trustee in bankruptcy sought declarator that he remained vested in the debtor's one-half *pro indiviso* share of the property and was entitled to insist on an action of division and sale. Alternatively, he sought declarator that the defender was infeft in that share as heir of provision by virtue of a special destination and was personally liable to the creditors of the debtor to the extent of the value of that share.

The court held that, in raising the action, the trustee was enforcing the rule that a substitute cannot take any greater right than was possessed by the institute and was doing so as part of his obligation and right to manage the estate.[188] Lord Sutherland held that:[189]

> 'At the time when the property passed to the defender it was of little or no value because it was burdened by the debts of the debtor. She could only take the property subject to that qualification. Because of the peculiar provisions relating to special destinations the property ceased to be vested in the trustee and became vested in the defender on the death of the debtor … [The truste] is, accordingly, in my opinion perfectly entitled in his own right to raise an action against the heir of provision for the purpose of restoring to the trust estate the value of the property which is equivalent to the value of the debts by which it was burdened.'

Lord Caplan held that after sequestration, the trustee had a vested right to the whole of the right which the instituted debtor had in the property. Even after the debtor died, the trustee in a question with the heir of provision retained a right to the value of the property insofar as it was required for creditors' claims.[190] Lord Sutherland held that the share of the deceased husband (the institute) had vested in the trustee, who was liable for the debtor's debts which had been constituted against the estate by valid

187 2000 SLT 406.
188 On institutes and substitutes see paras **11.13–11.17.**
189 *Fleming's Trs v Fleming* 2000 SLT 406, at 410.
190 2000 SLT 406, at 414.

claims. On the death of the debtor, his share passed under the special destination with the same qualifications.[191]

(2) Nominations

7.26 Nominations are a form of will-substitute, in which a person has nominated a beneficiary for property held by a third party to be paid out to them on death. In most cases this is money or capital. The capital sum will be paid directly to the beneficiary by the institution holding the funds without the executor's involvement in most cases. They can arise in many different forms and there are various rules regulating nominations depending on their provenance. The classic example is funds held in a pension scheme, whereby the deceased scheme member may have made a nomination of a family member to receive a lump sum on the scheme member's death.[192] Consideration of the scheme rules is required in every case, but these nominations are typically not often binding on the scheme administrators or scheme trustees but are taken to be the deceased's precatory wishes as to who the funds should pass to directly on death.

Other forms of nomination exist, which are permitted and regulated by statute, which are binding on the institution to pay the nominated beneficiary. These derive from reserved legislation from the UK Parliament, and the rules in England & Wales are identical to Scotland.[193] These typically relate to older forms of modest savings accounts or schemes, or funds held in a mutual society or a trade union. The provision of a nomination in such cases is because it was viewed that 'the poorer members of a society' should have 'the power to make provision for the disposal, at their death, of this small sum without the expense being incurred of the making of a will or of administering this part of their estate'.[194]

191 2000 SLT 406, at 410.

192 See a discussion of the rules in English law in A Braun, 'Pension Death Benefits: Opportunities and Pitfalls' in B Häcker and C Mitchell (eds), *Current Issues in Succession Law* (2016).

193 See A Learmonth et al (eds), *Theobald on Wills*, 20th edn (2025), paras 1-009–1-012.

194 *Eccles Provident Industrial Co-operative Society* v *Griffiths* [1912] AC 483, per Lord Mersey at 490.

The juridical nature of nominations is a matter of debate and rather undertheorised in Scots law.[195] Somewhat confusingly, nominations have been held to be writings of a 'testamentary nature', but it should be emphasised that it is only where the rules that regulate such schemes allow for a nomination that has testamentary effect.[196] A nomination of a qualifying type has also been seen as a form of special destination.[197]

Revocation of a nomination can be achieved only by the forms prescribed by their governing statute, or the scheme rules, and they cannot be revoked by subsequent testamentary writings such as a will unless referred to specifically.[198] If a will does purport to revoke the nomination, the beneficiary named in the will may acquire a right to the fund and the nominee will retain only a power of administration over it but, again, this will depend on the terms of the particular rules and regulations concerned.[199] The entire area is far from certain.

(3) Policies of life assurance

7.27 The proceeds of policies of life assurance may not always form part of the deceased's estate and beneficiaries of life policies and pension schemes can be named in much the same way as in nominations. Life policies may also be taken out jointly and contain a survivorship destination.

Where the proceeds of the policy are payable to the deceased or his or her executors or assignees, they will form part of the estate. In *Muirhead v Muirhead's Factor*[200] the deceased had effected two insurance policies on his own life. The terms of the policies stated that the sum due on the policyholder's death was payable to his executors. The defender averred that since the sums were merely contingent and not payable until after his death, they did not fall into the fund available for legal rights. The view of Lord President Inglis was that:[201]

195 See D Carr, 'Will-Substitutes in Scotland' in A Braun and A Röthel, *Passing Wealth on Death: Will-Substitutes in Comparative Perspective* (2016), 96–97.
196 *Clark's Exrs v Macaulay* 1961 SLT 109; and *Gill v Gill* 1938 SC 65.
197 *Ford's Trs v Ford* 1940 SC 426.
198 See *Clark's Exrs v Macaulay* 1961 SLT 109; and *Ford's Trs v Ford* 1940 SC 426.
199 *Young v Waterson* 1918 SC 9.
200 (1867) 6 M 95.
201 (1867) 6 M 95, at 98.

> 'It seems impossible to resist the conclusion that the sums in these policies form part of the executry estate … If this money did not form part of the executry estate I do not know what is to become of it – it is not heritable but moveable, and as nobody can take it but as succeeding the deceased, it must be included in the free executry estate.'

Alternatively, the policy may not be payable to the deceased or his or her executors or assignees and, where it is not, it may not be written in trust. Where it is not, and the policyholder intends that the proceeds should be payable directly to a beneficiary rather than being payable to his or her executor for administration along with the rest of the estate, he or she merely names that person as the beneficiary under the policy or assigns the policy to them. Where the policy is written in trust, it will not form part of the deceased's estate if the policyholder states that the policy is for the benefit of a third party; for example, a spouse, a spouse and children or a civil partner. This arrangement is regulated by the Married Women's Policies of (Scotland) Assurance Act 1880[202] which now applies to husbands and civil partners as well as to wives.[203] There is no requirement that the policyholder intimates or delivers the policy to the beneficiary but, once taken out, the right immediately and irrevocably vests in the beneficiary. It will pass to the beneficiary's estate if he or she predeceases unless either a survivorship condition is written into the policy or the policy contains a destinationover; that is, it stipulates who is to benefit if the first beneficiary predeceases.[204]

Thus, the proceeds of a policy of life assurance on the life of the deceased (whether the premiums were paid by the deceased personally or not)[205] may or may not be payable to the executry estate. If they are, the proceeds will form part of the moveable fund available for legal rights.[206] The fact that the proceeds do not become payable until death – and, therefore, are not *in bonis* at the time the deceased died – is irrelevant.[207]

202 Married Women's Policies of Assurance (Scotland) Act 1880, s 2 [as amended by the Married Women's Policies of Assurance (Amendment) (Scotland) Act 1980].

203 Civil Partnership Act 2004, s 132.

204 See paras **11.12ff**.

205 *Chalmers' Trs* (1882) 9 R 743.

206 See **Ch 5**.

207 *Beveridge v Beveridge's Exrx* 1938 SC 160.

(4) Endowment policies

7.28 Where a policy is payable neither to the deceased's executor nor directly to a beneficiary nominated in the policy, it will usually be because the policy has been assigned as security against a mortgage debt.[208] A joint life policy can take one of two main forms, each having different consequences in relation to the estate of the first of the joint policyholders to die.[209] Very often, this will be an endowment policy where both spouses assign the policy as security over a mortgage. In the first type, the proceeds of the policy are payable to the estate of the first deceased. If the executor pays the outstanding debt over the house in full, using the proceeds of the life policy to do so, one of the spouses has effectively paid the whole of the debt notwithstanding that each is liable for half of the debt individually. Consequently, the surviving spouse is liable to the estate for half the sum, in order that the total value of the estate is not diminished. In the second type, the proceeds are payable to the survivor. The position is reversed, and the estate will be liable to the survivor for half the proceeds. This sum will be a debt on the estate and payable before any right in succession.[210]

(5) Mortis causa donations

7.29 There is, or was, a final form of will-substitute in the form of a donation *mortis causa.* A donation *mortis causa* was a gift 'whereby one in contemplation of his death gives anything to another, or grants a right in his favour, revocable at the granter's pleasure'.[211] It was not a legacy but a gift having testamentary effect. In *Morris v Riddick*[212] Lord President Inglis defined it as:[213]

> 'A conveyance of an immovable or incorporeal right, or a transfer of moveables or money by delivery, so that the property is immediately transferred to the grantee, upon the condition that he shall hold for the

208 See paras **4.31–4.32**.
209 See G Gretton 'Life Policies and the Law of Succession' [1988] *JLSS* 141.
210 See *Christie's Exr v Armstrong* 1996 SLT 948; and para **4.32**.
211 Bankton *Inst,* I.9.18.
212 (1867) 5 M 1036.
213 (1867) 5 M 1036 at 1041.

> granter so long as he lives, subject to his power of revocation and, failing such revocation, then for the grantee on the death of the granter.'

By the time the Scottish Law Commission reviewed this form of gift in 2009, it was considered that they were unknown in modern practice.[214] As such, the Succession (Scotland) Act 2016 abolished the donation *mortis causa*, though it is possible to make a gift expressly conditional, such as only taking effect on the donor's death.[215] In such cases, a transfer of possession could take place in the lifetime by a donor to a donee, but it will be expressly agreed that ownership will not pass to the donee until the donor has died.[216] When the donor dies, only then will the right of ownership pass to the donee, and thus the gifted property will not form part of the deceased donor's estate from the moment of death. Whilst convoluted, it may still be possible for a gift to operate as a will-substitute in the manner described.

214 Scottish Law Commission, *Report on Succession* (SLC Report No 215, 2009), paras 7.38–7.41.

215 2016 Act, s 25. However, see the difficulties with the wording of the legislation noted in S Macdonald-Mulvihill, '*The Scots Law of Donation*', thesis, University of Edinburgh (2024), Ch 6.

216 On the rules of transfer under a gift or donation, see K Reid, *The Law of Property in Scotland,* 2nd edn (2026), Chs 21–24. In most cases, it is suspected, the gift will be of corporeal moveables, of which see the rules discussed by Reid at paras 1118–29.

Chapter 8

The capacity of the testator and influence of others

INTRODUCTION

8.1 Since giving effect to a testator's intention is the paramount consideration in testate succession, it follows both that he or she must have been capable of forming an intention to test, and that it was formed freely. While formal validity refers to the form and manner of execution of the deed, essential validity refers to the requirement that the testator expressed his or her true testamentary intention within that deed.[1] The *animus testandi* must be the product of a disponing mind, and a disponing mind requires both mental capacity and freedom from the imprecations of others. This means that although a deed may conform precisely to the requirements of validity in relation to its formal execution, it may be void if the testator lacked testamentary capacity or be liable to reduction if the execution was subject to pressure from another person, particularly a person who obtains a benefit under the deed.

There are two types of challenge to the capacity of the testator. The first is where the testator lacks testamentary capacity entirely; he or she may be incapax because he or she was too young to execute the deed, or was mentally disordered, or was affected by illness to the point of being unable to appreciate the effect of the deed. As Stair states, 'the power of testing is not competent to pupils, idiots, [and] furious persons in their furiosity'.[2]

With the second type, it is not that the testator lacks testamentary capacity altogether, but that they suffer from a mental or emotional facility that others may take advantage of. Given that a will may be reduced only on the grounds of either formal or essential validity and not

1 See **Ch 7**.
2 Stair *Inst* III.8.37.

simply because its terms seem to be unfair, Lord McLaren's observation is unsurprising:[3]

> 'Amongst objections to wills involving the question of personal disability, there is none more frequently urged, or with more fatal effect, than that of insanity, or facility, on the part of the testators.'

What was true in the nineteenth century remains the case in the twenty-first, and in most cases where a challenge is made to a will, the issues turn more on their own particular facts than on any contentious point of law. In practice, incapacity and facility (together with circumvention or undue influence or both) may be averred as alternatives, since the boundaries between them are blurred and the strength or weakness of the testator's mind is a matter of degree. The evidence is weighed on the balance of probabilities; there may never be a definitive diagnosis of the testator's state of mind but only a set of facts from which inferences can be drawn. Whether the deed is void or voidable depends on the factors militating against its validity[4] and the practical result of a successful challenge may be intestacy since the remedy sought by the pursuer will be either total or partial reduction.[5]

CAPACITY OF THE TESTATOR

(1) Children

8.2 The Age of Legal Capacity (Scotland) 1991 Act provides the age of general legal capacity at 16. However, there is an exception for

3 J McLaren, *The Law of Wills and Succession as Administered in Scotland,* Vol I, 3rd edn (1894), para 492.

4 It will be void *ab initio* if the capacity of the person to form an intention is totally lacking in relation to its execution, but voidable if the person possesses sufficient capacity but has been the object of pressure or importunity by a third party.

5 An action of reduction in relation to a testamentary deed may be brought in either the Court of Session or sheriff court under s 38(g) of the Courts Reform (Scotland) Act 2014. Reduction may be sought by itself or with other, non-reductive conclusions such as declarator. If it is brought on its own, then the pursuer must show that a practical result will follow: *Skerret v Oliver* (1896) 23 R 468. Partial reduction can apply to two situations: first, where only one or some, but not all, of the provisions in a single deed are reducible: *Broadley v Wilson* 1991 SLT 69; second, where the testamentary disposition includes a codicil or codicils and only these are voidable: *Horsburgh v Thomson's Trs* 1912 SC 267; and *West's Tr v West* 1980 SLT 6.

testamentary capacity contained in s 2(2). In relation to testamentary writing, testamentary capacity is acquired at the age of 12.

Sections 3(3)(a) and (b) of the Age of Legal Capacity (Scotland) Act 1991 exclude from the definition of a 'prejudicial transaction' the exercise of testamentary capacity by a person under the age of 16. This means that a will executed by a child between the ages of 12 and 16 cannot be challenged solely on the ground that it was against the child's interests to make it and any challenges to the essential validity of the will must be made on the same grounds as if the child were an adult. Apart from the eventuality of an early death by a child who owns property and dies testate, the rules operate on the basis of the principle that a later will revokes an earlier will.[6] Since a later will in terms inconsistent with an earlier one revokes the former by implication, a will made by a child under the age of 16 will be revoked at the date of any future testamentary writing. Issues of capacity in relation to children who die at a young age remain of at least theoretical significance, although they are unlikely to be of practical relevance.[7]

(2) Adults

8.3 When a will is challenged on the basis of averments that the testator lacked testamentary capacity, the onus of proof is on the pursuer to show that the testator's mental condition vitiated the validity of the deed. The essential validity of a will depends on *animus testandi* on the part of the testator and the original justification for reducing deeds for lack of capacity seems to have been to protect the testator's heirs from disinheritance. Lord McLaren states that, 'the right of the heir ought not to be taken away except by the testamentary act of a person in full possession of his mental powers'[8] and he summarised the conceptual foundation of lack of testamentary capacity as 'import[ing] not only a want of judgment, but the absence of will – the disponing mind'.[9] He observed, however, that 'in the present state of the law, it is hopeless to attempt a definition of the

6 See para **7.15**.
7 See A Barr and L Edwards, 'Age of Legal Capacity: further pitfalls (i) succession and trusts' 1992 *SLT (News)* 77.
8 J McLaren, *The Law of Wills and Succession,* 3rd edn (1894), para 494.
9 ibid para 492.

state and degree of mental alienation which renders the person so affected incapable of making a will.'[10]

Nonetheless, the courts have made several attempts. In *Sivewright v Sivewright's Trs*, a general and straightforward test was formulated:[11]

> 'A testator must be able to exercise a rational appreciation of what he is doing. He must understand the nature of his act. But, if he does, he is not required to be highly intelligent. He may be stupid, or he may be improperly, as far as ethics go, activated by ill-feeling … The question is simply whether he understands what he is about.'

When deciding whether the testator understood what he was about or not, the court is concerned with whether, even if suffering from a mental illness, he or she knew what a testament was and what the effects of its provisions would be. It cited with approval the *locus classicus* of the test of testamentary capacity in English law, *Banks v Goodfellow* in which the necessary conditions for the power of testation were enumerated:[12]

> 'It is essential to the exercise of such a power that a testator shall understand the nature of the act and its effects; shall understand the extent of the property of which he is disposing; shall be able to comprehend and appreciate the claims to which he ought to give effect; and, with a view to the latter object, that no disorder of the mind shall poison his affections, pervert his sense of right, and prevent the exercise of his natural faculties – that no insane delusion shall influence his will in disposing of his property and bring about a disposal of it which if the mind had been sound would not have been made.'

Evidence of the testator's mental condition and evidence of his or her appreciation of the testamentary provisions that he or she has made are therefore distinguishable, but related, and the latter may also constitute evidence of the former. Unsoundness of mind is a matter of degree and of duration and a testator may not be generally or permanently but only intermittently or temporarily *incapax*. If a will is to be reduced, its provisions must therefore have been the product of a particular delusion operating as a compelling influence on the mind of the testator at the time of execution.[13]

10 ibid para 493.

11 *Sivewright v Sivewright's Trs* 1920 SC (HL) 63, per Viscount Haldane at 64.

12 (1869-70) LR 5 QB 549, per Cockburn CJ at 565.

13 *Sivewright v Sivewright's Trs* 1920 SC (HL) 63 and *Nisbet's Trustees v Nisbet* (1871) 9 M 937.

Thus, the court attempts to strike a balance between, on the one hand, safeguarding the interests of relatives or other persons with an interest in the will and, on the other, respecting and giving effect to the testator's wishes as actually expressed, however singular these may appear to others. The fact that the testator has made provisions which seem unfair or malicious – for example, where no provision has been made for children or for a person who may have spent years caring for him or her – does not mean necessarily that he or she lacked capacity. Lord Prosser summarised the position when he noted, 'it is no part of my function to prevent a testator from doing something which may seem unfair … hurtful though that may be to those who are thus excluded'.[14]

Most of the case law concerns wills where the testator has given the bulk of his or her estate to someone other than a close relative or relatives and they have had a strong interest in seeking to have the will reduced, the result being entitlement to the deceased's intestate estate.[15] The leading case on testamentary capacity is *Morrison v Maclean's Trustees*.[16] The testator, Colonel Alexander Maclean, had made a trust disposition in which the trustees were directed to pay an annuity to his housekeeper and to educate poor boys named Maclean. He had declared that he had no relatives, when in fact he had, and had left nothing to them. His relatives, who were his heirs under the rules of intestate succession, raised an action on the basis that the testator had been insane or, alternatively, he had been facile and subject to circumvention by his housekeeper. Various averments relating to both the testator's personality and behaviour and the nature of his relationship with his housekeeper were put forward but the court held that although the testator was eccentric, allegations that no rational person would have made a will in such terms were insufficient to prove that he was insane. The fact that a will may be morally objectionable to some people, particularly a testator's relatives, does not render it invalid.

In practice, solicitors are required to assess whether or not the testator has the requisite capacity when taking instructions, such as with the

14 *Brogan v Rennie* (6 August 1991, unreported), OH.

15 See **Ch 4**.

16 *Morrison v Maclean's Trs* (1862) 24 D 625.

drafting of a will.[17] This may involve requesting an opinion from a medical professional. Despite reasonable safeguards being employed by the profession, it can be the case that a will may be subject to challenge on the basis of incapacity. This can arise with professionally drafted wills, but it is more common where the testator has not availed themselves of professional advice.[18]

(a) Mental illness

8.4 As with actions based on other branches of the law, cases involving total incapacity in relation to the law of succession tend to focus on the more severe forms of mental illness such as schizophrenia and the advanced stages of senile dementia or Alzheimer's Disease. Yet, where the court has to decide questions of capacity as they affect the validity of a will, it must also deal with cases of milder forms of mental illness, 'cases where some severe or unexpected strain has disturbed the springs of that delicate mechanism by which the mind communicates with external nature'.[19] This kind of illness would include, for example, clinical depression.

A court will not find easily that a testator lacked testamentary capacity. A person may be suffering from distressing mental or emotional symptoms – or indeed be under severe misapprehensions about the state of the world

17 Law Society of Scotland, Practice Rules 2011, Rule B1.5, and accompanying guidance. There has been a political campaign for improved safeguards for a medical profession to attest to the granter's capacity, see S O'Neil, 'Calls for Willie's Law after sick dad signed assets away', *BBC News,* Sunday 9 November 2023, available https://www.bbc.co.uk/news/uk-scotland-tayside-central-67359407. In England & Wales, there is a so called 'golden rule' to have an elderly or infirm testator assessed by a medical practitioner, though it is merely best practice and has no legal effect, may not be appropriate in every case, and even if followed carries no guarantee that the testator indeed had capacity. The Law Commission of England & Wales have recently reviewed this area and recommended a new code of practice for assessing and determining testamentary capacity, see Report on *Modernising Wills Law,* Vol I (LC Report No 419, 2025), paras 2.133–2.192.

18 For further discussion, see R Kerridge, 'Wills made in suspicious circumstances: The problem of the vulnerable testator' (2000) 59 *Cambridge LJ* 310; J Kerrigan, 'Capacity – Recent developments' 2011 *SLT (News)* 221; and J Kerrigan, 'Capacity – More recent developments' 2015 *SLT (News)* 21.

19 J McLaren, *The Law of Wills and Succession,* 3rd edn (1894) para 493.

or other people – but know perfectly well what he or she is doing when making a will. As long as this is the case, the court is under a duty to respect his or her testamentary intentions. Similarly, while some forms of dementia may render the testator totally incapable of executing a valid deed,[20] milder or less advanced forms may render the person facile but not incapax.[21]

Ballantine v Evans[22] illustrates well the general difficulties of defining a degree of mental illness sufficient to render a deed void and the reluctance of the court to accept that the terms of the will are necessarily a manifestation of a delusion on the part of the testator. The testator had been suffering from severe depression and had committed suicide. He also appeared to have been suffering from a mild paranoia yet, as the court stated, 'the general powers and faculties of his mind were unimpaired'.[23] The testator's will was upheld on the basis that his 'delusion' that people were making accusations against him could simply be the result of a mistake: he had overhead certain remarks and had misconstrued them in the same way as any rational person could have done. Similarly, in *Smith v Smith's Trustees*[24] the testator had suffered a reactive depression following the death of his wife. His symptoms included a belief that his wife had returned to him after her death but the court held that this delusion had no bearing on the terms of the will which he had then executed.

The point at which the irrationality of provisions in the will become such as to raise doubts about the testator's capacity is not fixed but if they appear utterly perverse, the will may, in theory at least, be set aside.[25] This somewhat pragmatic means of ascertaining objectively the testator's capacity means that the rationality of testamentary provisions can, in some cases, be construed as evidence supporting (or not) an averment that the testator did not know what he or she was doing.

20 See, eg, *Boyle v Boyle's Exr* 1999 SC 479 where undue influence was also averred: see paras **8.12–8.13**.
21 See *Rennie v Stephen* (4 July 1991, unreported), OH.
22 *Ballantine v Evans* (1886) 13 R 652.
23 *Ballantine v Evans* (1886) 13 R 652, at 664.
24 *Smith v Smith's Trs* 1972 SLT (Notes) 80.
25 On the difficulties facing the court in balancing the right of the testator to favour whom he chooses and the objective merits of that person, see R A McCall Smith 'The deluded testator' 1973 *SLT (News)* 61.

Even if the testator was mentally disordered, a will executed during a lucid period is valid. This is a matter to be established as a question of fact. In *Nisbet's Trustees v Nisbet*,[26] the testator had been resident in a mental hospital for many years but, although confused, it was not apparent that he had suffered from any particular or general delusions. He appeared to have recovered at the time he executed the deed and the very rationality of the deed itself was held to be evidence of his capacity to have done so. Lord Ardmillan observed:[27]

> 'We cannot penetrate the profound mysteries of the sentient and intellectual constitution of man, nor trace the recondite discords which distract thought … We ought not, if we can avoid it, to interfere with the undoubted right to dispose of property by will. It is a great step towards decision, that the will is simple and rational, and not unjust.'

The case is also authority for the evidential rule that if it is admitted or proved that the testator has a history of mental illness, the onus is on the party seeking to found on the deed to prove that the will was not the result of that illness. This reverses the rule in cases where it is alleged that the testator lacked capacity when the will was executed.

(b) Physical illness, infirmity and the effect of drugs

8.5 Testamentary incapacity may also result from a severe physical illness or condition if the testator's mind is diminished by its effects.[28] Some of these effects may be induced by the prescription of drugs. For

26 *Nisbet's Trs v Nisbet* (1871) 9 M 937.

27 *Nisbet's Trs v Nisbet* (1871) 9 M 937, at 948.

28 Cases of this type can be seen as similar to those decided under the old law of deathbed, repealed in 1871, which abolished the right of reduction *ex capite lecti*. The common law presumption of incapacity where the granter executed a deed whilst ill from the disease of which he died was based on the fact that 'the decay of the vital powers is usually accompanied with a certain infirmity of the will, rendering the moribund person more or less accessible to the importunities of interested attendants': McLaren, *Wills and Succession*, 3rd edn (1894) para 333. Any such deed would be reducible in so far as it was prejudicial to the rights of the testator's heirs. See Stair *Inst* III.4.20, III.4.27-30; III.4.37-48; Erskine *Inst* III.8.95; Bell *Prin* § 1786–1815; *Pargillies v Pargillies* (1669) Mor 3304; *Ogilivy v Mercer* 10 Dec 1793 FC; *Maitland v Maitland* 16 May 1815 FC.

example, in *Laidlaw v Laidlaw*,[29] the will was reduced where it was proved that the testator had been almost comatose as a result of the administration of opiates when he had executed his will. In *Graham v Robertson*[30] the testator signed a will on the day before she died. She was in hospital suffering from acute septicaemia and in a confused toxic state as a result; in addition, she had suffered brain damage from a previous stroke. The combination of her medical condition, medical history, age, general health, and the drugs being administered to her led the court to the conclusion that the probability was that she did not possess the necessary testamentary capacity and the will was reduced. It follows that if drugs are taken voluntarily or the testator has consumed excessive alcohol, testamentary capacity may also be negated temporarily, to the extent that he or she is incapable of forming a rational intention.

The presence of illness and powerful medication can be seen recently in *Smyth v Romane's Exrs*.[31] Here the testator had cancer and was in significant pain in the final days and weeks of her life. Two weeks before her death, she executed a codicil which later went on to be challenged on the basis *inter alia* that the testator did not have capacity. In the judgment by Lord Glennie, which contains a useful exposition of the relevant principles and authorities in this area, his lordship noted that:[32]

> 'First, it is clear that testamentary capacity may come and go over time. A person may have rational moments followed by moments when he is incapable of thinking or acting rationally. In the context of testamentary capacity, a testamentary disposition will only be reduced if it can be shown that it was executed while the testator was incapable…A person suffering from a grave, debilitating and painful illness will have moments when he is able to discuss matters calmly and sensibly…while at other moments he may be in such pain or so tired that, though capable of reasoning clearly, he simply goes along with what is proposed even though it is not what he would otherwise have done.'

29 (1870) 8 M 882.

30 (3 March 1995, unreported) OH. See also the English case *Clancy v Clancy* [2003] EWHC 1885 (Ch) where the testator was admitted to hospital in the terminal stages of cancer and signed a will under the effects of sedative drugs.

31 [2014] CSOH 150.

32 [2014] CSOH 150, at para 51.

Having heard evidence from a range of persons present during the testator's illness, alongside medical professionals offering up evidence on the effect of the opiate medications being administered to the testator, his lordship concluded:[33]

> '[The testator] was almost constantly in great pain, was often suffering from nausea and would have been affected by the side-effects of the medications taken to relieve her pain. The side-effects, allied to the pain and nausea, would very likely have affected her consciousness and mental stamina. At times her mental capacity may have been affected. But I cannot conclude on the medical evidence alone that in any general sense she no longer had mental capacity throughout this period.'

In light of the evidence, Lord Glennie determined that at the time of instructing the changes and executing the will, the testator had 'full capacity' and that 'she understood what she was doing and she had the capacity to understand the assets at her disposal and the obligations to which she would or might wish to give consideration'.[34] Cases such as *Symth* serve to highlight that capacity may not be so certain as an 'on-off switch' and that despite experiencing significant pain or in receipt of powerful medication, there may yet be lucid periods in which the testator has capacity to make a will.

THE WRONGFUL INFLUENCE OF OTHERS

(1) General issues

8.6 The circumstances surrounding the execution of a will and the terms in which it is framed may lead to allegations that it was made as the result of someone persuading, coercing or otherwise influencing the testator to make it. This is most commonly the case where the testator has revoked a will and executed a new one in which a substantial legacy is given to a person who seems an unlikely or unusual legatee, thus arousing the suspicion that he or she somehow interfered with the testator's free will in executing the deed.

33 [2014] CSOH 150, at para 73.
34 [2014] CSOH 150, at para 125.

A challenge to a testamentary disposition on the ground of the total incapacity of the testator is based on averments that the testator did not possess the requisite will or 'disponing mind'. By contrast, a challenge on the grounds of facility and circumvention or undue influence is based on the testator having a disponing mind – he or she has known what a will is and has understood the provisions contained within it – but a mind so affected by another person's will that the will cannot be said to have been the product of the testator's own will at all. In the case of undue influence, the testator and beneficiary must have had a fiduciary or quasi-fiduciary relationship which the beneficiary has exploited for his or her own ends but in relation to *mortis causa* deeds, averments of undue influence are unlikely to be proved unless the testator was also facile.[35]

Averments of actual fraud may be made but, unless 'one or more specific, identifiable instances of deception or misrepresentation by which the deceased was induced to act in a way which he would not otherwise have acted' can be proved, the action must fail.[36] Given the difficulties of proving any such instances, the bases of a challenge are the closely related doctrines of facility and circumvention and undue influence.[37] While fraud involves deception by a third party and both facility and circumvention and undue influence involve pressure,[38] Institutional authority refers to pressure as a kind of deceit or moral fraud[39] and the terminology used in some of the recent cases assimilates fraud with the concept of circumvention or pressure.[40] Notwithstanding these semantic issues, where averments of facility and circumvention or undue influence are made, no specific instances of deception are required; rather, the inference may be drawn that the will could only have been the result of importunity on the part of another person who, taking advantage of the testator, managed to obtain a benefit that he or she would not normally have been given.

35 See paras **8.12–8.13**.

36 *MacDonald v McCallum* (29 August 2003, unreported) OH.

37 On the history of these doctrines, see W McBryde, *The Law of Contract in Scotland*, 3rd edn (2007), Ch 16.

38 See R Kerridge, 'Wills made in suspicious circumstances: The problem of the vulnerable testator' (2000) 59 *Cambridge LJ* 310, 318, for discussion of the distinction and why judges have tended to assimilate them.

39 See para **8.8** below.

40 eg, *Pascoe-Watson v Brock's Exr* 1998 SLT 40; *Anderson v The Beacon Fellowship* 1992 SLT 111; and *Whelans v Whelans* 1986 SLT 164.

As well as in some cases being averred in the alternative to averments that the testator lacked testamentary capacity, averments of the separate doctrines of facility and circumvention and undue influence also tend to be made in the alternative to each other.[41] It is common to find a 'two-pronged' attack in reported cases that a testamentary document is argued to be reducible either: (i) on the basis of facility and circumvention; and (ii) *esto* on the basis of undue influence (and vice versa).

The two doctrines are difficult to distinguish, if indeed they can be distinguished at all, and their boundaries appear blurred but in *Ross v Gosselin's Executors* the Lord President Clyde emphasised that the concepts should not be confused:[42]

> 'The essence of undue influence is that a person, who has assumed or undertaken a position of quasi-fiduciary responsibility in relation to the affairs of another, allows his own self-interest to deflect the advice or guidance he gives, in his own favour. On the other hand, the essence of circumvention and facility is that a person practises on the debility of another whose individuality is impaired by infirmity or age, and moulds the inclination of the latter to his own profit. I think it would be extravagant and fallacious to refuse to recognise the distinction between these two different kinds of questions, merely because they are both ultimately referable to the same broad category of fraud.'

This distinction appears to lie in the type of fraud that may be involved, the character or status of the beneficiary and the degree to which actual deception or coercion was involved.

(2) Facility and circumvention

8.7 The doctrine of facility and circumvention is the primary means in Scots law by which the apparently voluntary testamentary act of a vulnerable person may be challenged. If it can be shown that a testator lacked the mental fortitude to resist the importunity of another person in relation to his or her testamentary arrangements and that person subverted the testator's will to his or her own advantage, the will may be reduced.

41 As examples, see *Horne v Whyte* [2005] CSOH 115; *Pirie v Clydesdale Bank* [2005] CSOH 51; *Boyle v Boyle's Executor* 1999 SC 479.

42 *Ross v Gosselin's Exrs* 1926 SC 325, at 334.

Three elements must be present: (i) facility on the part of the testator at the time the will was executed; (ii) acts amounting to circumvention or circumstances leading to an inference of circumvention; and (iii) lesion, or loss. The relationship between them and the evidence required to prove them was summarised by Lady Smith in *Horne v Whyte*:[43]

> 'Direct evidence is normally required for the first and third of these elements but the second, for obvious reasons, is usually, where the granter of the challenged deed is dead, a matter of inference.[44] The three elements are clearly interrelated, they require to be looked at as a whole and the strength of a pursuer's case on one matter may compensate for weakness on other matters.'

The interrelationship between the elements is close: the greater the facility, the more likely it is that an inference of circumvention will be drawn; the weaker the evidence of facility, the more specific the evidence of circumvention must be; and unless there is both facility and circumvention, there cannot be lesion.

Doubt as to the testator's intentions will be generated only if someone has sought to take advantage of the testator's condition or personality. Where both testamentary incapacity and facility and circumvention or undue influence are averred, the 'weaker alternative' rule will be applied[45] as facility in one case may be total incapacity in another, depending on the quality of the available evidence in relation to the testator's mental impairment. In some cases, the averments must be taken as a whole and the will may be capable of reduction on both grounds.[46]

(a) Facility

8.8 Facility is weakness of mind such that the mind of the person affected is easily swayed by that of another. *Bell's Dictionary* defines it as 'a condition of mental weakness, short of idiocy, in which an individual is easily imposed upon and induced to do deeds to his own prejudice'.[47]

43 *Horne v Whyte* [2005] CSOH 115, at para 51.

44 Citing *Clunie v Stirling* (1854) 17 D 15; *Mackay v Campbell* 1967 SC (HL) 53; *Pascoe-Watson v Brock's Executor* 1998 SLT 40; and *Gaul v Deerey & Others* 2000 SCLR 407.

45 *Haigh and Ringrose Ltd v Barrhead Builders Ltd* 1981 SLT 157.

46 See, eg, *Williams v Philip* (1907) 15 SLT 396.

47 *Bell's Dictionary*, 7th edn (1890) 396.

In the leading case of *Gibson's Executor v Anderson*, Lord Justice-Clerk Alness described it as where 'a person is in such a mental state that he is unable to resist pressure, and … someone else can mould and fashion his conduct as he pleases'.[48]

The court will not find lightly that a testator was facile. For example, in the unreported cases of *Rennie v Stephen*[49] and *Brogan v Rennie*[50] it was held that, contrary to what was alleged by the pursuers, the testator had not been facile, far less *incapax* (as alleged in the alternative). Mild dementia does not amount necessarily to facility and expert evidence proved that dementia did not necessarily interfere with a person's judgment so that rational decisions could be taken in relation to important matters. Facility must, therefore, be shown to have a verifiable foundation in fact.[51] Age alone does not necessarily render a person facile and, as Lord Justice-Clerk Grant stated with some cogency in *Mackay v Campbell*:[52]

> 'If what the defender avers can amount to weakness and facility, the litigation index in regard to contracts and wills executed by the over-60's or the accident-prone of a pessimistic mind will undoubtedly turn sharply upwards.'

The forms which facility can take, and the causes from which it may derive, were summarised by Lord Justice-Clerk Inglis in *Morrison v Maclean's Trustees*,[53] where the pursuers had averred as an alternative to insanity that the testator had been facile and subject to circumvention by his housekeeper:[54]

> 'A man may be weak and facile from want of judgment or reason … [or] from mere nervousness and incapacity to resist solicitation … you must endeavour to see whether there is any correspondence between the kind of facility that is proved and the kind of arts that are employed against him.'

48 1925 SC 774, at 790.

49 *Rennie v Stephen* (4 July 1991, unreported), OH.

50 *Brogan v Rennie* 1991 GWD 31-1885.

51 *Ross v Gosselin's Exrs* 1926 SC 325; *West's Tr v West* 1980 SLT 6; and *Grant's Exrs v Grant* 1999 GWD 36-1772.

52 *Mackay v Campbell* 1966 SC 237, at 249–50. His lordship referred particularly to *Clunie v Stirling* (1854) 17 D 15 and *Horsburgh v Thomson's Trs* 1912 SC 267. See also *Wright v Cotias Investments Inc* 2001 SLT 353.

53 *Morrison v Maclean's Trs* (1862) 24 D 625.

54 *Morrison v Maclean's Trs* (1862) 24 D 625, per Lord Justice-Clerk Inglis at 635.

If facility is proved, its cause or nature may be due to a number of possible factors: for example, the effects of bereavement and illness,[55] dementia short of total incapacity,[56] or alcoholism.[57] It may be manifested as mere suggestibility on the part of a testator who is 'easily got round'.[58] On the other hand, it may be that the testator, while eccentric but not facile, fully intended to benefit a person to whom he or she had become attached and to favour that person in his or her will more generously than any family members.[59] Even if the testator is facile, he or she may also have been a stubborn personality highly suspicious of other people wanting his or her money. In this case, an implication of circumvention may well be negated.[60]

(b) Circumvention

8.9 Even if it is proved that the testator was facile when he or she executed the deed, this alone will not be sufficient to reduce it without averments of circumvention.[61] Circumvention is simply pressure of some kind exerted on the testator by a third party, and what it amounts to in a particular case always depends on the actual condition of the testator and the surrounding facts and circumstances. *Bell's Dictionary* defines circumvention as 'deceit or fraud'[62] and Stair writes that circumvention 'signifyeth the act of fraud whereby a person is induced to a deed or obligation by deceit'.[63] Fraud, in this context, is 'improper practices and

55 *Munro v Strain* (1874) 1 R 522.

56 *Horsburgh v Thomson's Trs* 1912 1 SLT 73.

57 *Pascoe-Watson v Brock's Exr* 1998 SLT 40.

58 *Whelans v Whelans* 1986 SLT 164.

59 *Morrison v Maclean's Trs* (1862) 24 D 625.

60 See the comments of Lord President Clyde in *Ross v Gosselin's Exrs* 1926 SC 325 at 333; Lord Prosser in *Brogan v Rennie* (6 August 1991, unreported), OH; and Lord Justice-Clerk Alness in *Gibson's Exor v Anderson* 1925 SC 774 at 790.

61 *Lord Advocate v Davidson's Judicial Factor* 1921 2 SLT 267; *McDougal v McDougal's Trs* 1931 SC 102.

62 *Bell's Dictionary*, 7th edn (1890) 181.

63 *Inst*, I.4.8. As Stair makes clear, the rules relating to facility and circumvention are identical in Scots law in the different branches of the law. That is, there is no essential difference in the meaning or application as between *mortis causa* and *inter vivos* deeds of the principle that the granter of the deed must have been acting on the basis of his or her own free will. The only difference relates to the quality of the evidence required. The same does not apply to undue influence: see paras **8.12–8.13** below.

solicitation by interested parties'[64] and fraud and circumvention 'shades of the same thing'.[65] The degree of circumvention required to invalidate a deed is inversely proportionate to the degree of facility: that is, the slighter the facility, the greater the circumvention required and the higher the degree of facility, the weaker any evidence of circumvention has to be.

(c) The nature of the circumvention

8.10 Where the person who is alleged to be facile is alive, facility must not only be proved but there must also be averments either of specific acts of circumvention or at least sufficient averments of facts and circumstances from which an inference of circumvention may be drawn.[66]

Where the granter is dead, less in the way of evidence is required than if he or she were alive. He or she is unable to give evidence as to the facts surrounding the execution of the deed in question and circumvention will more readily be inferred. Erskine states that 'where lesion in the deed and facility in the granter concur, the most slender circumstances of fraud or circumvention are sufficient to set it aside'.[67] There is no need, therefore, to aver or prove any specific act of circumvention since, given its nature it is unlikely that it would in any case be possible. Given the nature of circumvention, it is unlikely that it will be possible to prove that it has occurred. As McLaren noted, 'the arts that may be practised by a beneficiary to procure the testator's signature to a will are not easily discoverable'[68] and, just as facility is a question of degree, so is circumvention a question of circumstances. In *Parnie v MacLean,* Lord Kyllachy stated:[69]

> 'Things that might be right to do with a strong-minded person become wrong when done for your own benefit towards a person who is … facile; … the question [is] whether, facility existing, there had been either distinct machinations, tricks, importunities, solicitations, even suggestions,

64 *Morrison v Maclean's Trs* (1862) 24 D 625, per Lord Justice-Clerk Inglis at 635.

65 *Gibson's Exor v Anderson* 1925 SC 774, per Lord Blackburn at 788, citing Lord Kyllachy in *Parnie v MacLean* (unreported).

66 See, eg, *Wright v Cotias Investments Inc* 2001 SLT 353.

67 Erskine *Inst*, IV.1.27.

68 McLaren, *The Law of Wills and Succession,* 3rd edn (1894), para 492.

69 *Parnie v MacLean* is unreported but is cited and approved in *Gibson's Exr v Anderson* 1925 SC 774 at 788; and *Anderson v The Beacon Fellowship* 1992 SLT 111.

> towards the testator while the testator's facility was such that she was not in a position to resist … It is not necessary that there should be deceit … The degree of circumvention would depend on the degree of facility.'

In *Clunie v Stirling*, it was held that in the case of a person who was very facile, persuasion alone was sufficient to overcome the testator's will to the advantage of the beneficiary. Lord Justice-Clerk Hope noted that:[70]

> 'The actual mode or particular acts of circumvention may not be discoverable or easily proved … It is seldom possible to ascertain the particular acts or practices by which either a facile old man, or a person whose power of judging of the fitness and propriety of entering into particular arrangements as to his affairs, has been weakened.'

If there was a motive for the defender to mislead and induce the deceased to enter into a transaction for his or her own or for another's benefit, and only persuasion acting on a facile mind could have brought about this result, there need therefore be only averments of the kind of circumvention involved or the kinds of circumstances from which the inference may be drawn.[71] The very fact that the means of bringing about a change of the testator's will are questionable may itself throw a question mark over the state of his or her mind.[72]

In *Horne v Whyte*,[73] the testator was a 'physically enfeebled' and 'mentally enfeebled' widower who had become highly dependent on his housekeeper and was frightened she would leave him. She had acted as a 'gatekeeper' between him and his family, had taken charge of his finances and had obtained significant sums of money from him towards the end of his life and for which she was unable to account. The testator had executed a codicil to his will, in somewhat suspicious circumstances, in which he reduced the legacies to members of his family that he had made in his previous will and greatly increased the legacy to his housekeeper. His fear of, and dependence on, the housekeeper, as much as the medical evidence as to his physical and mental condition, pointed to facility on the part of the testator. Her actings in relation to his affairs supported the inference

70 *Clunie v Stirling* (1854) 17 D 15 at 17–18.
71 *McDougal v McDougal's Trs* 1931 SC 102.
72 *Munro v Strain* (1874) 1 R 1039, per Lord Neaves at 1045.
73 *Horne v Whyte* [2005] CSOH 115.

that only circumvention on her part could have caused him to change his will as he did.

The degree of facility on the part of the testator and the type of circumvention are thus inextricably linked. It may, accordingly, be possible to draw the conclusion that only persuasion or impetration could have brought about the result and to reduce the deed if it can be inferred sufficiently strongly that the defender had a motive to mislead or induce a facile testator. At the other end of the spectrum, the circumvention may be severe and overcome the will of a person who is not facile in the sense of mental impairment but vulnerable because of age or infirmity. Impetration of the testator's will includes intimidation[74] and this may take the form of physical intimidation or psychological or emotional pressure. There may not be evidence of any specific acts but, rather, 'a general course of threats and harshness'.[75] In *Cairns v Marianski*, there was evidence that the deceased, a man who had been upwards of 86-years-old at the time when he gave the defender his money, was afraid of him. Lord Justice-Clerk Hope approved the text of note that the judge at trial had given to the jury and which read:[76]

> 'The expressions 'weak', 'facile' and 'easily imposed on', are flexible terms, intended to cover cases of a very different character, and may embrace the case of a very old man whose intellect may not be weak, if at all impaired, but who may be easily frightened – timid and nervous from age – afraid of violence – compelled from dread, and from the desire of ease, and with the helplessness and dependence of age, to submit to the ascendancy of another, and incapable of exercising resolution so as to resist violence of temper.'

(d) Lesion

8.11 Clearly, the terms of a will cannot be to anyone's lesion (or loss) if they were the product of the testator's free and independently formed intention, even if those terms cause disappointment in certain people.

74 *Horsburgh v Thomson's Trs* 1912 1 SLT 73. See also *Lindsay's Executor v Outlook Finance Ltd* [2021] CSOH 82.

75 *Love v Marshall* (1870) 9 M 291, per Lord Kinloch at 297.

76 *Cairns v Marianski* (1850) 12 D 1286, at 1295. Although this was a case of facility and circumvention *inter vivos*, the donor was dead when the case was decided.

Where the testator is facile and circumvention is proved or inferred, clearly there is lesion to a range of persons; a beneficiary under a previous will; a person likely to have benefited under a will executed freely be the testator; or a person who would take the intestate estate if the will is reduced. In some cases, a family member may fall into each of these categories. It is also recognised that in every case of facility and circumvention, there is lesion to the testator, notwithstanding that he is deceased, in that his or her ideas and inclinations in relation to the disposal of his or her estate have been interfered with by another person.[77]

(3) Undue influence

8.12 In the absence of any particular mental, psychological, emotional or physical weakness on the part of the testator, it may be that a challenge to the essential validity of a testamentary deed may be made on the ground of undue influence. The problem in such cases is to determine whether, on an objective view, the will is a product of the testator's 'free and deliberate will'[78] or of another person's controlling influence. In *Allcard v Skinner* Lindley LJ described it in graphic terms:[79]

> 'What then is the principle? Is it that it is right and expedient to save persons from the consequences of their own folly? Or is it that it is right and expedient to save them from being victimised by other people? Courts of Equity have never set aside gifts on the ground of the folly, imprudence, or want of foresight on the part of donors … On the other hand, to protect people from being forced, tricked, or misled in any way by others into parting with their property is one of the most legitimate of all laws; and the equitable doctrine of undue influence has grown out of and been developed by the necessity of grappling with insidious forms of spiritual tyranny and with the infinite varieties of fraud.'

77 For example, in *Williams v Philip* (1907) 15 SLT 396 one of the issues for the court was 'whether [the testator] was weak and facile in mind and easily imposed upon, and whether the defender … taking advantage of his said weakness and facility, did by fraud or circumvention obtain or procure from the [testator] the will … to the lesion of the said [testator]?' See also R Kerridge, 'Wills made in suspicious circumstances: The problem of the vulnerable testator' (2000) 59 *Cambridge LJ* 310, 312.

78 *Weir v Grace* (1898) 6 SLT 101 at 104.

79 *Allcard v Skinner* (1887) 36 Ch D 145 at 183.

The purpose of the doctrine is to provide a remedy where the testator has placed trust and confidence in the beneficiary and that trust has been abused or exploited for his or her own self-interested advantage. Given the difficulties of proof, a finding of undue influence will be more easily made than facility and circumvention provided there is 'anything in the nature of weakness or facility' on the part of the testator.[80]

(a) The nature of undue influence

8.13 The doctrine of undue influence was received into Scots law from English law in the case of *Gray v Binny*[81] where Lord Shand defined it in the following terms:

> 'The circumstances which establish a case of undue influence are … the existence of a relation between the granter and the grantee of the deed which creates a dominant or ascendant influence, the fact that confidence and trust arose from that relation, the fact that a material and gratuitous benefit was given to the prejudice of the granter, and the circumstance that the granter entered into the transaction without the benefit of independent advice or assistance.'

Here, a son had entered into an *inter vivos* agreement with his mother to his own disadvantage and had received no independent advice.[82] As in English law, rather more than the absence of independent advice is required in relation to challenging the validity of *mortis causa* deeds.[83] Since the application of the doctrine does not depend on the facility of the testator, evidence of fraud or actual coercion is required. In *Forrest v Low's Trustees*,[84] where the influence of a solicitor over his client in executing his will was in question, Lord Kinnear held that reduction could be granted only if the solicitor had made any kind of misrepresentation to the testator or if the influence in question could have coerced the testator

80 *McKechnie v McKechnie's Trs* 1908 SC 93 at 98.

81 1879) 7 R 332 at 347. The doctrine of facility and circumvention does not exist in English law. On the reception of the doctrine see W H D Winder 'Undue Influence in Scots and English Law' [1940] *LQR* 97–112.

82 See also *Carmichael v Baird* (1899) 6 SLT 369.

83 Although the provision of independent advice is important, *Smyth v Romanes' Executors* [2014] CSOH 150.

84 1907 SC 1240, at 1258.

into acting as an instrument of his solicitor rather than as an independent agent. Similarly, in *Weir v Grace*,[85] it was held that:

> 'Influence, in order to be undue within the meaning of any rule of law which would make it sufficient to vitiate a will, must be an influence exercised either by coercion or by fraud.'

A 'dominant or ascendant influence' involves relationships classifiable as fiduciary or quasi-fiduciary. These have included relationships such as that of solicitor and client,[86] parent and child,[87] doctor and patient,[88] a man and his secretary,[89] a spiritual adviser over parishioners or disciples[90] and an art dealer and his clients.[91] The category has also been held to include a housekeeper and her employer[92] and an elderly woman and her taxi driver.[93] Such relationships always involve a degree of dependency – sometimes a very high degree – and the concept of *quasi*-fiduciary relationship may extend simply to any person who assumes control over the testator's financial or living arrangements.[94].

Although there are certain sorts of relationships, or relationships with certain sorts of qualities, to which the doctrine will most readily apply, more than the mere existence of such a relationship is required before an inference of undue influence will be drawn.[95] The person in

85 *Weir v Grace* (1899) 2 F (HL) 30, at 32.
86 *Stewart v McLaren* (1920) SC (HL) 148; *Weir v Grace* (1900) 2 F (HL) 30, [1899] F 261; and *Moira Tiarks v Norris Paterson* 1992 GWD 523-1328.
87 *Forbes v Forbes' Trs* 1957 SC 325; *Allan v Allan* 1961 SC 200 (parent over child); *MacGilveary v Gilmartin* 1986 SLT 89; and *Grant's Exrs v Grant* 1999 GWD 36-1772 (child over parent).
88 *Radcliffe v Price* (1902) 18 TLR 466.
89 *Re Craig, Deceased* [1971] Ch 95.
90 *Allcard v Skinner* (1887) 36 Ch D 145; *Anderson v The Beacon Fellowship* 1992 SLT 111; and *Catt v Church of Scientology Religious Education College Inc* [2001] CP Rep 41.
91 *Honeyman's Exrs v Sharp* 1978 SC 223.
92 *Horne v Whyte* [2005] CSOH 115.
93 *Gaul v Deerey* 2000 SCLR 407.
94 *Boyle v Boyle's Exor* 1999 SC 479 at 493; and *Horne v Whyte* [2005] CSOH 115.
95 In contrast to English law, the mere existence of such a relationship does not give rise to a presumption of undue influence, with the onus on the defender to rebut it. On the differences in Scots and English law, see W H D Winder 'Undue Influence in Scots and English Law' 1940 *LQR* 97.

the dominant position need not necessarily have coerced the deceased by means involving intimidation, threats or force so as to overcome his or her will;[96] rather, he or she is also under the more passive obligation not to abuse the relationship of trust, particularly if the testator is facile.[97] Where the relationship of trust and confidence does appear to have been abused, 'anything of the nature of weakness or facility … will make it easier to hold that a person acted under the undue influence' of that other person.[98] While facility is not essential to a finding of undue influence, it is unlikely to succeed without it and even in the context of an *inter vivos* deed, the party whose will has been unduly influenced has often been facile to some extent.[99]

It follows from the centrality of the notion of free agency and individual intention to the making of testaments that a testator is presumed to know what he or she is doing unless the contrary can be shown. It is difficult to resist the conclusion that it is impossible, in legal terms at least, to overcome anyone's will unless that person is, to some degree or another, facile since it seems unlikely that a rational testator would confer a benefit on anyone against his or her will. The connection between control over the testator and facility on the part of the testator was highlighted by Lord Eassie in *Boyle v Boyle's Executor* when he stated:[100]

> 'I am satisfied that [the testator's] signature of the July will was, at the least, procured by the use of the defender's control and influence over her at a time when she was plainly in a state of facility.'

As in *inter vivos* cases, undue influence is more likely to be found where the deceased has not obtained independent legal advice[101] and although this could be seen as the distinguishing feature, the involvement of a

96 In *Munro v Strain* (1874) 1 R 522 the deceased was facile at the time the will was signed but no inference of undue influence could be drawn since he had been induced to sign the deed in ignorance of its contents; his will had not been overcome. The case is anomalous in that the deed was reduced on the basis of essential error as the deceased was unaware that the effect of the deed was to cancel his previous will.

97 *Horne v Whyte* [2005] CSOH 115.

98 *McKechnie v McKechnie's Trs* 1908 SC 93, per Lord Justice Clerk Kingsburgh at 98.

99 *MacGilvary v Gilmartin* 1986 SLT 89; and *Anderson v The Beacon Fellowship* 1992 SLT 111.

100 *Boyle v Boyle's Exr* 1999 SC 479 at 493.

101 *Gray v Binny* (1879) 7 R 332.

medical practitioner when a will is executed by a facile person may have the effect of militating against allegations of undue influence as well as circumvention of a facile person.[102]

102 In *Horne v Whyte* [2005] CSOH 115 the testator's GP had visited him and had read the codicil giving a very substantial legacy to the defender. He had not, however, considered any question other than the testator's testamentary capacity, such as how the decision to execute the codicil had come about.

Chapter 9

Construction of wills and rectification

INTRODUCTION

9.1 Wherever the terms of a will are in dispute for being open to more than one interpretation, the underlying aim of the court is to discover what the testator intended it to mean.

In cases of doubt, discovering the testator's meaning may involve complex and, indeed, tortuous lines of reasoning. The court has to grapple with the inherent contradiction between the testator's subjective intention and his or her objective demonstration of that intention[1] and, at the same time, bear in mind the practical consequences of any particular determination which it makes.

A number of rebuttable presumptions have been formulated to assist in the task of interpreting provisions of wills where the meaning of a provision or set of provisions is ambiguous or ambivalent, as long as they are not radically uncertain. For example, did the testator intend not to include his own child or children in the will? How are members of a class to be ascertained and how did the testator intend that a gift be divided between them? What did he or she intend should happen to a legacy if the beneficiary predeceased? Who did he or she intend to benefit when it appears there may be more than one candidate? Did the testator intend the right to a legacy to vest immediately or be postponed until a condition attached to the legacy had been purified? Questions of construction are intrinsic to questions about the substantive law of succession. This is implicit or explicit in later chapters of this book and only the broad, general rules of construction are outlined here.

In questions of interpretation of wills, it may be identified that there is a mistake or error in the will. Whilst the general principles of interpretation may be able to resolve an error made by the testator personally, where

1 This point is discussed at some length by R Kerridge and J Rivers in 'The Construction of Wills' (2000) 116 *LQR* 287.

a third party has drafted the will at the testator's instruction there is a separate statutory power of the courts to order rectification under the Succession (Scotland) Act 2016.

GENERAL PRINCIPLES

9.2 The courts have developed general rules and principles of construction for testamentary documents, which are, by and large, consonant with general canons of interpretation.[2] The construction of a deed will always depend on the terms of the actual deed in question. Rules of interpretation are not applied slavishly and, as Lord Justice-Clerk Hope stated in *Robertson v Richardson*:[3]

> 'No rule of interpretation can ever be safely adopted, which is not to bend to satisfactory expressions or proof of the testator's intentions on the face of the particular deed which is to be construed.'

(1) The will should be construed to avoid intestacy

9.3 The general principle followed by the court in all cases is that a construction of a will that would create a whole or partial intestacy should be avoided whenever possible. As Lord Justice Clerk Alness commented in a case involving interpretation:[4]

> 'I approach consideration of the question with the following considerations in mind. First of all, there is the familiar presumption against intestacy. The Court always strives, if it is reasonably possible, to avoid the result that the testator or testatrix shall be deemed to have died intestate in regard

2 See Discussion Paper *on Interpretation in Private Law* (SLC DP No 101, 1996), Part VI; and H MacQueen, *MacQueen and Thomson on Contract Law in Scotland,* 6th edn (2024), paras 4.36–4.37. Woolman and Black, citing Lord Reid in *Credential Bath Street Ltd v Venture Investment Placement Ltd* [2007] CSOH 208 at para 38, argue that the traditional canons of construction may, at least in the case of contracts, be undergoing a period of modification in light of the developments to the courts' approach to contractual interpretation, see G Black, *Woolman and Black on Contract,* 6th edn (2018), para 8-17.

3 *Robertson v Richardson* (1843) 5 D 1117, 1123.

4 *Auld's Trustees v Auld's Trustees* 1933 SC 176 at 179. See also *Crozier's Trustee v Underwood* 1963 SLT 69, per Lord President Clyde at 73.

to a large portion of his or her estate. The presumption against intestacy is strong and important.'

The effect of the presumption against intestacy is that 'ambiguity will not render a deed void, unless it be such that no construction can be put on it'.[5] Indeed, holding that intestacy is inevitable is a 'counsel of despair'[6] which the court follows only with great reluctance. A court may go so far as to subvert other rules in order to avoid it.[7] In some cases, however, intestacy will be impossible to avoid. For example, a failure to name any beneficiaries would result in the will necessarily failing for uncertainty or, if beneficiaries were named but had all predeceased without issue entitled to take in their stead, it would fail for lack of an object.[8]

(2) The will should be read as a whole

9.4 A will is the totality of all writings and documentary documents that relate to the same subject matter and which convey the deceased's estate to executors.[9] This means that codicils should be read in conjunction with the will to which they are attached. Only if the provisions of a later testamentary document contradict or are wholly inconsistent with the previous testamentary document is the previous testamentary document considered to be revoked.[10]

Within a single deed, words and phrases and individual clauses should be reconciled so far as is possible to be consistent with its substantive provisions. Where the meaning of a particular provision or a word within it is unclear, it may be construed by reference to the whole deed or another provision within it and individual provisions read in the context of the whole.[11]

5 *Ewen v Ewen's Trs* (1830) 4 W&S 346, per Lord Wynford at 359.
6 *Macduff v Spence's Tr* 1909 SC 178, per Lord McLaren at 184.
7 See *Elrick's Tr v Robinson* 1932 SC 448; and *McGinn's Exrx v McGinn* 1993 SC 137. See also *Weatheritt's Exrs, Applicants* [2024] SC JED 3 where the presumption against intestacy was attempted to be used in a case where the testator had not subscribed at the end of the last page of her will. Unsurprisingly, the sheriff rejected this attempt to use a maxim of interpretation in such a way.
8 See paras **11.12** and **12.14**.
9 See para **7.2**.
10 See para **7.15**.
11 *Taylor v John Lewis Ltd* 1927 SC 891; and *Laing's Trustees v Horsburgh* 1965 SC 339.

(3) Words should be given their ordinary meaning

9.5 In construing a will, everyday words should not be given an artificial, secondary, or technical meaning.[12] Words that do have a technical or legal meaning will be construed in accordance with that meaning and ordinary grammatical constructions should be employed in seeking the sense of a particular provision.[13] Clearly, a word may have more than one ordinary meaning and must be understood within its particular context. It might also be noted that recourse to caselaw may be helpful to identify general rules, but one should be very cautious when taking an authority as a set rule for certain words or phrases previously before the courts. As Viscount Simon commented in an English case:[14]

> 'The duty of a judge who is called on to interpret a will containing ordinary English words is not to regard previous decisions as constituting a sort of legal dictionary to be consulted and remorselessly applied whatever the testator may have intended, but to construe the particular document so as to arrive at the testator's real meaning according to its actual language and circumstances.'

(4) Conflicting intentions should be reconciled wherever possible

9.6 Where the testator's intentions appear to conflict, the will should be construed so as to give effect to a consistent intention. If, for example, a will refers to a legacy of £150 to a particular legatee in a previous deed but the previous deed gives that legatee only £100, the higher figure stated in the later deed will be considered as expressing the testator's completed intention.[15] Where a deed refers to a legacy in a prior deed but the prior deed mentions no such legacy, the testator is deemed to have intended to give one by the later deed.[16] Alternatively, and depending on the wording, it may be that the testator intended that two legacies should be given to the same beneficiary.[17]

12 *Young v Robertson* (1862) 4 Macq 314, at 319.
13 *Stalker's Exrs* 1977 SLT (Notes) 4.
14 *Perrin v Morgan* [1943] AC 399, at 408.
15 *Forbes' Trs v Forbes* (1893) 20 R 248.
16 *Grant v Grant* (1851) 13 D 805.
17 See para **10.25**.

EXTRINSIC EVIDENCE AS AN INTERPRETATIVE AID

9.7 In order to determine the deceased's intentions, it may be necessary for a court to consider admitting extrinsic evidence to understand what the testator meant and how the document should be so interpreted. However, extrinsic evidence – that is, evidence from sources other than the document itself – will not ordinarily be admitted by a court as an interpretive aid.[18] This is a general rule which, like many general rules, has exceptions that are noted below. However, as part of the general rule, subjective evidence, such as statements made by the testator regarding their will, is excluded from admission as evidence in court.

Initially, restrictions on extrinsic evidence may seem rather odd. However, there are reasons for such an approach. Whilst a court seeks to uphold both the testator's testamentary freedom and their intentions for disposal of their estate, it is somewhat impossible to question a deceased testator directly as to what was inside his or her mind when executing the deed. Therefore, it is incompetent to speculate as to what their subjective intentions actually were. In this respect, it is not the testator's 'true' intentions that the court is seeking to uphold,[19] but those intentions which he or she has expressed in the document itself:[20]

> 'The question is not, of course, what the testator meant to do when he made his will, but what the written words he uses mean in the particular case – what are the 'expressed intentions' of the testator.'

What is written into the document is what the testator has expressly intended for their estate, which the court seeks to respect through using the canons of construction already noted above. Recourse to extrinsic evidence would therefore somewhat undermine the primacy that is placed in a testamentary document if such evidence were to be admitted in every dispute that came before the courts.[21] As such, a will must ordinarily be interpreted according solely to what appears to be the testator's intention

18 This is a generalisation as the law of interpretation of documents has somewhat been in flux in recent years, see further M Ross et al, *Walker and Walker: The Law of Evidence in Scotland,* 6th edn (2026), Ch 26.

19 *Fortunato's JF v Fortunato* 1981 SLT 277.

20 *Perrin v Morgan* [1943] AC 399, per Lord Chancellor Symon at 406.

21 Though see the developments in contract law in H MacQueen, *MacQueen and Thomson on Contract Law in Scotland,* 6th edn (2024), paras 4.31–4.35.

as expressed on the face of the document. As Lord Justice-Clerk Moncrieff stated in *Blair v Blair*:[22]

> 'I hold the law to be clear, that we must find the intention of the testatrix within the four corners of the deed which she has legally executed. We are, undoubtedly, to look at the whole deed; and I do not doubt, that if there be any doubt in the terms, we are to take into consideration the circumstances under which the deed was executed — that is, with reference to the state of the family, and any relative deeds duly executed, to which the testatrix was a party. Yet even as to these things, it is only if the terms of the deed appear to be in themselves doubtful in their import or legal construction, that it is either necessary or legitimate to affect or explain them by extraneous circumstances.'

(1) Ambiguity as a threshold for admission of extrinsic evidence

9.8 It will be apparent from the above quote from Lord Moncrieff that a major exception to the general rule is that admission of extrinsic evidence is permissible where there is ambiguity in the document. However, the court will not generally admit extrinsic evidence where the ambiguity contained in a document is patent (that is to say, obvious) rather than latent (or, not apparent from the face of the deed alone), since it is in the nature of a patent ambiguity that it may be resolved through interpreting the wording of the deed itself without resort to extrinsic evidence.[23]

For example, in *Yule's Trustees*[24] a testator had provided that on the death of the last survivor of his wife and children, the fee of his estate was to be paid to his grandchildren who were then alive, equally among them *per stirpes*. He also provided that: where any child died prior to the date of vesting, the lawful issue of any such a child or children would be entitled to take both the original and the accresced share which their parent would have had if he or she had survived. The question arose as to whether this provision relating to accretion applied only to the testator's children or whether it also related to his grandchildren. The deed contained only a patent ambiguity and no extrinsic evidence was led or admitted. The court construed the deed as meaning that the testator had made an error

22 (1849) 12 D 97 at 107.

23 *Logan v Wright* (1831) 5 W & S 242 at 246.

24 1981 SLT 250.

in expression and could only have meant that grandchildren as well as his own children should benefit by the provision.

In a case of a latent ambiguity, by contrast, the wording of the deed and the effect of the provisions are perfectly comprehensible except as applied to the particular facts at hand. In this case, it may be necessary to admit extrinsic evidence in order to ascertain the true facts to which the deed is intended to be applied. It may be impossible, for example, to identify the intended legatee or even the particular legacy without admitting extrinsic evidence.[25] Accordingly, extrinsic evidence may be admitted only where it is otherwise impossible to make sense of the will using the ordinary rules of interpretation. To uphold the deceased's intention, it becomes necessary to look at extrinsic evidence to understand how the document is intended to operate. The court should put itself 'in the testator's armchair'[26] and attempt, by other means, to ascertain what his or her intention may actually have been. In doing so, the surrounding circumstances of the document will fall to be considered. The courts in Scotland have adopted the Supreme Court's approach in the English case of *Marley v Rawlings*:[27]

> 'When interpreting a contract, the court is concerned to find the intention of the party or parties, and it does this by identifying the meaning of the relevant words, (a) in the light of (i) the natural and ordinary meaning of those words, (ii) the overall purpose of the document, (iii) any other provisions of the document, (iv) the facts known or assumed by the parties at the time that the document was executed, and (v) common sense, but (b) ignoring subjective evidence of any party's intentions…
>
> When it comes to interpreting wills, it seems to me that the approach should be the same. Whether the document in question is a commercial contract or a will, the aim is to identify the intention of the party or parties to the document by interpreting the words used in their documentary, factual and commercial context.'

This approach has been accepted in Scotland.[28] In *Gray's Exrs v Manson's Exr*,[29] the Lord Ordinary (the now Lord President Pentland) employed

25 See paras **11.2–11.11**.

26 *Boyes v Cook* (1880) 14 Ch D 53, at 56.

27 [2015] AC 129, per Lord Neuberger at paras 19–20.

28 See G Watt, 'Extrinsic evidence in the interpretation of testamentary writing' 2017 *SLT (News)* 11.

29 [2017] CSOH 25.

this approach, and several shrieval decisions have now followed *Marley*.[30] As one example, in *Carswell v Skelton*[31] a deceased farmer left a testamentary writing bequeathing 'my share of Midtown Farm'. However, the landholdings that the deceased owned actually consisted of more than just Midtown Farm and comprised other named farmland (known as Bent Farm), alongside farm machinery and other moveable property. The question for the court was: What property was intended to be bequeathed by the deceased under this legacy? Sheriff Gallacher considered that:[32]

> 'Applying the principles of interpretation as set out by Lord Neurenburg [sic] in *Marley v Rawlings*, it is clear to me that if placing oneself in [the deceased's] armchair, applying common sense and having regard to the factual context in which the farming business was, and had been for some time, conducted, that by using the phrase 'my share of Midtown Farm' [the deceased] wanted [the legatee] to inherit his entire share of the farming business, namely the land and whole assets and undertakings of the business so that, following his death, [the legatee] could continue to operate the farming business.'

Whilst, therefore, it is possible to use extrinsic evidence, it is worth remembering that the Supreme Court continued the older rule that direct evidence as to subjective intent on the part of the testator cannot be admissible. Instead, there must be an objective exercise in which the court places themselves in the testator's armchair and the context in which the will was made.

(2) Where admissible extrinsic evidence may be used

9.9 The following examples illustrate the sorts of circumstances in which extrinsic evidence may be admitted in order to resolve ambiguities and ascertain the facts to which the deed is to be applied where it is simply impossible to ascertain the testator's intention from the face of the deed alone.

30 *The Parachute Regiment Charity v Hay* [2019] SC ABE 18; *Scott-May v Scott-May* [2024] SC PER 13; *Alexander v Farroll* [2024] SAC (Civ) 18; and *Carswell v Skelton* [2025] SC HAM 54.

31 [2025] SC HAM 54.

32 [2025] SC HAM 54, per Sheriff Gallacher at para 177.

(a) To prove that the deed in question represents the testator's completed testamentary intention

9.10 Where questions such as whether a deed is intended to be a draft[33] or whether a revocation is effective[34] arise, this may involve looking at other documents such as letters sent to solicitors or beneficiaries.

(b) To translate a will written in a foreign language or to decipher a code

9.11 Language or code experts would be required to translate the will and certify its terms. Where special terms of art, peculiar to a certain trade or occupation, are used it may be necessary to admit expert evidence as to their meaning.[35]

(c) To ascertain which meaning is intended where several ordinary meanings of a word are possible

9.12 In older cases especially, reference to a child in a will may have been the first acknowledgment by the testator that he or she had a child. Questions have also arisen as to whether the testator intended to include only 'lawful' children[36] in a bequest. Whilst this is primarily a question which can be derived from the terms of the deed and the law in force at the time,[37] questions of fact may arise so that the identity of the child and its whereabouts may have to be ascertained by extrinsic evidence. Similarly, questions have arisen as to whether the testator intended to include grandchildren within the meaning of 'children'.[38] If a deed contains a patent error, it will not be appropriate to admit extrinsic evidence when a construction can be arrived at from the terms of the deed alone.

33 See paras **7.2–7.4**.
34 See paras **7.8** and **7.12–7.13**.
35 *Goblet v Beechey* (1829) 3 Sim 24.
36 *Scott's Trs v Smart* 1954 SC 12; *Hay v Duthie's Trs* 1956 SC 511. On 'lawful children' see paras **2.9–2.13.**
37 *Wright's Trs v Callender* 1993 SLT 556. See paras **11.8–11.11**.
38 For conflicting views see *Ranken* (1870) 8 M 878; and *Rhind's Trustees v Leith* (1866) 5 M 104. See also paras **11.7–11.8**.

(d) To identify the subject or object of a legacy

9.13 Where it is obvious that provisions in a will are inconsistent, the legacy may lapse for uncertainty.[39] There is a latent ambiguity if more than one person fits the description of the legatee named in the deed. *Nasmyth's Trustees v National Society for the Prevention of Cruelty to Children*[40] lays down the rule that where more than one object fits the description in the deed, extrinsic evidence may be led to ascertain which object the testator intended to refer to. In *Cathcart's Trustees v Bruce*[41] extrinsic evidence, in the form of letters, was admitted to ascertain which, if either, of two possible beneficiaries were intended as the objects of a legacy since neither of two possible individuals were accurately named.[42]

(e) To rebut the presumption against double provision or prove what the testator knew in relation to the property

9.14 The question may arise as to whether the testator knew that he or she did or did not own the property that is to be bequeathed to a beneficiary. This is particularly relevant in ascertaining whether, for example, the testator intended to give more than one legacy to the same beneficiary;[43] or whether he intended, in the knowledge that he or she did not own a particular thing, that it be purchased by the executor for a beneficiary.[44]

RECTIFICATION OF A PROFESSIONALLY DRAFTED WILL

9.15 It is entirely possible that there may be an error in an effective will when it has been prepared by another person. For example, a solicitor may have been instructed to draft a will but has muddled the intended legatees,

39 See W H D Winder 'Mistakes as to legatees' 1953 *SLT (Notes)* 149.

40 *Nasmyth's Trs v National Society for the Prevention of Cruelty to Children* 1915 SC (HL) 76.

41 *Cathcart's Trs v Bruce* 1923 SLT 722.

42 See paras **11.2–11.3**.

43 See paras **10.20–10.24**.

44 See para **10.19**.

or has inserted the wrong property (or values thereof) into a legacy. Unless a testator has the skills of a qualified lawyer, it would be unreasonable to expect them to identify such errors before executing the document. Such errors may go unnoticed until the testator later dies, and an examination of the will by the executor or the legatees identifies an issue that the will does not seem to reflect what the testator had intended nor instructed.

In such cases, and others,[45] where a will has been drafted by another person but it fails to reflect what was seemingly instructed by the testator, it is possible to apply to court under section 3 of the Succession (Scotland) Act 2016 for an order to rectify the will after the testator's death. In doing so, the court will order rectification to give effect to the testator's original instructions.[46] Such applications must ordinarily be made within six months of the death of the testator, or within six months of confirmation being granted.[47]

Unlike the position with extrinsic evidence in interpretations generally, and the limited exceptions in which it will be admitted, the use of extrinsic evidence is expressly allowed in order to ascertain the deceased's instructions and intentions in the making of the will.[48] In *Finnie v McClure*,[49] the deceased had requested solicitors to make a will in favour of his cohabitant and his sons. The firm had prepared the will but had erroneously omitted the cohabitant as a residuary beneficiary of the estate, leaving the residue to pass to the sons alone, despite the testator's instructions. The court allowed the use of extrinsic evidence through the cohabitant's witness statements, alongside the email correspondence the testator had with the firm, to determine that the will was not as instructed.

45 See the examples provided by the Scottish Law Commission in recommending reform, Report *on Succession* (SLC Report No 215, 2009), para 6.2.

46 2016 Act, s 3(2).

47 2016 Act, s 4(1).

48 2016 Act, s 3(3).

49 2022 SLT (Sh Ct) 199.

PART 4:

INTERPRETATION OF WILLS

Chapter 10

Legacies

INTRODUCTION

10.1 Providing that a testament conforms to the legal requirements for formal and essential validity, the deed is binding. If, however, a testator's intentions in relation to the substantive provisions made in the deed are unclear, problems may arise in relation to their interpretation. General principles of construction of wills were set out in **Chapter 9**, but this chapter and **Chapter 11** examines the construction of the provisions of testamentary documents in more detail. This chapter focuses on how legacies are classified; how they are ranked if the value of the estate is insufficient to pay a legacy, either wholly or partially; how the existence of the subject of the legacy is determined; how a legacy to multiple beneficiaries may be divided; and how multiple legacies to the same beneficiary may be interpreted.

What the testator intends the subject of the legacy (the bequeathed property) to be must be ascertained as far as possible from the wording of the deed itself but, in some cases, the question must be determined with the help of legal presumptions or extrinsic evidence. It may be, for example, that the subject has been destroyed, sold, or given away or, for some other reason, does not form part of the estate. The thing may not exist in the same form; it may either have never existed or may never have been owned by the testator.

The nature of the subject determines the way in which the legacy is classified. This is important when the value of legacies exceeds the total value of the estate and legal presumptions must be applied to regulate the order of preference in which legacies are paid to beneficiaries. There may also be difficulties of construction in relation to conditions which may be attached to a beneficiary's entitlement. Conditions may be classified in different ways and the type of condition may have implications for a number of related issues, including whether they are actually enforceable[1]

1 See **Ch 12**.

and when the beneficiary may acquire a vested right to it.[2] Alternatively, the testator may not have made a valid bequest of the subject at all if he or she has failed to express his or her intention in a manner which has binding effect.

CLASSIFICATION OF LEGACIES

10.2 In general, the category into which a legacy falls depends on the nature of its subject but any type of thing may be the subject of a conditional legacy. The classification of legacies is of fundamental importance in determining a number of related questions. It will determine, for example, whether what appears to be an absolute gift to a beneficiary is actually worthless or unenforceable or, conversely, whether an apparently empty provision can be construed as a valid bequest. A number of further questions may require to be answered:

- Does the subject of the legacy exist, or does it exist in a form in which it can be paid to a particular legatee?
- Is the legacy of a type that is subject to being reduced in amount in order to pay another type of legacy?
- Must the legatee comply with any conditions attached to a legacy?
- Is the apparent legacy a legacy at all?

What may form the subject of a legacy is virtually without limit. Other than to bear in mind the basic issue of whether property is heritable or moveable,[3] it is pointless to discuss in detail the qualities of any one type of thing, far less attempt to draw up a list of which kinds of things may be the subject of a legacy. In any case, the way in which a legacy is classified depends on how the subject is described; in some cases, the thing forming the subject of a legacy may be classified in more than one way, depending on the terms in which the bequest is made. The type of legacy given to a beneficiary is rarely specified as such in the deed in which it is given; rather, the question of which category it falls into is a matter of construction.

2 See **Ch 13**.
3 See paras **3.2** and **4.11–4.14**.

The difficulty in defining the category into which a legacy should fall is largely caused by the categories themselves being neither particularly clear nor readily comprehended. The sources of definition are the Institutional writers who were considering the matter at a time when the main purpose of classification was to identify which part or parts of an estate were to fall to the heir and which were payable to other beneficiaries. In order to achieve flexibility in meritorious cases brought by persons other than heirs, the categories necessarily became blurred. Lord McLaren gives an example.[4] A testator made a bequest to his daughters of a specified sum that he had provided was 'to be paid out of arrears of income due from the Monteath trust estate'. It turned out that the arrears of income were insufficient to pay the legacy. On the face of it, the legacy was a demonstrative legacy[5] and liable to lapse. By a majority, the court held that the gift was *not* necessarily to be made from a specific fund but that the wording of the bequest simply indicated a source from which money might be found to pay the legacy. The legatees were entitled, therefore, to claim their legacies from the residuary estate since this was the only fund from which the legacy could be met. Clearer cases are explained below but in more marginal ones, a classification must necessarily be deduced from general rules. This section sets out the categories into which a legacy may fall and the implications and possible consequences of a legacy being classified in a particular way.

(1) Precatory legacies

10.3 A legacy is said to be precatory where its terms do no more than express a wish or hope of the testator. The testator might make a bequest such as '£10,000 to Ross in the wish that he puts it to use in looking after his son, Paul'. On one view, the legacy has a binding provision attached that the monies *must* only be used for Paul's care and upbringing. On another view, the wording is merely expressing the testator's wish for what Ross *should* do with the bequeathed property. It is the latter view that is precatory, rather than 'imperative', and a precatory legacy is where

4 J McLaren, *The Law of Wills and Succession as Administered in Scotland,* 3rd edn (1894), para 1040, citing *Douglas' Exrs v Scott* (1869) 7 M 504.

5 See below at **10.5**.

the testator's wish amounts to no more than a spurious kind of condition which the beneficiary is free to ignore.

The use of the word 'wish' or 'prefer' in relation to the bequest does not of itself mean that it is precatory. Rather, the words may be effective as a rather passive expression of the testator's completed intention and, consequently, the imposition of an imperative condition. In *Thompson v McLeod*,[6] the testatrix had left the residue of her estate to her brother and sister but had added a provision that she 'should like' a third party to 'have my wearing apparel for disposal as she thinks fit, and any bits of jewellery etc. after my said sister has taken what she desires'. The Inner House determined the use of 'like' was a form of command to the executor and therefore enforceable.

As a generality, a provision that can be construed as a polite form of command is imperative and binding when directed towards the executor. However, a provision is likely to be considered precatory where it is attached to a legacy and directed towards the legatee.[7] In *Smart v Smart*[8] a husband had appointed his wife as executor and left a legacy of his remaining estate to her. However, he added a provision to the legacy that 'If my wife should remarry or die I wish all my real and personal estate to be equally divided between my surviving sisters and brother'. A dispute arose as to how these this term was to be interpreted. Clearly the wife could not be given the remaining estate absolutely for it then to be deprived from her, or her own estate, upon her death or remarriage. Such an interpretation would effectively constitute a *pseudo* liferent held by the wife. Lord President Clyde, along with others on the bench, considered the 'wish' expressed by the husband to be merely precatory:[9]

> 'In my opinion the clear and unambiguous sentence bequeathing to the wife "all my other real and personal estate" is not qualified by the precatory clause which follows referring to what would be the testator's "wish" in the event of his wife's remarriage or death. If both sentences had been expressed in equally direct and unmistakeable terms, they would have been contradictory, and might, or might not, have proved irreconcilable.

6 950 SLT (Notes) 18.

7 *Garden's Exr* v *More* 1913 SC 285, per Lord President Dunedin at 289; and *Walker's Exr* v *Walker* 1953 SLT (Notes) 59, per Lord Sorn at 60.

8 1926 SC 392.

9 1926 SC 392, at 400.

> But the contrast between them is sharp. The first is as clear in intention as it is imperative in form; while the second seems to be no more than an expression of how the testator would like his absolute legatee to dispose of the estate in the event of her death or remarriage.'

In *Milne v Smith*,[10] the testator owned a business alongside a separate partnership that he ran with his brother. In his will, he made a legacy bequeathing his interests in both the business and the partnership to his brother and his son with a provision that 'it being my wish that both these businesses should be combined by my son and my brother' and ran together as a single enterprise. In considering whether this provision had testamentary effect and was binding on the beneficiaries Lord Stott observed:[11]

> 'An expression in a testamentary document may be imperative in its real meaning even when appearing in the form of a request and that applies whether the request is addressed to trustees or appears in words attached to a legacy and addressed to the legatee … Where the words of request are attached to a legacy they are to be given their ordinary meaning and not treated as imperative unless it appears that it was the intention of the testator so to use them. The question is of course always one of the construction of each particular deed and the deed must be considered as a whole.'

On his analysis of the deed, Lord Stott determined that 'when one considers the nature of the bequest as a whole it is impossible to draw from it any inference that what is in form a precatory provision was intended by the testator as imperative'.[12]

(2) Specific legacies

10.4 A specific legacy is a legacy which has a determinable subject. Common examples are corporeal property such as a house or car but the subject of a specific legacy can also be incorporeal property. To be a specific legacy, the subject of the legacy must be specified distinctly but

10 *Milne v Smith* 1982 SLT 129, OH. See also J McLaren, *The Law of Wills and Succession,* 3rd edn (1894), para 633.

11 1982 SLT 129, at 130.

12 1982 SLT 129, at 130.

this may be expressed in the singular or the plural. For example, a legacy of 'my collection of china' is a specific legacy in the same way as 'the gold watch given to me by my grandfather'. If the testator had been given more than one gold watch by his grandfather, the legacy would be specific only if it could be shown which one the testator had intended to give to the particular beneficiary.

A legacy of shares may also be specific; for example, 'one-half of my shares held in *Boom! Plc*'. The subject of a bequest may also be worded generally, as in 'all my moveable property' and be classed as specific. A specific legacy may be heritable or moveable. If the subject of a specific legacy has been destroyed or disposed of by the testator *inter vivos*, the legacy is not payable and the beneficiary will have no right to claim any alternative unless one is specified. If there are insufficient funds in the estate to pay legacies of other types, payment of the specific legacies will have priority over the rest.[13]

(3) Demonstrative legacies

10.5 A demonstrative legacy is a sub-category of a specific legacy, the difference being that not only is the amount of the legacy specified but also the fund or source of which the legacy is to be paid. A demonstrative legacy can take the form of, for example, '£100 from my *Grin* bank account' or 'one-half of my preference shares held in *Boom! plc*'. It follows that a legacy can be classified as demonstrative not only when the subject and source is specified (such as in the example just given) but also when the testator directs trustees as to the way in which the legacy is to be managed. Thus, where a testator directed that money was to be invested in a particular fund for a particular beneficiary, the legacy was not specific but demonstrative.[14] The significance of the category is that a demonstrative legacy ranks after a specific legacy but before general legacies.

13 See paras **10.13–10.14**. According to Bell, a specific legacy is equivalent to a *mortis causa* assignation of the property, whilst a general legacy confers only a *ius crediti* to the beneficiary; Bell, *Prin* § 1875–1877. This distinction is, however, of less importance since the whole of a deceased's estate now vests in the executor: Succession (Scotland) Act 1964, s 1.

14 *Dewar v Kirk Session of Torryburn* (1864) 2 M 910.

(4) General legacies

10.6 A general legacy may also be pecuniary, but the nature of the subject does not allow it to be distinguished from other things of the same class. Erskine defines a general legacy as:[15]

> 'A legacy not of a special article or debt, but of a certain quantity or value which may be measured in money (as is usual) or in goods of a specified description.'

For example, the legacy of a fixed sum of money such as £100 is a general legacy. It may be paid from any source of funds since the fund out of which it is to be paid is not specified. Since money has no distinguishing characteristics and it is impossible, therefore, to differentiate one amount of £100 from any other amount of £100, the legacy is general.

(5) Residual legacies

10.7 The residue is the balance of the estate that is left after other legacies have been paid and any claims for legal rights satisfied. An exact valuation of the testator's property in advance of death is almost impossible to obtain; accordingly, a testator can dispose of his or her entire estate by means of specific, demonstrative or general legacies only if they equal the value of the estate on death or exceed it (in which case they will be reduced).[16] One purpose of a residue clause, therefore, is to dispose of the whole estate that remains after any such legacies have been paid since, if the value of the estate exceeds the total value of any specific, demonstrative or general legacies and the testator has nominated no residuary legatee, any estate remaining after payment of specific legacies will fall into intestacy. Because a residuary legatee takes the whole estate which is not payable to any other beneficiary, a bequest of residue which lapses will fall to be distributed according to the rules of intestate succession. Provided that a residuary legatee is nominated, any legacies which fail or lapse will fall to the residue. Likewise, if a spouse or child elects to claim legal rights in preference to accepting testamentary provisions, the legacy to which he or

15 Erskine *Inst* III.9.2.

16 See paras **10.13–10.14**.

she was entitled will fall to the residue. Since the amount of the residue is unspecified, it follows that legacies which are specific are payable before the value of the residue can be ascertained.

In the main, however, the residue of an estate is not generally such an amount as happens to be left over after other types of legacy have been paid. The name is slightly misleading as more often than not, the residue is the largest proportion of the estate and provisions giving specific legacies can be seen more as a deduction from the value of the residue. Indeed, a universal settlement of the whole of a testator's estate is usually expressed as a gift of residue, the residue being simply the residue of the estate after the payment of debts. The residuary legatee is often the primary beneficiary, to whom virtually all of the estate is bequeathed, with specific legacies being given to minor beneficiaries as tokens by which the testator wishes to demonstrate his or her regard for them. Common examples in the past were where a small specific legacy would be left to a faithful servant or poor relation. In contemporary wills, specific legacies may more usually be made to grandchildren, with the bulk of the testator's estate being gifted to a partner or children as residue. Residuary legacies are first to be reduced if there are insufficient funds to pay all the specific, demonstrative or general legacies. This seems to be explicable historically since, prior to the Succession (Scotland) Act 1964, the recognition of the privileged position of beneficiaries of specific legacies was the only means by which the absolute rights of the heir-at-law and the next-of-kin could be postponed to others.

(6) Conditional legacies

10.8 Where the entitlement of a beneficiary to a legacy is qualified by the requirement that certain conditions specified in the deed are fulfilled, it is classified as a conditional legacy. A conditional legacy is not, however, a category of legacy of its own, in the same way as a specific, demonstrative, general or residual legacy. A conditional legacy can fall into any of these categories: it is the attachment of a condition to the gift, rather than the nature of the subject itself, which distinguishes it. The significant characteristic of a conditional legacy is that the right of the beneficiary, or object of the legacy, is contingent on the occurrence – or not – of a specified event. If the condition is enforceable, and the condition is not met, the legacy will lapse unless a secondary beneficiary is entitled to take in his or her stead. Whether the condition attached to the legacy is enforceable and the consequences of a condition being purified at some future date are considered in later chapters[17] and the focus here is simply to describe the kinds of conditions that may be attached.

Conditions can be classified into two main types: potestative and casual, with casual conditions being in the form of either suspensive or resolutive conditions. What distinguishes them is essentially that whereas purification of a potestative condition is within the power of the beneficiary, purification of a casual condition is outwith the power of the beneficiary because it involves the occurrence of a natural event or the act of a third party.

(a) Potestative conditions

10.9 Where the right of a beneficiary to a legacy is conditional upon the performance of an act which is within his or her power to perform, the condition is potestative. A large body of case law has developed which limits the kinds of acts that a testator can legitimately require of a beneficiary before he or she obtains a right to the legacy. Generally, the enforceability of a potestative condition will depend on whether it is of a type considered by the court to be reasonable. It will not be enforceable if it is contrary to public policy, immoral, impossible or uncertain.[18] If the condition is not enforceable for any of these reasons, the beneficiary will be entitled to the legacy as if the condition did not exist.

(b) Casual conditions

10.10 A condition is defined as casual where the condition refers to a contingent event and purification of the condition cannot be achieved by any act that is within the power of the beneficiary to perform. The occurrence of the event specified by the testator as the event that will bring the beneficiary's right into being or, alternatively, negate it, is not something over which the beneficiary has any control. Rather, his or her

17 See para **12.4** and paras **13.13–13.20**.

18 See paras **13.13–13.20**.

right to the legacy is conditional upon either a natural event or the acts of others. There are two sub-categories of casual conditions: suspensive conditions and resolutive conditions.

(i) Suspensive conditions

10.11 The effect of a suspensive condition attached to the terms of a legacy is that the time when the legacy will vest in, or be paid to, the beneficiary is suspended until the condition is fulfilled.[19] Henderson defines a suspensive condition in the following way:[20]

> 'Where the legatee's right is dependent on his survivance of a time or event, or his attainment of majority, vesting is clearly suspended. These conditions enter into the description of the beneficiary, and define the party whom the testator intended to favour. They are personal, for if they happen at all they must happen in the lifetime of the legatee.'

Where the condition is attached to the beneficiary personally, vesting will be postponed, *pendente conditione*, until the condition is purified. In this case, the consequence of the beneficiary dying before he or she acquires a vested right to the subject of the legacy is that it will not form part of his or her estate on death. The bequest to that legatee will lapse and its subject will be distributed to some other person, such as a conditional institute, substitute,[21] a residuary legatee, or a person entitled to succeed to the intestate estate. Alternatively, if a condition is attached only to the beneficiary's right to payment of the legacy, the question of lapse of the legacy is not at issue since vesting in the beneficiary must have occurred already and the condition is not, in that case, suspensive of vesting.[22]

The distinction between conditions that postpone vesting and conditions which postpone only payment is based on the Roman law distinction between *dies certus* and *dies incertus*. Where a condition refers to a *dies incertus*, the maxim *dies incertus testamentis conditionem facit*

19 See para **13.11**.

20 R Candlish Henderson, *The Principles of Vesting in the Law of Succession*, 2nd edn (1938), 5.

21 See paras **11.13–11.15**.

22 See para **13.11**.

applies. This means that unless the contrary is stated expressly, a legacy which is subject to a condition which must, by its nature, be satisfied eventually, will vest immediately. Where, however, the condition refers to the occurrence of an event which may never happen, vesting will be postponed. The distinction is illustrated in the case of *Mackintosh v Wood*.[23] A testator directed her trustees to pay a sum of money to her son on her daughter's death or marriage. She then executed a codicil in which she directed that the trustees were to pay her son a further sum on her daughter's marriage. The second legacy was therefore subject to the suspensive condition, personal to the son, that he survive the period between his mother's death and his sister's marriage. However, he died before the daughter's marriage. The first legacy was held to have vested *a morte*, on the basis that the daughter's death was *dies certus*. By contrast, vesting of the second legacy had been postponed, since it was dependent on a *dies incertus*, and therefore lapsed on the son's death.[24]

The type of suspensive condition attached to the second bequest to the son in *Mackintosh v Wood* was a survivorship clause, specifying that the beneficiary must survive until the occurrence of an uncertain event in order to acquire a right to the legacy. More frequently, a survivorship clause will require the beneficiary to survive the testator for a specified period of time.[25] The condition must be an integral part of the provision in question and the courts will not construe a deed so as to hold that a testator must have intended a survivorship clause to be attached to a legacy by inference from other provisions contained in the deed,[26] or that it may be inserted separately, elsewhere in the deed.[27]

23 (1872) 10 M 933.

24 On the face of it, the payment to the son on the daughter's marriage was not subject to a personal condition and thus not capable of suspending vesting. Although the condition referred to a *dies incertus* which operated to suspend vesting, the condition related to factors which were not only outwith the legatee's control, but which related to the actions of another person. The condition appeared, accordingly, to have been resolutive. This, however, was not the case: the son was not a conditional institute, and his potential right could not be defeated by the prior claim of any other person. See paras **11.12–11.14**.

25 *Rattray v Rattray's Trs* (1868) 6 M 476; and *Yeates v Paton* (1880) 8 R 171.

26 See paras **13.13ff**.

27 *Miller v Finlay's Trs* (1875) 2 R (HL) 1.

Example

X gives a legacy to A 'providing that she survives me by 30 days, whom failing to B'. The legacy does not vest in either A or B until it is ascertained whether A survives for 30 days. A dies 10 days after the testator and the legacy vests in B.

Similarly, if it is a condition of receiving the legacy that the legatee reaches, say, the age of 25, vesting is postponed until that time and with it the right to demand payment from the executor. In *Graham's Trustees v Graham*[28] the testator's trust disposition and settlement contained the following provision: 'upon my son William attaining the age of thirty years, I direct my trustees to convey to him the properties of A and T'. William survived the father but died before attaining the age of 30. The court held that his right to the properties was conditional upon him reaching that age. It followed that the direction was construed as stipulating not the date of payment but the date of vesting, since the prospect of William living until the age of 30 was *dies incertus*. By contrast, where it was provided that 'the heir succeeding under this settlement must have attained the age of twenty five years' it was held that, having regard to the deed as a whole, vesting was not suspended.[29] Rather, he was not entitled to payment until the age of 25 was attained.

It is therefore a matter of construction whether the gift is contingent upon: (i) the beneficiary reaching the specified age or surviving the specified event; or (ii) whether, on the other hand, the beneficiary acquires the right immediately with payment being postponed.[30] If the latter, this will depend on the age of the beneficiary and other terms of the deed as a whole; for example, a beneficiary can demand payment at any time in respect of any vested right as a beneficiary that they hold under a trust, providing they are aged 18 or above.[31]

(ii) Resolutive conditions

10.12 Whereas a suspensive condition will postpone vesting, the effect of resolutive conditions is that vesting is immediate, subject to being

28 *Graham's Trs v Graham* (1899) 2 F 232.

29 *Wemyss Petitioners* (2 March 1994, unreported).

30 See para **13.13.**

31 Trusts and Succession (Scotland) Act 2024, s 58.

defeated on the contingency of a specified event taking place or not. The contingent event is one which is entirely extraneous to the beneficiary and over which they have no control. For example, a legacy which specifies that the right of beneficiary A will be defeated if another person, B, has a child. Put the other way round, the legacy to A is conditional on B not having a child. If, in this example, the event has not occurred at the date of the testator's death (ie, B has not had a child), A's conditional right vests immediately. His right will, however, have been defeated if B has had a child, an event outwith the control of A. T B Smith explains resolutive conditions in the following terms:[32]

> 'Suspensive conditions, which depend upon factors personal to the legatee – such as attaining majority or survivorship – usually postpone vesting until the occurrence of the stipulated uncertain event. On the other hand, resolutive conditions (which are not personal to the legatee) do not postpone vesting but make vesting liable to defeasance if the uncertain event contemplated by the testator takes place.'

There is no particular form of words which distinguishes a resolutive from a suspensive condition. It all depends on the words used in the deed and the meanings which can be drawn from them. One way of understanding resolutive conditions is to regard the position of the beneficiary in whom the right immediately vests (but whose right will be defeated on the occurrence of the specified contingency) as reversing the normal position of institutes and conditional institutes.[33] In a sense, the first vested person is a conditional institute; their institution is conditional upon some other person *not* fulfilling a condition that will defeat his or her right. The institute's right is to be preferred if, and only if, the resolutive condition is purified. Instead of vesting being suspended, the right vests for the time being in one beneficiary *a morte*, until or unless an event which is outwith the control of that person does *not* occur. At that point, the right becomes absolute. If the contingent event *does* occur, the beneficiary in

32 TB Smith *A Short Commentary on the Law of Scotland* (1962), 435. Henderson explains the distinction between suspensive and resolutive conditions in similar terms in *The Principles of Vesting in the Law of Succession*, 2nd edn (1938), 4: 'A suspensive condition prevents vesting *pendente conditione*; whereas a resolutive condition admits of vesting, but renders the right or interest so vested liable to withdrawal in the event of the condition happening.'

33 See paras **11.13–11.16**.

whom the right has vested (B) is divested of that right and it vests in the primary beneficiary (A) who has emerged since vesting took place. In other words, the doctrine attempts to bring some conditional legacies within the general preference for early vesting by allowing immediate but conditional vesting. The real significance of resolutive conditions relates to the date of vesting of the legacy.[34]

RANKING OF LEGACIES

(1) Abatement

10.13 If the value of the estate is insufficient to pay some or all of the legacies bequeathed by the testator in full, they must be ranked according to their classification to determine the order in which they may be paid. This may be necessary for a number of reasons; for example, the testator's debts have consumed a large part of the estate or because he or she disposed of part of his or her estate *inter vivos*. Alternatively, a spouse, civil partner or children may have elected to renounce legacies bequeathed to them and claim legal rights because these have a greater value. In this case, the share available to legatees whose legacies comprise moveable property must be abated (reduced) if their claims amount to a greater share of the moveable estate than any legacies to which they were entitled.[35]

In order to pay higher ranking legacies, lower ranking legacies will be reduced first, the amount depending both on their values and the funds available to pay them. The will may specify the order of abatement but the fact that they are numbered in the will is not construed as the testator instructing which beneficiaries are to have priority over others. In *McConnel v McConnel's Trustees*[36] the testator had bequeathed various legacies to various beneficiaries but the funds in the estate were insufficient to pay all of the legacies in full. The legacies in question had been numbered from nine to thirteen in the will and a special case was brought to the court to determine whether priority should be given to the legacies in the order in which they were numbered. If not, the question

34 See paras **13.21–13.26**.

35 See **Ch 5**.

36 *McConnel v McConnel's Trs* 1931 SN 31, HL.

was which, if any, of the five legacies had priority over the other. Having considered certain of the provisions in the whole deed, the court took the view that legacy number ten had priority over the others. Although giving no reason for the decision, the House of Lords gave its opinion that there were no grounds for holding that the legacies were to rank according to the numbers allocated to them in the deed.

(2) Order of abatement

10.14 Where no order of abatement is specified in the will, presumptions at common law will apply and the way in which legacies are classified determines the order of abatement. The presumption is that they abate in the following order: residuary legacies; general legacies; demonstrative legacies; and specific legacies. Residual legacies abate first and will abate down to nil before general legacies are abated. General legacies abate equally between themselves in proportion to the shortfall they are required to make up, but only after the residue has been exhausted.[37] Demonstrative legacies will abate in the same way as general legacies but only once the specific fund from which the legacy should be paid from is exhausted. Specific legacies abate last.[38]

Presumptions as to ranking apply universally, including where an election for legal rights is made in preference to a legacy. In *Tait's Trustees v Lees*[39] the surviving spouse of the testator elected to claim *ius relictae* from the estate in preference to the provision made for her under the will, because the value of the *ius relictae* was greater than the value of the residue. The pursuers argued that the first payments due to be made out of an estate were debts; legal rights were a debt; and thus there could be no residue until all the debts were paid. Legal rights were a debt on the estate[40] and therefore the *ius relictae* should be borne out of the whole estate before the value of the residue could be computed. This would mean that each legatee should, without distinction, contribute to the *ius relictae* in proportion to the amount of his or her legacy which, in

37 J McLaren, *The Law of Wills and Succession,* 3rd edn (1894), para 1067.

38 *Tennent's Trs v Tennent* 1946 SC 420.

39 (1886) 13 R 1104.

40 See para **5.2.**

this case, would amount to one-half of each of the specific, general and residual legacies. Lord Justice-Clerk Moncrieff dealt with the position of legal rights in relation to the estate as a whole by observing:[41]

> 'Whatever may be the nature of *ius relictae*, whether a claim for division or a claim for debt, this at all events is certain, that the testator has no power to test upon it … So far as the nature of the right is concerned I think the distribution must proceed as if the testator had dealt in his settlement with nothing but what he was entitled to test upon, and as if he had not tested or endeavoured to test on that portion of the moveable succession which fell under the *ius relictae.*'

Lord Craighill summed up the reasoning of the court when he held that 'the ordinary rule is as applicable to this case as it would be in a case in which the deficiency is created by the payment of ordinary debts'.[42] The claim for legal rights was accordingly to be paid from the residual legacies only.

CANCELLATION OF LEGACIES

(1) Ademption

10.15 Clearly, a beneficiary cannot receive a legacy to which he or she has a putative or expectant right if its subject does not exist. The legacy will be cancelled, or adeemed. Ademption will, quite clearly, apply in certain obvious cases; for example, the testator has died after being sequestrated and the value of claims by creditors exhausted the property within the deceased's estate. Some cases are not quite so straightforward and ademption will also apply where the subject has never existed or, if it did at one time, it no longer does at the date of death. This should be distinguished from where there is a misdescription by the testator of the thing that he or she intends to bequeath. McLaren cites the case of *Door v Geary*,[43] where the testator bequeathed a black horse but in fact owned only a white one. It was held that the subject of the legacy did exist, on the

41 *Tait's Trs v Lees* (1886) 13 R 1104, at 1110.

42 *Tait's Trs v Lees* (1886) 13 R 1104, at 1111.

43 See J McLaren, *The Law of Wills and Succession,* 3rd edn (1894), para 384, citing *Door v Geary* 1 Ves sen 225.

basis that the testator had only one horse and where there is only one thing of the type, effect can be given to the legacy, even if it is misdescribed. If, on the other hand, the testator demonstrably owns no horses at all, the bequest cannot take effect[44] unless it can be read as a *legatum rei alienae*.[45]

The doctrine of ademption relates to the existence of the thing which forms the subject of a specific legacy and derives from Roman law.[46] If a testator had intentionally disposed of the thing before his death, this was considered to be a form of revocation and indicated his *animus adimendi*. Deciding whether a legacy had adeemed thus depended on how the will was construed to ascertain the testator's intention. However, over time the doctrine of ademption changed into a more 'mechanical' test that disregards intention. As explained in the English case of *Stanley v Potter*:[47]

> 'The idea of proceeding on the *animum adimendi* has introduced a degree of confusion ... I believe it will be a safer and clearer way to adhere to the plain rule which I before mentioned, which is to inquire whether the specific thing given remains or not.'

This view was accepted into Scots law[48] and the question of ademption is now simply regarded as a 'mechanical' question of fact, with the general test for ademption being simply: Whether the thing bequeathed is within the deceased's patrimony at death? Accordingly, questions of whether the

44 This is on the basis of the maxim *falsa demonstratio non nocet*.

45 See para **10.19**.

46 See R Paisley, 'Ademption: Various meanings of the term', in A Steven et al (eds), *Nothing So Practical as a Good Theory: Festschrift for George L Gretton* (2017).

47 *Stanley v Potter* (1789) 2 Cox Eq Cas 180, 26 at 29, following *Ashburner v Macguire* 2 Br CC 108.

48 See Lord Justice-Clerk Moncrieff in *Anderson v Thomson* (1877) 4 R 1101, at 1110. He applied the English rule set out in *Stanley v Potter* (1789) 2 Cox Eq Cas 180 only because it was so firmly established that he had no alternative, whilst observing that it was 'utterly at variance with any concept of jurisprudence'. On the development and rationale of the rule see W H D Winder 'The Ademption of Legacies' 1959 *SLT (Notes)* 185. Intention is the test of conversion (Erskine *Inst* II.2.14), express or implied, but decisions on ademption have been careful to distinguish it from conversion, albeit that the relationship between them remains unclear: see, eg, *McArthur's Exrs v Guild* 1908 SC 743, (1908) 15 SLT 1023; *Macfarlane's Trustees v Macfarlane* 1910 SC 325, 1910 1 SLT 40; *Heron v Espie* (1856) 18 D 917; *Pollock's Trs v Anderson* (1902) 4 F 455; and *Turner v Turner* [2012] CSOH 41.

testator intended the legacy to adeem by disposing of the property in their lifetime is now generally irrelevant.[49]

The presumptions towards ademption developed by case law need not be applied if the testator has foreseen the possibility that the thing may cease to exist and taken steps to avoid ademption by inserting an anti-ademption clause into the legacy.[50] This means that the same type of property may be the subject of the legacy even if it is not the particular item. For example, if the testator bequeaths 'my house at 1 High Street' and sells that house prior to his death, the legacy adeems. If what he or she intended was to give his or her house to a beneficiary regardless of which house it happened to be, the testator could make this clear and enforceable by describing the subject more generally in terms such as 'my house at 1 High Street, Glasgow, or such other residence that I may own at the time of my death'.

(2) Ascertaining the existence of the subject

10.16 Whether the thing remains may not always be clear and the basic test set out in *Stanley v Potter*[51] has been refined so that the question is whether the *substance* of the original gift, if not the actual thing, remains unchanged. In *Ogilvie-Forbes' Trustees v Oglilvie-Forbes*,[52] the testator had made a bequest of a liferent in his heritable estate. He then formed a private company in which he retained a controlling interest and transferred his heritage to it. The question for the court was whether the heritage was substantially the same thing or not. It held that although the heritage remained in exactly the same form when it was sold, the testator had exchanged the heritage for the shares in the company. Because shares in a company are not identical with the assets of the company, the thing bequeathed had been exchanged for something different. As Lord Sorn noted, 'it avails nothing to trace the new thing back to the thing bequeathed'.[53] The court held that where the question of whether

49 *Cobban's Exrs v Cobban* 1915 SC 82.

50 See A Barr, *Drafting Wills in Scotland,* 2nd edn (2009), paras 4.16–4.17.

51 *Stanley v Potter* (1789) 2 Cox Eq Cas 180, 26 at 29, following *Ashburner v Macguire* 2 Br CC 108.

52 *Ogilvie-Forbes' Trs v OgilvieForbes* 1955 SC 405.

53 *Ogilvie-Forbes' Trs v Ogilvie-Forbes* 1955 SC 405, at 414.

the same things exists is in doubt, the legacy will not adeem if subject is substantially the same thing:[54]

> 'The question is, whether a testator has at the time of his death the same thing existing, it may be in a different shape, — yet substantially the same thing.'

Ascertaining the subject of the legacy and, therefore, whether or not it is a specific legacy and liable to ademption, may not always be straightforward. Erskine defines a specific legacy as 'a determinate subject which belonged to the deceased'.[55] This includes a vested but unpaid right, such as a debt. Where the legacy consists of a right to payment of a debt, the legacy will adeem if the debt is paid prior to the testator's death.[56] Where stocks and shares are the subject of the legacy, stocks are not specific[57] and will not adeem but shares are specific and will adeem (provided that the particular shares are specified). If specified shares are sold and shares in a different company purchased, they are not substantially the same thing and a legacy of the original shares will adeem. However, if the shares are converted into stock in the same company the legacy will not adeem since its subject is substantially the same thing.[58] A legacy of money identified as being in a particular bank account will adeem if the money is placed in a different bank account.[59]

(3) Uncompleted transfers of property

10.17 If missives in a sale of heritage have been completed but there has been no conveyance to the purchaser before the seller dies, the property will not adeem. In *McArthur's Executors v Guild*[60] it was held that a specific legacy is not adeemed if the disposal by the testator is incomplete or under a suspensive condition. A testator had bequeathed to his daughter

54 *Ogilvie-Forbes' Trs v OgilvieForbes* 1955 SC 405, per Lord President Clyde at 411.
55 Erskine *Inst* III.9.10.
56 *Stanley v Potter* (1789) 2 Cox Eq Cas 180; *Cobban's Exr v Cobban* 1915 SC 82.
57 *Re Gillins, Inglis v Gillins* [1909] 1 Ch 345; *Re O'Connor's Will Trusts, Westminster Bank Ltd v O'Connor* [1948] Ch 628, [1948] 2 All ER 270.
58 *Macfarlane's Trs v Macfarlane* 1910 SC 325.
59 *Ballantyne's Trs v Ballantyne's Trs* 1941 SC 35.
60 1908 SC 743.

a specific legacy of a hotel but before his death he had sold it, subject to the suspensive condition that the purchaser obtain a licence. The licence was granted the day after the testator's death. The court held that at the time of his death, the testator remained the owner of the property since the condition had not been purified. Applying the factual test of ademption laid down in *Stanley v Potter*,[61] it held that the sale was only completed by the granting of the licence, before which point the hotel had become the subject of an enforceable legacy for the daughter, subject to the terms of the contract.[62] Thus, whilst she could acquire ownership, she was under an obligation to convey the property to the purchaser and, in return, had a right to receive the agreed purchase price.[63]

The doctrine of ademption applies equally to moveables. In *Tennent's Trustees v Tennent*[64] the testator had bequeathed shares to his son but before his death had sold them. The sale was not completed in that the share certificates were neither stamped nor registered. As the shares remained owned by the deceased, the property remained available to pay the legacy, and had not adeemed.

(4) Ademption where testator is incapax

10.18 Although the general rule is that the intention of the testator in relation to his disposal of something is not the test of ademption,[65] there is a limited exception. Intention remains the test where the act of transfer is not the act of the testator but of a third party acting for the incapax. In this case, the testator's original intentions as to the destination of the subject within a legacy, as expressed in his or her will, override the act of the third party in disposing of it so that ademption does not apply.

In *Macfarlane's Trustees v Macfarlane*,[66] the testator had lost testamentary capacity following execution of his will. A *curator bonis* was appointed and he sold all the shares that the ward owned in a particular

61 Here, the proceeds of the sale and not the heritable property itself were payable to the beneficiary: see para **4.13**.

62 *Stanley v Potter* (1789) 2 Cox Eq Cas 180.

63 *McArthur's Exrs v Guild* 1908 SC 743, per Lord Kinnear at 750.

64 1946 SC 420.

65 *Ogilvie-Forbes' Trs v OgilvieForbes* 1955 SC 405.

66 1910 SC 325.

company. When the ward died, the question for the court was whether legacies of shares in the company to each of his three sisters had adeemed. The court held they had not, on the basis that:[67]

> 'No act of a *curator bonis* can avail to affect the order of his ward's succession, or its character in the distribution of it between heir and executor, unless it can be shewn not only that it was a proper and necessary act of administration on the part of the curator, but that it would have been a necessary and unavoidable act on the part of the ward if *sui juris*.'

While the sale may have appeared necessary from the curator's point of view in preserving their ward's estate, it was not necessary in relation to the maintenance of the ward. The curator had sold the shares without knowledge of the terms of the trust disposition and settlement and, in any case, sale by the ward would not have been necessary had he remained capax.

The exception continues to apply in respect of guardians or attorneys in modern times. In *Turner v Turner*,[68] an attorney appointed by a subsequently incapacitated adult had sold their ward's house in order to avoid it being dilapidated after the ward had moved into residential care. The terms of the will had not been examined by the attorney as a legacy of the house had actually been made. Lord Tyre, relying on *Macfarlane,* found that the legacy had not adeemed given the sale was unnecessary as the ward had sufficient funds to meet their caring fees and the sale had been considered a 'prudent' act rather than a necessary act. Whilst the property itself may no longer be in the deceased's estate, the legatee was entitled to the sale proceeds, or value of the disponed property, alongside its fruits instead.

LEGATUM REI ALIENAE

10.19 If the testator does not own the property that is the subject of the legacy either when he or she executes the will or at the date of death, the legacy may not necessarily adeem. Instead, it may be interpreted as

67 *Macfarlane's Trustees v Macfarlane* 1910 1 SLT 40 per Lord Dundas at 44, citing with approval *Kennedy* (1843) 6 D 40; *Moncrieff* (1856) 18 D 1286; and *M'Adam's Exr* (1904) 7 F 179.

68 [2012] CSOH 41.

a legacy *rei alienae*, an implicit instruction by the testator either that the subject is to be acquired for the benefit of the legatee or that a sum equal in value is to be substituted for it, in order to give effect to the bequest.[69] It is based on a principle of construction derived from Roman law[70] rather than being a doctrine in its own right. In order for the bequest to be presumed to contain such an instruction, the testator must have been aware that he did not own the thing at the time he made it. Only then can the terms of the deed be construed in such a way as to demonstrate that it was his or her intention that the bequest be effectual. It will not be paid if the testator simply made a mistake in thinking that he did own the thing.[71] There must be certainty as to the subject of a legacy and the legacy will fail if the value of the thing specified in the legacy cannot be ascertained.[72]

The onus is on the legatee to show that the testator was not aware that he did not own the thing. In *Meeres v Dowell's Executor*[73] the testator had bequeathed a legacy of furniture and other household effects that he had already disposed of by ante-nuptial contract. The pursuer raised an action for the proceeds of their sale but did not aver that the testator had known that the items were not within his power of disposal. The court held that such knowledge could not be inferred from the fact that the furniture had previously been disposed of under the marriage contract by the testator himself.

LEGACIES TO MULTIPLE LEGATEES

10.20 Where a legacy is bequeathed to more than one person and must be shared between the beneficiaries, it may not be clear from the face of the deed how much the beneficiaries are to receive and how the legacy is to be divided between them. This is particularly an issue where the beneficiaries are members of a class, such as the children of a particular person or of the testator, and principles of construction will be applied in order to determine the questions that arise. Where the bequest clearly is a

69 Erskine *Inst* III.9.10.
70 Justinian *Inst* II.20.4.
71 Erskine *Inst* III.9.10; Bell *Prin*, § 1882–1884.
72 *Macfarlane's Trs v Macfarlane* 1910 SC 325.
73 1923 SLT 184.

class gift, questions as to how the class is to be ascertained is a separate matter considered in **Chapter 11**.

(1) Class gifts

10.21 Where a bequest is to a class, the members of the class will usually be members of the same family but, in order to ascertain membership of the class, it must first be established whether the testator intended the bequest to be a class gift at all. If so, the next stage is to establish how the legacy is to be divided between the beneficiaries. The testator may not have specified the scheme of division between members of the class and presumptions may have to be applied since the terms of the bequest may be internally inconsistent and it may be necessary to construe the testator's meaning from conflicting provisions. The share to which each member is entitled will depend on whether the testator's intention was to bequeath the legacy to an individual who happens to be a member of a class or whether it is intended that he or she take as a member of the class. If the testator has given a bequest to named individual beneficiaries who happen to belong to a class, it will be presumed that he or she intended the gift to be given to them individually. This means that, should the class become enlarged after the deed is executed, the additional members of it will not be included.[74]

Example

X bequeaths a legacy 'to A, B and C' without any reference to the fact that A, B and C are siblings. After the deed has been executed, another sibling, D, is born. The objects of the bequest are construed as A, B and C as named individuals and not A, B and C as members of a class. Accordingly, this is not a class gift and D is not entitled to a share.

Where it is impossible to ascertain the amount of the legacy the testator intended to bequeath, the legacy will be void for uncertainty.[75] The testator may have been clear about the class of persons who are to benefit

74 *White's Trs, Petrs* 1957 SC 322.
75 *Morgan v Morris* (1858) 3 Macq 134.

but mistaken as to their number and thus the amount they were each to receive. In that case, there may be merely a patent ambiguity about what the subject of the legacy actually is and the court will construe the testator's intention in a manner that gives a logical effect to it.[76] For example, in *Maclehose v Boyes*[77] a testator gave legacies to the children of A and B but was mistaken as to how many children A and B actually had. He specified that the children were to receive £400 each, amounting to a total of £1,200. There were in fact four children, so that the total should have been £1,600. It was held that each was entitled to £400 and not that each was entitled to only one-quarter of £1,200.

Alternatively, the testator may have named individual members of the class simply for the avoidance of doubt as to the intended beneficiaries. Here, it will be presumed that he or she intended the class as a whole to benefit. Where payment of the legacy is postponed, but vesting has taken place *a morte*, the existing children's vested right may be subject to partial defeasance in favour of an unborn child.[78]

Example

X bequeaths a legacy 'to A, B and C, the children of M'. A, B and C are siblings and after the deed has been executed another sibling, D, is born. The objects of the legacy are the class of children of M, and therefore include D.

Where the beneficiaries are the testator's own children, a bequest in terms such as 'to my children A and B' will not necessarily exclude a later born child, C. The effect of a legacy to children *not* being considered as a class gift would be that the excluded subsequently born member or members may have been entitled to invoke the *conditio si testator sine liberis decesserit*.[79] If that presumption were invoked, the consequence would be the reduction of the will, with the estate falling into intestacy.

76 See **Ch 9**.

77 *Maclehose v Boyes*, 28 Feb 1815, FC.

78 See paras **13.27ff**.

79 *Menzies' Factor v Menzies* (1898) 1 F 128; *Young's Trs v Young* 1927 SC (HL) 6, 1927 SLT 2. See para **7.16**.

(2) Division of the legacy

10.22 Where a legacy is given to multiple beneficiaries, the question of how the legacy is to be divided between them may arise. Unless the testator has expressed in some other way his or her intention as to what the relative shares which each beneficiary is to receive are to be, the division of the gift between them will be either *per capita* or *per stirpes*. While these forms of division are set out in statute in relation to legitim and the intestate free estate,[80] the division in any particular case of testate succession will depend on construing the testator's intention unless it is clear from the face of the deed.

A division is *per capita* where the fund is divided equally between the legatees whether they have been named individually or not. However, if one or more of the beneficiaries has predeceased, it may be that the predeceasing beneficiary's share transmits not to other members of the class by way of the doctrine of accretion[81] but to their children under either an express destination-over, or an implied destination-over under s 6 of the Succession (Scotland) Act 2016.[82] In this case, the division of the fund is more likely to be *per stirpes*. The fund is divided between the head of each *stirps* (or branch of the family) and subdivided between the individual members of each *stirps* depending on the degree to which they are related to the testator. The number of children of a predeceasing head of the *stirps* determines the amount of the legacy each will receive.

(a) Stirpital division

10.23 The concept of *stirpital* division is relatively clear; the fund is divided into as many parts as there are *stirps*. The difficulty in testate succession in dividing the legacy between members of a class lies not in the concept of stirpital division itself but in determining its application to a particular case. The Succession (Scotland) Act 1964, ss 6 and 11 set out the formula for its application in relation to the division of the intestate free estate and the legitim fund respectively. In the case of legacies in

80 See paras **6.36** and **5.8–5.9**.
81 See para **11.20**.
82 See para **11.22**.

a testament, by contrast, there is no universally accepted method of identifying the head of the *stirps* and thus how the legacy ought to be divided.[83]

Example

X bequeaths a legacy of £3,000 'to the issue of my brother A and my sisters B and C *per stirpes*'. A and B have one child each, and C has two.

Approach A
If A, B and C are each heads of a *stirps* the fund will be divided into three. A and B's children receive £1,000 each and C's children receive £500 each.

Approach B
If the issue of A, B and C are each head of a *stirps* the fund will be divided into four equal parts, with each child receiving £750.

The legatees in this example are not named individually but as a class: 'the issue of A, B and C'. The issue of A, B and C are all of the same degree of relationship to the deceased (all are nieces and nephews) and it will be presumed that, in this case, each of the children is head of a *stirps*. Thus, there are four *stirps* and the fund will be divided equally between the children.[84] Effectively, the result is a *per capita* distribution. As a consequence, the testator might more simply have bequeathed the legacy 'to the children of A, B and C equally between them'.[85]

A direction by the testator that division is to be *per stirpes* is construed as expressing the testator's intention that the intended *stirps* are those who survive at the date of vesting, with the share of a predeceasing head of a *stirps* being shared equally amongst any surviving children that legatee may have. The effect of such a direction is accordingly the same as if the bequest had included a destination-over and, in this case, the children of any surviving *stirps* cannot claim a share of the legacy.[86]

83 This can lead to problems in interpretation and drafting of a will, see A Barr, *Drafting Wills in Scotland*, 2nd edn (2009), para 5.8ff.

84 *Campbell's Trs v Welsh* 1952 SC 343.

85 See *Thomson v Cumberland* 16 November 1814, FC; and *Bogie's Trs v Christie* (1882) 9 R 453.

86 *Turner's Tr v Turner* (1897) 24 R 619; *Bailey's Trs v Bailey* 1954 SLT 282; *Boyd's Tr v Shaw* 1958 SC 115.

Example

A testator bequeaths a legacy of £3,000 'to the issue of A, B and C *per stirpes*'. A has one child and B has two. C has two grandchildren, the children of her predeceasing child. Each of the children is head of a *stirps*, with C's two grandchildren being members of the *stirps* of a different degree of relationship to the deceased from the children of A and B. The children of A and B receive £750 each and the grandchildren of C £375 each.

A legacy may, unusually, be given to a head of a *stirps* and his or her children, such as 'to A and her children and B and her children equally between them'. Here, the legacy will be divided equally between those legatees named individually and the children named as a class *per capita.*[87] Where it is expressed as, for example, 'to A and B and their children should any predecease me', the primary legatees will be A and B, with their children taking only in the event of their parent's predecease; in this case, the children are conditional institutes and not the primary legatees.[88] If A's children do take in place of A, division will be *per stirpes* with A's children receiving the share that A would have received had she survived.[89]

Occasionally, the question may not be simply whether the shares are to be *per capita* or *per stirpes* but which of the members of a class are entitled to take at all. In *McGinn's Executrix v McGinn*[90] the executor had bequeathed a house to 'my dear family'. He added that 'if they wish to sell it, then I think the fairest way would be each one of the four members at home...a share...in proportion to their contribution to the upkeep of it'.[91] When all but one of the children died, the survivor sold the house and the widow of one of the other children, who had not lived in the house, raised an action for payment of a share of the proceeds. Having regard to the presumption against intestacy and the wording of the deed as a whole, the court held that the bequest was not void for uncertainty. Rather, the testator's statement as to the division of the proceeds of sale was simply

87 *Cobban's Exrs v Cobban* 1915 SC 82.
88 See paras **11.13–11.16**.
89 *Laing's Trs v Sanson* (1879) 7 R 244.
90 *McGinn's Exrx v McGinn* 1994 SLT 2.
91 *McGinn's Exrx v McGinn* 1994 SLT 2, at 3–4.

the expression of a precatory wish without binding effect and accordingly, the pursuer was entitled to a share of the proceeds.[92]

(b) Liferent and fee

10.24 Where a legacy is given to more than one beneficiary, it may not be clear whether the testator intended for the executor to transfer ownership of the subject to the beneficiaries or intended to bequeath different real rights to different beneficiaries. Unless there are directions to the contrary or it is clear from reading the will as a whole, the general presumption is that the subject of the legacy is given in fee; that is, ownership of the property. When a legacy is given without limitation of time, it is also presumed that it has been given as ownership.[93] However, it may be that, either expressly or by implication, the testator intends the gift to be split into two separate rights, that of liferent and fee.

A proper liferent is a subordinate real right to use the property and enjoy its fruits or income without destroying its substance.[94] A proper liferent may be granted over heritable or moveable property and may or may not be qualified. The common law rules apply by default only to proper liferents, where liferent and fee vest simultaneously in the liferenter and fiar and both acquire a real right in the subject, provided that the relevant formalities are completed.[95] It is not the purpose of this chapter to describe in any detail the characteristics of the separate rights and obligations of liferent and fee.[96] Rather, it is to note that the status of the legatee in relation to the subject of a legacy may be a matter of construction if not set out plainly in the deed. Not only is this important in relation to the rights of the individual concerned but it may also be important in relation to the rights of another beneficiary. If, for example, property is bequeathed 'to A in liferent and B in fee' it will be of great importance to B to know that he or she has no right to sell the property until A's liferent has terminated.

92 See para **10.3**.

93 J McLaren, *The Law of Wills and Succession,* 3rd edn (1894), para 1039.

94 Erskine *Inst* II.9.39; Bell *Prin*, § 1037.

95 In practice, many improper liferents are also created under a trust.

96 See the specialist text, though rather outdated in its terminology, W Dobie, *Manual of the Law of Liferent and Fee in Scotland* (1941). A more introductory analysis can be found in G Gretton and A Steven, *Property, Trusts, and Succession,* 5th edn (2024), Ch 23.

MULTIPLE LEGACIES TO A SINGLE LEGATEE

10.25 Where more than one legacy has been bequeathed to the same beneficiary, it may not be clear whether the testator intended that person to be entitled to each of the individual legacies. Providing that the beneficiary has been identified correctly and the multiple bequests are actually intended for the same person and not two different people, it may be necessary to establish whether the testator also intended that the object of the bequests receive more than one. The question is whether the legacies are cumulative or whether they are substitutional.[97] Where there is doubt as to the testator's intention, rules of interpretation must be brought into play. Extrinsic evidence may be admitted only when the legacies appear, *prima facie*, to be substitutional and thus where the beneficiary may be disadvantaged by an interpretation limiting his or her entitlement to succeed.

The general rule is that where more than one varying legacy to the same beneficiary is contained in the *same* deed, the legacies will be presumed to be cumulative. On the other hand, if more than one identical legacy is given to the same beneficiary within the same deed, the legacies will be presumed to be substitutional. If, for example, the testator bequeaths £300 to B twice in the same will, it will be presumed that the testator intended B to receive only one legacy of £300 and that this was forgetfulness on the part of the testator.[98]

Where multiple legacies are bequeathed to the same legatee in *different* deeds, these legacies are presumed to be cumulative:[99]

> 'When a testator by one or several instruments gives two or more legacies or other benefits to the same individual, he presumably intends that they shall all have effect, and in the absence of any expression or other indication to the contrary, the law takes this to be his intention accordingly.'

The presumption applies regardless of whether the subjects of the bequest are identical,[100] despite the rule of interpretation that wills and codicils

97 Though in the case of a special legacy, there is only one thing to be bequeathed, such as in the case of a legacy of a house.

98 See J McLaren, *The Law of Wills and Succession as Administered in Scotland,* 3rd edn (1894), paras 1322ff.

99 See *Arres' Trs v Mather* (1881) 9 R 107, per Lord Young at para 109. See also *Edinburgh Royal Infirmary v Muir's Trs* (1881) 9 R 352.

100 *Hooley v Hatton* (1773) 1 Bro CC 390; *Stirling v Deans* (1704) Mor 11442; *Arres' Trs v Mather* (1881) 9 R 107.

are to be read together as if they were the same instrument expressing the testator's intention.[101] It may be rebutted, depending on the circumstances. If, for example, identical bequests have both been made by way of codicils and each codicil makes clear that they are in substitution for legacies bequeathed by way of a previous will, the legacies will be presumed to be substitutional.[102] On the basis of the ordinary rules of construction, it follows that where the provisions of a subsequent document contradicts the provisions of the earlier document, the provisions of the first will be deemed to have been revoked.[103]

101 See para **9.4**.

102 See 'Wills and Succession', Volume 25 in *The Laws of Scotland: Stair Memorial Encyclopaedia,* para 858. See also *Resch's Will Trusts, Re* [1969] 1 AC 514; and *Le Cras v Perpetual Trustee Co Ltd* [1967] 3 All ER 915, PC.

103 *Beattie v Thomson* (1861) 23 D 1163; see also paras **7.15** and **9.4**.

Chapter 11

Legatees

INTRODUCTION

11.1 Just as it may be a matter of construction how the subject of a legacy, or the thing bequeathed, is to be classified and ascertained, so may identifying the legatee or object of the legacy. This chapter focuses on how the testator's intention in relation to the person to whom the subject is bequeathed may be interpreted.

First, the legatee must be identified; having been identified, his or her survivance must be ascertained.[1] If the legatee has predeceased, the consequence is that the legacy may lapse, falling either to the residue or to intestacy. Similarly, a legacy may carry a condition that requires it to be purified for the legacy to be vested or to be distributed. If purification of the condition has not occurred, or cannot occur, then the legacy may lapse in the same manner as a legatee failing to survive the deceased.

The testator may, however, have envisaged that a legacy may lapse, and inserted provisions in the will whereby an alternative legatee will be substituted for the original legatee if the original legatee fails. If the testator has not provided expressly for an alternative candidate, it may be that presumptions fall to be applied in order to avoid the lapse of the legacy. The device of the destination-over prevents a testator's intentions from being frustrated, or at least allows some approximation of them to be established. The rules relating to alternative or substitutionary legatees are a combination of rules of construction and substantive doctrines, but different types of device or destination have their own rules as to their application and these require careful consideration.

1 See **Ch 1**.

IDENTIFYING LEGATEES

11.2 The person whom the testator intends as the legatee, or the object of a legacy, may not always be clear. If the testator has simply forgotten or has never been quite clear about the beneficiary's name, it may be possible to identify him or her from other information contained within the deed without resort to extrinsic evidence. If this is impossible, extrinsic evidence may be admissible in order to avoid intestacy.[2] Provided that the testator appears to have had some identifiable beneficiary in mind when expressing his or her testamentary intentions, the task of the court will be to attempt to give effect to that intention. Legal presumptions apply where the objects are described as a spouse or as a class. If it is impossible to identify the beneficiary from the deed itself or by extrinsic evidence, the legacy lapses for uncertainty.[3]

(1) Individuals and groups of individuals

11.3 Errors as to the spelling of the beneficiary's name are ignored where his or her identity is otherwise clear.[4] Where, however, it appears that the wrong name entirely is attached to a description of the beneficiary, the testator's intention may be construed to give effect to what seems to be the most plausible construction. For example, a testator gave a legacy to 'my late brother James's son'. His late brother James had a daughter but his brother David had a son. The court held that James's daughter was the intended beneficiary, on the ground that the testator was more likely to have forgotten the sex of his brother's child rather than his brother's name.[5]

Where it would otherwise be impossible to identify the intended beneficiary, extrinsic evidence may be admitted. For example, where two people amongst a number of possible beneficiaries bore similar names but neither name corresponded exactly to the beneficiary nominated in the deed, letters from the deceased were admitted to show who was the

2 See **Ch 9**.

3 See paras **11.3** and **12.14**.

4 *Keiller v Thomson's Trs* (1824) 3 S 279.

5 *Macfarlane's Trs v Henderson* (1878) 6 R 288.

most likely candidate.[6] In *Keiller v Thomson's Trustees,*[7] the testator had bequeathed a legacy to 'Janet Keiller or Williamson'. There were two possible claimants: Agnes Keiller, who was a widow of a man called Wedderspoon, and her sister, Janet, who was married to a man called Whitton. The court admitted evidence of five previous wills and eight codicils to show that there had been a mistranscription of Wedderspoon to Williamson.[8] If the intended legatee is manifestly unknown to the testator – perhaps because he or she was unborn at the date of execution of the deed – the issue to be addressed is not one of identification of the legatee but of ascertaining the testator's intention as to the time of vesting.[9]

Where the testator has made a gift in very general terms, such as a sum of money 'to my friends', such friends to be identified by a named person and approved by trustees, this may be sufficient to identify the intended beneficiaries, provided that the description is sufficiently clear.[10] Where the gift is merely to 'my friends', with no means of selection indicated, the bequest will be void for uncertainty. In this case, the testator will be considered as having been wholly lacking in testamentary intention for the legacy. Accordingly, in *Salvesen's Trustees v Wye*[11] a legacy to 'any poor relations and friends or acquaintances of mine' without any further indication as to the means of their selection was void. In any case, the terms in which the bequest was made included the word 'and' so that the objects had to be read conjunctively. In consequence, the entire clause would fail if identification of any of the objects enumerated were impossible. A 'poor relation' could be identified but as it was impossible to know how to identify 'friends' or 'acquaintances',[12] and so the whole bequest was void.

6 *Cathcart's Trs v Bruce* 1923 SLT 722.

7 *Keiller v Thomson's Trs* (1824) 3 S 279.

8 For a full discussion of the kinds of cases where the identity of both the subject and object were in doubt, see J McLaren, *The Law of Wills and Succession as Administered in Scotland,* 3rd edn (1894), Ch 20.

9 See **Ch 13**.

10 *Crichton v Grierson* (1828) 3 W & S 329.

11 *Salvesen's Trs v Wye* 1954 SC 440.

12 On certainty and uncertainty of objects see W Wilson and A Duncan, *Trusts, Trustees and Executors,* 2nd edn (1995), para 7-08.

(2) Spouses or civil partners

11.4 If a testator makes a bequest to his or her spouse or civil partner, or the spouse or civil partner of another person, without adding the person's name, the general rule is that the intended beneficiary is the person to whom the testator or the other person was married or partnered at the date of payment of the legacy.

In the case of the testator's spouse, this means that the intended beneficiary is anyone the testator was married to at the time of his or her death, since that person will still be the spouse in question even if payment is postponed until some time after the deceased's death. However, where the beneficiary was the former spouse or civil partner of the deceased, subsequently divorced or partnership terminated, then a reference by description to the testator's spouse or civil partner in a legacy will be treated as if he or she had predeceased the testator and the legacy will lapse.[13]

The position may be rather different when the spouse in question is the spouse of a third party. The third party may have remarried in the period between the execution of the will and payment of the legacy, with the consequence that the spouse married to that person at the time of the testator's death may well not be the person to whom the testator intended to refer.[14]

Example

H has a son, J, and leaves a legacy to 'my son's wife'. At the date H executed the will, J was married to K. At H's death, J had remarried to Q. As a generality, Q would be entitled to the legacy in preference to K.

Where the name of the spouse is added to a more general description, the beneficiary will be presumed to be the person of that name regardless of whether he or she remains the spouse.

(3) Class gifts

11.5 A gift is to a class where the beneficiaries are identifiable not as individuals or as members of a group of individuals but as members of

13 See paras **2.22** and **2.24**.

14 *Burns's Trs Petrs* 1961 SC 17.

a class definable by their status. This will most frequently be a class of relatives, described variously as 'my siblings', 'my children', 'my issue', 'my descendants' or 'my heirs'. In older deeds, particularly, such bequests may present special problems of identification. Not only must definitions of the class be understood but, depending on when the testator died, the persons who can be identified correctly as members may fall to be determined according to the law which was in force at the relevant time, the meaning of the relevant time depending on the particular rules in question.

(a) Time when the class is ascertained

11.6 The normal rule in relation to class gifts is that the members of the class are to be identified at the date of the testator's death.[15] Thus, if the testator bequeathed a gift to 'my nieces' of whom there were two at the time the will was executed but three when he died, the gift would be to all three nieces. If the gift is qualified, however, by words such as 'my nieces who are alive at the time of my death' and a third niece is born some time after the death, she would be excluded from the bequest.[16] If the third niece had predeceased the testator, the consequence of the qualification would be that accretion would apply to her share of the legacy.[17] If vesting is postponed, the class will be identified at the time of vesting unless the testator has specified another date. If payment alone is postponed, it may or may not be that it is at the date of payment that members of the class fall to be identified.[18]

(b) Defining the class

11.7 The eligibility of members of a class described as 'children' in post-1964 and post-1986 deeds is relatively straightforward. Legacies to 'children' or 'issue' are to be interpreted as including all children, including

15 *Gregory's Trs v Alison* (1889) 6 R (HL) 10 but this applies only if vesting occurs *a morte testatoris*: see Ch 13.

16 *Carleton v Thomson* (1867) 5 M (HL) 151. If no such qualification was made and the date of payment was later than the date of vesting, the shares of the first-born nieces would be subject to partial defeasance on the birth of the third: see para **13.27**.

17 See para **11.20**.

18 *Wood v Wood* (1861) 23 D 338; J McLaren, *The Law of Wills and Succession,* 3rd edn (1894), para 1261.

posthumous children, adopted children and, since 1986, children whose parents were not married to each other.[19] Where the objects of a legacy are described as 'heirs', this is construed to mean persons who would be entitled to succeed if the testator had died intestate.[20] The term 'next of kin' is entirely obsolete in this context but in effect means the same as 'heir'.

Two distinct but possibly coincident types of difficulty may arise in determining who is entitled to a legacy, the object of which is described as a class in any of these ways. First, there is the question of whether 'children' or 'issue' includes grandchildren and more remote descendants. This point is why the specific phrase 'descendants' has come into fashion within wills and trusts to attempt to remove any doubt. Second, there is the question of whether the definitions of 'children', 'issue' or 'heirs' to be applied are those which applied at the date of execution of the deed, the date of the testator's death or the date of vesting, if this is postponed.

(c) Bequests to 'children' or 'issue'

11.8 Where the objects of a bequest are described as 'children', *prima facie* the children of a predeceasing beneficiary have no entitlement to succeed in his or her place.[21] Additionally, grandchildren will not normally be included within the class of 'children' *in addition* to surviving children unless the contrary is clear from the terms of the will.

Example

A bequeaths a legacy to 'the children of B'. A was a friend of B. One of B's three children predeceases A, survived by their own child, G. G cannot

19 Legitimacy (Scotland) Act 1959, s 1; Law Reform (Miscellaneous Provisions) (Scotland) Act 1968, s 5; Law Reform (Parent and Child) (Scotland) Act 1986, s 1(4)(c); Succession (Scotland) Act 1964, s 23(4); Family Law (Scotland) Act 2006, s 21. See paras **2.9–2.13**.

20 Unless the will makes clear that any person who would come into the categories set out in the Succession (Scotland) Act 1964, s 2 is expressly excluded: *Nelson's Trs v Nelson's CB* 1979 SLT 98; and *Borthwick's Trs v Borthwick* 1955 SC 227.

21 In the wholly anomalous case of *Ranken* (1870) 8 M 878 a bequest to 'children' was held to include grandchildren in a situation where the old *conditio si institutus* could not be applied: see J McLaren, *The Law of Wills and Succession,* 3rd edn (1894), para 1252.

take her parent's share. Only B's two surviving children are entitled to the legacy.

The only case in which any entitlement arises for a child of a predeceased beneficiary is where a destination-over to children can be implied under s 6 of the Succession (Scotland) Act 2016, or for older deeds the *conditio si institutis*, both of which are discussed below.[22]

The term 'issue' is not synonymous with 'children' and the class of beneficiaries who may be included in a legacy to 'issue' is wider than that included in a legacy to 'children'. The testator's use of 'issue' as a description of the legatee is construed as an intention to include not only children but also grandchildren or more remote descendants within the class should children fail to survive. At one time, 'issue' had no technical meaning and the question of whether the testator intended to include descendants generally, or children only, depended on the context of the bequest.[23] Later, the courts preferred the view that the ordinary meaning of the word included direct descendants of every degree[24] and this construction has been followed since.[25]

Since a person or persons conditionally instituted under a destination-over will take the place of the institute only if the institute should fail to survive, descendants will be excluded if their surviving ascendant survives the testator. Thus, a bequest to 'issue' does not mean that all surviving descendants of the legatee take the legacy simultaneously; remoter descendants will take only if nearer descendants have predeceased the testator.

Example

X bequeaths a legacy 'to the issue of my friend A'. At the date of execution of the will, A had three children, each of whom had one child. At the date of X's death, one of A's children had died. The class therefore comprise A's two surviving children and the child of the predeceaser.

22 See para **11.22**.

23 *Young's Trs v McNab* (1883) 10 R 1165, per Lord President Shand at 1168: "issue' and 'lawful issue' are merely words of popular signification and ... we must take them to mean just what we can gather to be the meaning intended to be attached to them by the testator as far as we can apprehend in the normal way by examining the whole terms of his settlement'.

24 See *Turner's Trs v Turner* (1897) 24 R 619, per Lord Kinnear at 621.

25 See *Bailey's Trs v Bailey* 1954 SLT 282; *Boyd's Trs v Shaw* 1958 SC 115.

The term 'issue' is also often used in the context of an express destination-over, as in 'to A and his issue'. This does not mean that if A and his issue survive the testator they all take a share of the legacy; rather, the word 'and' is construed to mean that A's issue will take in his or her place, should A predecease the testator.

(d) Identifying the class where legal definitions of status have changed

11.9 Changes to the law of status which determine who is to be included within a class of beneficiary described as 'children', 'lawful children', 'issue', and 'heir' etc. Legacies to legatees described in these ways have raised difficulties in relation to determining the date on which members of such classes are to be defined and under which set of rules they are to be identified. Legislation since 1968 concerning 'legitimacy', adoption and the classes of persons entitled to succeed on intestacy has had a significant impact on the categories of person entitled to inherit in testate and intestate succession alike. Prior to the Succession (Scotland) Act 1964, the Law Reform (Miscellaneous Provisions) (Scotland) Act 1968 and the Law Reform (Parent and Child) (Scotland) Act 1986, 'issue' was construed so as to include only 'lawful' issue. As a consequence of reforms introduced by the Acts, a reference to 'issue' now includes all children, whether adopted or whether their parents were married to each other, in any will executed after the relevant dates.[26]

Further, the Succession (Scotland) Act 1964, s 2 abolished the status of the 'heir-at-law' and of 'next of kin' and substituted a ranked list of relatives entitled to succeed on intestacy.[27] In post-1964 wills, therefore, an 'heir' is simply a person who would be entitled to succeed to the intestate estate under s 2 of the 1964 Act.[28] These statutory changes have given rise to a number of cases where the relevant legislation was passed either (i)

26 Succession (Scotland) Act 1964, s 23; Law Reform (Miscellaneous Provisions) (Scotland) Act 1968, s 5 and Law Reform (Parent and Child) (Scotland) Act 1986, s 1(4)(c); Family Law (Scotland) Act 2006, s 21.

27 See **Ch 6** but note that such an express reference to 'lawful issue' will still exclude any such children.

28 See, eg, *Grant's Trs v Simon* 1925 SLT 136, 139.

after the date on which the will was executed but before the death of the testator, or (ii) after the date of execution but before the date of vesting.

(e) Changes to the law between the date of execution of the deed and the death of the testator

11.10 Where changes to the law have taken place between the date on which a will has been executed and the date of the testator's death, the common law rule is that the law to be applied is the supervening law in force at the date of the testator's death, not the law in force at the date of execution of the deed.[29] The justification for the rule is that between the date of expressing his or her testamentary intentions and death, a testator can be presumed to have become aware of any change in the law affecting the law of succession and would have had the opportunity to change his or her testamentary intentions to take account of the changes, had he or she chosen to do so. This approach was taken by the court in applying the Intestate Moveable Succession (Scotland) Act 1855 which introduced representation by children of predeceasing heirs in moveable succession but did not state expressly which wills were to be included.[30]

However, legislation relating to the status of children of unmarried parents *exclude* the common law rule. The Law Reform (Miscellaneous Provisions) (Scotland) Act 1968,[31] the Law Reform (Parent and Child) (Scotland) Act 1986[32] and the Family Law (Scotland) Act 2006[33] each provide that their provisions apply only to deeds executed *after* the dates of their coming into force.[34] Thus, the question of whether these statutes which came into force after the execution of a will apply to the legacy does not arise unless there is an express provision in the will to the contrary.

29 *Nimmo v Murray's Trs* (1864) 2 M 1144; and *Maxwell v Maxwell* (1864) 3 M 318.

30 *Nimmo v Murray's Trs* (1864) 2 M 1144, per Lord Justice Clerk Inglis at 1149. The question at issue related to the applicability of changes to the class of heirs in *mobilibus* introduced by the Intestate Moveable Succession (Scotland) Act 1855 to deeds executed before that date but coming into operation after it.

31 1968 Act, s 5(3).

32 1986 Act, s 1(4)(b).

33 This does not feature in the 2006 Act itself, but see its amendments to s 1(4) of the 1986 Act.

34 That is, to all wills executed on or after 25 November 1968, 8 December 1986, and 4 May 2006 respectively.

Example

A executes a will in 1980 and dies in 2020 aged 80. The will provides for a legacy to 'the issue of B'. By the date of the testator's death, B had two children but never married. In the intervening period between execution and death, the 1986 Act and 2006 Act had changed the law relating to the status of these children. However, the legislation has no effect on the deed because it came into force after its execution.[35]

(f) Changes to the law between the death of the testator's death and the date of vesting

11.11 More difficult questions may arise when vesting has been postponed[36] and the law has changed since the testator's death. In *Wright's Trustees v Callender*[37] the provisions of the testator's trust disposition and settlement were complex. The testator, who had died in 1917, bequeathed a legacy of the fee of the residue of his estate to such grandchildren as survived the date at which the liferent expired, together with any issue of any grandchildren who might have predeceased at that date. As the terms made clear, vesting was postponed until the expiry of the liferent and, accordingly, identification of the beneficiaries of the fee was also delayed until that date.

The testator's widow had been granted the power to alter any provisions of the deed and she had exercised the power by varying the terms so that the residue was to be held in liferent for the grandchildren and their issue in fee. The share of any predeceasing issue was to accresce to the others and their issue in the event of their predeceasing without leaving issue. The widow died in 1932 and vesting of the fee took place in 1989 when the last of the liferenters died.

The main question to be decided was whether all of the grandchildren's issue were entitled to the fee.

35 Cases decided in similar conditions include *Allan v Adamson* (1902) 9 SLT 404; and *Purdie's Trs v Doolan* 1929 SLT 273, OH.

36 See paras **13.4–13.6**.

37 1993 SCLR 415.

One of the grandchildren had three children but, at the times they were born, their mother was not married to their father. Some years later, in 1954, the parents married and the children became legitimated subsequently under the provisions of the Legitimacy Act 1959 and the Legitimation (Scotland) Act 1968.[38] The court held that although the issue were to be identified at the date of vesting, they were to be identified in accordance with the law in force at the testator's death in 1939. Paraphrasing the opinions of an earlier case on which the decision relied,[39] Lord Keith stated that:[40]

> 'These opinions indicate that a testator is not to be regarded as having contemplated that there might be a change in the law between his death and the opening of the succession and that the more natural intention to attribute to him is that the succession should be regulated by the law as it stood at the time of his death.'

In summary, the new law will prevail where it has changed after the date of execution of the deed but before the testator's death, unless excluded by the statute in question. Where the law has changed after the testator's death, the common law rule will prevail.

FAILURE OF THE LEGATEE

11.12 The law of succession is concerned with the transmission of rights in property from a deceased person to a person or persons nominated as beneficiaries of his or her estate. It is clear that, as a general principle, a beneficiary must survive the testator in order to acquire the right. It follows that simply put: the dead cannot inherit.

If the legatee does not survive, the question arises as to who, if anyone, may have become entitled to that legacy in the legatee's place. Clearly, the testator may have changed their will in response to the legatee's death, in which case the problem does not arise. If the testator does not, the legacy will lapse unless the right is transmitted to an alternative beneficiary. Similarly, if the object of a legacy has failed to purify a suspensive condition attached to the legacy (such as surviving a certain

38 See para **2.11**.
39 *Cockburn's Trs v Dundas* (1864) 2 M 1185.
40 *Wright's Trs v Callender* 1993 SCLR 415, at 420.

period or event),[41] the legacy will lapse unless the right is transmitted to an alternative beneficiary. Erskine states:[42]

> 'When a legatee dies before the testator, the legacy is not transmitted to the legatee's executors; both because legacies are granted from the testator's special regard to the legatee himself, and because they do not become due, *dies non cedit*, till the death of the testator; and nothing can pass from one to his heir or executor till it be due to himself … A conditional legacy falls if the legatee dies, before the condition can be fulfilled.'

Erskine makes clear that the doctrine of *delectus personae* applies to legacies. However, in some circumstances, it may be overridden in order to prevent lapse. The testator may have considered the possibility that the object may fail and have provided for an alternative person to take the legacy if this happens. If the testator has not made such provision, it may be possible to apply legal presumptions to impute an intention to the testator. In this case, the deed may be construed in such a way that an alternative object can be identified and lapse of the legacy avoided. The consequence of lapse is that the legacy will fall to residue; if, however, it is the residuary legatee who fails, or there is no residuary legacy, then the residue will fall into intestacy.

The means of avoiding lapse of a legacy is by way of a destination-over, express or implied. Whereas representation in legal rights and intestate succession entitles children and remoter descendants to claim from an intestate estate in place of their predeceasing parent,[43] the doctrine does not apply to testate succession. However destinations-over have the same effect but they are not confined in application to the original legatee's descendants. An express destination-over gives effect to what the testator's actual intention was, and an implied destination-over imputes intention by means of legal presumptions. Where it is express, the wording of the deed will be a variation of the form 'to A, whom failing to B'. In other words, B is named as an alternative object in the event of A's failure.

A legatee is known as an institute; that is the person nominated by the testator and in whom the right will be instituted. Where a legacy contains a destination-over, either express or implied, to an alternative legatee, the alternative legatee is known either as the conditional institute or the substitute.

41 See para **13.11**.

42 Erskine *Inst* II.10.9.

43 Succession (Scotland) Act 1964, ss 5 and 11; see paras **5.7–5.9** and **6.35–6.36**.

CONDITIONAL INSTITUTES AND SUBSTITUTES

11.13 Where a destination-over is express or implied, the effect is that A is the primary legatee (or first choice) and known as the 'institute'; that is, the person in whom the gift is instituted. B is the secondary legatee and will take the gift only in the event of the failure of A, so can be considered as a 'second choice' or 'reserve' candidate. There are two categories that second choice candidates can fall into, being either: (i) conditional institutes, or (ii) substitutes. Both are discussed below.

A conditional institute is effectively a reserve candidate. If in a legacy 'to A whom failing B' and A has predeceased the testator, then the destination will give the right under the legacy to B. A's executor loses any potential to claim the property as the right has vest in B instead.

Substitution is more complex. Substitution implies that the property is to pass to B on A's death. Thus, if A survives the testator, A inherits the legacy until their death, at which point the property (if all or part still remains in A's patrimony) is to pass to B.

There is no particular form of words which amounts to a valid declaration that the intention of the testator is to exclude conditional institution and to provide for substitution instead.[44] The deed in which the bequest to the beneficiary is contained will identify the primary object (even if the person or persons conforming to its description cannot be ascertained individually until some future date)[45] but will not necessarily specify whether the second person is a conditional institute or a substitute. In this case, presumptions will be applied in classifying the alternative object. For deaths before the commencement of the Succession (Scotland) Act 2016 on 1 November 2016, determining the status of the alternative legatee depended on the subject of the legacy and what species of property it is classified as being.[46]

44 *Greig v Johnston* (1832) 6 W & S 406, per Lord Brougham at 420.

45 Legacies may be given to a class of persons who are not born at the time of the deed as well as to a living individual: see paras **13.21ff.**

46 In the old law, different classifications for the alternate object could be reached depending on the species of property as either heritable or moveable. A legacy of heritable property with a destination was presumed to be a substitution, whereas a legacy of moveable property was presumed to be a conditional institution. See further A Barr, *Drafting Wills in Scotland,* 2nd edn (2009), para 5.27.

For deaths on or after 1 November 2016, then s 8 of the Succession (Scotland) Act 2016 applies.[47] Under s 8, where property is to pass to 'A, whom failing B' then the statute presumes that B is a conditional institute rather than a substitute – subject to the terms of the wills or the demonstrable intention of the testator. This applies regardless of the species of the property and simplifies the law. Where the destination-over is implied rather than expressed, the alternative beneficiary will always be a conditional institute and not a substitute.

(1) Conditional institution

11.14 Where B is a conditional institute, his or her right is conditional on A's predeceasing the testator or failure to survive a particular event. If A does survive and the legacy vests in him or her, B's conditional institution 'flies off' and A's right becomes absolute.[48]

Example

X bequeaths a legacy of £5,000 in the form 'to A whom failing B' in a deed executed in 2018. The testator dies in 2025, survived by A and B. The legacy vests in A (the institute) and B's contingent right is cancelled.

In determining B's right, the key issue is whether the legacy has vested in A; quite clearly, this will be impossible if A has predeceased the testator. Accordingly, A can acquire a right to the legacy only once the fact of his or her survivorship has been ascertained.[49]

Survivorship may mean survivorship of the testator's death but may, alternatively, mean survivorship of another event. If the legacy is subject to a suspensive condition, such as surviving a liferenter, vesting in A may be suspended until the expiry of the liferent. Henderson explains the position as follows:[50]

47 The Succession (Scotland) Act 2016 (Commencement, Transitional and Saving Provisions) Regulations SSI 2016/210.

48 Succession (Scotland) Act 2016, s 8.

49 See para **13.13**.

50 R Candlish Henderson, *The Principles of Vesting in the Law of Succession,* 2nd edn (1938), 50.

> 'As, therefore, a conditional institution provides for the disposal of the subject in the event of the institute's death before a given time, by the creation of an alternative interest, it makes the institute's right conditional upon his surviving that time, and therefore in the meantime suspends vesting.'

This means that neither the institute nor the conditional institute can acquire a right until or unless the requirement for survivorship of either is established.

Example

X bequeaths the residue of her estate to A in improper liferent and in fee to B, whom failing C. C's right to the fee is conditional on B's failure. B's right is conditional upon surviving the liferenter. B survives the testator but dies before the expiry of the liferent. C survives both the testator and the liferenter, and she acquires a right to the fee at the date of the liferenter's death.

(2) Substitution

11.15 Where B is a substitute, his or her interest is not conditional on A's failure but is postponed to A's right.[51] That is, a substitute has a right to the subject of the legacy not only if A fails before acquiring an absolute right but also, *prima facie*, on A's death if the legacy has vested in A. Thus, if A predeceases the testator, B will take the legacy in A's place just as if he or she were a conditional institute. If A survives the testator and acquires an absolute right, B's conditional right does not 'fly off' but will become absolute if he or she survives the death of A.

As a result of s 8 of the 2016 Act, an interpretation of substitution by a court is somewhat unlikely. However, the testator may still wish to use such destinations expressly.[52] Where there is a document of title, normally where the subject is heritable property, the destination to B as substitute will be replicated in the conveyance of the property to A. Thus,

51 J McLaren, *The Law of Wills and Succession*, 3rd edn (1894), para 1131.

52 Express wording to this effect can be quite troublesome to draft, see A Barr, *Drafting Wills in Scotland*, 2nd edn (2009), para 5.27.

a disposition of heritage by the executor in favour of A will contain a destination reflecting the intended substitution of B upon A's death. This will be in a form of a destination in favour of B being inserted into the title.[53] Hence, the legacy to B contains a double contingency: B will take in the event that he or she survives the testator but A predeceases; B will also take the legacy if both A and B survive the testator but A predeceases B.[54]

Notwithstanding the continuing conditional right of B, the institute is free to evacuate the destination during his or her life.

Example

X bequeaths a legacy with A as institute and B as substitute in a deed executed in 2018. The testator dies in 2022, survived by both A and B. The legacy vests in A but the property is later conveyed to him subject to a destination to B, to take effect on A's death. A sells the property, evacuating the destination to B. B cannot receive the property on A's death as it is no longer within A's patrimony.

The terms of the substitution are binding on the testator's executors in conveying the property to the institute but they are not binding on A.[55] A is therefore empowered to sell the property or otherwise dispose of it during life or by *mortis causa* disposition in which he bequeaths it to a beneficiary of his or her choosing. The institute is under no obligation to limit his or her freedom to deal with the property in order that it remains intact for the substitute on death, even assuming that the substitute survives the institute. If the institute's rights were to be limited in this way, the testator would effectively have bequeathed only a liferent to the institute and not ownership.

(3) Construing the testator's intention

11.16 Section 8 of the 2016 Act provides a presumption of conditional institution for all destinations but this can be rebutted from the express

53 On special destinations see paras **7.19–7.25**.

54 See Henderson, *The Principles of Vesting,* 2nd edn (1938), 52. See also para **13.19**.

55 J McLaren, *The Law of Wills and Succession,* 3rd edn (1894), para 1131.

terms of the will where the testator intended otherwise. However, ascertaining the testator's intention can be difficult.

Crumpton's Judicial Factor v Barnardo's Homes[56] provides a useful illustration of the complexities of construing the testator's intentions in relation to whether the second beneficiary is a conditional institute or a substitute. The testator had given a pecuniary legacy of £8,000 to her nephew and his 'heirs, executors and administrators absolutely' but added 'in case my nephew shall die without issue, I appoint the said £8,000' to be divided equally between certain charities.

The wording of the first part of the bequest made clear that the legacy was an absolute right and that the nephew's heirs and executors were secondary legatees. Thus, if the testator's nephew should predecease the testator, his right to the legacy would not lapse but would devolve to his heirs and executors and be payable on her, the testator's, death. The wording of the second part, however, meant that the nephew's right was conditional upon his having children; failing this, the charities were to take. In a later clause in the will the testator had then added that if her nephew survived her he was also to receive a legacy of £500. This was subject to the provision that both that legacy and the legacy of £8,000 were to be placed in trust for him and he was to receive only the interest. This provision therefore appeared to cancel the legacy of the fee of £8,000 and substitute a liferent of that sum and the £500.

The nephew survived the testator but died intestate and without children. The question to be addressed by the court was whether the charities were conditional institutes or substitutes, since the issue of whether the nephew's executors or the charities were entitled to the legacy turned on its resolution. Barnardo's Homes argued that the testator had clearly intended that the later provisions of the will were to qualify the earlier, reducing the interest given to her nephew to a liferent and leaving the fee to the substitutes originally named (the charities). The court held that there was only one event in which the charities were to take and that was if the nephew died without issue. Although he had indeed died without issue, Lord President Strathclyde held that:[57]

56 1917 SC 713.
57 1917 SC 713, at 719.

> 'The natural meaning of those words is died without issue prior to the death of the testatrix, and not died at any time before or after her death. Otherwise … the words 'heirs, executors and administrators absolutely' would be destitute of meaning.'

Accordingly, the fee had vested in the nephew *a morte testatoris*.[58] The charities were merely conditional institutes, the condition being the death of the nephew without issue prior to the death of the testator. The condition never having been purified, their contingent right had 'flown off' when the fee vested in the nephew.

DESTINATIONS-OVER

11.17 A destination-over is the legal device by which a right is conferred on a secondary or substitutionary legatee in the event of the failure of the primary or original legatee. The clearest category are express destinations-over, where the testator has foreseen, and made provision for, the contingency that the primary legatee fails to survive or to purify a condition. By contrast, an implied destination-over arises *ex lege* and will be applied where possible in order to impute an intention to the testator as to the destination of the legacy, in preference to lapse. It may be that several forms of destination-over appear to be applicable in the same case. In consequence, principles have developed in order to determine priority between the potential rights of different classes of substitutionary legatee.

(1) Express destinations-over

11.18 In an express destination-over, the testator specifies expressly the alternative beneficiary (or class of beneficiaries) who is to take the legacy if the institute should fail. Having contemplated the possibility of the failure of the institute, the testator may also have attached a survivorship clause to the legacy, effectively a suspensive condition that the beneficiary survives him or her for a specified period of time. This is a form of conditional legacy, operating to suspend vesting until the condition has been purified.

58 See paras **13.3–13.4**.

Example

X bequeaths a legacy to A 'on the condition that he survive me by 30 days, whom failing to B'. A survives the testator for only 25 days. The legacy passes to B.

Where there is an express destination-over to a beneficiary and his or her issue, the word 'and' can be construed as meaning the same thing as 'whom failing'. However, a gift in these terms such as 'to A and her children' or 'to A and her issue' is, strictly speaking, a clause of devolution. In a clause of devolution (otherwise known as a 'derivative destination'), the children or issue acquire a right as the *representatives* of A rather than as alternative legatees. A's issue are not conditional institutes as such, whose right is contingent on their not only surviving A but also surviving the date of payment of the legacy if this is later than the date of vesting.[59] Rather, the issue are entitled to take in A's place whether or not A survives. This is because the property vests in A as the head of a line of descent and not as an individual. In the event of A's predeceasing either the testator or the date of payment, his or her right is defeated in favour of children or issue of that line.

Therefore, the word 'and' in this context is construed as meaning that the gift is to A with an implied destination to his children, A taking as head of a line of descent.

Example

X gives a legacy 'to A and his issue'. A and his three children survive X. The legacy vests in A at the date of X's death but payment is postponed until some years later. A dies before the date of payment and the legacy is payable to the children of A, including to the estates of any who have failed to survive until the date of payment.[60]

The effect is therefore rather like that of substitution: the right of the children arises independently of whether A survives.[61] Such a construction

59 See paras **13.4–13.6**.

60 See para **13.20**.

61 *See Hendry's Trs v Hendry* (1872) 10 M 432, per Lord Kinloch at 437; and *Wardlaw's Trs v Lennox's Exrs* 1940 SC 286.

applies only, however, where the second-named beneficiaries are children and does not imply a destination where it is used in relation to any other person or class.[62]

(2) Implied destinations-over

11.19 A destination-over can be implied as well as express. Implied destinations may operate *ex lege* as a set of presumptions applied to the construction of deeds and may apply both where a competition between potential beneficiaries arises and where the testator's intention as to the destination of the legacy appears, from the face of the deed, to be obscure. Where destinations-over are implied, their effect is identical to that of express destinations-over. This means that a principled basis for the distribution of the estate can be formed where there is a dispute over the correct construction of the will, with the result that the legacy to which the principles are applied will not lapse. If, for example, a testator bequeaths a legacy to A but A has predeceased, the legacy may not necessarily lapse simply because the testator has omitted to provide for this contingency.

(a) Accretion

11.20 The doctrine of accretion may apply where a legacy is given to a group or class of persons rather than to a single beneficiary. It operates to imply a destination-over in favour of the survivors of the group should any of their number predecease the testator, or should the legacy for any other reason fail to vest in one of them. In effect, accretion is a form of survivorship destination; the *ius accrescendi* implies that the share of a predeceasing legatee accresces to the survivors of the group. In other words, a legacy to 'A, B and C' is effectively the same as 'to A, B, C and the survivor or survivors of them'. In the event of either A, B or

62 This is because the rule is derived historically from the right of heirs to succeed to heritage The proper use of the word 'and' in contradistinction to 'whom failing' is a matter of some importance: 'and' is 'properly used only to connect a destination to heirs with the name of the individual from whom the succession is to be traced, not to introduce a distinct nomination or line of heirs': J McLaren, *The Law of Wills and Succession,* 3rd edn (1894), para 796.

C predeceasing, his or her share will be distributed between the remaining survivors.[63]

Example

Q leaves a legacy of '£5,000 to X, Y, and Z'. X predeceased Q. X's share of the legacy will be redistributed to Y and Z. £2,500 will be given to Y and £2,500 will be given to Z.

Each individual in the group or class can be taken as both an institute *and* a conditional institute,[64] as Lord McLaren explained:[65]

> 'Where a legacy or share of succession is given to a plurality of persons collectively, without any words importing a severance of interests, each of the legatees is understood to be instituted in the entire bequest, subject only to the condition of sharing it with any of the others in whom a right may vest.'

In making the bequest in such terms, the testator has somewhat made clear that the surviving members of the group are to take the legacy rather than the share of any predeceasing members falling into the residue or the intestate estate.[66] Whether the doctrine is operable in any given case will depend on whether the legacy is given jointly or severally to the group or class. This can be ascertained by analysing the words used by the testator and applying the test of accretion to the particular terms in which the bequest is phrased. The test is whether words of severance have been used

63 Identifying the beneficiaries may not always be straightforward if the legacy is for example 'to the children of A': see paras **11.5–11.11.**

64 'The right of survivorship may be defined to be the conditional institution of all the individuals of a class who may survive a certain event, consequent upon the failure of those who may die before that event': J McLaren, *The Law of Wills and Succession,* 3rd edn (1894), para 1143. The event may, for example, be the expiry of a liferent when the right of fee vests in the survivors who, as conditional institutes, take the share of any predeceasing member of the class. It may also be attaining a certain age or purifying some other condition. Depending on the wording of the deed, the event may be the testator revoking the legacy to one of the beneficiaries: *Fraser's Trs v Fraser* 1980 SLT 211.

65 J McLaren, *The Law of Wills and Succession,* 3rd edn (1894), para 1300.

66 See *Barber v Findlater* (1835) 13 S 422; *Tulloch v Welsh* (1838) 1 D 94; and *Breadalbane's Trs v Pringle* (1841) 3 D 359.

and accretion will apply only whenever the bequest is expressed in terms that amount to a joint destination.

(b) Joint and several institution

11.21 The use of the word 'jointly' expresses the testator's intention for accretion most clearly[67] but a bequest made in terms such as not to imply a severance of each legatee's interest will imply a *ius accrescendi* in the surviving members of the group.

Example

X bequeaths a legacy of £1,000 'to A and B'. A predeceases the testator. A's share accresces to B, who takes the whole legacy of £1,000.

A legacy to a number of persons will normally be construed as joint and it is only if there is any indication to the contrary that it will be construed as several. In *Andrew's Executors v Andrew's Trustees*[68] a legacy was expressed as being 'to my said sisters Eliza and Alexandrina'. The word 'joint' was not actually used but the fact that there were no words of severance was enough to construe the legacy as joint. One sister had predeceased the testator and her share was held to have accresced to the survivor.

If the legacy is worded in such a way as to include 'words of severance', the legacy will be held to be several. A common situation will be where the testator uses the term 'equally'. The consequence is that each member of the group is entitled only to the proportion of the legacy which he or she originally had.

Example

L leaves a legacy of '£6,000 to M, N, and O, equally between them'. M predeceased L. M's share of the legacy will not be redistributed to N and O. £2,000 will be given to Y and £2,000 will be given to Z. The final £2,000, being M's share, lapses and will fall into the residue of the estate.

67 Stair *Inst* III.8.27; Bell *Prin*, § 1879.
68 1925 SC 844.

The general rule was laid down in *Paxton's Trustees v Cowie*[69] where the Lord President (Inglis) held that it was long settled that:[70]

> 'When a legacy is given to a plurality of persons named or sufficiently described for identification 'equally among them' or 'in equal shares' or 'share and share alike', or in any other language of the same import, each is entitled to his own share and no more, and there is no room for accretion in the event of the predecease of one or more of the legatees. The rule is applicable whether the gift is in liferent or in fee to the whole equally, and whether the subject of the bequest be residue or a sum of fixed amount or corporeal moveables.'

Words of severance will be construed as bequeathing equal shares *only* where the members of the group to whom the legacy is given are named or designed individually. Where the legacy is to a class, such as 'my sons equally between them' or 'the children of B share and share alike', the words of severance will not prevent accretion.

A legacy to more than one legatee will usually be construed as a class gift, not only where the group of legatees are not named individually, but also where they are all related to each other. A legacy to children 'to be divided equally' will be construed as a legacy to whichever members of the class survive at the time of vesting[71] so that the share of a predeceaser will accresce to the others.

In *Muir's Trustees v Muir*[72] the testator had directed his trustees to accumulate the whole residue of his moveable estate 'for behoof of and equally among the children' of his only child until they were 25 or, in the case of granddaughters, until they married, whichever was the sooner. At his death, six grandchildren had been born and two were born after his death. Only one of the granddaughter's born during the testator's life survived him but she died unmarried before the age of 25. Distinguishing *Paxton's Trustees v Cowie*[73] on the ground that the intended legatees were not named or sufficiently described for identification at the testator's death,

69 (1886) 13 R 1191.

70 (1886) 13 R 1191, at 1197.

71 J McLaren, *The Law of Wills and Succession,* 3rd edn (1894), para 1150; *Rutherford v Turnbull* 38 NE 37 (1821); *Douglas v Douglas* (1864) 2 M 1008; and *Lockwood's Trs v Falconer* (1866) 4 M 1036.

72 (1889) 16 R 954.

73 (1886) 13 R 1191.

the court held that the surviving granddaughter's share had not vested in her at that time.[74] Accordingly, her share had accresced to the others and fell to be divided amongst them.[75]

The case also illustrates the fact that predecease need not be the only contingency which brings the doctrine into operation. The legacy may fail to vest for other reasons; here, it was the legatee's failure to purify the suspensive condition that she attain the age of 25 or be married which prevented the legacy from vesting in her.[76]

THE *CONDITIO SI INSTITUTUS SINE LIBERIS DECESSERIT* AND SECTION 6 OF THE 2016 ACT

11.22 The *conditio si institutus sine liberis decesserit* was a doctrine that even if no express provision is made for the contingency of a beneficiary's predecease, the testator would not have intended the legacy to lapse but rather that the legatee's children should take the legacy instead. It was heavily restricted and only applied where the testator had made a legacy to his children or other descendants, alongside any nieces or nephews that the testator had acted as *loco parentis* to them.

The Scottish Law Commission had recommended repealing the common law doctrine and replacement with a new statutory rule.[77] Section 29 of the Succession (Scotland) Act 2016 abolished the application of the *conditio si institutus* for any death on or after 1 November 2016.[78] Consequently, the old common law doctrine will not be discussed here in the interests of space.[79]

74 See paras **13.3–13.6.**

75 See also *Menzies' Factor v Menzies* (1898) 1 F 128 ('to the grandchildren of my brother equally among them share and share alike') and *Roberts' Trs v Roberts* (1903) 5 F 541 ('my sons equally among them').

76 If there had not been such a condition, the fact that two of the children were born after the testator's death would have meant that vesting in the children alive at his death would have been partially defeated by the subsequent birth of others. See para **13.26**.

77 See the discussions in Report *on Succession* (SLC Report No 124, 1990), paras 4.50ff; and Report *on Succession* (SLC Report No 215, 2009), paras 6.22ff.

78 The Succession (Scotland) Act 2016 (Commencement, Transitional and Saving Provisions) Regulations 2016 SSI 2016/210.

79 For further reading on the *conditio si institutus* see J R Scott 'The *Conditio si Institutus*' 1958 *SLT (News)* 229 and the previous edition of this work at paras 9.22–9.30.

For more recent deaths, Section 6 of the 2016 Act was introduced. This rule operates where a legacy has been bequeathed to a descendant of the testator, but that descendant has died but survived by their own issue. It does not apply to predeceased legatees who may be a spouse, cohabitant, collateral, or ascendant of the deceased, or their issue thereof, nor any non-familial legatees such as friends or colleagues. It is limited to the direct descendants of the testator and does not apply to stepchildren or accepted children who have not been formally adopted by the testator.

Where the direct descendant has predeceased, the legatee's own issue (however remote) can claim the legacy instead.

Example

David made a legacy in favour of his son Angus. Angus predeceased David but is survived by his own child, Joe. Joe can receive Angus's legacy.

Section 6 will only operate where there is no wording in the legacy to exclude its application, or evidence that the testator intended otherwise.[80] Determining when s 6 is excluded can be difficult to ascertain from the intentions of the testator alone based on what is available as admissible extrinsic evidence, but in the case of an express destination-over to an alternate legatee, then it is clear that the testator had intended otherwise from the terms of the will itself.

Example

David made a legacy in favour of his son Angus and made his brother Robert a conditional institute. The legacy reads 'to Angus, whom failing Robert'.

Angus predeceased David but is survived by his own child, Joe. Joe cannot use s 6 of the 2016 Act to claim Angus's legacy as David clearly intended that Robert was to receive the legacy instead.[81] This is in contrast to the common law *conditio si institutus*, where it was held that the *conditio* prevailed over express destinations-over.[82]

80 2016 Act, ss 6(2) and 6(3).
81 2016 Act, s 6(3)(b).
82 *Devlin's Trs v Breen* 1945 SC (HL) 27.

In the case of a survivorship clause, for example 'to A and B, or the survivor' s 6 will again be excluded to prevent A or B's descendants from claiming their ancestor's share of the legacy.[83] This contrasts with the common law, whereby a descendant could exclude accretion to the survivor under the *conditio si institutus* and claim their ancestor's original share.[84] Instead, under the current law, the predeceased legatee's share will accresce to the surviving co-legatee and the descendants will have no claim.

How s 6 interacts with implied destinations can seem less clear initially. However, s 6 will take priority over an implied destination, as the share that the issue can receive is 'the share the deceased would have received if alive'.[85]

Example

H leaves a legacy of £10,000 to 'my two daughters, J and S'. J predeceased H but is survived by her own son, P. P is entitled to £5,000 as J's share as if she were alive. Implied accretion of J's share to S is excluded.

If any descendants are entitled to take by virtue of operation of s 6, then they take the same share as their parent would have received.[86] Where there is more than one descendant of the deceased legatee, then the legacy (or share thereof) will be distributed in the same manner as the distribution of the intestate free estate under the Succession (Scotland) Act 1964.[87]

83 2016 Act, s 6(3)(a).

84 Campbell's *Trustee v Campbell* 1915 SC 100; Crosbie's *Trustees v Crosbie* 1927 SC 159; and Mackinnon's *Trustee v Watt* 1933 SLT 192 (OH).

85 2016 Act, s 6(4).

86 2016 Act, s 6(4). As to what constitutes the parent's share, see the treatment in the old law under *Henderson v Henderson* (1890) 17 R 293.

87 2016 Act, s 6(5).

Example

L makes a will leaving her entire estate to 'my children equally between them'. L had two children, M and P. M predeceased L but is survived by two daughters, Q and R.

Under Section 6 of the 2016 Act, a destination-over is implied that Q and R are to inherit M's share. P receives half of the estate, and Q and R receive a quarter share each.

Chapter 12

Restraints on testamentary freedom

INTRODUCTION

12.1 Freedom to exercise the power of testation, or the *testamenti facti*, is not unconstrained, and restraints imposed by law take several forms. Illegality is an obvious restraint since a provision designed to effect an illegal purpose will be void. The rights of spouses, civil partners and children to fixed proportions of the moveable estate in the form of legal rights is another kind of restraint as it limits the amount that a testator can bequeath.[1] Legal restraints on certain other kinds of provision are also imposed either by statute or public policy and also arise intrinsically, in that the terms of the deed may be constrained by the legal effect of other rules and doctrines and by contradictions contained within the deed itself. A provision that fails to conform to restraints imposed on its effects will be invalid, with the consequences of invalidity differing as between the different types of restraint.

The purposes of restraining testamentary freedom are generally to ensure that property passes to a beneficiary absolutely and within a reasonable time of the testator's death; to prevent the testator from making provisions that appear wasteful or vain; and to free a beneficiary from the excessive control of the testator after his or her death. Whereas challenges to a will based on defects in the form and manner of execution are directed to the validity of the deed itself, restraints on testamentary freedom are directed to the substance of the provisions contained in the deed. The validity of provisions, or of conditions attached to bequests, is not determined by the means or circumstances by which the provisions in the deed came into existence but by their effect.

1 See **Ch 4**.

STATUTORY RESTRAINTS

12.2 There are statutory restrictions which apply to a *mortis causa* trust arising in a testamentary document alongside *inter vivos* trusts. These relate: to (1) restricting how long any income arising from trust capital can be accumulated for without it being made over to beneficiaries; and (2) restricting the operation of successive liferents to avoid a trust continuing in perpetuity where no successive beneficiary is able to obtain the fee in the trust property. These restrictions are intended to prevent a testator from being able to 'tie up property long into the future, thus removing the freedom of future generations to do as they wish with [the trust] property.'[2]

As a result of the 'revolution' of the Trusts and Succession (Scotland) Act 2024, these statutory restrictions are to be repealed for trusts (other than charitable trusts) coming into effect after commencement of the Act.[3] In respect of a *mortis causa* trust under a will, the trust will take effect at death. Therefore, new *mortis causa* trusts taking effect after commencement of the 2024 Act will be governed by the new *laissez-faire* system, rather than the restrictive old statutes.[4]

Consequently, it is not proposed to discuss the rules here in light of their imminent repeal, but in respect of extant trusts that pre-date the commencement of the 2024 Act readers are directed to other works on general trust law.[5]

POLICY RESTRAINTS

(1) Legacies that benefit no one

12.3 It appears from a number of cases decided in the nineteenth century that the power of testation must be exercised responsibly and

2 Report *on Trust Law* (SLC Report No 239, 2014), para 18.2.

3 2024 Act, s 45.

4 See Report *on Trust Law* (SLC Report No 239, 2014), para 18.80.

5 See J Kessler and W Grant, *Drafting Trusts and Will Trusts in Scotland,* 2nd edn (2018), Chs 8 and 14 and Report *on Trust Law* (SLC Report No 239, 2014), Ch 18. For an older but still relevant account, see the previous edition of this text at paras 10.2–10.9.

does not extend to the direction of purposes which the court may consider to be wasteful of assets. In both the *McCaig* cases, discussed below, an analogy was made between the terms of the testators' directions and a direction that all the testator's money was to be thrown into the sea; just as the latter would be an abuse of the *testamenti facti*, so was the former. Thus, a general rule of public policy has emerged in relation to testaments that legacies which do not appear to confer a benefit on any particular beneficiary or group of beneficiaries or on the public will be void. Most of the cases in which bequests have been struck down on this ground have involved testators who have directed the erection of memorials to themselves and which the courts have considered to be extravagant, pointless or even risible. While modest memorials will be permitted, such as a headstone and payments for its maintenance, payments which are indefinite and unreasonable will not.[6]

Not all the provisions in this category that have been struck down expressly or exclusively on the basis of public policy; some have been struck down as inconsistent with other legal rules. In *Mackintosh's Judicial Factor v Lord Advocate*,[7] the court made clear that what may be an abuse of the testamentary power or contrary to public policy depends on the circumstances of the case. Here, the testatrix had directed that her entire estate be spent on a mausoleum for herself and her uncle and aunt, who were to be disinterred and re-buried with her. She had been born outwith marriage and, under the law in force at that time, was not legally related to them.[8] The court held that the direction was not an abuse of the *testamenti factio*[9] and that the extent of the expenditure that would be involved was not contrary to public policy. Nevertheless, the direction was struck down on the basis that the testatrix had no authority on which to order her relatives' exhumation.

6 See para **1.24**. In *Lindsay's Exr v Forsyth* 1940 SC 568 the testator directed that a sum of money be spent on placing flowers on her grave in perpetuity and the provision was struck down.

7 1935 SC 406.

8 See paras **2.9–2.10**.

9 The decision was based on English authorities, on which point Lord President Clyde ventured to 'repeat a remark (which I am afraid I have often made) … that I cannot understand why the light which the law of our own country sheds on a question such as this should be deliberately hidden under a bushel of alien authority': *Mackintosh's JF v Lord Advocate* 1935 SC 406 at para 409.

In all cases, however, the public policy element has been implicit if not explicit and clearly directed at preventing a testator from depleting an estate so as to exclude from the succession persons who would otherwise succeed to it. That there is also a clear moral element to the question which was alluded to by Lord President Clyde when he observed that, 'just as a mad person cannot make any will, so a sane person cannot make a mad will'.[10]

The example par excellence of such memorials concerns the McCaig siblings.[11] In the first *McCaig* case,[12] the testator had directed that the income from his estate should be used in perpetuity to build towers and statues of himself and his family on his estate, justifying the expenditure on the ground that it was designed to provide inspiration and encouragement to Scottish artists. His sister challenged his will, and the provision was struck down, on the ground that his heirs in intestacy would be disinherited without any beneficial interest being created in favour of anyone else. Lord Kyllachy stated:[13]

> 'If it is not unlawful, it ought to be unlawful, to dedicate by testamentary disposition … the whole income of a large estate to objects of no utility, private or public, objects which benefit nobody, and which have no other purpose or use than that of perpetuating at great cost, and in an absurd manner, the idiosyncrasies of an eccentric testator.'

He added that there was no rule against 'a testamentary disposition directed to the providing, on a customary and rational scale, of a burial place for a testator or a suitable monument to his memory'.[14] In the event, Lord Kyllachy found the trust purposes to be invalid not on grounds of public policy but on the doctrine that heirs could not be divested of their rights except where a beneficial right was constituted in a third party. He also found that the directions were repugnant, on the basis that the heir's right was postponed to trust purposes which were invalid.[15]

10 *Mackintosh's JF v Lord Advocate* 1936 SC 406, 411.

11 See R Rennie, 'Folly, Guilt and More Folly: The *McCaig Cases*' in J Grant and E Sutherland (eds), *Scots Law Tales* (2010).

12 *McCaig v Glasgow University* 1907 SC 231.

13 Lord Kyllachy cited Bell's *Prin* § 1682 and 1691–1692, *Ross v Ross* (1860) Mor 5019, *Gardner v Ogilvie* (1857) 20 D 105 at 109 and *Neilson v Stewart* (1860) 22 D 646, 650.

14 *McCaig v Glasgow University* 1907 SC 231, 242.

15 See para **12.11**.

Although her case succeeded, the sister then (bizarrely) went on to make almost identical provisions in her own will. In the second *McCaig* case,[16] which concerned her testamentary provisions, a provision for a similar purpose was also struck down, but this time for reasons of public policy since no heirs could be found. The particular principle of public policy articulated by the court was that although a person can do what he or she likes with his or her money during life, this was not the case after his death since the law would not support the useless waste of assets.[17]

In *Aitken's Trustees v Aitken*[18] the testator was the last of a family connected with the burgh for several centuries. He directed that part of Musselburgh High Street be demolished so that a massive statue in bronze, featuring the testator mounted on a horse, could be erected on the site. The Town Council objected to the scheme and the trustees presented a special case to the court to test the validity of the directions. Attempting to reconcile the two grounds of invalidity on which the *McCaig* cases were decided, the court held that a bequest would be invalid if it conferred neither a patrimonial benefit on any person nor a benefit upon the public. 'Public benefit' was to be construed as meaning that the purpose of the bequest was not immoral or contrary to public order. In this case, the court held that although 'interest in one's ancestors and pride in one's ability to trace them for many generations, and in their respectability if not their distinction, is a typical, and in some respects a not unlaudable, trait of the Scottish character', the provisions of the deed were 'an irrational, futile and selfdestructive scheme to carry out not unreasonable purposes'.[19] By contrast, in *Campbell Smith's Trustees v Scott*,[20] a bequest of a large amount of money to build a monument to commemorate an army regiment was held to be neither extravagant nor contrary to public policy. It appears therefore that the individual to be memorialised must have been especially distinguished if such memorials are to be permitted.

Memorials to the testator need not necessarily take the form of statues and mausoleums. In *Sutherland's Trustees v Verschoyle*,[21] the testatrix

16 *McCaig's Trs v Kirk-Session of United Free Church of Lismore* 1915 SC 426.
17 *McCaig's Trs v Kirk-Session of United Free Church of Lismore* 1915 SC 426, 438.
18 1927 SC 374.
19 1927 SC 374, per Lord Sands at 381 and 383.
20 1944 SLT 198.
21 1968 SLT 43.

directed that her 'valuable art collection' be housed, arranged and displayed in perpetuity. This entailed purchasing a building especially for the purpose and employing a resident caretaker. The art collection was described as 'a heterogeneous conglomeration with no group of material sufficient to provide or illustrate any historical or educational theme such as might attract scholar, student or even the general public'[22] and was worth only about £12,000. The court agreed with the principle expressed in the *McCaig* cases that while only in exceptional cases should it interfere with the expressed wishes of a testator, in this case the direction was wasteful and thus contrary to public policy.

(2) Invalid conditions

12.4 A bequest may be given conditionally as well as unconditionally, and, as in the case of bequests which do not appear to benefit anyone, the conditions which may be attached to bequests may be struck down as contrary to public policy.[23] Again, certain sorts of conditions may be seen as an unacceptable abuse of the testator's power. Conditions which may be invalid relate to the placing of unacceptable restraints on the freedom of the beneficiary, but they differ from provisions that are repugnant in that they do not relate to the freedoms associated with rights of ownership and are not incompatible with them. Rather, they attempt to restrict the beneficiary's personal freedom.

The types of conditions which have this effect are potestative conditions; that is, conditions which make the beneficiary's right to the gift contingent on the performance of an act which is within his or her power to perform.[24] A condition will not be enforced if it is incompatible with ideas of morality or public policy or because it is in fact or in law impossible. For example, in *Miller, Petitioners*,[25] the testator had provided that the beneficiaries

22 1968 SLT 43, per Lord Justice-Clerk Grant at 46.

23 See J Chalmers, 'Testamentary Conditions and Public Policy' in K Reid et al (eds), *Exploring the Law of Succession: Studies National, Historical and Comparative* (2007).

24 Bell states that 'conditions physically impossible are in settlements held to be *pro non scripto*. And if unlawful or *contra bonos mores* they are regarded by law as impossible', *Prin* § 1785.

25 *Miller Petrs* 1977 SLT 67.

were to 'always provide a home for me during the remaining years of my life'. The court held that this condition had been satisfied when the testatrix died in hospital without taking up residence in the home which the beneficiaries were willing and able to make available for her.

Impossibility, in this context, includes the promotion of an illegal or immoral purpose, so that the act simply cannot be performed by the beneficiary in conformity with law. In some cases, the terms in which the condition is expressed may mean that the intention of the testator is radically uncertain, so that it cannot be known what performance would actually entail.

(a) The effect of invalidity

12.5 The attachment of an invalid condition to a legacy does not render the legacy void (and thus not payable to the beneficiary); rather, the condition is treated as *pro non scripto* and the legacy is given effect to as if the condition did not exist. McLaren states the position:[26]

> 'In the jurisprudence of Scotland, it is a universal rule that a bequest or voluntary provision, coupled with an unlawful or impossible condition, is effectual, the condition being held either *pro non scripto* or treated as satisfied because the executor or legatee has done all that is possible to satisfy the testator's requirement.'

Thus, an invalid condition will be treated in one of two ways, depending on whether purification by the beneficiary is possible; possible, in this context, meaning not only that the beneficiary can actually perform the condition but also, more broadly, that it is not illegal or *contra bonos mores*.

If purification is possible, it is enough that the beneficiary has done everything in his or her power to purify it by the date of vesting.[27] In

26 J McLaren, *The Law of Wills and Succession,* 3rd edn (1894), para 1094, following Erskine *Inst* III.3.84: 'No person can lay himself under an obligation to perform what is naturally impossible; or to do any immoral or unlawful action, which is said to be legally impossible; because what is forbidden, either by the rule of reason or by positive institution, is, in the consideration of law, out of our power.'

27 A potestative condition does not postpone vesting, only a suspensive condition has this effect; see **Ch 13**.

this case, the condition will be treated as purified, and the legacy will be payable. Alternatively, if it is impossible for the beneficiary to purify the condition – either because it is outwith his or her power to perform it or it is illegal or *contra bonos mores* – the condition will be treated as *pro non scripto*. For example, in *Simpson v Roberts*[28] the testator had bequeathed a liferent to her housekeeper-companion on condition that she would still be in her service at the date of her death; and, should the testator be survived by her husband, the beneficiary was required to be still in his service. The husband survived the testatrix and, on his remarriage, dismissed the beneficiary. The court held that the condition was potestative; the employee had done all in her power to fulfil it, and it had been frustrated by the act of the husband. Accordingly, she was deemed to have satisfied the condition. Similarly, where the beneficiary's right to a legacy was conditional upon caring for any of his pets but, at his death, the testator did not own any pets, the court held that since fulfilment of the condition was impossible, the legacy was payable as if the condition had been met. Only if the testator had in fact owned a pet and the beneficiary had refused to care for it would the condition have been enforceable.[29]

(b) Construction of conditions

12.6 It may be a matter of construction whether the direction contains a condition which is impossible to fulfil (in which case the legacy will be payable) or a trust purpose which has failed (in which case it will not). In *Dunbar v Scott's Trustees*,[30] the testator had directed his trustees to pay £2,000 to A if he, the testator, had not already purchased him a commission in the Army before his death. The purchase of Army commissions was abolished before the testator's death. The question of whether the money was payable to A depended on how the testator's intention was to be construed. Did he intend it to be a condition of the legacy that A purchase a commission? If so, purification of the condition was impossible: it would be treated as *pro non scripto* and the money paid to A. Alternatively, was

28 *Simpson v Roberts* 1931 SC 259.

29 *Watson v National Children's Home* (1995) 92(37) LSG 24.

30 *Dunbar v Scott's Trs* (1872) 10 M 982.

the money to be paid to A in order to fulfil a particular trust purpose? If so, the purpose had failed and A had no right to the money. The court held that the testator could be presumed to have intended the money to be payable since the purchase of commissions had been abolished in his lifetime. If this was not what he intended, he could have changed his will.

It is also a matter of construction whether a condition is truly a condition or merely a wish. If it is merely a wish, it will be precatory and the question of whether or not the condition is enforceable will be irrelevant.[31]

(c) Grounds of invalidity

12.7 There is sometimes an overlap between provisions that are unenforceable on grounds of public policy or morality, and provisions which are uncertain.[32] A condition that is unenforceable *prima facie* may be struck down not because it is *contra bonos mores* but because it is so vague that its meaning cannot be ascertained. Holding that a condition is uncertain means that it is unnecessary for the court to set out what it considers the requirements of morality or public policy to actually involve. Where, for example, a condition attached to a legacy does not actually prohibit the marriage of the beneficiary but attempts to impose conditions about the qualities of the prospective spouse, this may be seen as uncertain rather than contrary to public policy, and the effect will be that the condition is treated as *pro non scripto*. If the condition in question is valid, it is sufficient that it has been purified at the time of vesting and it follows that if the act that is the condition of acquiring the right to the legacy is of a continuing nature, the beneficiary is entitled to observe the condition or not, as he or she chooses, once the legacy has vested.

The kinds of conditions that have been considered judicially can be categorised according to the types of acts by the beneficiary that the testator has attempted to control.

(i) Marriage

12.8 Conditions which relate to the choice of a beneficiary's spouse or which attempt to restrict or interfere in marital relationships are nearly

31 See para **10.3**.

32 See para **12.3**.

always unenforceable. A condition which places an absolute prohibition on the marriage of the beneficiary will be struck down.[33] A legacy for the benefit of an unmarried child will not be struck down if being single is not a condition of the legacy but is merely descriptive of the person who is the intended beneficiary or purposive in that it confers a benefit on children while they remain unmarried.[34] Similarly, it is a valid condition of a liferent that it continues only as long as the liferenter remains unmarried,[35] and it is a common and valid condition of a liferent that it terminates on the re-marriage as well as on the death of the liferenter.

It might seem surprising today to encounter a condition restricting a beneficiary's right to marry a particular person or class of person, but it is not outwith the bounds of possibility. There are a number of English cases on this issue,[36] mostly relating to prohibitions on marrying a person of a specified religion or nationality.[37] A condition that confers a benefit on spouses only if they remain apart will be unenforceable[38] but a condition aimed at conferring a benefit on spouses who remain together will not. In *Barker v Watson's Trustees*,[39] the testator directed in a codicil to his will that if, at the time of his death, his daughter was not reconciled with her husband, the legacy to her children was to be considerably reduced. In a second codicil, he amplified his intention by stating that by 'reconciled' he meant 'living together as man and wife'. At the date of the second codicil and the testator's death, the daughter was residing in an institution where she was receiving treatment for her addiction to laudanum. She had been

33 J McLaren, *The Law of Wills and Succession*, 3rd edn (1894), para 1096 states that restraints on marriage which amount to a total prohibition in either form or effect are illegal. See also *Ommanney v Douglas* (1796) 3 Pat 448; *Aird's Exors v Aird* 1949 SC 154; *Young v Johnson and Wright* (1880) 7 R 760.

34 *Sturrock v Rankin's Trs* (1875) 2 R 850. *Cf* the decision of Lord Justice-Clerk Alness in *Barker's Trs* 1929 SC 109 at 117.

35 *Kidd v Kidd's Trs* (1863) 2 M 227; *Smith's Trs v Smith* (1883) 10 R 1144.

36 *Perrin v Lyon, Lyon v Geddes* (1807) 9 East 170, LC; *McKenna v Bank of Ireland* [1947] IR 277; *Clayton v Ramsden* [1943] AC 320, HL; *Re Selby's Will Trusts, Donn v Selby* [1965] 3 All ER 386.

37 It has been argued that the Scottish courts would interpret such conditions in a similar way to the courts in England. See Wilson and Duncan, *Trusts, Trustees and Executors*, 2nd edn (1995), 110.

38 *Re Moore, Trafford v Maconochie* (1888) 39 Ch D 116, CA. In Scotland, it is more likely to be held to be *contra bonos mores*.

39 *Barker v Watson's Trs* 1919 SC 109.

admitted before her father's death and her husband had told her that return to him was impossible 'unless the laudanum habit is broken for ever', and he was threatening to begin proceedings for a separation unless it was. Their child brought an action on the basis that, his mother's situation being what it was, the condition in the will was either *contra bonos mores* or impossible and should be held to be *pro non scripto*. By a majority, the court held that, by looking at all the facts and even in taking a generous construction of the deed, the condition was valid.

(ii) Residence

12.9 Conditions which attempt to restrict the freedom of an individual, either by placing a prohibition on his or her living at a particular address or with a particular person, or, conversely, stipulating that they should, may be invalid. It all depends on the circumstances of the case and whether or not it is reasonable to insist that the beneficiary comply with the condition. In *Reid v Coates*,[40] the testator gave a legacy to his nephew subject to the condition that he would not live with his mother. Since the condition involved nothing unlawful, the condition was allowed to stand. In *Fraser v Rose*,[41] by contrast, the testator made a legacy to his daughter conditional on her ceasing to live with or in any respect be under the influence of her mother. The court held the condition to be *contra bonos mores* since not only was the character of the mother 'pure and irreproachable' but the condition was contrary to the Commandment to 'honour thy father and mother'. More pragmatically, the court noted that, without the benefit of the legacy, the daughter would be destitute.[42]

Whether a condition as to residence is held to be *contra bonos mores* also appears to depend on whether the parties involved are related to one another. If they are not, the condition seems more likely to be allowed to stand. In *Balfour's Trustees v Johnston*[43] the condition that the testator's daughter cease to communicate with or take an interest in an orphan

40 *Reid v Coates* 5 Mar 1813 FC.

41 *Fraser v Rose* (1849) 11 D 1467.

42 See also *Grant's Trs v Grant* (1898) 25 R 929, where a condition that a young beneficiary did not live with her parents was struck down as *contra bonos mores*.

43 *Balfour's Trs v Johnston* 1936 SC 137.

whom she had taken into her home was held to be valid. Lord President Normand stated *obiter* that no authority had been cited before the court:[44]

> 'Which would justify us in extending the principles applicable to the relationship between parent and child to an association between parties between whom no tie of blood exists, and it is obvious that different considerations apply to the two cases.'

Since the test of the enforceability of a condition is whether its fulfilment is dependent on the beneficiary doing something that is in his or her power to do, the condition may be valid when it relates to doing something regarding another person. In *Wemyss v Wemyss's Trustees*,[45] the testator directed that his son should not allow his mother, the testator's divorced wife, to reside on the estate; after considering its reasonableness, the court held this to be a valid condition. A positive direction that a beneficiary should reside in a particular place may also be valid. The question of what 'reside' actually means leaves the issue open to uncertainty but, at the same time, the test of residence, while not necessarily easy to satisfy, may not be particularly strict,[46] and the term 'occupy' has been interpreted without difficulty.[47]

INTRINSIC RESTRAINTS

(1) Legal rights

12.10 Legal rights are a restraint on testamentary freedom in that, technically, a testator is free to bequeath only the dead's part of his or her moveable estate.[48] Since spouses, civil partners and children (or remoter issue) have automatic rights to a share in the moveable estate that vests on the death of the testator by way of *ius relicti*, *ius relictae*, rights under s 131 of the Civil Partnership Act 2004 and legitim, the effect is that any

44 *Balfour's Trs v Johnston* 1936 SC 137, 143

45 *Wemyss v Wemyss's Trs* 1921 SC 30.

46 McLaren states that 'we incline to think that a condition enjoining residence in a particular place is lawful, on the principle that the testator may desire his representative to keep up a connection with the locality of his choice, and that the condition is sufficiently complied with by having a home or place of residence in the locality, and occasionally visiting it': *The Law of Wills and Succession*, 3rd edn (1894), para 1095.

47 *Veitch's Exr v Veitch* 1947 SLT 17.

48 See **Ch 3**.

bequests of moveable estate that exceed the dead's part are, potentially, liable to ademption.[49] Legal rights may thus be seen as a limited form of 'forced heirship', common to continental legal systems where a portion of the deceased's estate is reserved for his or her spouse or partner or issue, the portion and the entitlement of persons in family relationships with the deceased depending on the particular legal system.

(2) Repugnancy

12.11 The doctrine of repugnancy applies where the testator has attempted to restrict the beneficiary's rights in a way which is inconsistent with the vesting of their unqualified right to demand the transfer of ownership of the property.[50] It is most likely to arise where the deceased has created a trust. Where: (i) a legacy gives the legatee a right as a beneficiary under a trust, and (ii) the right vests in a legatee of full age, but (iii) the truster has directed the trustees to retain ownership or control of the property, the direction may be repugnant and, accordingly, invalid.

For example, if a sum of entrusted money is bequeathed to a beneficiary who has reached the age of 18 at the time the legacy vests,[51] but the bequest includes a direction to trustees that the money is not to be paid until he or she reaches the age of 25, the beneficiary can simply demand payment immediately and seek to vary the terms of the trust.[52] Where the terms of a bequest are held to be repugnant, the effect is the same as if an invalid condition had been attached; its terms will be construed so as to give effect to it as if the repugnancy did not exist.

A legacy of an alimentary *fee* is a contradiction and therefore repugnant, because a fee (that is to say, ownership, or the right to acquire ownership depending on the context) entitles the beneficiary to dispose of the property or otherwise deal with it as he or she wishes.[53] Only an alimentary *liferent*

49 See paras **10.15–10.18**.

50 A beneficiary may acquire a vested right subject to a resolutive condition; in this case, the right vests subject to defeasance and therefore does not conform to the tests laid down in *Yuill's Trs v Thomson* (1902) 4 F 815: see paras **13.20–13.25**.

51 See **Ch 11**.

52 Trusts and Succession (Scotland) Act 2024, s 58.

53 *Douglas-Hamilton v Duke and Duchess of Hamilton's Trs* 1961 SC 205; *Wilkie's Trs v Wight's Trs* (1893) 21 R 199; and *Watson's Trs v Watson* 1913 SC 1133.

will entitle trustees to administer the income bequeathed to a liferenter beyond the liferenter's control (albeit the liferenter can seek to vary or terminate the trust).[54] A direction that a legacy of a fee is given for alimentary use only will therefore be repugnant if this means that a legacy of the fee is to be administered on behalf of a person who has acquired a vested right to it. The only exception is if the beneficiary is under 18 because he or she has no right to demand payment until reaching full age.[55] A direction to trustees to buy an annuity or other property for the beneficiary will also be repugnant unless it is for the alimentary use of the beneficiary.[56] In this case, the legacy will be of an alimentary liferent. If there are no trustees, it is incompetent for an executor to purchase such an annuity using bequeathed property since vesting of the legacy in the beneficiary means that he or she is entitled to demand payment from the executor and to deal freely with the property as they choose. If the executor were to buy an annuity the beneficiary could, accordingly, sell the annuity for its cash value.[57] The same applies to directions to buy or sell any heritable property for the beneficiary; he or she is entitled to payment of the capital value of the legacy instead.[58]

(3) Distinguishing conditional gifts and repugnancy

12.12 The interaction of conditional gifts and repugnancy can tend to be confused. Where a condition on the legacy is imposed, the right of the beneficiary is contingent in some way; if the condition is potestative, for example, it is conditional upon the performance of some act by the beneficiary, provided that this is possible.

By contrast, where a legacy is repugnant, the beneficiary's right to the legacy is not conditional in any such way but is absolute. What may render a legacy as repugnant is that the testator has made directions as to the manner in which the subject of the legacy is to be used or managed and

54 Trusts and Succession (Scotland) Act 2024, s 62.

55 However, see s 24 of the Trusts and Succession (Scotland) Act 2024 which gives trustees a default discretionary power to advance capital.

56 *Branford's Trs v Powell* 1924 SC 439.

57 *Brown's Trs v Thom* 1916 SC 32, 1915 2 SLT 278; and *Dempster's Trs v Dempster* 1921 SC 332.

58 See para **4.14**.

has, therefore, attempted to restrict the normal incidents of unqualified ownership which the beneficiary has a vested right to receive.[59] For example, if a testator leaves a legacy of property in which ownership will pass without any qualification to the legatee – then the legatee should have the full incidents of ownership to the property bequeathed. If the testator then makes further provision in their will stipulating that the property so bequeathed is to be redistributed on the legatee's death to another party, then this is a contradiction with the legatee's unqualified right of ownership given it has restricted one of the main incidents of ownership, namely the power to bequeath it.[60] Consequently, the provision is repugnant.

On the other hand, if a testator has attached conditions to the legacy, then any conditions attached to that direction become conditions of the gift itself.[61] Consequently, the legacy is not unqualified and the conditions cannot, therefore, be repugnant.

What may look, at first sight, like a repugnant gift may not be at all if the gift was never intended to be unconditional.[62] Thus, if a legatee is bequeathed a legacy of a house on the condition that it is to be subject to a liferent in favour of another – this condition is not repugnant with the legatee's ownership. In that example, the legatee's powers of management over the property may be restricted in some way by the existence of the liferent, but this is part of the qualified right of ownership that the testator has made provision for in their will. In itself, this is not repugnant with the bequeathed right as the testator did not intend to give the legatee unencumbered ownership.

In *Gore-Browne-Henderson's Trustees v Grenfell*,[63] the testator had disponed his whole estate to trustees. One of the directions to trustees was a direction to convey certain heritable property to a cousin 'absolutely', but subject to the condition that the trustees were to offer a lease of the property to a suitable tenant, the tenant to be selected by the North of Scotland Agricultural College. Since the gift to the beneficiary was not unqualified, it was not repugnant. Further, the testator had not made a direct gift to the beneficiary but a disposition to the trustees in order to

59 See *Nathan v Leonard* [2003] 4 All ER 198.

60 See the facts of Cochrane's Executrix v Cochrane 1947 SC 134.

61 *Donaldson's Trs v Macdougall* (1860) 22 D 1527, at 1541.

62 Scott-May and others v Scott-May [2024] SC PER 13.

63 *Gore-Browne-Henderson's Trs v Grenfell* 1968 SC 73.

carry out trust purposes and the beneficiary's right was subject to those trust purposes being carried out.

A condition attached to the gift may operate to suspend vesting rather than merely qualify it.[64] Since the beneficiary cannot acquire an indefeasible right to the legacy until the condition has been fulfilled and, again, the bequest will not be repugnant. For example, in *Derek Green v Daniel Graham Harrison,*[65] a testator had bequeathed heritage to his two sons, A and B, equally between them and the survivor of them. The bequest was subject to the condition that if both survived him, A should have the right to purchase B's half share, to be exercised within one year of the testator's death and at a price specified in the deed. In a codicil, the testator then added to the bequest the condition that if A was unmarried at the date of the testator's death, A should have a right of occupancy of the house without prejudice to his right to purchase B's share within one year. A was in fact married at the date of the testator's death. The question for the court was whether the bequest was repugnant, in that A's option to purchase B's share was inconsistent with B's unqualified right to obtain ownership which vested in him at the testator's death. It held that vesting was postponed until the expiry of the one-year period and, therefore, there was no repugnancy.

(4) Exception to repugnancy

12.13 Even if it is clear that the beneficiary has been given a vested, unqualified and indefeasible right but directions to trustees contradict the terms of the gift, it may be that the bequest is not repugnant but that the single exception to the rule applies. That is, where other trust purposes cannot be secured without retention of the property by the trustees, the direction remains valid and payment of the beneficiary's right may be deferred. If trustees are directed to hold capital on behalf of the beneficiary until certain trust purposes are fulfilled, the word 'hold' will *prima facie* denote the existence of a trust and not a direct right for the beneficiary to obtain ownership; in this case, the terms of the bequest are not contradictory,

64 See paras **13.6–13.8**.

65 *Derek Green v Daniel Graham Harrison* (7 December 1983, unreported), OH.

and there is no repugnancy.[66] In *Miller's Trustees v Miller*, the court held that, although the court will always try to relieve a beneficiary of any trust management that is cumbrous, unnecessary, or expensive:[67]

> 'Where there are trust purposes to be served which cannot be secured without the retention of the vested estate or interest of the beneficiary in the hands of the trustees, the rule cannot be applied, and the right of the beneficiary must be subordinated to the will of the testator. This is a necessary qualification, because there may be contingent liabilities, the amount of which cannot be precisely ascertained, and for which it may be necessary to retain such a sum as the trustees judge to be sufficient.'

This decision was affirmed in *Yuill's Trustees v Thomson*,[68] where the court held that for the rule to apply three conditions had to be met. First, the initial gift should be absolute and unqualified; second, the right should be indefeasibly vested in the beneficiary; and third, there should be no trust purposes that can be secured only by retention of the property by trustees. If all of these criteria are met and the bequest does impose a direction which is inconsistent with the legacy, the beneficiary has the right to claim payment or demand a conveyance as soon as he or she reaches the age of 18 and the direction to trustees will be invalid. If the testator does not wish the beneficiary to take the legacy until a later age, provisions should be made in the deed to suspend vesting of the right until that time.[69]

(5) Uncertainty

12.14 Whether or not the substance of a provision is uncertain is primarily a matter of construction of the deed. If it is impossible to construe a deed so as to deduce what the testator intended, a single provision, or indeed the deed itself, may be challenged. When a legacy is a universal settlement, so that the whole estate is bequeathed to one person, the entire deed may be void from uncertainty if that person cannot be ascertained or identified. For example, in *Wood v Wood's Executrix*[70] a testament was

66 *Veitch's Trs v Rutherford* 1914 SC 182.
67 *Miller's Trs v Miller* (1890) 18 R 301, per the Lord President at 305.
68 *Yuill's Trs v Thomson* (1902) 4 F 815 at 819.
69 See paras **13.4–13.6**.
70 *Wood v Wood's Exrx* 1995 SLT 563, OH.

reduced as being void from uncertainty on the ground that, apart from the appointment of his sister as executor, the testator's sole provision was 'I give everything I have to her to share out as she knows I would wish it.' On the basis that only a testator has the power to bequeath his or her own property to others, devolution of the power to test in its entirety will render the deed void. On the same basis, a particular provision within the deed may also be void from uncertainty.[71]

The court will, however, attempt to give effect to a direction wherever possible, by construing the bequest strictly within the terms of the deed itself rather than by reference to other branches of the law, including the law of contract. In *Shepherd's Trustee*,[72] the testators had given a pre-emptive right to their eldest son to buy their house after their deaths and had further stated that he should have 'not less than five years to pay up the balance of the price'. If he declined the offer, the house should then be offered to his two younger brothers, in order of their age. His brothers argued that the declaration regarding payment of the price was void from uncertainty since it would be impossible for the executor to frame an offer which would satisfy the requirements for certainty of a contract of sale. The court held that the question was not to be resolved by looking at what would constitute a valid contract under that branch of the law. Rather, the test was of whether the executor, approaching the matter with proper care and properly advised, would be able to carry such an instruction out;[73] in the instant case, there would be no such difficulty.

71 *Salvesen's Trs v Wye* 1954 SC 440.

72 *Shepherd's Trustee* 2003 SC 345.

73 Following the test in *Hood v Macdonald's Trustee* 1949 SC 24.

Chapter 13

Vesting

INTRODUCTION

13.1 Without dashing the reader's hopes of an easy or quick chapter, it is worthwhile to begin the discussion on vesting with the observations on the area by Professor George Gretton:[1]

> 'The stage in the university course when the law of vesting must be considered has traditionally been one of unhappiness for lecturer and student alike. The lecturer begins by saying that the subject is one of considerable difficulty and frequent obscurity, while the student is perplexed and hopes that that subject will not be examined.'

Despite its complexity, the law of vesting serves an important purpose in property law by identifying when a person has obtained a right in their patrimony. It is of particular importance in succession law in determining when a beneficiary of an estate has obtained a right in respect of the deceased's property such that they can lawfully demand the property be transferred to them. However, beyond this bare explanation, the definition of vesting itself is rather troublesome.[2]

Vesting of succession rights has been defined as the point in which the beneficiary of an estate obtains 'a right of property'.[3] One would argue that this definition does not work as it implies the beneficiary acquires some form of real right in the property, which would certainly not accord with modern understandings of trust and succession law, nor of general property law, in Scotland.[4] More controversially, it has been said that

1 G Gretton, 'What is vesting?' (1986) 31(6) *JLSS* 148, 148.

2 The term 'vest' itself derives from the Latin *vestire* ('to clothe with' or 'put on' a garment). Note, that vesting is not a concept unique to the law of succession; vesting occurs whenever something is acquired by a person who did not have rights over it previously, including *inter vivos* transfers such as sale, gift or assignation.

3 *Haldane's Trs v Murphy* (1881) 9 R 269, per Lord Young at 295.

4 In respect of the right of a beneficiary under a trust, see K Reid, 'Patrimony Not Equity: The Trust in Scotland' in R Valsan (ed), *Trusts and Patrimonies,* (2017), 122–23.

vesting involves 'the creation in a beneficiary of rights of ownership or *dominium* in property which formerly comprised part of the estate of a deceased person'.[5] This definition does not make sense, for what is the point in an executor obtaining ownership through confirmation to manage and distribute an estate if the beneficiaries already hold the right of ownership? The law of vesting is an area which academics and the wider legal community have grappled with for some time.[6]

It is not proposed to reopen debates here, but in succession law, vesting might be said to be the moment when a beneficiary acquires a right within their patrimony. It is, in most cases, a personal right that vests rather than a real right, or ownership.[7] The personal right is enforceable against the executor to demand payment or transfer of the property so that they can obtain ownership. No single perfect definition may be possible, but at the very least, vesting is when a beneficiary acquires a right in their patrimony. The exact classification of the right may be debated but, in most cases, it is not ownership that vests under the law of succession, but a personal right to demand a conveyance or payment of the subject from the executor. For example, if X leaves a legacy of '£10,000 to A', it should not be open to A to simply appear at X's bank, claim they are the owner, and withdraw the monies from their account (irrespective of the practice or policy of the bank). The monies must be paid to them by the executor. Similarly, if Y in his will leaves 'my Ming vase to B', it would seem perverse that B could attend the deceased Y's home and remove the vase without any approval by the executor.

Without a clearer authority on the issue, the debates in this area will continue, and inconsistencies in definitions and reasoning can be found amongst the various sources on vesting in Scots law. The inconsistencies give rise to the subject's complexity as many older authorities often do not

5 'Wills and Succession', Volume 25 in *The Laws of Scotland: Stair Memorial Encyclopaedia*, para 902.

6 See the 'vesting debate' of the 1980s: G Gretton, 'What is vesting?' (1986) 31(6) *JLSS* 148; G Maher, 'The rights and wrongs of vesting' (1986) 31(10) *JLSS* 396; W Gordon, 'The wrongs and rights of vesting' (1987) 32(6) *JLSS* 281; H Patrick, 'What is a real right in Scots law?' (1988) 33(3) *JLSS* 98; and S Styles, 'Vesting and the law of property' (1989) 34(9) *JLSS* 338.

7 This author ascribes to the theory of Gretton in G Gretton, 'What is vesting?' (1986) 31(6) *JLSS* 148.

speak of vesting in a way in which modern property law is now understood to be.

SPES SUCCESSIONIS

13.2 Until vesting has occurred, a (prospective) beneficiary of an estate has merely a *spes successionis* – a 'chance of acquiring a right in the subject'.[8] Although a *spes* may be assigned,[9] the prospective beneficiary has no right to demand payment or transfer of the property under a *spes* (though they may seek to enforce breaches of trust)[10] and the right to succeed will not form part of their estate if they die before the right vests in them.

At vesting, a hope of succession becomes a right of succession. It is at the moment of vesting that a contingent, or expectant, right becomes concretised and the right vests in the beneficiary's patrimony. As an example, whilst a testator is alive, a legatee cannot demand payment of a legacy under the testator's will because they have a mere *spes* rather than a concretised right until the testator's death. Should the testator change their will and revoke the legacy, the *spes* 'flies off' and vanishes, and the legatee has no right to the property formerly bequeathed after the testator's death.[11]

THE SUBJECT AND TIMING OF VESTING

13.3 In most cases, vesting of a right of succession in a beneficiary's patrimony takes place on the death of the person from whom the succession

8 RC Henderson *The Principles of Vesting in the Law of Succession*, 2nd edn (1938), 1.

9 Moveable Transactions (Scotland) Act 2023, s 1(4) (note that s 61 excludes from the definition of 'claim' a non-monetary right relating to land, thus a *spes* concerning a right to succeed to heritable property is excluded from the operation of the 2023 Act and governed by the common law, see *Reid v Morison* (1893) 20 R 510, per Lord Rutherfurd Clark at 512). On the wider common law position, see *Trappes v Meredith* (1871) 10 M 38, per Lord President at 40; *Carter v McIntosh* (1862) 24 D 925 per Lord Kinloch at 931; and W Wilson and A Duncan, *Trusts, Trustees and Executors,* 2nd edn (1995), paras 10-38–10-43.

10 See *Rae v Meek* (1889) 16 R HL 31.

11 Though see the difficulties where a contract to test has been utilised, and potential remedies open to a disappointed legatee in such cases, see para **7.12**.

opens (whether testate or intestate). The beneficiary acquires a personal right to succeed, which is enforceable against the future executor, who will not yet be confirmed to the estate. While vesting undoubtedly creates a right in a beneficiary, it cannot be said to vest ownership until or unless the subject is actually delivered or conveyed to them and ownership is transferred.[12] Further, vesting of the right and payment of the subject of the legacy may not take place simultaneously and, in some cases, the beneficiary may not be entitled to delivery or payment until some considerable time after the right has vested.

The practical effect of vesting of a right in a beneficiary's patrimony is that it gives rise to a series of rights and obligations. As observed by Lord Young in *Haldane's Trs v Murphy*,[13] a question of vesting is always 'a question of capacity to transmit and, as far as I know, never had or can have any other practical significance'. Thus, a beneficiary's vested right becomes attachable by creditors, even if its payment is postponed to some future date[14] and a vested right will form part of the beneficiary's estate if he or she dies before delivery or payment.[15]

Although the general presumption is that vesting takes place *a morte testatoris*, on the death of the testator, the resolution of 'hard cases' has involved the creation of rules which permit other possibilities; namely postponed, intermediate and defeasible vesting. Cases in which such problems have arisen necessarily involve legacies with suspensive or resolutive conditions attached; further, most of the cases of this kind

12 The beneficiary does not acquire a real right in heritable property until title has been registered, or in corporeal moveables until delivered, whether actually or constructively. There is also a nice question about ownership of the property during the *haereditas jacens* when an executor has not yet obtained confirmation. Clearly, however, the estate cannot vest in an executor prior to confirmation unless the deceased has employed a trust disposition and settlement, see K Reid, *The Law of Property in Scotland*, 2nd edn (2026), para 1211. The consequence is that although a right may vest in a beneficiary *a morte*, the beneficiary has no one from whom to obtain a valid title until that time. Whether this issue will be considered in greater detail by the Scottish Law Commission's executry law project remains to be seen.

13 (1881) 9 R 269 at 295. Similarly, Lord Fullerton stated in *Newton v Thomson* (1849) 11 D 452 at 456 that, in less technical language, vesting meant simply 'any power of disposal'.

14 *Jamieson v Clark* (1872) 10 M 399.

15 See para **4.3**. See also G Gretton and W McBryde 'Sequestration and the *spes seccessionis*' (2000) 4(2) *Edin LR* 129–146.

have occurred where the estate is the subject of a continuing trust and the ultimate beneficiary has died before the date of payment of a legacy.[16] It may then fall to be established, retrospectively, whether he or she died holding a vested right, or a merely contingent right or *spes*. This will then determine the destination of the right; that is, whether it is vested in the primary beneficiary, will vest in a secondary or alternate beneficiary, falls to residue, or lapses into intestacy.

DISTINGUISHING BETWEEN VESTING AND PAYMENT, AND POSTPONEMENT OF VESTING AND PAYMENT

13.4 It is important to distinguish between two key dates: (i) the date of vesting, when the beneficiary receives a right to succeed to a subject; and (ii) the date that a beneficiary is entitled to demand payment or transfer of that subject. In the normal case, these are (in principle) simultaneous and occur at the point in which a person dies and the succession to their estate opens.[17] Since a person dying intestate has not expressed any testamentary intention for the relevant property falling into intestacy, his or her intention is presumed by law to be in accordance with the rules set out in the Succession (Scotland) Act 1964, so that vesting of prior rights and rights to the intestate estate is also *a morte* alongside legal rights. However, in the case of testate succession, the testator may have modified the date of vesting or the date of payment of legacies. It is open to a testator to: (i) postpone the date of vesting; (ii) postpone the date of payment or transfer of the property; or (iii) postpone both.

16 A simple bequest 'to A in liferent and B in fee' does not in itself prevent vesting of the right to the fee *a morte*: *Carleton v Thomson* (1867) 5 M (HL) 151, per Lord Colonsay at 154. Only if a suspensive condition is attached will this be the case. See paras **13.13–13.17.**

17 In practical terms, a lapse of time between vesting and payment is inevitable in every executry. An estate will remain as a *haereditas jacens* until the executor obtains confirmation (if at all) and the beneficiary will have no person in order to enforce their personal right against during this period. Additionally, an executor must normally wait six months after death before payment of any legacies can be made in order to ensure that all claims by creditors have been settled and payment of legacies will in most case be made at that point, see **4.29**.

(1) Vesting

13.5 As noted above, in the normal case, vesting occurs *a morte testatoris*, on the death of the testator. However, it is entirely possible for the testator to postpone vesting of the right until the occurrence of a specified event or condition being satisfied.

(2) Payment

13.6 Even if a right has vested, it is open to the testator to modify the date of entitlement to payment or transfer of the property. It does not necessarily follow that vesting of the right will automatically mean that the beneficiary is entitled to payment or transfer of the subject of that right at the same time as vesting. Clearly, however, vesting cannot take place after payment since this would be a contradiction; payment is dependent on the right having vested.

An example of postponement of payment can be seen with improper liferents. The testator gives a right to the income arising from capital to an improper liferenter, but the right to receive the capital is given to another legatee (the improper fiar). In such cases, the fiar holds a vested right but does not yet have a right to demand payment. Payment or transfer to the improper fiar is postponed until the liferent has been extinguished.

What arises from the distinction between payment and vesting, alongside the power of the testator to modify either, is that vesting may be postponed, or entitlement to payment may be postponed, or both vesting and entitlement to payment are postponed for lengthy periods. In rare cases, and only where no other construction is possible,[18] vesting may take place at some intermediate time between the death of the testator and the date the beneficiary becomes entitled to payment. It is also possible that vesting can be accelerated, in that the date of vesting is brought forward due to some extraneous event.[19]There are five possible permutations of the relative dates of vesting and payment that will be touched upon below:

(1) vesting is immediate and payment is made soon after;

(2) vesting is immediate, but payment is postponed until some future date;

18 *Marshall v King* (1888) 16 R 40, per Lord President Inglis at 43.

19 See para **13.28.**

(3) vesting is postponed until the date of payment;

(4) vesting takes place at some intermediate date between the death of the testator and the date of payment;

(5) vesting is postponed, but payment is accelerated.[20]

In determining when vesting occurs, the courts have, as a result of a substantial volume of cases in the area, developed general principles to employ when examining and interpreting a testamentary document. Like much of interpretation, the cases can be fact-specific depending on the terms of the legacy, and more weight may be attached to some principles than others. Nevertheless, the general principles serve as worthwhile guidelines for the area.

GENERAL PRINCIPLES OF VESTING

(1) Ascertaining the testator's intention

13.7 Ascertaining the date of vesting is essentially a matter of ascertaining the intention of the testator as expressed or implied in the deed. The time of vesting may have been made explicit, and in this case the terms in which that intention is expressed will be conclusive. Where it is not expressly provided, the time of vesting will be construed from the deed as a whole. As Lord Colonsay said in *Carleton v Thomson*:[21]

> 'When a question arises under a *mortis causa* settlement, whether the benefit given is or has become a vested right, the intentions of the testator, in so far as they can be discovered or reasonably inferred from the deed, taken as a whole, and from the circumstances legitimately collected under which the deed is made, should have effect given to them. It is a *quaestio voluntatis*. That is the cardinal rule and guide.'

20 There are no reported cases where this has happened but an executor may make a payment to a beneficiary on account if it is clear that the right will vest and there will be funds in the estate to make payment, but payment will not be made as a matter of right. One might see the operation of s 10 of the Succession (Scotland) Act 2016 as a form of payment without vesting when payments are made to the deceased beneficiary's estate without the right having vested.

21 (1867) 5 M (HL) 151, at 153.

In some cases, however, construing the intention of the testator might not be a straightforward matter. In accordance with the general rule of the construction of deeds, effect will be given to the actual words used by the testator (or truster). The court will not attempt, by intuitive processes or extrinsic evidence, to decipher what his or her subjectively true intention may have been.[22] It will look at the deed as a whole (including any codicils) as well as any particular provisions within any part of it, subject to the rule of last resort that if it is otherwise impossible to determine the testator's intention, effect will be given to the last dated deed to have been executed or the last relevant provision in a single deed.[23] As Lord Colonsay's *dictum* makes clear, the court may also look at the circumstances surrounding the testator when the deed or deeds were executed and place itself 'in the testator's armchair' to understand what the deed intends for.[24]

Certain presumptions have been formulated to assist in interpreting the testator's intention as to the time of vesting, but all, or indeed, any, of them may be rebutted if it can be shown that the testator's true intention was other than that which a presumption derived from a previous case would imply. Ordinary and not technical meanings are to be given wherever possible; the expression of the testator's intention, where it can be discerned by looking to the words used, is thus primarily a question of fact and not of law.[25] As Lord President Dunedin pointed out in *Tweeddale's Trustees v Tweeddale*:[26]

> 'No decision in this branch of the law can ever be authority for another ... The decision of the proper construction of the will of A can never, as authority, rule the construction of the will of B.'

Nonetheless, in the absence of any clear indication of a contrary intention, the courts will infer an intention consistent with the normal meaning of a word or provision as established by previous cases.[27]

22 See **Ch 7**.
23 *Constantine v Constantine* (1801) 6 Ves 100; and *Livingston's Trs v Livingston's Trs* 1939 SC (HL) 17.
24 *Scott's Trs v De Moyse-Bucknall's Trs* 1978 SC 62. See **Ch 9**.
25 *Young v Robertson* (1862) 4 Macq 509 at 514.
26 *Tweeddale's Trs v Tweeddale* (1905) 8 F 264 at 273.
27 *Barclay's Trs v Inland Revenue* 1975 SC (HL) 1 per Lord Reid at 13.

(2) The presumption of immediate vesting

13.8 It is obvious that the earliest possible time that vesting can take place is on the death of the testator; that is, *a morte testatoris*. Unless there is an express provision directing some other time or the construction of the deed otherwise requires it, it is presumed that the testator intended vesting to take place as soon as possible:[28]

> 'In general, legacies are held to vest *a morte testatoris*, unless the contrary be clearly indicated; and, as a general rule, when the term of payment is not postponed by reason of interests personal to a third party, the presumption that it was intended to vest from the testator's death will not be avoided.'

In the simple case where a testator dies having made a bequest to a beneficiary without further destination and without the attachment of conditions, the default rule will apply and the legacy will vest *a morte*. Any legacy expressed in the present tense, using phrases such as 'I leave' or 'I bequeath' will be construed as directing that vesting be immediate, unless this is inconsistent with any other provision of the will.[29] Even if the terms of a testament are ambiguous and there are two possible constructions that may be put on the provision, there is a presumption that the construction which favours early vesting will be preferred.[30] If there is ambiguity as to whether the testator intended the postponement to relate to vesting or payment, vesting will be *a morte*, unless there is evidence pointing to a contrary intention, and payment only will be postponed. The presumption is rebuttable, with the onus of rebuttal lying on the party seeking to found on postponed vesting.

Unconditional legacies vest immediately because the acquisition of the right of succession is not contingent on the occurrence or performance of any event, and like the nature of legal rights which vest *a morte*; they arise automatically, are entirely unconditional and must be discharged expressly.

28 *Finlay's Trs v Finlay* (1886) 13 R 1052 per Lord Justice-Clerk Moncrieff at 1055.
29 *Hamilton v Ritchie* (1904) 21 R (HL) 35.
30 Bell *Prin* § 1879.

CONDITIONAL LEGACIES

13.9 The difficulties with vesting, and the laments thereof, always involve legacies with conditions attached. It is useful to illustrate the problems with an example:

> A leaves a legacy of £25,000 to B and C, to be paid when they turn 18. B and C are currently 14 years old.

On one view, at A's death, B and C have a vested right to receive £25,0000, albeit payment has been delayed until they attain the age of 18. On another view, B and C have no vested right until they turn 18 (upon which date they are also entitled to payment). These differing interpretations illustrate how it can be difficult to ascertain when vesting has occurred.

Where conditions are attached to a legacy, it can be hard to determine whether a right vests *a morte*, or whether it vests at a later date. The different types of conditional legacies and their principal features were outlined in **Chapter 10**, and each has implications for vesting. Much caselaw has been generated in the treatment of conditional legacies. One may argue that much of it is contradictory to the point that it is unhelpful.[31] However, an overview of the relevant rules is offered here but in any particular case, the construction of the document and the intention of the testator are of paramount importance.

(1) Potestive conditions

13.10 Where the condition is potestive,[32] vesting is immediate unless postponed for some other reason. Payment will occur when the condition is purified. However, if the condition is unclear, impossible or *contra bonos mores* and thus treated as *pro non scripto*, both the legacy and the entitlement to payment vests immediately as if the condition did not exist. If the condition is valid, it is enough that the beneficiary has done everything within his or her power to fulfil the condition at the date of the testator's death, at which point the legacy will vest.[33]

31 One does not escape the conclusion that it may just be helpful for the courts to 'start again'. Unfortunately, the doctrine of *stare decisis* does not operate in such a way.

32 See para **10.9**.

33 *Miller, Petrs* 1977 SLT 67.

(2) Suspensive conditions

13.11 If vesting is not *a morte* but postponed, it will usually be postponed until the date of payment because a suspensive condition[34] has been attached to the legacy. The example given above, with B and C and the legacy of £25,000,[35] is an example of a suspensive condition. Where a suspensive condition is attached to a bequest, the question arises as to whether the testator intended either: (1) vesting of the right to be postponed until purification of the condition; or (2) vesting of the right to be *a morte*, but entitlement to payment is postponed until purification.

The determination of vesting in these cases is often to consider whether the condition involves a certain future event (*dies incertus*) or an uncertain future event (*dies incertus*). A certain future event is one that is bound to happen, such as the death of a person. Thus, a legacy payable on the death of another person is a certain event. All people are bound to die at some point in time, even if the date is unknown, so that is a certainty. In principle, with conditions relating to the occurrence of a certain event, the legacy will vest *a morte* but payment is deferred until the event has occurred.

In contrast, an uncertain future event is something that may or may not occur. In the example above, of B and C and the legacy of £25,000, B or C may turn 18, or they may not. That is an uncertainty of life, and either may die before reaching a certain age. In such cases, the general principle is that vesting is suspended until the *dies incertus* occurs. However, much can turn on the construction of the document itself and determining the date of vesting is really a matter of construing the intention of the testator, and not a matter to be decided at the discretion of the executor or trustees.[36] Trustees and executors may have discretion as to the date of payment, but where there is a direction to administer the estate pending completion of trust purposes (including the payment of debts where the term of payment is not specified), this will not operate to postpone vesting in the beneficiaries but only the date in which the legatee becomes entitled for the legacy to be paid to them.[37]

34 See para **10.11**.

35 See para **13.9**.

36 *Scott v Scott's Exrx* (1877) 4 R 384.

37 Similarly, where trustees agreed that payments of capital to two beneficiaries were to be conditional upon them granting indemnity in relation to the third, the court held that payment but not vesting had been postponed: *Stenhouse's Trs v Lord Advocate* 1986 SLT 73, OH.

Survivorship clauses, destinations-over and derivative destinations are all effective as forms of suspensive condition and may all result in postponement of vesting, depending on circumstances and the construction of the deed in question. Each can include niceties in their application, which are discussed further below.

(3) Resolutive conditions

13.12 Where a resolutive condition is attached, vesting of the right depends, broadly speaking, on the contingent occurrence of an event relating to a third party.[38] Vesting can take place *a morte* in the conditional beneficiary, subject to the possibility of divestiture of the right in favour of a primary beneficiary (should they so emerge). This again involves niceties as to its operation, and further analysis is given below.

SUSPENSIVE CONDITIONS AND POSTPONED VESTING

(1) Survivorship clauses

(a) Survivorship clauses and individuals

13.13 A clause of survivorship may be attached to a bequest to operate as a suspensive condition to suspend vesting *a morte* and postpone it to a later date. It may be a condition of the gift that, for example, the beneficiary must survive for the duration of a liferent before he or she may become vested in the right to the fee (but in this case, a destination-over may well be attached).[39] It is also fairly common, particularly in the case of bequests between spouses, for a simple clause of survivorship to be attached to a bequest.[40] If it is a condition of the bequest that the beneficiary survive for a specified period, such as 30, 60 or 90 days after the death of the testator, vesting will occur at the end of the period if and only if the beneficiary survives it. The crucial question in determining when the legacy is to vest is which of two meanings is to be given to words of survivorship. Are

38 See para **10.12**.

39 See paras **11.12–11.5**.

40 See para **1.13**.

the words a condition of the gift, so that the beneficiary must survive a certain event or for a certain period in order to purify the condition and thus postpone vesting? Or are they merely a description of the intended beneficiaries in whom the legacy will vest *a morte*?

Alternatively, the period of survivorship may not be specified exactly but require the beneficiary to survive until he or she reaches a certain age, and this may be many years after the death of the testator. For example, in a bequest in terms such as 'to A on his 21st birthday', vesting may occur *a morte*,[41] but payment has been postponed until A's 21st birthday. If, however, the legacy is not being held by trustees in order to enable other trust purposes to be carried out, A has the right to demand payment from the executor at any time after his or her 18th birthday.[42] Only if it is clear that it is a condition of the legacy that A actually reaches his 21st birthday (in other words, a *dies incertus*) will vesting be suspended as an uncertain event.[43]

(b) Survivorship clauses and groups or classes

13.14 A survivorship clause may be attached to a group or class of beneficiaries under a legacy. The terms of the bequest may state that failing the survival of one or more of the beneficiaries, the right of a predeceasing legatee accresces to the other legatees and vests in them instead. Forms of words which express such an intention include, for example, 'to A, B and C, and the survivors of them' or 'to the issue of A surviving'.

Such a provision may raise basic questions that are not always easy to answer: what is the event that must be survived for the right to vest, and on what basis is the survivor to be ascertained and identified? The answer to these involves an examination of the decision of the House of Lords in *Young v Robertson*.

41 *Alves' Trs v Grant* (1874) 1 R 969.

42 A beneficiary at full age (18) in whom a right has vested has the right to demand immediate payment provided that the fund is not required to fulfil trust purposes, Trusts and Succession (Scotland) Act 2024, s 58. See also the power of a court to modify the trust on a material change of circumstances under s 65 of the 2024 Act.

43 *Cattenach's Trs v Cattenach* (1901) 4 F 205. See para **10.11**.

(c) The rule in Young v Robertson

13.15 The general rule relating to vesting and the construction of survivorship clauses within a class or group is laid down in *Young v Robertson.*[44] In *Young,* the testator had bequeathed the residue of his estate to his wife in liferent and to several grandnephews and grandnieces in fee, stating expressly that if any of the legatees died without issue before the fee vested, their share should be divided equally among the survivors of them.

The question for the court in *Young* was whether the fee had: (1) vested *a morte* in all of those legatees who survived at the death of the testator, or (2) vested in the remaining surviving legatees at the expiry of the liferent. In the leading judgment, Lord Westbury held:[45]

> 'I apprehend it to be a settled rule of construction, that words of survivorship occurring in a settlement (that is, in a will,) should be referred to the period appointed by that settlement for the payment or distribution of the subject-matter of the gift.'

Payment of the fee was postponed until the expiry of the liferent, but the survivorship clause precluded ascertainment of the fiars until that date; accordingly, vesting was suspended until the expiry of the liferent when the survivors could be ascertained. This represents the general rule: where a survivorship clause is attached to a legacy to two or more individuals or a class and payment is postponed, vesting will be suspended until the date of payment when survivorship can be ascertained. At the date of payment, the legacy will vest only in those beneficiaries who have survived to that date.[46] In consequence, the expectant right of any potential beneficiary who fails to survive the period between the death of the testator and the date of payment will lapse, and his or her potential share of the legacy will not form part of his or her own estate. In explaining the reasoning behind the rule, Lord Westbury stated:[47]

44 (1862) 4 Macq 314.

45 (1862) 4 Macq 314, at 319.

46 If it cannot be determined who survived, then s 10 of the Succession (Scotland) Act 2016 will apply. See paras **1.16–1.19**.

47 *Young v Robertson* (1862) 4 Macq 314 at 319. It is notable that Lord Westbury uses English terminology of life estate rather than liferent.

> 'If a testator gives a life estate [a liferent] in a sum of money or in the residue of his estate, and at the expiration of that life estate directs the money to be paid or the residue to be divided among a number of objects and then refers to the possibility of some one or more of those persons dying, without specifying the time, and directs in that event the payment or distribution to be made among the survivors, it is understood by the law that he means the contingency to extend over the whole period of time that must elapse before the payment of distribution takes place … In such a gift the survivors are to be ascertained in like manner by a reference to the period of distribution, namely, the expiration of the life estate.'

The court held that ordinary meanings should be given to the expression of the testator's intention. The very fact he had contemplated that one or more legatees may predecease the expiry of the liferent, and had provided that their shares be destined to the survivors, led to the logical conclusion that vesting could not take place at any date earlier than the date of payment of the fee; namely at the expiry of the liferent. The *ratio* of *Young* has since been widened to include any case 'where there is an express gift to survivors of an accrescing share'[48] and has not been restricted to only where a liferent delays payment.[49]

The construction of the deed turns in every case on the particular wording used by the testator. Only where the words used by the testator permit, will the rule in *Young v Robertson* be applied; namely, that where survivorship is attached to a bequest, vesting will necessarily be postponed to the date of payment when the survivors can be ascertained. The primary question to be resolved, therefore, is whether: (1) survivorship is to be construed as a condition of the gift so as to postpone vesting, or (2) merely as a description of the intended beneficiaries in whom the legacy will vest *a morte*.

In *Webster's Trustees v Neil*,[50] the testator had directed his trustees to pay income from the residue of his estate to his widow and the capital to the children of his brother on the expiry of the widow's liferent. The provision in favour of the children was worded 'to A, B and C and the survivors or survivor of them, equally between them, share and share alike'. The testator was survived by his widow, A, B, and C. However,

48 *Miller's Trustees v Brown* 1933 SC 669, per Lord Hunter at 686.
49 See *Freeborn's Trs v Bennett* 1940 SC 517; and *Stirling's Trs v Stirling* 1977 SC 139.
50 (1900) 2 F 695.

A subsequently died and only B and C survived at the expiry of the widow's liferent. The question for the court was whether, as a result of the survivorship clause, the right to the fee had vested in A, B, and C at the testator's death, or whether vesting was suspended until the date of payment. The court held that the words of survivorship did not refer to the date of payment but to the death of the testator. Accordingly, the children's share of the residue had vested at that date, and A's successors were entitled to claim A's share of the fee. The court held that the points at issue were capable of solution by reading the will 'without much aid from decided cases'.[51] Two constructions of the deed were possible, and it held that it should 'lean to the one which favours immediate vesting'.[52]

(d) Intermediate vesting and survivorship inter se

13.16 The rule established in *Young v Robertson*[53] did not resolve the problem that where none of the beneficiaries survived the date of payment, then the legacy would simply lapse. Since vesting could take place only at one of two possible times, the death of the testator or the date of payment, lapse was the inevitable consequence. The decision in *Lindsay's Trs v Sinclair*[54] introduced the concept of intermediate vesting to resolve this apparent anomaly. Here, it was held that a reference to the 'survivor' of two or more beneficiaries might be construed differently from the plural 'survivors', although the authorities are in some doubt.[55]

The facts of *Lindsay's Trs* were that the testator directed that the fee of heritable property was to be given to his two sons, A and B, subject to the *proviso* that if either of them died without issue before the expiry of

51 *Webster's Trs v Neil* (1900) 2 F 695, per Lord Justice Clerk Kingsburgh at 697.

52 *Webster's Trs v Neil* (1900) 2 F 695, per Lord Justice Clerk Kingsburgh at 699. The terms of the bequest also contained a destination-over; see paras **13.18–13.19**. The facts of this (and similar cases) raise the question of whether the construction given to such a clause in a particular case may depend on its actual consequences. For example, whether the legacy will lapse into intestacy or pass to a non-family member. In *Webster's Trustees*, the bequest was to the children and the survivors or survivor of them, whom failing their church.

53 *Young v Robertson* (1862) 4 Macq 314.

54 (1885) 12 R 964. The concept of intermediate vesting was first put forward in *Newton v Thomson* (1849) 11 D 452 but was merely *obiter*.

55 *Cf Playfair's Trs v Stewart's Trs* 1960 SLT 351.

the liferent, his share was to pass to the survivor. Both sons predeceased the liferenter without leaving issue, but B had outlived A for a period of time. If the rule in *Young v Robertson* had been applied and vesting postponed until the expiry of the liferent, the part of the testator's estate which comprised the subject of the legacy would have become intestate. The court held that the property had vested in B on the death of A, on the basis of Lord Shand's view that:[56]

> 'It seems to me that the only object the truster had in view in inserting the survivorship clause was to provide for the case of one of the two sons predeceasing the widow. That event having occurred [on the death of the first son], it cannot be said the vesting was to be still postponed until the death of the widow.'

The use of the singular 'survivor' may thus imply that the legacy will vest in whichever one of a group of beneficiaries turns out to be the longest liver; that is, it refers to survivorship of the beneficiaries *inter se* and not to survivorship at the time of payment of the legacy. In this case, the consequence is that vesting takes place at the time when one of the group or class has outlived the rest, unless it is clear that some other date is intended, even if this is before the date of payment.[57]

Similarly, in *Macfarlane's Trustees v Macfarlane's Curator Bonis*[58] the testator had made a bequest 'to A in liferent, and B and C in fee' but with the condition that if either B or C should predecease A, the survivor should take the whole fee. B and C died before the date of payment, but B had survived C for a period of time. The question was whether the legacy had vested in B at C's death. Lord Blackburn stated that wherever there is a gift of the fee with a destination-over to the survivor of two persons without any further destination-over to issue:[59]

56 *Lindsay's Trs v Sinclair* (1885) 12 R 964, at 967. This was followed in *Gardner v Hamblin* (1900) 2 F 679; and *Ferguson's Trs v Readman's Exrs* (1903) 10 SLT 697. *Cf Aitken's Trs v Aitken's Trs* 1930 SLT 509 (OH) where the destination was to 'survivors one or more'. It was held to be irrelevant that a plurality of survivors would have taken a vested right only at the expiry of the liferent but this is the only case in which a destination to 'survivors' has been held to imply intermediate vesting.

57 See also *Livingston's Trs v Livingston's Trs* 1939 SC (HL) 17.

58 1934 SC 476.

59 *Macfarlane's Trs v Macfarlane's CB* 1934 SC 476, at 481.

> 'I think that the construction of such a destination is settled and that, during the lifetime of the liferenter no rights vest in any of the persons entitled to share in the fee until there is only one survivor of them left, when the right to the whole fee vests in that survivor whether he predeceases the liferenter or not.'

Lord Fleming concurred, holding that the term 'survivor' imported survivorship between B and C *inter se* and, accordingly, that it was not a condition of the bequest that the longest liver should survive the liferenter. The contingency which had suspended vesting, namely, that B and C predecease the liferenter, had ceased to operate when the class had reduced to one, and the legacy vested in B.[60]

(e) Exclusion and limitation of intermediate vesting

13.17 Where both words are used, as in a bequest 'to A, B, C, and the survivor or survivors', there is no implication that survivorship *inter se* is intended. As Lord Guest observed in *Playfair's Trustees v Stewart's Trustees*,[61] 'if vesting is to take place on the death of the last survivor but one, there could only be one survivor and the term 'survivors' would be meaningless'. Where the words 'survivor' or 'survivors' are both used, the second meaning will be preferred, and a bequest to 'survivors' therefore contains an implied destination-over, in the form of accretion, of the share of any predeceasing legatee, to those who survive at the date of payment.

A legacy expressed as being to certain beneficiaries *and* the survivors makes clear that on the failure of any, or indeed all of them except one, the other or others are to take their share. If any of the group or class dies before the date of vesting, then the deceased member's share will accresce to the others. That result might be disapplied where there is an express destination-over for the share to pass instead to a conditional institute, and accretion is overridden in such cases.[62] If none survive at the date of vesting, the legacy will lapse unless there is a further destination. In the

60 1934 SC 476, at 483.

61 *Playfair's Trs v Stewart's Trs* 1960 SLT 351, at 353.

62 It should be noted that s 6 of the Succession (Scotland) Act 2016, whereby direct descendants of the testator have a destination implied to them if their ancestor predeceases, is likely excluded here due to the survivorship wording, 2016 Act, s 6(3)(a).

case of a common calamity involving all the members of the group, and it simply cannot be ascertained who survived, then the result may be that the legacy is simply divided equally between the deceased member's estates, leaving aside questions of vesting.[63]

The solution of intermediate vesting may, however, be seen as being concerned primarily with avoiding intestacy and thus conforming with a fundamental principle of the construction of wills.[64] None of the decisions in this area can be taken as establishing any fixed principles of construction. Certainly, case law permits intermediate vesting in principle, but whether this will occur in any particular case depends entirely on the terms of the actual deed concerned.

Importantly, in *Laing's Trustees v Horsburgh*,[65] the court held that no general principle can be drawn from cases which allowed intermediate vesting. Here, the testator had provided that a legacy was to be taken by A and B 'equally or to the survivor of them' but had in explicit terms made clear that survivorship was to be ascertained at the date of payment; accordingly, the rule in *Young v Robertson*[66] applied. The court also stated that it did not consider *Macfarlane's Trustees v Macfarlane's Curator Bonis*[67] to be authority for a general proposition that a reference to a single 'survivor' implied survivorship *inter se*. Both Lord Justice-Clerk Grant and Lord Strachan reviewed in some detail the cases cited in support of a contention made to the court that *Macfarlane's Trustees* laid down a general principle. They concluded that the cases where survivorship was held to refer to survivorship *inter se*, and thus to intermediate vesting, turned on their own construction. Further, it did not appear that *Young v Robertson* had always been cited before the court which had decided them. The court held that, far from being a precedent, *Lindsay's Trustees v Sinclair*[68] had been decided on the basis of the particular words used by the testator and not on any rule of law.

63 2016 Act, s 10. See paras **1.16–1.19**.
64 *Lindsay's Trs v Sinclair* (1885) 12 R 964.
65 1965 SC 339.
66 (1862) 4 Macq 314.
67 1934 SC 476.
68 (1885) 12 R 964.

(2) Destinations-over

(a) Conditional institution

13.18 The purpose of a destination-over is to prevent the lapse of a legacy should the primary beneficiary, the institute, die before vesting has occurred.[69] In a sense, it contains a form of survivorship since it is a condition of the gift that the primary beneficiary, the institute, survives the date of vesting in order to defeat any contingent right that the conditional institute may have. Conversely, if the institute fails to survive vesting, then the conditional institute may receive the legacy instead. In the case of a simple destination-over where the legacy and payment both vest *a morte*, the matter is relatively straightforward.

Example

K leaves '£10,000 to A, whom failing B'. If the institute (A) has survived the testator, the right will vest in their patrimony, and no right will vest in the conditional institute (B). B's right 'flies off'. Alternatively, if A has failed to survive the testator *a morte*, the legacy will vest in B instead.

It has been said that the rule in *Young v Robertson* establishes a presumption that the use of a destination-over shows the testator's intended to delay vesting until the date that the legacy becomes payable – at which time the survivance of both the institute or the conditional institute will be ascertained.[70] Where the testator has expressly or implicitly postponed payment of the legacy, then vesting may occur at the date the legacy becomes payable – upon which the destination will become operative to determine in whose patrimony, either the institute's or the conditional

69 See paras **11.12–11.21.**

70 See *Freeborn's Trs* v *Bennett* 1940 SC 517, per Lord Moncrieff at 521, yet see the Lord President's dissent at 524. There is considerable debate and inconsistencies in the case law in respect of vesting with conditional institutions and the application of *Young*. Only an introductory overview can be provided here without being drawn into debate. A modern treatment is needed, but see W Candlish Henderson, *The Principles of Vesting in the Law of Succession,* 2nd edn (1938), Ch IV.

institute's, the legacy will vest. As Lord Reid noted in *Barclay's Trustee v Inland Revenue*:[71]

> 'When a gift is payable at a date later than the date when the deed takes effect, and it takes the form of a gift to A whom failing to B whom failing to C the normal rule is that vesting is suspended or delayed until the date of payment, so that if A, B and C all predecease the date of payment none of them takes anything.'

Consequently, if the institute dies in the period between the testator's death and a postponed payment date, then the legacy vests in the conditional institute at the time the legacy becomes payable instead.

Where a legacy has an alternate legatee as the institute's own successors, such as 'to A and her heirs', this is taken as a destination-over.[72] In *Hay's Trustees v Hay*,[73] the testator gave a liferent of his whole estate to his wife, and then directed on her death to convey his heritable property in favour of his brother 'and his heirs'. The brother survived the testator's death but predeceased the wife. A question arose as to whether the legacy had vested in the brother *a morte* before his subsequent death, and consequently his own testamentary trustees were entitled to demand the property, or whether his heir had acquired a vested right at the expiry of the liferent. In the absence of any suspension of payment, the court held the legacy had vested in the brother *a morte*. In *Bowman v Bowman*,[74] there was a suspension of payment, but the court held that a destination to legatees 'or to their respective heirs' was to be treated as a conditional institution and the legacy vested in the legatees *a morte* upon proper construction of the testator's intentions.

Where vesting has been postponed, the heirs of the deceased legatee (as conditional institutes) may have changed in the time between the testator's death and the date of vesting. A question can arise as to whether the heirs of the institute are to be taken as those: (i) at the testator's death; or (ii) at the date of payment. This will be a matter of construction of the deed. In *Wylie's Trustees v Bruce*,[75] the testator had granted an improper liferent to his wife, and on her death, to convey the fee to his cousin 'or his heirs'. The cousin

71 1975 SC (HL) 1, at 13.
72 McLaren, *The Law of Wills and Succession*, 3rd edn (1894), para 1441.
73 (1890) 17 R 961.
74 *Bowman v Bowman* (1899) 1 F (HL) 69.
75 1919 SC 211.

survived the testator but predeceased the widow. The cousin's first-born son, who was initially the cousin's heir, had also predeceased the widow, but his second-born son survived the death of the widow. A question arose as to whether the second-born son was entitled to the fee and the right had vested in him (or whether others were entitled to the property). A court of thirteen judges held that vesting and ascertainment of the heir were taken as at the date the heirs were entitled to payment, rather than those heirs existing at the testator's death. There Lord Dundas noted:[76]

> 'It stands to reason, and the [previous] cases illustrate, that, in this sense, a man may have one heir at his death and another at some later period; the question is, at what date did the testator intend the heir to be looked for whom he called as an independent conditional institute to the legatee.'

Where the conditional institute is a class, or a group, where accretion or survivorship amongst them applies, then following *Young* vesting will be determined at the date the legacy becomes payable to allow the class to be ascertained.[77]

(b) Substitution

13.19 When there is a substitution,[78] and there appears to be no expression by the testator of an intention to the contrary, vesting in the institute will be *a morte*. However, vesting in B will occur at any time the institute dies, whether before or after payment of the legacy. The destination to B means that B takes the legacy either: (i) as an alternative to A, if A has failed, or (ii) after A, if A has survived but dies without evacuating the destination. If A survives the testator but dies before payment, then the legacy will immediately vest in B.

> **Example**
>
> A testator gives a legacy of a liferent to her husband and the fee to A, whom failing B. Payment of the fee is therefore postponed until the expiry

76 1919 SC 211, at 226.

77 *Thompson's Trustees v Jamieson* (1900) 2 F 470, per Lord Kyllachy at 484; *MacDonald's Trustees v MacDonald* 1974 SC 23; and *Baillie's Trustees v Whiting* 1910 SC 891.

78 See para **11.15**.

of the liferent. The right to the fee vests in A *a morte*. However, A dies before the expiry of the liferent without having evacuated the destination, and the right to the fee vests in B at A's death.

If B were a conditional institute rather than a substitute, his or her contingent right would be defeated as soon as the legacy vested in A. Substitution does not mean that the property in question is owned by both A and B simultaneously. Rather, B's right is postponed to A's antecedent right as institute and it is a condition of the gift to A that B subsequently takes the property on A's death, whenever that might occur. If payment is immediate, the effect of substitution is to create a special destination in favour of B.[79] B will take the property on A's death as well as on A's predecease, subject to A's right to evacuate the destination *inter vivos* or *mortis causa*.[80] B's right will lapse, therefore, only if A evacuates the destination; otherwise, the legacy will vest in B on A's death. Because substitution means that vesting is not suspended, the right of a substitute may vest subject to defeasance if the legacy is also subject to a resolutive condition.[81]

(c) Clauses of devolution and derivative destinations

13.20 Where the conditional beneficiaries are beneficiaries under a derivative destination, also known as a clause of devolution,[82] such as in a bequest 'to A and A's children' or 'to A and A's issue', vesting in A will not be postponed. If A does not survive vesting, A's original share will pass to his or her children and not any increase in that share brought about by the lapse of a legacy to another beneficiary.[83] There may, however, be express directions to the contrary.[84] Further, there may also be a destination-over, such as in a bequest 'to A and A's issue and in the event of the predecease of A's issue, to B'. Alternatively, the gift may be subject to a survivorship

79 See para **11.15**.
80 *Crumpton's JF v Barnardo's Homes* 1917 SC 713.
81 *Houston v Houston's Trs* (1894) 2 SLT 118. See paras **10.12** and **13.22ff**.
82 See para **11.18**.
83 *Henderson v Henderson* (1890) 17 R 293, per Lord President Inglis at 296.
84 *McNish v Donald's Trs* (1879) 7 R 96; and *Cumming's Trs v White* (1893) 20 R 454.

clause, such as 'to A and A's issue and the survivor or survivors of them'. In these cases, vesting will likely be suspended and it may be that the share of any issue of a predeceaser is enlarged in preference to that of a conditional institute.[85]

RESOLUTIVE CONDITIONS AND DEFEASIBLE VESTING

13.21 Where a legacy is given to the 'issue' or 'children' of a specified person and there are no such issue or children in existence at the time of the testator's death, the question arises as to whether vesting of the legacy must be postponed until it can be ascertained whether they will emerge. If a legacy is given to 'the children of B, whom failing B having any issue, to C', it would seem to be somewhat unfair if vesting in C were to be postponed indefinitely until the status of B and their potential for procreation or adoption of children became ascertained. Partly to solve problems such as this, the doctrine of vesting subject to defeasance emerged as the alternative and, arguably, simpler solution to a situation where an executor has to retain a legacy for a prolonged period.

(1) The rationale of the doctrine

13.22 The idea that vesting need not necessarily be indefeasible and that vesting in someone, even if it may be temporary, is preferable to leaving legacies pending was developed in order to deal with the perceived difficulty of suspending vesting over a long period of time. To this end, the court devised the doctrine of defeasible vesting, which would enable a legacy to vest in a conditional beneficiary, subject to his or her right being defeated if a primary beneficiary emerged and the resolutive condition were fulfilled. Given the highly contingent nature of any resolutive condition being fulfilled, the reality was that there was every possibility that, ultimately, a conditional institute, rather than the institute, would

85 *Neville v Shepherd* (1895) 23 R 351; *Cattenach v Thom's Exrs* (1858) 20 D 1206; and *Bell v Grieve* (1840) 2 D 880. Cf *White's Trs v Chrystal's Trs* (1893) 20 R 460. See also W Candlish Henderson, *The Principles of Vesting in the Law of Succession*, 2nd edn (1938), Ch V.

acquire an indefeasible right to the legacy in question. The rationale for the doctrine was expressed by Lord Blackburn in introducing the aim, if not the application, of the doctrine into Scots law:[86]

> 'It is in general for the benefit of the objects of the testator's bounty that they should be able to deal with their expectant interest at once, which they can do if their interest is vested, though subject to be divested by the happening of a subsequent event, but which they cannot do if their interests are kept in suspense and contingency until that event has happened.'

In approving the doctrine, Lord McLaren gives a useful summary of the purpose behind it:[87]

> 'The determination of the rights of a class known and ascertained at the testator's death ought not to be suspended because of the possible interests of an unknown and sometimes non-existent class having a prior place in the destination, the rights of the last-mentioned class being safeguarded by the conditional character of the vested right.'

In cases where the terms of the bequest contain what can be construed as a resolutive condition, the application of the doctrine of vesting subject to defeasance does offer solutions, but if the aim of the doctrine was straightforward, its application is complex.

(2) The nature of defeasible vesting

13.23 The basic test of whether a legacy vests defeasibly in the conditional institute, pending the emergence of an as yet unborn or unidentifiable institute, is whether the terms of the bequest include a resolutive, as opposed to a suspensive, condition. An example is a legacy expressed in a form such as 'the residue of my estate to A in liferent, and to the issue of A in fee, and in the event of A dying without issue, to B'.

At first sight, this legacy seems no different from the cases previously described, in that it contains a destination-over and therefore would operate

86 *Taylor v Gilbert's Trs* (1878) 5 R (HL) 217 at 221. The doctrine was not actually applied in the case and Lord Blackburn's dictum was aimed at resolving the problem of how to allocate the shares of a predeceasing beneficiary when no provision for accretion to the surviving beneficiaries had been made.

87 McLaren, *The Law of Wills and Succession*, 3rd edn (1894), para 1491.

to suspend vesting. The difference, however, lies in the fact that there is no express or implied requirement that any beneficiary survive; rather, it is that an ultimate beneficiary should emerge. The effect of a resolutive condition is the reverse of a suspensive condition: vesting is immediate, subject to being defeated upon the occurrence of a specified contingency. There is no particular form of words to distinguish a resolutive from a suspensive condition. It all depends on the words used in the deed and the meanings that can be drawn from them.

In *Taylor v Gilbert's Trustees*,[88] the testator had directed his trustees to hold and apply[89] the residue of his estate in the following, rather complicated, terms:

(1) one-third to A in liferent and her children in fee;

(2) one-third to B in liferent and her children in fee;

(3) one-third to C, D, E and F in liferent equally and their children equally among them *per stirpes*;

(4) if A and B died without issue or such issue died before attaining majority or being married, the two one-third shares to A and her issue and B and her issue should accresce to C, D, E and F and their children, respectively, in liferent and fee equally among them *per stirpes* with respect to their own share of the residue.

A and B died without issue. C left one son who attained majority but predeceased A and B. The question for the court was whether C's son had a vested right to the share of the residue accruing from A and B. By scrutinising the words used by the testator, particularly his repeated (and, furthermore, explained) insistence on a *per stirpes* division, the court construed his intention to be that the children of C, D, E and F should each take a share of the fee of his estate. There were personal conditions

88 *Taylor v Gilbert's Trs* (1878) 5 R (HL) 217. Previous cases had adopted solutions with a similar result but no doctrine as such was elucidated: see *McKinnon v McDonald* (1765) Mor 5279; Stair *Inst* III. 5. 50; *Stewart v Nicholson* (1859) 22 D 72; *Grant v Grant's Trs* (1859) 22 D 53; *Martin's Trs v Milliken* (1864) 3 M 326; and Bell's *Prin* § 1642.

89 A direction to convey the property to the beneficiaries at the termination of a liferent is treated identically to a direction to hold for them: *Cumming's Trs v Anderson* (1895) 23 R 94.

attached to the legacies to A and B, namely that their children were not to take unless they attained majority or were married. Normally, therefore, such conditions would suspend vesting. Nonetheless, Lord Gordon held that:[90]

> 'As soon as these conditions were fulfilled I think the children each became possessed of a vested right in the fee. There was no condition that the children should survive the liferentrices … Of course the payment of the fee was postponed till the death of the liferentrices, but this did not affect the vesting.'

Despite the contingencies specified in regard to the accrued shares of A and B which may have defeated the rights of C, D, E and F, namely that A and B left issue who attained majority or got married, Lord Gordon agreed with Lord Blackburn that these contingencies were:[91]

> 'In no respect a condition of the legacy. It is only an event before the arrival of which it cannot be known whether the devolving clause has or has not taken effect in favour of the conditional institute. But when that is once ascertained, [C's son] simply takes from the date of his majority or marriage – that is to say, it vests, and whether he predeceases or survives the liferentrix is a matter of no moment.'

The general proposition laid down in *Taylor v Gilbert's Trs* is therefore that, providing that the words of the deed itself permit of such a construction, vesting of a legacy in terms such as 'to A in liferent and the issue of A in fee, whom failing to C' will be subject to defeasance.

(3) The development of the doctrine

13.24 From *Taylor v Gilbert's Trustees*[92] is derived the rule that for vesting, including defeasible vesting, to occur, the gift must be made in such terms as to confer upon the beneficiary an unqualified legacy and not be subject to a further destination qualifying the beneficiary's right. A destination-over attached to the gift will point, therefore, to postponed

90 *Taylor v Gilbert's Trs* (1878) 5 R (HL) 217 at 219.
91 *Taylor v Gilbert's Trs* (1878) 5 R (HL) 217 at 220.
92 *Taylor v Gilbert's Trs* (1878) 5 R (HL) 217.

vesting and tend to rebut the presumption of defeasible vesting.[93] Early cases which followed the decision in *Taylor v Gilbert's Trustees*[94] did permit the doctrine to be applied in fairly wide circumstances. For example, in *Smith's Trustees v Smith*,[95] a truster directed that his widow should receive an annuity, the household furniture and occupation of the house during her life, provided that she remained unmarried. If she did remarry, the annuity was to be reduced 'with neither free house nor furniture'. The question was whether the truster had created a liferent over the house and furniture or given a right of fee subject to forfeiture in the event of a second marriage. The widow had not in fact remarried at the time of the action and Lord Justice-Clerk Moncrieff held that there was 'no practical inconvenience in declaring and giving effect to the obvious intention of the truster, viz that the widow has a right of fee subject to forfeiture'.[96]

Later development of the doctrine was concerned to clarify both the kinds of terms in which such a provision may be made and the kinds of events, which are the subject of the resolutive condition, which may (but not necessarily must) rebut the presumption of defeasible vesting. In *Steel's Trustees v Steel*,[97] Lord President Ingles set out the distinction between the situations in which vesting is suspended and where it takes place subject to defeasance. Essentially, vesting is suspended where the institute cannot be known or ascertained at the date of the testator's death but takes place *a morte,* subject to defeasance, if the liferenter or liferenters died leaving issue. Unless the facts in a particular case suggest a different solution, the presumption is therefore that a destination-over to an individual or class of individuals who cannot be known or ascertained until the death of the liferenter will suspend vesting. If, conversely, the individual or class is known or ascertained, vesting will be *a morte* but subject to defeasance if the liferenter leaves issue.

In both *Taylor* and *Steel's Trustees* it was held that, provided these criteria were met, and there were no other reasons to exclude it, there could

93 This has not always been followed, however: see *Scott's Trs v De Moyes-Bucknall's Trs* 1978 SC 62.

94 (1878) 5 R (HL) 217.

95 (1883) 10 R 1144.

96 (1883) 10 R 1144, at 1147.

97 (1888) 16 R 204 at 208.

be vesting subject to defeasance in a bequest to A in liferent and A's issue in fee, whom failing to a third party.[98] Vesting subject to defeasance will also take place where a legacy is given to A with a subsequent direction to trustees to reduce the gift to A to a liferent and his or her issue in fee. If A does have issue but they predecease the date of payment, vesting in A will not be defeated.[99]

Subsequent judicial consideration of the doctrine and its relationship to suspended vesting made clear that a bequest that provides for a series of contingencies will invariably contain suspensive conditions within its terms and thus rule out defeasible vesting. This led to the formulation of the 'double contingency' rule whereby, as long as any suspensive condition is attached to the legacy, vesting will be postponed.

(4) The double contingency rule

13.25 The general principle to be derived from the case law is that for an event to be a 'defeating event', there can be no existing object between a claimant and his or her right, but merely the possibility of a prior beneficiary becoming entitled to the bequest.[100] In accordance with this principle (but subsequent to wider applications of the doctrine having been held to be correct),[101] the court in *Johnston's Trustees v Dewar*[102] restricted its application to where, but for one single contingency, namely the birth of issue to a specified person or the survivance of issue, vesting would be absolute. The provisions of the bequest at issue were that the testator gave a sum of money to his granddaughter, A, in liferent, and to her issue, if any, in fee. Failing his granddaughter having any issue, he directed that the sum should be given to his two daughters, B and C, and, should one of them fail to survive, their issue, and failing them, to his next of kin, D. Vesting of the bequest was not, accordingly, conditional upon the occurrence of the single contingent event of whether or not the

98 See also *Corbett's Trs v Pollock* (1901) 3 F 963; *Moss's Trs v Moss's Trs* 1958 SC 501; and *Munro's Trs v Monson* 1962 SC 414.

99 *Lindsay's Trs v Lindsay* (1880) 8 R 281.

100 *Gardner v Hamblin* (1900) 2 F 679; see also comments made obiter in *Thompson's Trs v Jamieson* (1900) 2 F 479.

101 See, eg, *Smith's Trs v Smith* (1883) 10 R 1144.

102 1911 SC 722.

testator's granddaughter had issue, but also upon the contingencies that B and C and their issue survived. A survived the testator but died without issue. B and C and their issue survived the testator but predeceased A. The question before the court was who was entitled to the fee.

Lord Kinnear held that where a gift was made in such terms that it would take effect absolutely at the death of the testator but for the single contingency of the possible birth of issue to a particular person, it would be presumed that the gift vested in the conditional beneficiary, subject to defeasance in the event of the birth of the issue in question. The presumption for vesting subject to defeasance could arise only where there was 'the possibility of issue without further destination on their failure'.[103] In this case, the gift was subject to contingencies other than whether the liferenter had children or not, namely that of the daughters failing to survive, and failing them, their issue, and failing them, the next of kin. The parties entitled to succeed were therefore held to be D, those of the testator's next of kin who survived the liferenter.

Despite some judicial acceptance[104] of the test laid down in *Johnston's Trustees*, vesting subject to defeasance may still apply if more than one contingent event appears to be attached to the bequest.[105] First, there is the matter of construing the deed to determine whether it contains double or multiple contingencies at all. A bequest that appears to contain plural contingencies may not actually do so, since it is a question of how a single contingency is to be defined. If more than one defeating event is specified but it is as an alternative or parallel contingency rather than one event in a chronological series, this will not be construed as a double contingency.[106] Likewise, if the terms of a contingent event are repeated, for example in a bequest 'to A in liferent and A's issue in fee whom failing to B in liferent and B's issue in fee whom failing to C', this is not treated as a double contingency but considered as essentially the same one.[107]

103 1911 SC 722, at 730.

104 *Lees' Trs v Lees* 1927 SC 886, 1927 SLT 621. But *cf Bannatyne's Trs v Watson's Trs* 1914 SC 693, 1914 1 SLT 469 where it was observed that defeasible vesting may be possible where more than one contingency was specified.

105 Dicta in *Bannatyne's Trs v Watson's Trs* 1914 SC 693 suggested that defeasible vesting may be possible where more than one contingency was specified.

106 *Coulson's Trs v Coulson's Trs* 1911 SC 881.

107 *G's Trs v G* 1937 SC 141.

Secondly, there is the question of whether, even if the bequest manifestly does depend on more than one contingency, defeasible vesting may not necessarily be barred. In *Moss's Trustee v Moss's Trustees*,[108] Lord President Clyde took the view that the dictum of Lord Kinnear in *Johnston's Trustees v Dewar* relating to double contingencies was 'unsound'. Apart from the fact that it had not been central to the decision in that case, it was 'not an accurate nor a comprehensive statement of the law'.[109] He also held that there was no discrepancy between the decisions in *Lees's Trustees v Lees* (where it was stated that the doctrine had never been applied where there was a double contingency) and *G's Trustees v G* (where it was held that alternative defeating events did not amount to a double contingency at all). Both were concerned with different categories and *Lees's Trustees* was distinguishable from the instant case. The Lord Justice-Clerk (Thomson) went further. Where the contingency in question related to the possible birth of issue to two or more particular persons this was a single and not a double contingency:[110]

> 'The condition to be resolved remains essentially the same, and I cannot see that it matters whether the issue which may emerge to defeat B comes from one source or two. The contingency is the emergence of issue from a liferenter or liferenters ... It is a single contingency with two possible aspects.'

Commenting that it was clearly Lord Kinnear's intention not to stretch any construction of the testator's intention too far in relation to vesting and to take practical considerations into account, the Lord Justice-Clerk said that he did not, in any case, see any logical reason for limiting the doctrine to one contingency. If one resolutive condition does not suspend vesting, there seemed to be no reason why two should necessarily do so and, where there are two conditions and neither is inconsistent with immediate vesting, there seemed no reason in principle why their conjunction should have the opposite result. Moreover, in previous cases there had been two contingencies, including *Taylor v Gilbert's Trustees*,[111] the very case where

108 1958 SC 501.

109 1958 SC 501 at 507.

110 *Moss's Trs v Moss's Trs* 1958 SC 501 at 509.

111 *Taylor v Gilbert's Trs* (1878) 5 R (HL) 217. In another House of Lords case, *Gregory's Trs v Alison* (1889) 16 R (HL) 10, there were two contingencies which were quite distinct in character but there was no suggestion that the doctrine was to be limited to one.

the doctrine was first established. Rather than devising a rigid formula in advance of any particular case, openness to possibility in particular cases was required:[112]

> 'There is no rule of thumb about the effect of single or plural contingencies. As the doctrine rests ultimately on a presumption that the testator intends the legatee to be vested rather than that his interest be suspended, that presumption must yield to anything in the deed that points to a contrary intention. If there be a series of complicated contingencies calling for construction there may well be in them or elsewhere in the deed indications that the testator intended that vesting should be postponed ... What one can safely say on the wider topic of 'double contingency' is simply this. In approaching the task of discovering the testator's intention it is not necessarily fatal to the application of the presumption that the testator has put in the deed more than one resolutive condition.'

(5) Scope of the doctrine

13.26 The reason why the scope of the doctrine remains unclear is that there have been few cases in which it has been tested. All that can be said is that the views expressed in *Moss's Trustees v Moss's Trustees*[113] certainly point to the logical validity of a wider application than the decision in *Johnston's Trustees v Dewar*[114] would allow. In saying that, it is not clear that this view has prevailed.[115]

Not only is the rule relating to plural contingencies in some doubt, but the issue of which types of factual situations the conditions may refer to in order to defeat conditional vesting is hardly less ambiguous. There is little case law on the subject, but there is some authority for the view that there can be circumstances other than the birth of a child in which vesting subject to defeasance may be permitted.[116] These relate to an apparently disparate

112 *Moss's Trs v Moss's Trs* 1958 SC 501, per Lord Justice-Clerk Thomson at 511.

113 *Moss's Trs v Moss's Trs* 1958 SC 501.

114 1911 SC 722.

115 *Nicolson's Trs v Nicolson* 1960 SC 186.

116 *Yule's Trs v Deans* 1919 SC 570, 1919 2 SLT 129; *McCall's Trs v McCall* 1957 SLT (Notes) 16, OH; *Craig's Trs v Dun's Trs* 1957 SLT (Notes) 3, OH; *Cathcart's JF v Stewart* 1948 SC 456, 1948 SLT 392; *Stainton v Forteviot Trust Ltd* 1948 SC (HL) 115, 1949 SLT 39; and *Grant's Trs v Crawford's Tr* 1949 SLT 374, OH.

range of circumstances but they all have one thing in common: they can be seen as analogous to the emergence of issue to the primary beneficiary and thus can be justified as being within the ambit of the doctrine.[117] It has to be said, however, that the analogy is somewhat convoluted. For example, in *Yule's Trustees v Deans*,[118] the testator had provided that a proportion of the income from his estate was to be used to maintain his son in an asylum. If his son recovered his faculties he was to receive the fee, failing which it was to be distributed to various third parties. The son died without recovering his faculties and the third parties argued that the fee had vested in them *a morte testatoris* subject to defeasance if the son had in fact recovered. Lord Skerrington held that the condition was resolutive since it was not one which was personal to the legatees, the third parties. Interestingly, although he noted that vesting subject to defeasance was considered as exceptional in nature and ought not to be readily extended, he stated that 'suspended vesting and conditional vesting are mere matters of legal machinery, and it is the duty of the Court to utilise either the one or the other as it may consider just'. In finding that in this case the fee had vested *a morte* subject to defeasance if the son had recovered, Lord Skerrington stated:[119]

> 'I reject the notion that conditional vesting must not be applied to any case merely because there is no precedent for it. It must not, however, be invoked, however great may be the temptation, in any case where by so doing we should subvert some firmly established rule of construction.'

Defeasible vesting is therefore a somewhat elastic concept. A condition will be resolutive if, and only if, the effect of its operation would be to take something away from the beneficiary, unless the beneficiary is not known or cannot be ascertained. The terms of the condition itself must involve the birth of a child to someone else or the survivance of an existing child, unless the terms of the condition can be seen as analogous to such an event. The condition cannot contain a double contingency, unless an apparent double contingency can be reduced logically to a single one or, possibly, a court is willing to allow plural contingencies in a suitable case. Whilst the aim of the doctrine is to enable the beneficiary to deal with his or her

117 *Hicks' Trs v Lord Advocate* 1973 SC 199, per Lord Fraser at 213.
118 *Yule's Trs v Deans* 1919 SC 570.
119 *Yule's Trs v Deans* 1919 SC 570 at 575.

expectant interest at once,[120] the doctrine may be applied retrospectively, and years may pass between the death of the testator and a court holding that the bequest had actually vested in the beneficiary *a morte*. Finally, although it has been said that the effect of the doctrine is to confer absolute ownership on the primary beneficiary,[121] on some views at least, the vested right remains conditional until there is no possibility of the right being defeated by the occurrence of the contingent event in question.[122]

VESTING SUBJECT TO PARTIAL DEFEASANCE

13.27 The doctrine of vesting subject to partial defeasance is rather different to, and very much simpler in nature than, the doctrine of vesting subject to defeasance. It applies solely to class gifts[123] where membership remains incomplete at the date of the testator's death. The normal rule is that if a legacy is given expressly to a class, the members of the class fall to be identified at the date of the testator's death.[124] A legacy to 'my children' is thus payable to all of the testator's children alive at his or her death, including posthumous children. A legacy to 'my heirs' is payable to those meeting this description at the date of vesting;[125] and a legacy to a class such as 'B's issue' is payable to those of B's children, grandchildren or remoter issue who are alive at the date of payment.[126] If, however, the date of payment is postponed, vesting of class gifts may be subject to partial defeasance. The legacy will vest in whichever members of the class are alive at the testator's death, but their right will be partially defeated by the emergence of additional members of the class. Once the right has vested, the share of any legatees who die before the date of payment will not accresce to the survivors of the class but pass to their executors.[127]

120 *Taylor v Gilbert's Trs* (1878) 5 R (HL) 217 at 221.

121 *Steel's Trs v Steel* (1888) 16 R 204.

122 McLaren, *The Law of Wills and Succession,* 3rd edn (1894) para 1491.

123 See paras **11.5–11.11**.

124 *Gregory's Trs v Alison* (1889) 6 R (HL) 10 but this applies only if vesting occurs *a morte testatoris*.

125 *Wylie's Trs v Bruce* 1919 SC 211; and *Barr's Trs v Inland Revenue* 1943 SC 157.

126 *Wood v Wood* (1861) 23 D 338.

127 *Carleton v Thomson* (1867) 5 M (HL) 151.

Where there is a legacy to A in liferent and to B's children in fee, the fee vests immediately in such children of B as are alive at the testator's death, subject to partial defeasance by the birth of any children born later and during the currency of the liferent. The value of the share of each child alive at the testator's death will be diluted if B subsequently has more children.

Example

X dies in 2010. He directs that a legacy be given 'the income to A in liferent and to B's children in fee'. At the time of the testator's death B has only one child (C). In 2012, B has another child (D) and in 2013 another child, E, is born. At the death of the testator, the whole fee vests in C. When D is born, half of C's share is defeated, and that half vests in D. When E is born, a third of C's share and a third of D's share are defeated and the two shares vest in E. D dies before the date of payment. Her share passes to her executor and not to C and E.

If it is a condition of the gift that the class survives until a certain time – such as the expiry of the liferent – vesting will be suspended. If there is a condition attached that the beneficiaries reach a certain age, vesting will be suspended until the first member of the class reaches that age, subject to partial defeasance when other members reach it. If the legacy is payable before the last member attains the required age, it will vest only in those members who have reached that age.[128]

ACCELERATED VESTING

13.28 Vesting of a legacy may be accelerated in certain circumstances. This is typically when a liferent is terminated early. The kind of circumstances in which this might take place would be where liferent has been renounced, perhaps because a surviving spouse has elected to claim legal rights, or a condition of expiry of the liferent is the liferenter's marriage. In such cases, s 7 of the Succession (Scotland) Act 2016 provides that the fee will vest in the fiar(s) on the termination of the liferent. However, this default rule is subject to the terms of the document or other obligation.

128 *Scott's Trs v Scott* 1909 SC 773.

It may be the case that the testator wished any renounced income to be reinvested in order to pay legatees before the fee is to pass to the fiars. In such cases, vesting may continue to be suspended.

Much will turn on the reading of the document itself, and the testator's intention must be construed from the words used in the deed.[129] Where the testator has made clear his or her express intentions as to when vesting is to take place those intentions will not be altered by the court. Given the paramountcy of the testator's intention in construing a will, the courts will not be prepared to effectively write a new one which makes different provision entirely from that envisaged. This point was underlined iIn relation to the question of early vesting in *Jack's Trustees v Jack* where Lord Kinnear held that:[130]

> 'Where vesting and not mere payment is dependent upon the death of the liferenter, nothing that the liferenter does in the way of abandoning his or her right can accelerate the period of vesting, because the testator has fixed it finally, and it is not for anybody else to make a new will for him.'

129 *Jack's Trs v Jack* 1913 SC 815; *A v B's Trs* 1941 SLT 193; and *Gray's Trs v Neilson* 1946 SN 81.

130 *Jack's Trs v Jack* 1913 SC 815, at 826.

Index

[all references are to paragraph number]